D0154356

Let Us Fight as Free Men

POLITICS AND CULTURE IN MODERN AMERICA

Series Editors
Margot Canaday, Glenda Gilmore, Michael Kazin, and Thomas J. Sugrue

Volumes in the series narrate and analyze political and social change in the broadest dimensions from 1865 to the present, including ideas about the ways people have sought and wielded power in the public sphere and the language and institutions of politics at all levels—local, national, and transnational. The series is motivated by a desire to reverse the fragmentation of modern U.S. history and to encourage synthetic perspectives on social movements and the state, on gender, race, and labor, and on intellectual history and popular culture.

Let Us Fight as Free Men

Black Soldiers and Civil Rights

Christine Knauer

PENN

UNIVERSITY OF PENNSYLVANIA PRESS

PHILADELPHIA

Copyright © 2014 University of Pennsylvania Press

All rights reserved. Except for brief quotations used for purposes of review or scholarly citation, none of this book may be reproduced in any form by any means without written permission from the publisher.

Published by
University of Pennsylvania Press
Philadelphia, Pennsylvania 19104-4112
www.upenn.edu/pennpress

Printed in the United States of America
on acid-free paper

10 9 8 7 6 5 4 3 2 1

Library of Congress Cataloging-in-Publication Data
Knauer, Christine.
    Let us fight as free men : black soldiers and civil rights / Christine Knauer. — 1st ed.
    p.   cm. — (politics and culture in modern America)
    Includes bibliographical references and index.
    ISBN 978-0-8122-4597-4 (hardcover : alk. paper)
    1. African American soldiers—History—20th century. 2. United States—Armed Forces—African Americans—History—20th century. 3. World War, 1939–1945—Participation, African American. 4. Korean War, 1950–1953—Participation, African American. 5. African Americans—Civil rights—History—20th century. 6. African Americans—Political activity—History—20th century. 7. Segregation—United States—History—20th century. 8. United States—Race relations—History—20th century. I. Title. II. Series: Politics and culture in modern America.
E185.63.K58   2014
355.0089'96073—dc23   2013046747

In Loving Memory of My Mother
Hannelore Knauer

Contents

Introduction

When Grant Reynolds volunteered for the army at the beginning of the Second World War, he did so with much patriotism and high hopes. He wanted to support the nation's cause and believed in the necessity of the mission to halt fascism across the globe. But he was also convinced that he could make a difference for his African American comrades and improve their position in and outside the military. Born in 1908, Reynolds had already made a name for himself as a civil rights activist in Cleveland, Ohio, where he was a reverend in the Mount Zion Congregational Temple and president of the local branch of the National Association for the Advancement of Colored People (NAACP). His service as a chaplain in the armed forces, he thought, would be another opportunity for him to fight for the black cause and strengthen black soldiers in their daily struggles with segregation and discrimination in the military. While preparing soldiers for war stateside, the outspoken chaplain became their confidant and spiritual advisor, as he shared their experiences. Even as an officer, he faced frequent prejudice and acts of humiliation. He was barred from living or eating with white officers. To uphold strict segregation of the races, the army built a separate living quarter just for the black chaplain.[1]

The absurdity and brutality of the system of laws and customs lumped under the label "Jim Crow" emboldened Reynolds to revolt against the oppressive system. Throughout his time in the military, he openly and vigorously demanded desegregation and equal treatment of black recruits. His commitment earned him respect among black soldiers, but also incurred the army's wrath. By transferring him from one base to the other, they tried to silence him for his relentless activism. In 1944, the army chose a more effective and permanent way to rid itself of Reynolds. Based on a questionable psychiatric evaluation that described him as showing "paranoid trends" and "being involved in affairs that are none of his business," he received an honorable discharge. His outspokenness about the mistreatment of African Americans in the armed forces, to the chagrin of his superiors in the army, had caused "considerable commotion."[2]

Grant Reynolds was furious when he had to leave the army against his will. He felt mistreated and campaigned for his return. The NAACP opposed the army's handling of civil rights activists in their ranks in a letter to Truman K. Gibson, civilian aide to the secretary of war. The army ignored the complaints.[3] Reynolds was not reinstated nor was the underlying issue, segregation, critically reconsidered. Although the army could rid him from its ranks, Reynolds returned to civilian life fighting, unwilling to back down. In protest of the organization's support of President Franklin D. Roosevelt whose "wilful degradation of the sensibilities of American Negro fighting men" could no longer be "countenance[d]," Reynolds gave up his membership in the NAACP.[4]

Intent to elicit change in the armed forces, Reynolds published four articles on the status of black soldiers in the NAACP monthly magazine *The Crisis* in 1944, despite his membership resignation.[5] In provocative terms that worried army officials, he charged that the War Department intentionally destroyed the morale of African American soldiers and spread Southern customs of segregation and white supremacy all around the country and the world.[6] Reynolds contended that the African American soldier would fight if ordered to do so, however, his fight would be for personal survival, not for people who continuously led "a vicious attack on his manhood" and "domestic nazis," who turned him and his comrades into "military scapegoats." This constant degradation of black soldiers, Reynolds claimed, could "some day explain the difference between defeat and victory."[7] He predicted that, after the war, the armed forces should not be surprised to find returning black soldiers "engage in bloody, conflict" at home in order to be granted the privileges and rights that they had fought for in the war.[8]

Reynolds did not "engage in bloody, conflict." Neither did the great majority of black soldiers returning from the war. His charged threat, however, exemplified black Americans' growing unwillingness to back down. African Americans returned as second-class citizens to America, but roused by their war experience and the unmet promises during the Second World War, they continued to fight for full civil rights and integration in all aspects of life.[9] White reactionary calls for a return to an old social order founded on clear racial hierarchies, segregation, and white supremacy would not stop them.[10] Thus, the postwar period saw an intensification of the fight for military desegregation and debates on the meaning of military service. For many African Americans, it would become a fight over equal access to the military, control over history and historical memory, and recognition of black manhood.

This book examines African Americans' reflections on military service, desegregation, and black soldiers in the immediate postwar world. The increase in African American activism had its roots in the black experience and service in the Second World War, as black soldiers assumed a special position at the front line of the fight for racial equality. Often, African American soldiers were the most prominent and most common victims of white racial violence, and the most offensive symbol of African American (male) strength, prowess, and self-confidence. For most African Americans, the statement in an editorial in the *Los Angeles Sentinel* in 1948 rang true: "The insults [of segregation and discrimination] cut deeper when they are wearing the uniform of their country and being adjured to fight to preserve democracy."[11] Indeed, the mistreatment of blacks in the military proved a powerful rallying point among African Americans. Demands for equality were based on African Americans' willingness to serve despite, and concurrently because of, the oppressive limitations they faced. Black soldiers' war record helped them claim agency and demand full and equal integration into American society as a whole.

Segregation was an evil that needed eliminating, but so did the tarnished image of black soldiers. Thus, African Americans were on a mission to salvage the reputation of World War II black soldiers and obtain the full citizenship rights they had fought for during the war. Black men had served their military duty despite Jim Crow,[12] now black veterans returned to collect the recognition and rights due to them as men. Thus, the time period covered here begins with the end of the war. Civil rights groups and the African American press had always paid special attention to military service. Organizations like the NAACP and the National Urban League (NUL) continued to push for military integration after the Second World War. A. Philip Randolph, founder of the Brotherhood of Sleeping Car Porters (BSCP) already known for his unconventional protest methods, and his partner, former army chaplain Grant Reynolds, managed to corner President Harry Truman when they told draftees to refuse to serve in a segregated military.[13] Their call for draft resistance at a time of national insecurity was a peak in the civil rights fight for military desegregation in 1948, with Randolph at the center. It represents, as historian John D'Emilio has aptly described it, "a new moment in twentieth century national politics."[14] The movement went far beyond traditional civil rights tactics and left gradualism behind.[15] It upset white America deeply, but was also highly contested among African Americans, who agreed on the need for military desegregation but could not agree on the strategy. Most blacks felt obliged to pledge their allegiance to the nation and their willingness to bear arms, distancing themselves from Randolph's civil disobedience campaign. Nonetheless, the campaign highlighted pent-up frustration and growing impatience with the unequal status of blacks in the military as well as in society as a whole. The ensuing debates on military integration and service were deeply gendered, entrenched in ideas of masculine behavior and male rights and obligations. Moreover, they led to Truman's Executive Order 9981 on July 26, 1948.[16]

Contrary to current popular perception, however, Executive Order 9981 did not effectively bring segregation in the U.S. armed forces to an end. It merely said that "there shall be equality of treatment and opportunity for all persons in the armed services without regard to race, color, religion or national origin," and that the adjustments should progress "as rapidly as possible," but "without impairing efficiency or morale."[17] It did not specify demands for concrete change in the military. In fact, the executive order did not even mention the terms "integration" or "segregation." However, it did put pressure on the military to question and adapt its ossified structures, which were deeply ingrained in racial hierarchies and ideas of alleged white superiority. It was not until the Korean War that military segregation could be put to an, albeit reluctant, end. The continuously troubled course of the Korean War that, at times, brought the United States to the verge of military defeat made desegregation a necessity. In dire need of replacements, the army in particular could not maintain segregation and simultaneously fill its rapidly dwindling rank and file. For decades, military officials had maintained that racial integration would hamper military efficiency and morale, yet the realities of the Korean War effort and African Americans' fighting proved them wrong.[18]

The fight for military integration proved one of the most prominent sites for the "convergence for foreign policy matters and domestic civil rights activities."[19] In a brutal fashion, the Korean War again brought the African American struggle for equality beyond national boundaries. The international crisis and the renewed call to arms could not silence the criticism of and protest against American domestic and foreign policy. Cold War hysteria had a dual effect on the civil rights movement and the quest for equality; while it delimited and thwarted the movement's mission, it concurrently spurred black activists' fight and rhetoric. Hence, left-leaning African Americans and whites were not the only ones to voice criticism of the United States for its foreign involvement and domestic failures. Blacks used the Korean War to criticize American foreign policy, American concepts of race, the notion of black inferiority, and the continued exclusion and segregation of blacks. The conflict was the last time that black soldiers fought in all-black units in a war involving the United States.

Lee Nichols, the first journalist to study military integration in the United States in depth, went so far as to refer to this transformation as "one of the biggest stories of the twentieth century."[20] African Americans and white integrationists hoped that military integration would set the norm in American society.[21] It might have been, as historian Richard Dalfiume notes, a "quiet racial revolution . . . with practically no violence, bloodshed, or conflict"[22] that evolved in a short period of time. Others paint a similar picture of this development, calling it "a proud milestone in the march of American democracy" or "a turning point in the black man's military position."[23] Despite its significance, the African American military service and struggle for racial integration in the military after the Second World War remains a relatively unexplored chapter of American history. Most civil rights historians have concentrated their focus on the domestic front of the civil rights movement, placing particular emphasis on *Brown v. Board of Education of Topeka*, the Montgomery Bus Boycott, and developments beyond.[24]

In 1996, historian Michael Klarman drew attention to this problematic starting point in civil rights history: "The many scholars who have treated *Brown* as the inaugural event in the modern civil rights movement have difficulty accounting for the momentous civil rights developments of the late 1940s and early 1950s."[25] Others followed in challenging the "traditional periodization of the civil rights movement by highlighting the considerable ferment in race relations during the 1930s and 1940s."[26] Recent research has extended the chronology of the "long civil rights movement"[27] as far back as the Progressive Era and has uncovered in more detail that there was vibrant civil rights activism that predated Martin Luther King, Jr.[28] In fact, the civil disobedience tactic famously orchestrated by King in leading the Montgomery Bus Boycott had already been used by A. Philip Randolph when protesting military segregation in 1941 and 1948. Still, historians neglect the fact that the integration of the military preceded *Brown* and set the stage for further civil rights changes.

Those studies that do focus on military desegregation track the implementation of integration mostly "from the top down."[29] Little research has been published on the perception of these events in public discourse or on the experiences of the American population in general, and of African Americans in particular. Despite a growing number of studies, African American soldiers as symbols and agents in war and peace, the civil rights activism for military integration, as well as the Korean War still have not received the attention they deserve.[30] This leaves essential and formative elements of both the postwar civil rights movement and the conflicts in the African American community in the dark. Yet these developments provide meaningful insights into issues of African American agency and identity. This account takes a fresh look at the fight for and progress of military desegregation after 1945.

African Americans had long pushed for equality in and desegregation of the armed forces as part of their general struggle for equality and full civil rights in American society. With the outbreak of the Second World War, military and war service again garnered much attention among African Americans. Black soldiers' highly contested presence in stateside training camps and war zones worldwide and their efforts in the name of American democracy were essential elements in the African American fight for civil rights and equality. Although military officials claimed that the armed forces were based on a "separate-but-equal" doctrine, equality did not exist. The mere act of separation and its underlying concept of black inferiority prevented equal treatment or respect. Blacks and whites could not serve in the same units. They trained and lived separately. Although black officers existed, white officers were still the norm and often disliked serving with blacks, whom they considered a career hindrance. Most military officials stuck to their long-held ideas of black inferiority and inability to serve in the same capacity as white soldiers, whose heroism and fighting ability they never doubted.[31] In the North and South, white supremacy barred African Americans from the ideal of the "citizen soldier" who had direct influence on American political life in return for his service in the military.

Access to full civil rights was (and still is) intrinsically linked to full military service. "In the United States, as in Europe, citizenship and eligibility for military service have gone hand in hand."[32] African Americans were fully aware of this link and determined to use it to their advantage in an attempt to expand their citizenship rights. Frederick Douglass, a former slave and influential author and reformer, had encouraged blacks to fight in the Civil War to prove their value as potential citizens. "Once let the black man get upon his person the brass letters, U.S., let him get an eagle on his button, and a musket on his shoulder and bullets in his pockets, and there is no power on earth which can deny that he has earned the right to citizenship in the United States."[33] W. E. B. Du Bois, a leading African American intellectual and cofounder of the NAACP, argued, "Nothing else made Negro citizenship conceivable, but the record of the Negro soldier as a fighter."[34] The notion that the "right to fight" and with it the patriotic realization of one's civic obligations represented the ultimate path to constitutionally guaranteed rights was fundamental to the African American understanding of military service. African Americans hoped that military service and performance in war would help "in the long drawn struggle still to be, for the betterment of conditions for their race."[35] According to a dominant understanding of the social contract between citizen and nation, military service and performance in battle prove national loyalty. Denying or restricting the eligibility of a certain group of people in service not only bars the affected group from enjoying educational advantages and better career options, but also denies them equal citizenship and the ability to express it. Access to military service and service itself "generated hierarchies among men in terms of their access to the perquisites of citizenship."[36]

Manhood is, as Steve Estes and Adriane Lentz-Smith, for instance, have shown, deeply embedded in the African American struggle for military service and full civil rights.[37] No other institution has been as much shaped by, as it has produced discourse on masculinity and manly valor than the military and war. As historian Michael Geyer points out: "War is systematically implicated, in terms of gendered, masculine identity, in the constitution of civil society. . . . War is at the very core of the modern definition of the (male) citizen as public and private person. The means to express this definition is the language of male obligation."[38] Segregation, especially in the military, created a hierarchy of manhood, which implied that white men were superior to blacks. The disenfranchisement, marginalization, and denigration of black masculinity in favor of hegemonic white masculinity were not limited to the military. However, the military represented one of the most visible and controversial sites of discrimination, oppression, and derogation. In general, white supremacy defined African American men in a derogatory context as representing "subordinated and marginalized masculinities."[39] Whereas white masculinist discourse attempted to disempower black men, relegating them to second-class citizen status, blacks invoked their own masculinist discourse, countering and threatening white masculine hegemony through their military service and their public discourse on black men's military prowess. They sought to occupy the dominant masculine ideal characterized, most prominently, by heterosexuality, power, authority, and (compassionate) toughness. The rhetoric and strategies of the African American struggle for military service and integration reveal claims to and assertions of manhood that directly challenged white men and often resulted in an ardent defense of white male supremacy.[40]

Although African American women were not excluded from the struggle for military integration, they and their quest for civil rights remained in the background. Especially during the Second World War, they fought for the integration of all military branches. While the draft did not apply to them, numerous African American women wanted to serve their country as part of the Women's Army Corps (WAC) or Women Accepted for Volunteer Emergency Service (WAVES) and as nurses, but could do so only in segregated outfits. Black nurses' fight mattered to the public and the civil rights movement. During World War II, Walter White, NAACP executive secretary, cooperated with Mabel Keaton Staupers, long-time head of the National Association of Colored Graduate Nurses, to achieve the full integration of black nurses into the United States Army Nurse Corps (ANC). They achieved this major step in 1945.[41] Despite their collaboration, the movement in general focused on men and applied deeply masculinist rhetoric to rally supporters and draw white people's attention to the issue of military segregation. Women certainly played a major role in the movement as financiers and grassroots activists, but they remained in the background all too often, as it was especially black veterans who felt entitled to civil rights after World War II.[42] Wartime experiences and military participation challenged the relationships between whites and blacks. The fight for military racial integration, however, affirmed traditional male and female gender roles in the United States.

A close look at the postwar struggle for military integration and African Americans' reflections on the Korean War unravel two equally important aspects of the fight for equality in military service and society. The control over the image of the black soldier in segregated as well as integrated environments became as fundamental to the African American civil rights movement as the actual fight for integration; they went hand in hand. The continuous slurring of the African American soldier and of all-black units represented a major issue for blacks and their civil rights efforts. African

Americans had not only long suffered from and struggled with their enslaved, segregated, or discriminated status in the body politic, but also with their excluded or undermined place in American discourse, history, and memory. White Americans often forgot—or rather intentionally overlooked—blacks. If they were included, it was in a stereotypical representation: black men were either impotent slave characters or oversexed brutes, both unable to live or perform in a modern society without white control and guidance.[43] Exclusion from and misrepresentation in public discourse, whether contemporary or historical, have been efficient instruments used to subdue and oppress blacks in American society.[44]

Fully aware of this exclusion and misrepresentation and its detrimental ramifications for their social status, African Americans made efforts to gain power over their representation in history and collective memory. They struggled to include their experiences and achievements in white public discourse. As literary scholars Robert O'Meally and Geneviève Fabre maintain, "blacks and whites . . . have been engaged in a struggle over what to say about America's past and how to say it."[45] The control over and modification or even replacement of representations and images have been essential to the eventual obliteration of what cultural critic bell hooks calls the "imperial gaze—the look that seeks to dominate, subjugate, and colonize."[46] A prerequisite to fight for the end of military segregation was the improvement of the black soldier's image in the public. These attempts at image control shed light on how blacks defined manhood and citizenship, as well as national and racial allegiance. The figure of the black soldier as an agent and symbol has a long tradition and was not new to the postwar era. Nonetheless, the postwar period stands out not only for the unprecedented wave of black protest it generated against military segregation, but also for its success in achieving desegregation of the armed services.

Looking at the issues at stake through (gendered) image control also allows for a reassessment of Dalfiume's evaluation of African Americans' response to military integration, especially during the Korean War, which he has described as "confused." Dalfiume asserts that African Americans were "obviously not aware of the extent of the revolution occurring within the Army in Korea."[47] Certainly, articles in African American newspapers reported on the combat excellence of segregated all-black units, yet they concurrently condemned segregation and demanded the full integration of troops. Such contradictory reports emerged long before the Korean War. The diverging attitudes toward integration and the African American performance in segregated units are not, however, "confused." Rather, they serve as a testament to the multiple and seemingly conflicting strategies African Americans used to build racial pride, pledge patriotism, establish a positive image of the black soldier, and demand integration as a necessity for the efficiency and improvement of the armed forces and society as a whole. African Americans were well aware what was taking place in the military in Korea and tried to take control of the situation.

African Americans could not and did not create a single strand of argument that wholly praised integration and interracial brotherhood in battle while ignoring black segregated units. Continuously emphasizing the negative effects of segregation and the positive effects of integration on black morale and their combat discipline and performance, to some degree, underscored the image of African American inferiority and unreliability. Most black people believed that segregation and discrimination negatively affected African American soldiers and their performance in combat. However, rather than discrediting blacks who served in segregated units, African Americans instead discredited the system lauding black achievements against all odds and finding fault with white commanders in Korea.

The fact that the Korean War was fought against Asians, who were perceived as yet another race, adds another important dimension to the conflict. It complicated the debate within both black and white communities in the United States. Blacks were caught between claims of racial sensitivity and interracial cooperation purported by many in the black elite, and the reality of the predominance of racial stereotypes and hierarchies. As a case study, the Korean War illustrates that African Americans longed to be an equal component of the American nation, at the expense of Asian people. At the same time, they opposed white supremacy and the exclusionary and humiliating discourse within and outside the military. The Cold War empowered their efforts for civil rights and integration in the military and further catapulted racial inequality in the United States onto the international stage. White supremacy and segregation proved to be serious burdens in the American struggle for worldwide leadership and support from African and Asian peoples. Segregated U.S. armed forces signified the most visible worldwide record for American failures in race relations.

The book consists of eight chapters and an epilogue, which together outline the essential role of African American soldiers as symbols and agents in the post-World War II struggle for military integration and civil rights through the end of the Korean War. The chapters are organized chronologically, as well as thematically. While attempting to analyze the African Americans' discourse in relation rather than in clear opposition to mainstream discourses, the book tries to avoid a division along racial lines. For reasons of simplification and for the purpose of diversification of terminology, "African American" and "black" in all their forms are used interchangeably. Degrading or offensive terms are only used in quotations of primary sources.

Although the focus of this study is the postwar struggle for military integration and the special meaning of the Korean War among African Americans, it is impossible to study these developments without looking at the African American experience during the Second World War in some depth. Consequently, the first two chapters chronicle African Americans' involvement and experience in, as well as assessment of the war—a war that was fought in the name of democracy and oppressed peoples, while racial discrimination and segregation continued in the United States. The next three chapters examine the efforts of A. Philip Randolph, the famous labor leader, and Grant Reynolds, the former army chaplain, to achieve racial desegregation of the American military service, especially their early attempts to convince Congress and President Truman to integrate the American military, their heatedly debated civil disobedience campaign, Truman's Executive Order 9981, and reactions of African Americans to its passing, as well as the difficult beginnings of military integration. While the order was certainly a daring move at a time when segregation and discrimination had steadfast places in American society and politics, it was hardly an unambiguous call for integration. The final three chapters of the book delve into African Americans' involvement in the Korean War, now somewhat misleadingly remembered as the first war fought by an integrated military. The bloody and costly war left room for serious criticism of American foreign and domestic policy not only expressed by communist or strongly left-leaning civil rights activists, but also by African Americans in general. Black soldiers' conflicting experiences of segregation and integration, discrimination and camaraderie, victory and defeat shaped the image of the war at home.

The book records a struggle for civil rights by merging cultural and social history with military history in its broadest sense. It does not mean to unravel the state and military decision-making processes on the path toward integration of the armed forces or the war in Korea. Neither is it a history of warfare or military strategy. It does not assess and rate the performance of African American soldiers in the Korean War. Rather, the book sheds light on the African American community and its interactions with white America. It uncovers African American ideas and discussion on military service and the struggle for racial integration in the armed forces after the Second World War as formative elements of both the postwar civil rights movement and the African American community. Blacks still considered military service a valuable asset in their lives and essential to the struggle for civil rights in American society. In early postwar America, black military service was not yet officially something to challenge or with which to tamper. However, some black activists and soldiers did exactly that, using a variety of different methods in an attempt to change the United States for the better.

Chapter 1

Fighting for Respect

For A. Philip Randolph, it was a fight with "gloves off."[1] The black labor leader was no longer willing to accept the mistreatment African Americans experienced on a daily basis. Long before America's direct involvement in the Second World War, Randolph was among the many African Americans who vehemently articulated their growing impatience and dissatisfaction with their social and political status in the United States. The war created millions of new jobs, especially in war industries. But despite the need for workers in all lines of work, discrimination and segregation continued. Moreover, the military intended to uphold segregation based on the discriminatory and oppressive "separate but equal" doctrine. African Americans now advocated most vigorously for a modification of employment regulations to ensure equal employment opportunities for blacks and the desegregation of the armed services. They attempted to capitalize on the correlations between segregation at home and fascist oppression abroad. In the light of the vastly growing criticism of fascism, their demands seemed more pressing than ever before. Racism in the armed forces, according to the African American *Carolina Times*, was "downright dumbness" in an international war in which Americans wanted to distinguish themselves as a democratic country.[2] Blacks' frustration grew, spurring their activism against the perpetuation of inequality.[3]

In an attempt to push President Franklin D. Roosevelt to improve the lot of African Americans and make America live up to its own standards, Randolph founded the March on Washington Movement (MOWM), one of the most prominent and groundbreaking grassroots movements at the time. He was convinced that a mass demonstration in Washington would

be the most effective way to fight the employment inequalities in government and government-related industries as well as the military segregation
faced by African Americans.[4] Based on Gandhian principles of nonviolent
protest,[5] the "first crisis concerning the racial management of the war"[6]
fought injustices in the labor market and in the military. The movement's
slogan, "We loyal Negro-American citizens demand the right to work and
fight for our country,"[7] represented its unique rhetoric, which paired
American patriotism with severe social criticism and used unprecedented
strategies in the fight for equality and civil rights.

The movement's primary goal was to instigate the issuance of an executive order by the president that would abolish racial discrimination in the
armed forces and national defense industry, something Roosevelt was reluctant to do. According to Randolph, the president continued to treat African
Americans as "half-men," and patience was no longer an option in breaking Roosevelt's reluctance.[8] Many African Americans hailed and supported
Randolph's call for an African American mass march on Washington. They
were impressed with its unprecedented radicalism and hoped it would be
effective in the struggle for fair employment and equality.[9] The significance
of Randolph's campaign lay in its expression of black agency; it was about
making change happen rather than waiting for white cooperation and support. Building and showing racial pride and self-reliance were essential elements of the march.[10]

The federal government initially demanded that the march be canceled,
contending that it would only stir racial hatred. Yet the campaign organizers remained unwilling to comply with President Roosevelt's request; this,
along with the rising number of African Americans planning to participate
in the demonstration, began to worry government officials and the president. Randolph continued to vouch for blacks' Americanism, patriotism,
and willingness to "fight for Uncle Sam!" However, it was essential to rid
society of African Americans' status as "half-men; as semi-citizens, begging
for a pittance."[11] Using rhetoric of manhood, Randolph demanded recognition and respect for black men, and called for black civil rights. His calls
grew increasingly impatient. He informed Roosevelt that 100,000 people
were planning to participate in the march and that only issuance of an
executive order that banned all racial discrimination in the war industries
and armed forces could prevent the march from taking place.[12] Despite
serious reservations within the government, the president acquiesced to the
demands, at least partly.

On June 25, 1941, President Roosevelt issued Executive Order 8802 that prohibited employment discrimination based on race, creed, color, or national origin in federal agencies and war-related industries. The order furthermore established the Fair Employment Practice Committee (FEPC) to monitor employment in defense industries and government agencies. Its issuance dealt a rather considerable blow to Jim Crow.[13] Roosevelt, however, was not willing to end segregation in the military. To the dismay of many of his followers, Randolph called off the march on Washington.[14] Yet his activism against discrimination and segregation of the armed forces remained steadfast; he considered the issue to be of too much importance and too much of a problem for the continued success of the black labor movement to give up.

As Randolph established the MOWM as a permanent organization, he continued to push for equality in the defense industry and, despite financial problems, to reinforce the movement's efforts to achieve military desegregation.[15] Under its auspices, Dwight and Nancy Macdonald published a pamphlet *The War's Greatest Scandal: The Story of Jim Crow in Uniform* that graphically outlined the injustices and violence experienced by black soldiers at the hands of their white countrymen. The pamphlet claimed to present "a true picture of jimcrowism in the armed services and to enlist the mind and will of all Americans, Negro and white, who are concerned with democracy."[16]

Mirror Image

The Japanese attack on Pearl Harbor on December 7, 1941, subdued anti-interventionist tendencies held by some African Americans.[17] Disagreements within the black community abounded with regard to African Americans' involvement in the war effort and the extent to which it should exist, as well as attitudes toward European, African, and Asian powers, and Communism. However, the overwhelming majority of blacks still considered military service necessary, believing that an Axis victory would be a far worse outcome for all, should the war effort fail. Most blacks wanted to join the war effort, but they also intended to make a clear case for their right to equality and full civil rights and express their unwillingness to accept white supremacy.[18] The war years represented "crucial period in African American history generally as well as in black engagement with foreign affairs." Residing in more urban and Northern areas, the African American population became even more "engaged with national and international political events than ever before." This increased interest in politics was coupled with growing influence of blacks in the urban, northern political sphere as voters and government actors.[19]

The black press presented a powerful platform for black leaders and intellectuals to discuss the war. They exchanged ideas, led discussions, and affected a large readership.[20] The 1930s and 1940s were, as historian Brenda Gayle Plummer has argued, "black journalism's golden age." Growing in circulation by 40 percent, black newspapers affected the lives of many more African Americans and their take on life as an oppressed minority in the United States than ever before.[21] They criticized the hypocrisy of fighting for democracy abroad, while denying social equality to blacks or minority groups in general at home. The African American press and civil rights movement announced the launch of the "Double V" campaign to triumph over the enemies of democracy abroad as well as over segregation at home. The *Pittsburgh Courier*, the first to use the term, wrote:

> We, as colored Americans, are determined to protect our country, our form of government and the freedoms which we cherish for ourselves and for the rest of the world, therefore we have adopted the Double "V" war cry—victory over our enemies at home and victory over our enemies on the battlefields abroad. Thus in our fight for freedom we wage a two-pronged attack against our enslavers at home and those abroad who would enslave us. WE HAVE A STAKE IN THIS FIGHT. . . . WE ARE AMERICANS, TOO![22]

This call for racial pride and proof of patriotic allegiance demanded profound changes in America's racial hierarchy as well as a victory on foreign territories. The press linked military service and the end of discrimination to the international sphere. A successful defense of the nation would be possible only if national unity was achieved, while giving in to the racist demands of American Southerners would spell failure. Democracy, they claimed, had to be defended against vicious attacks, "RIGHT NOW and RIGHT HERE."[23] The link between the defeat of Hitler's Germany and Imperial Japan, and the defeat of "irresponsible and prejudiced white trash" in the United States became strong thematic trends in the African American press.[24]

As early as 1933, black newspapers had drawn parallels between the American South and Nazism to point to the inherent hypocrisy in fighting for democracy and equality abroad, while racist ideologies existed in strength at home.[25] In 1936, an incensed reader of the *Chicago Defender* even protested the participation "of our Negro brethren" in the Olympic Games in Berlin because "The Jews are being mercilessly persecuted in Germany, and for our boys to engage in the coming Olympics is an endorsement of Nazism."[26] In 1938, Roy Wilkins of the NAACP wrote: "The South approaches more nearly than any other section of the United States the Nazi idea of government by a 'master race' without interference from any democratic process."[27] During the war, George Schuyler, "an outspoken right-winger"[28] and columnist for the *Pittsburgh Courier*, noted that "what struck me . . . was that the Nazi plan for Negroes approximates so closely what seems to be the American plan for Negroes."[29] The fates of Jews in Germany and African Americans in the United States were positioned in direct relation to one another.

Throughout the war, black America aligned the Jim Crow South with Nazi Germany and listed racial violence and oppression of blacks in the United States as a victory for the enemy. In a letter to the *Chicago Defender*, a black recruit stationed in the South wrote, "We are shown many pictures of why we fight. They consist of how the Germans and Japanese treat other people . . . They must think we are blind not to see through all this. They talk of how the Germans and Japs do but never of how they treat thirteen million who help them fight."[30] The obvious parallels between Southern Jim Crow and Nazism were considered to be powerful tools in the struggle for equality. Claude Barnett, founder of the Associated Negro Press (ANP), asked President Roosevelt what blacks had "to hope and fight for? It is not enough to say that under Hitler conditions for the Negro would be worse."[31] Many black commentators pointed out an inevitable foreign loss of trust in the United States, should the self-proclaimed guardian of democracy and human rights continue to allow discrimination, segregation, and violence against minorities, foremost blacks. A few African Americans even considered Japan a haven of racial equality and a potential supporter in their fight against white supremacy.[32] With their willingness to serve in the military, blacks believed they had earned every right to protest, and especially among black soldiers, impatience with the unequal system was growing. African American newspapers printed numerous letters from black soldiers who condemned the mistreatment of themselves and their fellows in arms or avowed their willingness to resist and fight back against white domination.[33] Black soldiers represented the most visible and, despite their subjugated status, empowered men, who managed to seriously put white supremacy into question.

Jim Crow in Uniform

Despite a growing need for recruits during the Second World War, the military upheld restrictions on its induction and use of black soldiers. The Selective Training and Service Act of 1940 ruled that "any person, regardless of race or color" should be able to volunteer within the limits of the quota. Furthermore, it allowed "no discrimination against any person on account of race or color." At the time, African Americans hoped this would ensure more openness and equality in the system. However, the military found ways to circumvent these regulations, fearing that enormous numbers of blacks would seek to join the armed forces to evade unemployment or receive education and training.[34] Control over eligibility standards, for instance, provided the military the means to drastically limit African Americans' induction.[35] Moreover, segregation remained in place. The armed forces argued that they were not "a sociological laboratory; to be effective it must be organized and trained according to the principles which will ensure success. Experiments to meet the wishes and demands of the champions of every race and creed for the solution of their problems are a danger to efficiency, discipline and morale and would result in ultimate defeat."[36]

Restrictions and discrimination notwithstanding, blacks had joined the armed forces since the War of Independence, with the hope that, like Grant Reynolds, they could elicit change in the military through their service. Of the 12,343 conscientious objectors to the war, only 5 percent were African American.[37] While an overwhelming number of blacks did not choose this radical form of expressing protest against the war, they often displayed a scathing critique of the war's underlying hypocrisies.[38]

Black men's presence in the military again raised difficult questions about the functionality of segregation and issues of citizenship. Black soldiers would never be allowed to command white troops or be superior to white officers; hence, their chances of promotion were virtually nonexistent.[39] Two thirds of African Americans were allocated to service units, which were understood to be a "'feminized' position in relation to white male citizens."[40] They often had to perform menial labor and predominantly worked in supply, maintenance, and transportation; they were thus excluded from combat, the most prestigious position in the military. The uniform they wore was the same as that of white soldiers, but for the most part they remained excluded from the battlefield, "where manhood and citizenship were defined."[41] The placement of black soldiers in service units was a manifestation of black men's perceived inferiority. One soldier maintained, "Blacks were not going to be given a chance to prove themselves in combat . . . even if it caused the death of every cracker in the Pacific to keep it that way. The glory boys had to be white!"[42] Pictures of wounded African Americans were not released to the press, as army officials feared that the black press could capitalize on these images, using them to "unduly" emphasize the role of African Americans in the war effort.[43] The armed forces tried to keep the fighting, victories, and liberations, especially in Europe, white.[44] Pastor William H. Jernagin, director of the National Fraternal Council of Negro Churches, told Roosevelt: "Negro troops are begging for combat. . . . Our men who are prepared for combat want contact with the enemy."[45]

The growing involvement of blacks in the war effort resulted in an increase in the number of attacks on soldiers throughout the United States. The South, in particular, was highly incensed by African American civil rights claims and growing self-confidence. In 1942, the *Chicago Defender* perceptively summarized this fear and anger, stating that, "the Uniform of the Army when worn by an American of color is as a red flag waved before the face of any other enraged bull."[46] Violence against African American soldiers or between whites and blacks occurred on a daily basis.[47] The rising number of violent attacks on black soldiers in the South and of race riots on military bases in the North worried and incensed the African American population. To white supremacists, black soldiers represented everything which blacks should not be: armed and independent men serving the nation.[48] It was not only physical violence that African Americans faced; but they also combated their socially perpetuated image.

Struggling with the Image

The black press headlined the achievements and performance of black soldiers hoping to counter racial stereotypes and humiliating treatment. As

Figure 1. "Greater Love Hath No Man." Cartoon, *Chicago Defender*, July 1, 1944, 12. Reproduced by permission of copyright holder; further reproduction prohibited without permission.

exemplified in a cartoon in the *Chicago Defender* (Figure 1), black soldiers were a symbol of patriotism and black support for the American nation despite their "Jim Crowed" status. They played an essential role in building racial pride. Black soldiers concurrently embodied and denounced the nationwide hypocrisy of continuing racism amid calls for a democratic and liberated world; symbolizing everything that was wrong with the United States and right with the African American male. In his willingness to be present on the front, the black soldier was a powerful agent of change. His fate at home and abroad remained at the center of the black press's attention throughout the war.

Despite African American involvement, the Second World War appeared to be a "white men's war" in public discourse. In a letter to the *Richmond Times-Dispatch*, a white reader asked whether there were any black troops involved in the war at all. The lack of information on black troops in the white press was tangibly evident. The *Norfolk Journal and Guide* picked up on the story, charging that the white press rarely admitted to the presence of blacks on the front lines, especially in Europe. Few positive reports on black military men appeared in the mainstream press, yet "The identification by race is never omitted, however, when any infavorable [sic] news involving Negro service men or civilians is printed."[49] The black press furthermore reported that the War Department intentionally cut out African Americans from newsreel footage.[50] Censorship was especially applied to reports and pictures of black soldiers. A black soldier with guns, in charge of whites or in the company of a white woman, would not reach the home front. Many war stories upheld racial hierarchies.[51]

Gunnar Myrdal's 1944 book *An American Dilemma*, the most influential study of the status of blacks and race relations in the United States, corroborated this assessment and called for action. Based on extensive research on race relations and racial hierarchies in all areas of life, the Swedish sociologist argued that the "Negro problem" was a "white man's problem" that hindered the nation to live up to its own ideals and African Americans to realize their aspirations. Although the number of blacks in the service was growing, Myrdal maintained, it was nowhere near proportional. Despite all positive performances during the Spanish-American War and First World War, white leadership still considered black soldiers inadequate fighters, lacking both stamina and courage. He claimed that "white people, generally, know little or nothing about the Negro's performance as a soldier. Deliberate attempts have been made to minimize the Negro's military record."[52] Those developments certainly hampered black morale and investment in the war.

Early in the war, the armed forces and the African American news services attempted to establish a fruitful cooperation, as improving black morale and image was of essential importance to both groups. Statistical investigations revealed that at least 74 percent of black soldiers who read African American papers tended to be greatly influenced by their content.[53] To take some control over the images of black soldiers, African American press executives and, among others, the NAACP thought it essential to send their own correspondents into the war zones and distribute reports as widely as possible.[54] Claude Barnett, founder of the Associated Negro Press (ANP), and William H. Hastie, civilian aide to the secretary of war, maintained close contact.[55]

When he got into office, Hastie sought to improve and take control over the representation of blacks in the press. In a letter to Barnett in August 1941, even before the U.S. entrance into the war, Hastie complained about the racist depiction of black soldiers in the armed forces' news dispatches. "Incidents of this type are destructive of morale among the troops and nullify the Army's attempt at building good will by causing justifiable resentment among the civilian populace. No group within the Army should be singled out for stories or pictures emphasizing racial or religious characteristics."[56] Hastie and Barnett grew impatient and frustrated with the black soldiers' position in the armed forces. Hastie would pass off-the-record information to Barnett "permitting us to use it without quoting where advisable so that we can keep constructive items in the releases and thereby help to develop the best of morale."[57] A positive representation of blacks in the press, they thought, would help build black morale and self-confidence and destabilize racist stereotypes in white readers.[58] In a memorandum to Vice President Henry A. Wallace in April 1942,[59] Barnett stated that the black press functioned as a

> channel for correcting and overcoming misconceptions and unfortunate impressions. . . . Reports which at present make soldiers unhappy because they are filled with the idea that they are being mistreated; which worry the families because they think their sons are not getting a fair deal will be neutralized. Such a program will overcome the mischievous pattern wrought by those who are so busy dealing in complaints and rumors that they can't see the things which are good and inspiring.[60]

In short, the press ought to focus on positive accomplishments of blacks rather than on their negative experiences. In 1943, Roy Wilkins, assistant secretary of the NAACP, discussed with Hastie the War Department's growing awareness of the need for an "experienced Negro public relations officer with high enough rank and authority to get something done on what appears to be an increasingly bad situation." African American soldiers, Wilkins noted, felt mistreated and badly represented, and supported the war effort only "because a victory for the Allies seems to be the lesser of two evils." They were "on the verge of mutiny."[61]

Although African American newspapers executed the call for more positive reports on black America so as not to further hamper morale, they did not fully refrain from pointing out the grievances and mistreatments of blacks on the war and home front. They even did not deny the existence of low black morale. However, they vehemently contested most white people's assumption that lack of morale and poor performance resulted from an inherent black character trait and proved black male inferiority. They maintained that if bad performance occurred, it resulted from white mistreatment and white supremacy. Lack of morale, they argued, was not a sign of weakness or the absence of patriotism of black soldiers, rather it stemmed from frustration with the demeaning treatment at home and abroad. Low morale was turned into a powerful symptom of protest that uncovered the limits of American democracy.

It was necessary for the negative effects of Jim Crow to be outlined, yet overemphasizing and constructing them as completely debilitating for African American soldiers was not an option. It had to be made clear that black men were real men, able to fight despite all obstacles. Charley Cherokee, columnist for the *Chicago Defender*, was one of the many to lay out this conflict. He maintained that race prejudice prevented black Americans from standing "100 per cent behind the war effort." Cherokee and his colleagues intended to present black soldiers in their male prowess as equal if not superior to whites. In his sardonic examination of the African American and white relationship in the war, manhood played an essential role. Cherokee stated: "Mid this utter tropicolored confusion, stalwart Negro manhood sees the issues clearly: 'I am an American. I never stop fighting to save my country from prejudiced male puppies at home who would make it something less than a democracy. . . . Give me arms and ammunition and get out of the way!' That's colored America."[62] He constructed African American patriotism as superior to that of the majority of whites who claimed to love their country. This demonstrated that it was not a lack of their patriotism or manhood on the part of African Americans, but the continuance of race discrimination and segregation which resulted in the lack of their support of the war effort. Cherokee's description of whites as "prejudiced male puppies," or little dogs who were untrained, and not to be taken seriously due to their naïveté, took the gendered quality of his assessment to another level. According to Cherokee, an armed African American was, through his manhood and patriotism, a better protector and provider than anyone who was white-skinned and bigoted. The affirmative and celebratory closure of his article, "That's colored America," should leave no doubt in the reader's mind that black America was the essential foundation and safeguard of the country and its security. The celebration of black pride and manhood went hand in hand with a call to action by unifying blacks in a fight against white supremacists who tried to oppress and humiliate black soldiers.

Although news on black war achievements was directed at the African American reader, the improvement of the black image was certainly also directed at the white establishment. The press intended to change the negative image of black soldiers and exert pressure on the military and administration to implement integration in the armed forces. Christopher Sturkey, a black lieutenant in the war, recalled that the press helped destroy the white conception that blacks could be useful only in service units. He asserted that the reason "we finally got into the action [was] because of all the hell the Negro press was raising."[63] While the mainstream press still largely refrained from including African Americans in their reports on the war, some individuals saw the need for change. In June 1944, Marshall Field, the owner and publisher of *PM* and the *Chicago Sun*, two notable white newspapers, held a speech on "The Negro Press and the Issues of Democracy" before the Capital Press Club in Washington, D.C. He reprimanded that a "one-sided view of war [was] given to white America" that almost obliterated the substantial part African Americans played in fighting and war production. A public opinion survey revealed that the majority of white Americans thought that African Americans did not contribute much to the war effort. This opinion, Field noted, resulted from the mainstream press's continuous failure to report on African Americans. As a result, he demanded the official recognition of their role in the war effort.[64] Impressed with his call for inclusion of the black war efforts in war coverage, the African American press saw a way of ridding "the country of race animosities."[65] Finally, change seemed possible.

"The Undependability of the Average Negro Soldier"

Although the War Department maintained strict segregation, it hoped to get African Americans fully invested in the war effort. A feature-length morale film produced by the U.S. army was meant to help convince African Americans of their importance for and acceptance in the war effort. In 1944, *The Negro Soldier*, an official army film, to some degree presented black soldiers in a surprisingly nonstereotypical fashion.[66] The Office of War Information initially wanted to show the picture to an exclusively African American audience, but by 1945 civil rights activists had achieved its distribution to white viewers. They hoped the film would help quench racial stereotypes among white Americans. Although the movie did not mention segregation, Albert L. Hinton of the *Norfolk Journal and Guide*, like many others, believed "it has advanced the cause of race relations twenty-five years."[67]

In general, blacks hoped that white reports on black performance would change. As military officers publicly lauded black soldiers, improvement was tangible and the odds of an end to Jim Crow seemed greater than ever before.[68] In November 1944, the army needed replacements to defeat the last grand German attack and called for African American volunteers in white combat outfits. More than 2,500 blacks fought alongside whites. After this unprecedented move, a survey showed that the overwhelming majority of white soldiers supported racial mixing in their units.[69] Nevertheless, positive reports did not last. Military leadership and the white press scrutinized black soldiers' and black units' combat performances meticulously. Tales of failures deeply embedded in long-held stereotypes of black inferiority continued to shape mainstream coverage of blacks in the war. The all-black 92nd Infantry Division came under especially close scrutiny within and outside the armed forces. In fall 1944, the outfit deployed to Italy and was thus one of the few all-black outfits sent into combat in Europe. Although they had garnered some success, in February 1945 massive German artillery stalled their advance in northern Italy, which resulted in enormous casualties and enforced mistrust in black soldiers' fighting ability. The black units were pulled out of combat and downgraded; one regiment was turned into a service unit.[70]

To most African Americans, the 92nd was always the epitome of black male prowess and heroism. The African American press reported on the division's "superb fighting against the Nazis."[71] According to the black press, their armed members fought valorously for democracy, thus proving African American equality on a grand scale. The white press, on the other hand, seriously questioned the black press's coverage of the war. *Time* magazine described the positive reports as "wistfully played up."[72] Although Milton Bracker, *New York Times* war correspondent, admitted that racial inequalities existed, he maintained that black papers "unquestionably tended to over-emphasize the division's accomplishments, and the inevitable racial aspects of the situation." He asserted that African American newspapers were "super-sensitive" when reporting on blacks, whereas they were "not sensitive enough to the criterion of accuracy" and could thereby "do more harm than good in one of the most delicate problems facing the United States."[73] He believed that African Americans overemphasized race as a factor in the assessment of black soldiers' performance and treatment in the armed forces. An article in *Social Forces* corroborated Bracker's understanding of the black press and its position on the black soldier. It listed the case of the 92nd Infantry Division as evidence that the black press often printed stories "without carefully checking the facts, or are guilty of seizing a phrase, sentence, or fact, pulling it from its context and building a story of injustice and prejudice."[74]

The official reports on the unit were devastating. Information came back home describing African Americans who broke into mass panic and fled the front lines. The War Department blamed this withdrawal on the black soldiers.[75] The division's commander, Edward M. Almond, argued that the reasons for this withdrawal were "the undependability of the average Negro soldier to operate to his maximum capability, compared to his lassitude toward his performing a task assigned. While there are exceptions to this rule, the general tendency of the Negro soldier is to avoid as much as possible." With this assessment in mind, he recommended not to use any African American troops in combat, since they would not live up to the challenge and ultimately endanger the mission.[76] Almond's assessment, which defamed all black soldiers and turned individual war performances into a question of race and alleged racial inferiority, received much coverage in the white press. *Newsweek* ran a story on the 92nd's allegedly volatile record noting that "The most extensive and wholehearted effort by the United States Army to give American Negro troops a role in the war equal to that of white troops has so far been more productive of disappointment and failure than of anything else."[77]

Following these negative reports on the 92nd Division, Truman K. Gibson, African American civilian aide to Secretary of War Henry L. Stimson, went to Europe to probe the division and determine whether the allegations were true. Succeeding William H. Hastie, who had quit the position in 1943 in protest to the continued racist treatment of blacks, Gibson took a practical approach in his work for black soldiers and their needs at the War Department. Instead of making provocative statements and demands in the fight for segregation, he worked within the system, communicating more closely with his superiors than with black soldiers. From the very beginning of his work, many African American activists and parts of the press criticized his approach. In a letter to the ANP, George Fairchild, who was discharged from the 92nd due to a serious injury, described discriminatory practices at Fort Huachuca, Arizona, and commented on Gibson: "Brig. General Davis [the only black general] and Gibson failed to see the bad things that exist at this camp. I just can't understand as to why they would report to the War Department that everything back at Fort Huachuca is setting pretty. . . . Only Uncle Tom men are selected as Non-Commissioned Officers. College men are the lowest ranking men in the 92nd Infantry Division."[78] Many blacks considered Gibson an apologetic accommodationist who tried to please whites more than he helped African Americans.[79]

After six days with the 92nd Division in Italy, Gibson handed his final report to Major General Otto L. Nelson on March 12, 1945. In his report, "about 800 officers and hundreds of enlisted men expressed themselves in one way or the other." Gibson found that the 92nd often failed because of lack of training and inherent race problems. Gibson did not criticize division commander Almond, whom the black press viewed with suspicion; rather he noted that Almond had only the best in mind for his division. Gibson's criticism of blacks' treatment in the military in general and of segregation was rather mild. He demanded a change in promotion policy, more black officers, the building of racial pride that he considered missing among black soldiers, and more "background material on Negro troops" to be used for battle leadership. He did not mention the necessity to end segregation.[80]

In the white press, Gibson came across as an infallible witness. As "the official representative of the War Department," and "himself a Negro," he was a "critical as well as sympathetic observer." Thus, "his candid admission that the Negro combat troops in Italy have not acquitted themselves well cannot be waved aside as prejudiced evidence."[81] Black criticism and complaints could thereby be easily construed as proof of African American "oversensitivity." Milton Bracker stated that Gibson's findings had to be "taken most seriously because he is the official representative of the War Department and is a Negro." Concurrently, allegations of blacks "melting away" dominated the white press. The New York Times quoted Gibson asserting that the outfit had made "more or less panicky retreats, particularly at night when the attitude of some individual soldiers seemed to be 'I am up here all alone; why in the hell should I stay up here?'" Most liberal white papers and Gibson himself tried to abstain from "racializing" poor combat performance and making it a purely "Negro problem." Yet articles, like the War Department's probe itself, suggested that African American soldiers needed to be under close scrutiny.[82] The "Gibson Report" caused a heated discussion in the black press revealing the inherent pitfalls of linking civil rights to war records.

The black press and community in general disagreed on its assessment of Gibson's statements. Some papers applauded Gibson for his fair-minded assessment of blacks' involvement in the war. To Lem Graves, commentator for the *Pittsburgh Courier*, for instance, Gibson had done justice to the black soldier by "carefully" investigating their situation. Another *Courier* reporter noted that Gibson had provided actual "facts."[83] Positive reactions to Gibson's report stressed the civilian aide's explanations of illiteracy due to discrimination at home and his assertion that the division's failure did not allow racial generalization. They emphasized Gibson's praise for the soldiers' record and his (fairly muted) rejection of Jim Crow in the armed forces.

But black reporters and commentators were in a difficult situation, torn between dismissing the allegations in general and admitting faults, while justifying them by pointing to the harmful effects of segregation and discrimination. An African American journalist remarked, "only if colored troops perform poorly at any time is it duly chronicled for posterity. Unfortunately, whenever they do well in battle, it is often ignored or played up in subtle 'believe it or not' manner."[84] When it came to the performance of blacks in battle, too much was at stake. Many black papers took special issue with Gibson, as they dreaded the damaging effect of his statements to be inevitable. The claim for full and equal citizenship as well as the recognition of black manhood was deeply interwoven with military service and combat duty and a tainted war record meant a setback for African Americans' advancement. An attack on black soldiers was an attack on all blacks at home and abroad.

What infuriated and worried even the most understanding of Gibson's critics, was that Gibson's comments could easily be construed to affirm white stereotypes of black men. His statement that black soldiers "melted away" prompted the black public's outcry. Adam Clayton Powell, one of the few black members of the House of Representatives, accused Gibson of selling out and demanded his resignation so he would not further impair the relationship between blacks and the American government.[85] Even Gibson's predecessor, Hastie, warned of the negative effect of "the ignoring of combat successes and the exaggeration of combat failures."[86] In the case of African American soldiers, separating poor performance from race and racialization was almost impossible. Whites were mostly judged on an individual basis, and while admission to failure was embarrassing, it was excusable and did not reflect on the whole race. Blacks were judged differently. Thus tampering with the image of the black soldier ultimately endangered the fate of the entire community in its struggle for civil rights and equality, in which the black soldier and his war record played a unique role. Grant Reynolds, the former army chaplain, refused Gibson any right to speak on behalf of African American soldiers. He accused him of not attending to their needs and persistently ignoring discrimination in training camps.[87]

The NAACP tried to counter Gibson's statements on a large scale. In a seven-page letter to the *New York Times* rebutting Bracker's article on Gibson's report, Roy Wilkins, NAACP acting secretary, argued that, if black troops struggled, it was because the War Department failed them and did not give them a fair chance to show their abilities. Neither Bracker nor Gibson, Wilkins inferred, cared to understand the discriminatory situation black soldiers faced.[88] The official NAACP magazine, *The Crisis,* called Gibson's report on the 92nd Division "a betrayal of the Negro soldier in this war."[89] In a letter to Eustace Gay, editor of the *Philadelphia Tribune,* Wilkins noted, "I would say that he [Gibson] has thoroughly absorbed the point of view of the War department on the Negro soldier and that, far from being put on the spot by the press associations in Rome, he was merely voicing what he really believes to be the facts. . . . I consider that Mr. Gibson in Rome was guilty, to put it very mildly, of the greatest indiscretion."[90] Wilkins even demanded the civilian aide's resignation.[91]

The relations between Gibson and the NAACP, especially Wilkins, deteriorated almost beyond repair. Gibson attacked Wilkins, stating that the latter had contacted him in "bad faith and with malicious intent," unwilling to wait for his response. The only papers that represented him appropriately, he claimed, were the *Courier, Norfolk Journal and Guide,* and *Baltimore Afro-American,* as Wilkins's comments had too wide a distribution and dominated public discourse.[92] The controversy dragged on and Gibson sent his complaints over Wilkins's action to Walter White, NAACP executive secretary, and the Board of Directors, which on April 9, 1945, had empowered Roy Wilkins "to take action, after getting the facts, to counteract the effect of the statements attributed to Mr. Truman K. Gibson, Jr., regarding the 92nd Division." Ultimately, the board expressed "its lack of confidence in the leadership of Mr. Gibson." Instead of taking control of the image of black soldiers, the board complained, Gibson had participated in the "old

Army game" of oppressing black soldiers.[93] Many blacks considered Gibson and his reports on black soldiers a great loss "of strength needed for the coming fight for the 'new world a-coming.' "[94]

The *Chicago Defender* acted as the unofficial mouthpiece for Gibson's critics and accused Gibson of betraying the black soldier and the entire race.[95] In a long editorial a few days after the news conference in Rome, the *Chicago Defender* blatantly described Gibson as a "Negro 'Uncle Tom'" "who is black but thinks like a white." The controversy further exemplified the gendered discourse that shaped the discussion and issues at hand. The epithet was rife with gender implications intending to ridicule Gibson's manhood and emasculate him.[96] Rooted in slavery stereotypes, an "Uncle Tom" did not speak out against his master and obediently performed the tasks demanded of him.[97] The *Chicago Defender* asserted that rather than standing up for the black soldier, Gibson tried to please the white establishment, had a "do-nothing attitude on Jim Crow" with respect to the needs of black soldiers, and was an "'official apologist.'" According to the paper, his statements in Rome "shamed and embarrassed every Negro with the least bit of pride in his race." However, the most abysmal result of Gibson's report, the paper claimed, was that African American soldiers now had to fight three enemies; those abroad, the white supremacists at home, and what it called the "Uncle Toms" in their own race.[98]

The most animated responses came from *Chicago Defender* readers. Soldiers or veterans felt betrayed and defamed by one of their own. The writers called Gibson names like "Negro Rankin" and said he would "probably make a better right hand man for Hitler than for Stimson." One woman described Gibson as "a traitor to our beloved America . . . [and] a disgrace to the Negro race of America."[99] Another reader asked why Gibson was not serving in the war himself, instead of staying behind in the United States, thereby inherently questioning his manhood and willingness to risk his life for his country.[100] The infuriated readers demanded that Gibson be forced from his position immediately.

Numerous articles accompanied the Gibson discussion, listing black soldiers' acclaimed heroics, and often presenting white officers as witnesses to these achievements.[101] An ANP dispatch noted that General Mark Clark, commander of the Allied Forces in Italy, had called the 92nd Division "brave" and "glorious," and, moreover, had gotten "into a controversy with Truman K. Gibson, civilian aide to the secretary of war, about the contributing factors that caused their publicized retreat."[102] When General

Almond, first commanding officer of the 92nd Division and one of the first to chastise the division's record, received the Distinguished Service Medal (DSM), the *Chicago Defender* reflected on why Almond would win the highest honor, if his outfit had performed badly. The paper declared the award a late "tribute to the 92nd that gives rebuttal to slanders of its fighting ability."[103] Thus, in the eyes of the *Chicago Defender* even the army contradicted Gibson. The impatience with which activists and the black press battled the problematic comments and segregation and discrimination in the armed forces was palpable.

Public pressure weighed too heavily on Gibson for him to ignore the widespread criticism. One month after the press conference in Rome, he publicly refuted any allegations that he had ever called the 92nd Division a failure. He could not understand "how some people can, on the one hand, argue that segregation is wrong, and on the other hand, blindly defend the product of that segregation."[104] Not unlike arguments emerging in the white press, Gibson alleged that his critics glossed over black failures that ultimately resulted from segregation, the evil against which they all were fighting. The link between valorous military service and civil rights was so tight, however, that many critics feared admission to black faltering would only damage their claims to full civil rights as well as the inherent assertion of equal manhood. For many, protecting the image of black segregated units was an essential part of the fight. Most blacks did not deny that black units faltered, because of the special circumstances maybe even more than whites, but they could not accept the inevitable link between race and failure. To black critics, it seemed, Gibson failed to factor in that link when making his report public.

Gibson's follow-up press conference did not change much. Papers that had been on his side applauded him for his clarifications. Nevertheless, even Gibson's supporters argued that the 92nd might have faltered and "Gibson might not have been as wrong as some would like to believe that he was," but all in all, the failures were explainable, not limited to blacks, and, more important, temporary.[105] Others remained skeptical as to the results of his statements and work as a black advisor to the military. The NAACP collected documents that, if necessary, could seriously damage Gibson's reputation.[106] It also considered organizing a reception for the 92nd Division, for "the men deserve it, particularly in the light of the slander of them by Truman Gibson."[107] Although understanding of his problematic position working for the War Department, Julius Adams in the *New*

York Amsterdam News asked whether Gibson was "a real public servant or an Uncle Tom," a question that was still to be decided once the dust had settled. Others were already convinced that instead of representing blacks, Gibson had embraced the War Department position. More than once, Gibson's work was compared unfavorably to that of his predecessor, Hastie.[108] For his opponents, criticism of black soldiers should be productive, not deliver ammunition to white supremacists. When Gibson resigned from his post as civilian aide in November 1945, the *Chicago Defender* remarked that "Negro soldiers were able to give a sigh of relief," for Gibson had been "completely ineffectual—and often downright harmful to the best interests of the colored soldiers."[109] While his status among many African Americans would remain tainted for years to come, Gibson did not fall from grace in the armed forces. Moreover, Southern white supremacists reveled in Gibson's statement and would frequently refer to his assessments in their crusades against black civil rights.[110]

Although the Second World War had made the hypocrisies at home nationally and internationally all the more visible, it failed to bring an end to segregation and discrimination in the United States. Moreover, African Americans and especially African American soldiers had to face the same stereotypes and disregard for their service that they had faced in all previous wars. While the war ended victoriously for the United States and its allies, the African American "Double V" campaign, whose ultimate aim was to achieve equality in all areas of life, faltered. Moreover, attempts to correct and control the image of the African American soldier in public and military discourse failed. Nevertheless, black America was unwilling to back down.

At the end of the war, a growing number of African Americans, especially black soldiers, were eager to make their protest and demands for equal rights heard. Military service in World War II contributed to the growing unwillingness of black men to "accept the prewar structure of racial dominance."[111] In response to white disinterest, ignorance, and often condemnation of and physical violence toward African American soldiers in particular, the black press undertook enormous efforts to "set the record straight" by telling the African American side of the history of the war. Their fight for social equality and desegregation went hand in hand with the struggle against stereotypical representation or plain omission of black soldiers from the war's history.

Chapter 2

Coming Home

For African American soldiers, the return home came with the harsh realization that not much had changed in the United States. Well aware of their special position in the African American community, white supremacists used the defamation of black soldiers as a powerful strategy to disfranchise and degrade the black community. By May 1945, with the war in Europe over, many white Southerners felt more than ever that a "second Reconstruction" was taking place that had to be stalled. Regardless of a certain amount of social and economic progress for blacks and growing support among some white Americans for their needs, white supremacy survived the war, and in the eyes of many whites it was time to put African Americans "'into their place.'"[1] Moreover, white Southerners feared that white supremacy was seriously in danger and black social equality in all areas of life inevitably loomed. White segregationists saw the most blatant sign of change in African American soldiers and veterans, who returned from war impatient and ready to fight.[2] White fears of black equality and demands for civil rights aroused outbursts of defamation and violence against black soldiers.

"White Anglo-Saxon Is the Forgotten Man in America Today"

Always opposed to Roosevelt's Fair Employment Practice Committee, the white South balked at its postwar extension.[3] They initiated a general condemnation of African Americans and especially black soldiers. Starting at the end of June 1945, Mississippi senators Theodore G. Bilbo and James Eastland filibustered the extension of the FEPC by implementing racial slurs. They represented the radical and often "scorned" faction of an otherwise "measured counteroffensive" against the civil rights movement in the South and around the nation, which otherwise adapted its measures to a changing racial climate.[4]

On June 27, 1945, Bilbo began his diatribe in Congress by lashing out against African American civil rights activists, dubbing them un-American communists seeking to destroy the American nation with the FEPC. He painted a gruesome picture of their crusade for social equality, calling blacks an intellectually inferior race, whose ultimate goal was intermarriage with whites. Moreover, he claimed that the desegregated mixing of races would eventually lead to the liquidation of the white race and the American nation in general. Bilbo maintained that the only way to end discrimination was the relocation of all African Americans to Africa.[5] By the time Eastland took the floor on June 29, 1946, large parts of the white press, even in the South, had already chastised Bilbo for his racist tirades against the FEPC and black empowerment.[6] Yet, following Bilbo in tone and fervor, Eastland stressed that the "Negro race is an inferior race" and was, therefore, neither eligible nor capable of being elevated to equality in all sectors of life.[7]

Black soldiers' performance in combat became the most powerful argument in his attempt to destroy African American demands for equality at the end of the war. Eastland maintained that they were "an utter and dismal failure in combat in Europe. . . . I state that the conduct of the Negro soldier in Normandy, as well as all over Europe, was disgraceful, and that Negro soldiers have disgraced the flag of their country." Playing minorities and their performance in combat against each other, he claimed that the Japanese American division "distinguished itself in combat, and further, saved a Negro regiment from annihilation."[8] He chastised African Americans for having "run when the show-down came." He did not cite segregation as the root of their difficulties, but rather claimed it was their lack of ability and racial pride. Eastland inverted the system of oppression, when he asserted that the "white Anglo-Saxon is the forgotten man in America today. He is discriminated against, he is mistreated . . ." due to the rule of "minority groups and for the benefit of minority groups."[9] According to his reasoning, whites Americans were the oppressed people, deprived of equality and a fair chance. Blacks, on the other hand, represented the ruling race.[10] The accusation was a scathing one, especially in the light of what African Americans knew they had done for the nation and endured during the war.

Eastland tapped into a long-standing white fear, when he capitalized on the stereotype of black sexual predation and lust for white women. The vilification of black men as sexual predators and rapists of white women was a common justification for lynching in the South.[11] Eastland maintained that African American soldiers had gone on rape sprees, attacking women in France who had recently been liberated from German occupation. "Negro soldiers would go to farm houses and holler 'Boche! Boche!' as if they were looking for Germans, call the men of the families out into the yards, and hold guns on them while they went in and criminally assaulted the women members of the family." He claimed that African American soldiers committed more crimes against French women in a few days than German soldiers had during four years of occupation. Eastland complained that the NAACP and the Communist Party prevented prosecution of guilty black soldiers.

Information on an alleged mass rape of German women in Stuttgart by Senegalese soldiers in American uniforms surfaced.[12] Based on supposedly irrefutable reports of a "number of high-ranking American generals," his story was corroborated by, among others, senator Burton Wheeler who had traveled Europe to investigate its progress under occupation. Eastland maintained, "It was one of the most horrible occurrences of modern times." He furthermore explained that the alleged mass rape was caused by "certain racial characteristics," which existed "wherever their members may be found." The incident proved "that the Negro race is most assuredly an inferior race."[13] Although African Americans were not involved in the alleged incident, Eastland turned all blacks into potential rapists of white women. Blacks could never become equal to white Americans, because they represented "African standards in the United States today."[14] He reasoned that white American men had always behaved like gentleman soldiers, trying "to maintain American standards in the American army," but were now deprived of their well-deserved preferential treatment by an inferior minority.[15] The (alleged) rape of white women in Europe became the "mask behind which disfranchisement was hidden," in which white pride was established and black men were disempowered. Eastland's statement on sexual violence capitalized on white hysteria, which equated alleged black sexual power with political power.[16] While Eastland turned Germany and its white citizens into victims with which white America should associate, the statement fed long-standing fear among many whites of black domination and violence.[17]

The rape charge against black soldiers was an efficient rallying tool for those who supported Eastland's rationale. First sergeant Washington Davis, an African American soldier stationed in Germany, reported that white soldiers were spreading rumors that blacks would "steal, rape, cut your throats," in an attempt to disrupt otherwise good relations between "German Fräuleins" and blacks.[18] Such descriptive scenarios proved whites' anxieties that "postwar political self-assertion by black men pointed toward underlying sexual desires for white women."[19] Even moderate white supremacists would not support social equality and the possibility of interracial sex, a fact that made Eastland's argumentation especially noteworthy.[20] The threat of social equality of blacks and whites resonated with many whites in both North and South.

For months after the senate session, many African Americans continued to express their dismay over Eastland's statements on black soldiers. Numerous soldiers sent letters to the NAACP voicing their abhorrence of Eastland's comments. The NAACP complained to President Truman about the "disgraceful," "un-American," and "un-democratic" attacks and went so far as to demand Eastland's and Bilbo's impeachment.[21] Offended African Americans wrote to Eastland directly and demanded public repudiation to clear their names of the charges against them.[22] All leading African American newspapers ran stories refuting Eastland's attacks on black soldiers and African American claims for equality, which was intrinsically linked to black soldiers' image and performance record in war. These newspapers also received a plethora of letters from readers and soldiers expressing their utmost aversion to Eastland's attacks.[23] The message to Eastland was clear: the defamation of the black soldier insulted "13,000,000 Citizens"[24] who were willing to put up with neither his slurs, nor with the underlying attempt to continuously disempower and disfranchise them. They were not "merely" blacks, but citizens with the right to respectful treatment. Bilbo and Eastland's words instigated immediate grassroots activism. The *Philadelphia Tribune* reported on a grandmother who initiated a letter writing campaign to General George Marshall in a desperate attempt to get the "unfair, untruthful and hateful attack" publicly repudiated.[25] The article indirectly underlined the general impatience and rage Eastland's insults against black soldiers had caused among nonactivists.

The black press returned to invoking the similarity between Nazi and American reactionaries. Marjorie McKenzie, a *Pittsburgh Courier* columnist, called Eastland "a fascist without a label"; she also condemned the armed forces for upholding segregation while trying to teach democracy to Japan and Germany. For her, given the circumstances, this was clearly a futile task.[26] In an open letter to black soldiers assuring them that their valor and combat excellence were acknowledged at home, Evelyn Swann, a columnist for the *Norfolk Journal and Guide*, referred to Eastland as "a Hitlerized American" and called on returning soldiers to vote him out of office.[27] The comparison and equation of white racism in the United States with German Nazism was omnipresent and powerful. Newspapers even compared Eastland to Joseph Goebbels and his tactics: "The High Priest of lying [Goebbels] may be physically departed, but certainly his spirit is still with us, judging by the antics of Mississippi's Senator Eastland in the Senate last week when he went to the most vicious extremes in lying against Negro soldiers."[28] Moreover, the *Pittsburgh Courier* claimed that reactionary forces, or the "enemies of this country," were "fearful of their [blacks'] determination to be full citizens, else they would not resort to such desperate tactics in a vain effort to hold them back."[29]

In their quest for recognition as well as a voice, African American papers at times appropriated terms used by white supremacists. In order to describe white acts of degradation and violence against blacks, African Americans inverted white racism and its language, which often equated African American males with animals. The *Pittsburgh Courier* described Eastland as being of "the lowest species of animal."[30] Reduced to their physical body, they allegedly showed no or only limited signs of intellectual strength and therefore had to be controlled and oppressed for the sake and protection of the national and individual white body.[31] Now whites were portrayed as inhumane, barbaric, and beastlike threats to the black body and the body politic. The newspaper called on white and black Americans to rid themselves of the "Southern Senators and Representatives . . . from districts where the people, white and black, are effectually disfranchised."[32]

It took quite some time for whites to publicly refute Eastland's allegations in Congress. The *Philadelphia Tribune* fumed: "This vicious attack made upon American colored soldiers by Mississippi's Eastland comes as no great surprise to us. . . . But the fact that not one Senator, Republican or Democrat, arose to challenge his base and despicable lies clearly shows the low estate in which Negroes are held by American lawmakers."[33] Black activists lobbied intensely to win spokespersons for their case. Two weeks after Eastland's speech opposing the FEPC, the Senate heard a public refutation; a handful of senators spoke out in favor of black soldiers. Senators

James Mead and Robert Wagner, both Democrats from New York, took a stance in the Senate, praising African American soldiers' performance in World War II.[34] The black press applauded their efforts, as white support was considered a valuable asset to counter the allegations by Southern white supremacists like Bilbo and Eastland.[35] In early 1946, Helen Gahagan Douglas, representative from California and advocate for desegregation and racial equality, spoke for hours before Congress to pay the black soldier "respect and to express the gratitude of the American people for his contribution in the greatest battle of all time—the battle which decided whether or not we were to remain a free people."[36] These assessments of the African American performance in the war were meant to invalidate the alleged inferiority and lack of masculinity of African Americans. In the minds of both blacks and whites, valorous military service was still intrinsically linked to the right to full citizenship. Every attack on the image and record of the black soldier represented an attack on the black fight for civil rights. Although their military record was seriously tainted by white reports and allegedly even by one of their own, African Americans agreed on one thing: the rectification of the image of the African American soldier in the Second World War was a necessity.

Isaac's Homecoming

Isaac Woodard made his way back home on a Greyhound bus. For four years, he had served as a longshoreman in the U.S. armed forces and had been awarded two service medals, a Good Conduct Medal and a Battle Star. He had just returned from Japan to the States on February 7, 1946, happy and relieved that the war had left him unharmed. His family, his wife of five years in particular, were eagerly awaiting his return in Winnsboro, South Carolina. Life was looking good. With the training he had received and an honorable discharge from the military, he hoped to make a good life for himself and his family. Still in uniform, the black veteran got into an argument with the white bus driver, who did not want to wait for him to use the restroom in Batesburg, South Carolina. Woodard insisted and, according to his later testimony, blatantly declared, "God damn it, talk to me like I am talking to you. I am a man just like you."[37] The bus driver grudgingly waited, but could not let this African American get away with this audacious assertiveness. It was bad enough that he was in uniform, but a black man talking back to a white man was unbearable in a system of white supremacy. He was, in short, a "'a nigger not knowing his place.'"[38]

Following the argument, the bus driver did what many white Southerners considered a logical and rightful act: he called the police to take over and reinstate order. Woodard was arrested for creating "a disturbance" and taken to prison, but not before being gravely beaten. Somewhere in South Carolina, seven days after he received his army discharge papers, white police officers gouged Woodard's eyes out and blinded him for life. Without medical care, the twenty-eight-year-old veteran was left in jail for the night, and was fined the next day.[39]

At first, the incident did not attract much public interest. However, starting in summer 1946, it made headlines all across the United States and the world. James Hinton of the NAACP had gotten word of the incident and publicized it on a grand scale.[40] The civil rights organization received a "flood of letters" from blacks, as well as whites who were "aroused over Blinding of Negro Vet."[41] The *Atlanta Daily World* reported that a "correspondent for British and Indian newspapers described it as one of the most shocking examples of race hate and sadism he'd heard."[42] The *New York Times* and *Washington Post* covered the story and recounted the failings of the officials of the city of Aiken and the attempts of the African American community to help Woodard. Even Southern newspapers ran parts of the story.[43] President Truman received hundreds of letters and telegrams from ordinary citizens who expressed disgust over the atrocious crime. They demanded that the president ensure the prosecution of the perpetrators and that they receive the "full penalty"[44] for their crimes. Woodard's treatment drew renewed comparison between Nazi Germany and the South, even in white newspapers. To many, "homegrown hate-mongering fascist[s]"[45] proved to be not much different from "Hitler's Gestapo" or the "Japs."[46]

Woodard's case hit a sensitive nerve among the African American public, as returning black soldiers who had risked their lives for their nation abroad, now increasingly fell prey to white mobs. These attacks evoked memories of the events after the First World War, when an upsurge in racial violence and lynching occurred mainly directed against African American men returning from their service in the war.[47] *The Crisis*, the NAACP organ, reported that two-thirds of hate crimes against blacks targeted veterans.[48] The number of violent attacks or lynchings after World War II did not reach the heights of those that occurred at the turn of the century or after

World War I, but the news about violent attacks caught the attention of the African American and mainstream media more than ever before. Blacks tried to seize control over the narratives. White perpetrators became "beasts who parade as men"[49] "whom we would like to feel were totally unrelated to the human species."[50] This black narrative of racial violence deprived white men of their humanity and civilized masculinity, thus negating their claims of supremacy over blacks. It was a rhetoric designed to elevate black men, especially black soldiers, over white men, appropriating the discourse of white dominance without practicing the physical violence and subjugation of their white male counterparts. After a horrific lynching in Monroe, Georgia, during which two men, one of them a veteran, and their two female companions were slain by a white mob, the call for unity against white oppressions in the light of the war experience grew even stronger.[51] The hypocrisy of an allegedly democratic Americanism that did not exist for African Americans was omnipresent.

Woodard's fate was a rallying point. He did not die, but the violent attack on him was an attempted lynching on a black soldier. "We have resolved that now is the time for all Negroes to stick together for certainly at that rate we are going if we don't, we will all be lynched one by one."[52] For African Americans, Woodard epitomized America's faults in the treatment of the black minority, especially black soldiers. Just like after the First World War, fear, impatience, frustration, and real urgency to fight back dominated the African American community. In an interview with the *Chicago Defender*, Woodard called unmistakably and forcefully for an end to black acquiescence and restraint when he stated,

the real battle has just begun in America. They went overseas and did their duty and now they're home and have to fight another struggle, that I think outweighs the war.

The South is perpetrating ideas held over from the Civil War and if we are ever to attain our status as American citizens to share in the social, economic and political rights as stated in the Constitution we must hammer into submission those with ideas of keeping the colored man down.

Never once while overseas did I have an idea that such a thing as happened to me could exist. . . . I haven't allowed myself to become discouraged in any way and I'm planning to devote the rest of my life to helping my people to win a better way of life in this country.[53]

He presented himself as powerful, unwavering, and unwilling to give up. In African American discourse, Woodard became the epitome of black manhood and black self-confidence. The black press and the NAACP used him as a poster boy for African American resilience in the face of white oppression.

The figure represented and constructed in the public was a strong individual who, despite his disability, strived for independence and self-sufficiency. His unrelenting pugnaciousness provided the African American community with a symbol "of the horror of jim crow,"[54] the need for full civil rights, and the affirmation of black masculinity. Woodard was quoted, "I'm going to fight this thing through to the finish. . . . The way I feel now, I could go back down there and clean out the whole place. But I know the NAACP is right. We'll fight them through the law—and I believe we'll win."[55] The image of manhood he represented and was constructed to represent, belied every stereotype purported by whites. Woodard's strength, power, and will to carry on for the betterment of his race and the nation in a country that treated him with violent disrespect was considered to be rooted in his strong family bond, especially his love for his wife and his mother. He was living proof of "how military service had reinforced his sense of masculinity."[56] More than ever before, veterans—and Woodard was the quintessential representative—were no longer willing to acquiesce to white male supremacy and oppression.

The figure of Woodard presented in the black press corresponded with long-held ideas and ideals of white middle-class masculinity. Though he made clear that he was man enough to physically fight the Southern culture of supremacy and its representatives, his reason and intelligence ensured that he would reach his goals in a lawful—American—manner with the help of the NAACP, and not through violence or irrationality. Though aggressive in his expression, he remained restrained in his activism, which corresponded with respectable forms of masculinity. Hence—and most likely soothing for many white liberals—the case, the ensuing enragement, and calls for change in race relations never questioned the perfectible potential of the United States. Despite criticism, it was not so much rage that underlay calls for racial change, but patriotism. In both press reports and Woodard's description of himself, his disability—his physical imperfection—never calls his penetrating physical and mental strength, or his manhood, into question.[57]

The construction of Woodard as an American veteran and dedicated family man countered the stereotype of the dysfunctional black family and of an oversexed black male—the sexual predator—who was unable and unwilling to fulfill his duties as the head of the household, provider, and protector of his relatives.[58] Woodard's family, in which he was the provider and protector, the strong, black man in control despite the disability that was forced on him by white policemen, corresponded with white middle-class values of family life and bond. The gendered quality of patriotism, military service, and suffering was reinforced by an article's construction of Woodard's mother as emotional, fearful, and heartbroken over her son's disability and fate. While Woodard represented full, undefeatable masculinity, his mother, although not weak, represented the mourning woman, a role generally assigned to women in the national discourse of war and violence.

Black newspapers and the NAACP molded Woodward into an "American hero,"[59] who was as much a symbol of patriotism as of racial pride. The *New York Amsterdam News* called on the public to fight back just like Woodard did, "without the cankering bitterness of self-pity."[60] The African American response makes clear the growing frustration over lack of equal rights despite dedicated military service. The *Chicago Defender* wrote: "There is no need to rant or rave or describe in flowing prose what has happened to Woodard . . . how he must go through life frustrated, bewildered and handicapped; constantly wondering how an ironic fate took him through a war unharmed to be destroyed by those who should be forever grateful for his sacrifice."[61] Woodard became a symbol for America's moral demise and white Americans' ingratitude to a man who risked his life for them. The *New York Amsterdam News* maintained that "New Yorkers intend to indicate by their whole-hearted support of Isaac Woodard, not only their acknowledgement of him as a symbol of the fight of all men against racism and oppression, but also that they are behind him in his fight to make a new life from the broken remnants of the old."[62]

The brutality of the case as well as pressure from the NAACP and the public attention it yielded moved the federal government to prosecute the case, which the FBI under J. Edgar Hoover investigated. Despite all evidence, the jury found the defendants not guilty. A speaking tour organized by the NAACP helped to raise money for the blinded veteran. The NAACP also helped Woodard file a civil suit against the bus company, Atlantic Greyhound Corporation of West Virginia, but he also lost.[63] Ultimately, the public lost track of and interest in Woodard and he vanished into obscurity, although his case is still present in history and memory.[64] For a while, however, his military service abroad and his fight with and against the loss of his eyesight, described as "hopeless" by doctors, made him a quintessential representative of a black manhood, which refused to submit to white supremacy.

Facing a World of Humiliation

The South remained almost as segregated as before the war and the North was far from being a haven of equality. People who were seemingly more open to racial equality often reproduced long-held stereotypes of African American soldiers. Despite his assertion that discrimination, segregation, and the denial of educational equality severely set back African American soldiers in the armed forces during the Second World War, colonel Paul C. Davis of the Army War College at the Carlisle Barracks in Pennsylvania argued in an article in *Virginia Quarterly Review* "that, however innately equal to the white they [black soldiers] may be, they have in their present state of development psychological peculiarities (from the white ethnocentric view, weaknesses) some of which may cause serious failures in combat. . . . American Negroes are peculiarly sensitive to suggestion and panic easily."[65] For many whites, these alleged psychological "peculiarities" of blacks confined black men to a lower form of citizenship and masculinity.

The official publication of the American Veterans Committee (AVC), an interracial veterans' organization founded in 1944 as a liberal counterorganization to the segregated American Legion, published a letter from New York veteran Henry N. Sachs. Pledging his utmost faith in the AVC's interracial principles and his opposition to senator Theodore G. Bilbo and white supremacists in general, Sachs wrote, "Here are the FACTS: Negroes as a group make poorer soldiers than Whites. . . . It is unfortunate that the mental and educational standards of the Negro are quite low." He continued that only through strong-minded and able white leadership could African American soldiers perform successfully.[66] The underlying faith in white superiority and leadership required bringing "the Negro soldier" in line.

White leadership could help blacks attain white men's fighting ability. This argument was not uncommon among self-acclaimed integrationists, who were as damaging to the cause of racial equality and civil rights as the full-fledged segregationists whose racial slurs were to be expected. The defamation and discrimination continued. Some soldiers were even tempted to stay in Germany, as "obviously the conditions for Blacks were better."[67] Coming home could be a perilous, complicated, and long-drawn-out process in which black soldiers were especially disenfranchised.

Indeed, a quick and honorable discharge often proved difficult to receive for most blacks. The point system that regulated discharges favored troops with a long combat time, from which most African Americans had been excluded during the war. In their fight against blacks' disadvantaged status, the NAACP argued that the system "ignores the long service of hundreds of thousands of service troops." They were certain that the armed forces intended to humiliate and disadvantage blacks further.[68] Moreover, a disproportionate amount of black soldiers received "blue discharges"—a discharge without honor printed on a blue piece of paper.[69] The military issued such discharges to individuals who allegedly showed "undesirable habits or traits of character." Mostly associated with homosexuality, blue discharges were not only a stigma of subpar service but also alluded to sexual deviance.[70] They seriously hampered the future of black soldiers. With a blue discharge, a veteran had limited chances on the job market and in the application for the GI Bill.[71] In the South, the black soldiers' general prospects on the job market were especially bleak. Most jobs were unavailable to blacks, even to those with an honorable discharge.[72]

African Americans saw the blue discharges as part of "widespread conspiracy" against black soldiers, which further tarnished their public image.[73] African Americans represented only 6.5 percent of the entire army personnel. According to Adjutant General Edward F. Witsell, 10,806 black soldiers received a blue discharge; this amounted to almost 25 percent of the 48,603 blue discharges handed out between 1941 and 1945.[74] The issue was so important to African Americans that newspapers formed an alliance to fight for the end of blue discharges. The personal rights of black soldiers and the reputation of all African Americans and their patriotism seemed to be at stake with the continuance of such a high number of blacks receiving these denigrating releases from the armed forces. The NAACP also mobilized to fight these debilitating discharges. The organization had established a Veterans Affairs Office on January 1, 1945, and successively expanded its work to help black veterans in their struggle against overt and covert cases of discrimination, helping them find jobs and housing. A lawyer was added to the organization's staff, in charge of "courts-martial and blue discharge certificate cases of Negro veterans which are inordinately disproportionate because of race prejudice."[75] Senator Edwin C. Johnson, a Democrat from Colorado, helped to bring an official proposal before the Senate, which led to an investigation and report on the effects of blue discharges.[76] While the report did not once mention the disproportionately high number of blacks affected, it did admit to the detrimental consequences of undesirable discharges on soldiers and their advancement. It recommended abolishing blue discharges altogether.[77] The House Military Affairs Committee urged the army to review every blue discharge issued since the start of the war. To blacks, this move signified an increase in black influence on white decision-makers.[78] They were willing to fight back in all spheres.

"The Record Speaks for Them"

Driven by the continuous neglect or negative representation in general public discourse, African Americans continued their attempts to take control over representation of black soldiers; the war was over, but not the fight. At the end of 1945, Benjamin E. Mays, the president of Morehouse College, accurately described the situation when he stated in a *Phylon* article, "In many sections of America, one would hardly know that Negroes fought and died in this war. . . . When a Negro soldier dies, in many areas, no public mention is made of his death."[79] The objective was now to correct this image, and to include them as heroes in the memory of the war. Black columnist Lucius C. Harper asserted, "We have been denied our past glories but we claim them now in the wake of our Renaissance. . . . let us awake and transcend the glory that we have been denied."[80] Rewriting or writing blacks into the history and memory of the war that had just ended was an essential part of this "Negro Awakening" and the basis for black civil rights claims. The contentions over the role of African Americans in the war turned into a discussion over the question of who controlled the writing of history.

The black press continued its campaign to honor black servicemen. In 1946, the *Los Angeles Sentinel*, for example, published a weekly series titled "The Story of the Negro Soldier in World War II" that was, the paper claimed, "based on facts and figures gathered from the files of the War and Navy Departments."[81] With "Men in Uniform," the *Norfolk Journal and Guide* printed weekly information on black soldiers. The *Black Dispatch* and the *Afro-American* distributed a comic strip on African American involvement in the war effort. The comic underlined the importance of the service units and their willingness to fight and sustain under heavy bombings and artillery fire.[82] The NAACP hired Jean Byers, a white graduate of Smith College, to write an "authentic" history of blacks' involvement in the Second World War "to offset unfavorable reports circulated by prejudiced publications and individuals to discredit Negro fighting men."[83] These negative assessments of African American soldiers as fighters and patriots promoted the continuation of subjugation and the white justification of racial hierarchies in the American nation. Mostly published in black publications, the articles also addressed whites oblivious to or dismissive of blacks.[84] The intent of the articles was not only to establish racial pride within the African American community, but also to prove blacks' equality and right to equality to white readers.

The war stories provided the platform to "negotiate[d] and renegotiate[d]" most daringly "the terms of racial coexistence."[85] The objective to recognize black soldiers as heroes remained.

> Thousands of Negroes made the supreme sacrifice in World War II. . . . In the face of such odds, their heroism is the more brilliant, their sacrifices greater. It is incongruous to call these men, lauded by Ike Eisenhower himself, yellow. Disillusioned though they are, these men fought for democracy with a strength and devotion that cannot be gainsaid. As best they knew they fought gamely, punching to the end. Were Negro soldiers cowards? The record speaks for them.[86]

In their endeavor to exonerate the black soldier and retell the narrative of his performance in the armed forces, the black community tried to eschew a discourse of victimization. African Americans, despite all impediments of racism, managed to prove their valor and virility for their nation and their race.

The soldiers' use in service units during the war was presented in a new light. Though confining and humiliating, preponderant employment of blacks in service units was turned into a valuable and honorable task that made the victory of the combat troops possible. "[T]he fact remains that eight out of every ten Negro soldiers were in the service outfits, doing 'the dirty work.' . . . It meant building airports, bases, roads and highways under fire, in freezing cold and blazing heat. . . . And these were the men on whom depended the success of the Normandy invasion."[87] Although they served without weapons in the service forces, they protected themselves and performed their tasks heroically. Despite their predominant exclusion from the position of combat soldier, blacks merited the highest honors. Columnist Charley Cherokee in the *Chicago Defender* wrote, "Popular misconception is that the colored troops mostly assigned to Service Forces in World War II, were safe from danger way behind the lines. Actually, mostly deadly of bombing and strafing planes concentrated on supply troops behind the lines. Negro 'Service' G.Is sometimes had to drop their work and dive for cover, sometimes they fought back with one hand and worked with the other."[88]

The black press often attempted to invert the existing gendered racial hierarchies, making black soldiers superior to whites because of the double burden of being attacked without weapons to defend themselves. Strong black men in uniform remained primary symbols of powerful black masculinity in the struggle for civil rights.

In 1947, the Schomburg Collection of the New York Public Library in Harlem (now the Schomburg Center for Research in Black Culture), one of the largest research collections on blacks in the United States, prepared for Negro History Month.[89] The 1947 celebration in New York specifically focused on the efforts and fate of black soldiers in the American armed forces. The title of the conference held in the framework of Negro History Month was "The Negro Warrior: His Record and His Future." L. D. Reddick, curator of the Collection, asked President Truman to attend "this significant conference" or at least send a statement.[90] Truman did not attend the conference, but sent his greetings. Although he supported opportunities for black veterans and the use of black soldiers "in all capacities and in all Services," Truman skillfully evaded the issue of segregation in the military and civilian life, leaving the African American community to wait for a presidential push toward racial equality, especially for soldiers and veterans.[91] Reddick, disappointed by the president's hesitation, continued to pressure Truman to actively support racial integration. Instead of addressing segregation head-on, the White House staff referred Reddick's letter to the President's Committee on Universal Training, whose only black member was the infamous Truman K. Gibson.[92]

A well-known figure and activist in the African American community, Reddick was versed in analyzing the role of African American soldiers in the armed forces and in America's wars. During the Second World War, he had published an article deliberating on the future of blacks in peacetime.[93] Moreover, he later uncompromisingly pushed General Dwight D. Eisenhower for a clear commitment to the improvement of the status of black soldiers in the armed forces and to the end of segregation.[94] Rectification of the public image of the African American soldier after the war held special significance for him. He intended to publicly expose the misconceptions and stereotypes he saw purported in social science, military, and general accounts of the "Negro in the armed forces." In a letter to the editor of the *American Journal of Sociology*, Reddick clearly stated that seemingly evaluative scientific articles and general accounts of black soldiers were based on misconceptions and fostered "fabrication of the social myth of the Negro's role in World War II."[95] The well-respected journal had just published an article titled, "Race Prejudice and Negro-White Relations in the Army," which, like so many pieces in academic and nonacademic publications, examined African Americans' role in the war and the armed forces.[96]

What upset Reddick most was that this article upheld the idea that problematic relations between the races were fundamentally unsolvable, in both the military and the civilian worlds. The mutual distrust and antagonism between the two sides were, according to E. T. Hall, the article's author, virtually impossible to overcome. The majority of conflicts between the races Hall described in his article involved white women. Hall capitalized on and corroborated the detrimental stereotype that black men had a special interest in the white female. The article, Reddick argued, never questioned the underlying concepts of white supremacy and superiority that considerably disempowered black men. To Reddick's dismay, Hall did not take into consideration the power relations existent in the military— and society in general for that matter—thereby never allowing for a fair pairing of the races. Reddick did not contest that black and white antipathy existed, but disagreed with its construction as a given that relied on the misconception that "little could be done about racial discrimination and segregation *because* American society is as it is."[97]

The perceived misrepresentation of soldiers did not end in the immediate postwar period. In 1950, *Life* magazine published *Life's Picture History of World War II* celebrating the achievements and valorous deeds of soldiers and civilians in defeating the enemies of democracy, freedom, and humanity, but excluded African Americans.[98] Of over 1,000 pictures, the book contained only a single picture of a black soldier. He was shown mourning the death of President Roosevelt. Reacting to the publication, Joseph D. Bibb, a *Courier* columnist, protested once again that, "American histories have consistently failed to present the actual and factual achievements of colored Americans to posterity. American history is a tissue of lies and misrepresentatives."[99] In an incensed letter to the publisher of *Life*, Roy Wilkins, executive administrator of the NAACP, expressed his shock over the book's exclusion of African American soldiers, and their essential role and performance in the war. How could "one tenth of the population of America [that] had its share of men in the uniform of their country doing their best all over the world in the fight against Hitlerism and Japanese imperialism" be excluded from the publication, Wilkins asked Andrew Heiskell, *Life* magazine's publisher. He did not claim that "Negro troops won the war or won any great operation of it," but that their role, although mostly in service units, was so essential that it could not simply be ignored.[100]

Wilkins's argumentation sought to achieve equivalent recognition and respect for the service of mostly disregarded labor battalions predominantly made up of blacks, with that of the mainly white and most respected combat units. The letter listed a selection of indispensable and invaluable deeds of black support troops in Europe and Asia. He pointed out the danger that the next generation of Americans reading the book would not learn of the essential role blacks had played in the war. If publications like *Life* continued to exclude African Americans from their stories, future generations would "conclude that Negro Americans did nothing worthy of recording in World War II." Furthermore, he stated that "the American Negro has become used to this sort of treatment, but as hardened and cynical as he has become, I am sure he did not expect this sort of complete blackout in a publication of the TIME-LIFE-FORTUNE group. Underrating, yes, but not complete omission."[101] Wilkins ended his letter with a strong and worrisome argument, pointing to the looming conflicts with an ever-strengthening Communist Russia. He maintained that the book fed directly into the upsurge of Communism by disregarding blacks and propagating the racism the seemingly democratic West perpetuated. He made unequivocally clear that "It is a lily-white book emerging at a time when mere whiteness is fast losing significance. It will not help win the war of ideas in which we find ourselves, and it could have more than a little effect in any war of guns."[102] Three months earlier, in July 1950, the United States had committed troops to Korea to prevent Communist North Korean troops from taking control over the American-controlled part of the East-Asian country. Wilkins clearly alluded to the ongoing debate on whether the Korean War was a race war and the growing majority of nonwhite people in the world, who felt that the white culture of dominance that American democracy represented, at least in part, might not be the best solution for their oppressed status. Wilkins made use of the Cold War conflict as a weapon in African Americans' general struggle for equality, and specifically for their equal representation in the memory of the "good war" that was so essential in the national identity construct of the United States.

In response to Wilkins's protests, Heiskell claimed *Life* had done everything to gather information on the war, but had come up empty-handed in regard to a record of black service. While he apologized to some degree for the lack of positive portrayal of black American soldiers, the explanation disappointed Wilkins. Only under sustained pressure did Wilkins eventually pay the outstanding invoice for the books he had ordered before knowing that *Life*'s publication had omitted blacks almost entirely. He continued to disapprove of the fact that a "reference book" for "millions of persons" excluded one million black men and women in uniform and left the degrading impression on its readers that "Negro American citizens did nothing worthy of recording in World War II."[103] Bibb, the *Pittsburgh Courier* columnist, chimed in and condemned the book as "contorted, twisted and misrepresented." He contended that the only African American depicted was a "Negro GI dejectedly fingering out funeral paeans at Roosevelt's funeral." For most African Americans, this depiction must have been an insult to the actual role of black soldiers in the war and stood in full contrast to predominant ideas of manly valor. Bibb called for "keeping the record straight" and openly condemned the omission of African American soldiers and civilians from the story about the war.[104] African American men were thus excluded from this generation of World War II soldiers, which Susan Faludi has called the "template for postwar manhood."[105]

A Time for Change?

At President Truman's urging, the navy and air force began to rethink their attitude toward black soldiers after the war. In September 1945, the army established a board to reevaluate the "use of Negro manpower." War Department Circular 124 in 1946, known as the Gillem Report, admitted that certain unfair treatment of African American recruits had taken place during previous wars, but did not demand the end of segregation in the army nor make any suggestions for far-reaching changes. A large portion of the African American public considered the report a disappointment or even a failure.[106] The *Chicago Defender* called it a "weasel-worded report" that "some brass hats and their Negro lackeys built up. . . . [I]f the proposal for a peacetime army which flies the Jim Crow flag goes through, a pattern will be set for civilian life which will give the white supremacy forces a most powerful weapon to make Jim Crow the law of the land in civilian as well as army life, in the North as well as the South."[107] Other black newspapers shared this assessment.[108] Following the report, nothing really changed in the army with respect to African American soldiers. The army held onto its conviction that it was neither efficient nor socially acceptable to implement integration.[109] The negative image of black soldiers and their alleged untrustworthy performance in battle lay at the foundation of this reluctance. Mistrust and racism ruled the army's attitude toward black soldiers.

Like many others, Truman was appalled by the mounting racial violence, especially against black servicemen and veterans. In a letter to Southern politicians, he noted: "[But] my very stomach turned over when I learned that Negro soldiers, just back from overseas, were being dumped out of army trucks in Mississippi and beaten. Whatever my inclination as a native of Missouri might have been, as President I know this is bad. I shall fight to end evils like this."[110] In a September 1946 letter to Attorney General Thomas C. Clark, Truman suggested the establishment of a "commission to analyze the situation and have a remedy to present to the next Congress . . . I think it is going to take something more than the handling of each individual case after it happens—it is going to require the inauguration of some sort of policy to prevent such happenings."[111] On December 5, 1946, he established the President's Committee on Civil Rights by Executive Order 9808. The committee would make recommendations while investigating and assessing the civil rights situation and the status of minority groups in the United States. In June 1947, Truman even spoke before the NAACP in front of the Lincoln Memorial, pledging his support for civil rights.[112] Change seemed to be in reach.

On October 20, 1947, Truman's President's Committee on Civil Rights issued *To Secure These Rights*. The landmark study identified many of America's race problems and inequalities, pointing especially to the faults of the South and its system of segregation. It listed lynching, police brutality, the inequality in the justice system, and the continuance of involuntary servitude as primary problems. Also emphasized were inequalities with respect to employment opportunities, on-the-job discrimination, education, housing, health services, public services, and accommodation. The report condemned segregation and the separate-but-equal premise as unfair and as essentially contradicting the concept of American citizenship. It reasoned that segregation had not only created unequal facilities and opportunities, but also hostility between the races. Only by ending segregation could the American society attain equal rights and racial accord. It assigned the federal government a special role in the resolution of inequality and segregation, thereby interfering with the Southern stronghold on states' rights.[113]

The committee's report explicitly referred to the situation of minorities, especially blacks, in the armed forces. The promising experience of the Second World War in which white and black soldiers fought in integrated units led the committee to believe that "the majority and minorities of our population can train and work and fight side by side in cooperation and harmony." It further made clear that the status quo was an unbearable situation especially for black recruits. It concluded that discrimination and segregation in the military had to be ended under all circumstances, as it was not only unjust but also an incalculable military and foreign policy risk for the nation. "Morally, the failure to act is indefensible. Practically, it costs lives and money in the inefficient use of human resources."[114] Segregation and lack of minority rights were the U.S. Achilles' heel in the increasing conflict with Communism.

The report raised hope among African Americans, and President Truman praised it and its recommendations highly. Moreover, the White House was aware of the importance of the black voting bloc in the North. In November 1947, Clark M. Clifford, special counsel to the president, warned that African Americans held "the balance of power" and could no longer be appeased by empty gestures.[115] In his civil rights message before

Congress on February 2, 1948, Truman stated his dedication to the extension of civil rights and demanded clear decisions from Congress. It was a groundbreaking speech: for the first time, an American president had directly addressed civil rights issues and pointed at the faults and failures in U.S. race relations. With respect to African Americans in the military, Truman maintained that he had informed the secretary of defense to end all forms of discrimination in the armed forces as soon as possible.[116] The African American community celebrated. Channing H. Tobias, member of the President's Committee on Civil Rights and first black director of the Phelps-Stokes Fund, called the speech "a bold, courageous utterance of a man who realizes that the international program of the United States cannot be carried out effectively without serious consideration being given to the denials of democracy in the practices of the American people at home." Americans looking for peace could not ignore the international dimension of civil rights.[117] David K. Niles, White House administrative assistant, further commented on the impression of the president's civil rights moves and maintained that most commentators in the black press used "strong favorable language. . . . The message was referred to as the greatest freedom document since the Emancipation Proclamation."[118]

Southern whites were livid over the report and the subsequent presidential speech on civil rights. In the House of Representatives, Thomas Jefferson Murray, a Democrat from Tennessee, called the committee findings "full of slurs, libel, misrepresentation and untruths about the South and its way of life."[119] He was not alone in his opposition to the seemingly radical changes taking place and being demanded in the United States. As much as African Americans did not want to relent in their fight for civil rights, a large part of the white South and its Northern supporters clung to white supremacy. Further tensions were on the horizon.

President Truman's position on civil rights and racial equality of blacks was ambivalent and his actions often lagged behind his words. While his civil rights rhetoric increasingly broke new ground and, according to historian John Hope Franklin, managed to create an atmosphere of change that could support the betterment of race relations,[120] it did not result in decisive and far-reaching actions on behalf of black equal rights. Fearful of losing Southern support and splitting the Democratic Party, Truman remained cautious.

With disappointments accumulating at the end of the war, many African Americans grew increasingly impatient and more active in their pursuit of racial equality and integration, especially in the armed forces. Amidst the heated debate on universal military training, new civil rights groups formed and joined established organizations campaigning for a swift end to military segregation and discrimination. The memory of African American soldiers' treatment in World War II loomed large and spurred black activism.

Chapter 3

Stepping Up the Fight

Grant Reynolds returned to his civilian life earlier than he had expected. During his nearly three years of service as a black chaplain in the army, Reynolds not only gave spiritual guidance to African American soldiers, but also fought against segregation and discrimination in various stateside military bases. Known as a "troublemaker," he was forced to leave the army and voluntarily left the NAACP. Nevertheless, his fight for civil rights hardly ended with his service, as his experiences in the military had made him more frustrated and militant. Like the soldiers he advised during his time as a chaplain in the army, he was "a man come of age" who expected "a new definition of the American ideals of liberty, justice and equality to come out of the present war."[1] As soldiers returned home, militancy or at least activism was growing. Many veterans did not intend to go "back to business as usual," but they wanted to "change this nation so that there's more equality than there is now."[2] Reynolds did not resume his work as a pastor, but began to study law at Columbia Law School. As an active member of the Republican Party, he had publicly supported and spoken out in favor of Republican governor Thomas E. Dewey's run against President Roosevelt in the 1944 presidential race. Reynolds believed Roosevelt had betrayed African Americans, in particular black soldiers, while Dewey supported the African Americans' fight for full civil rights. Reynolds's allegiance to the New York governor paid off. Shortly after the war, Dewey appointed the fierce army veteran state commissioner of correction.

In 1946, Reynolds ran against Democratic representative Adam Clayton Powell, Jr., in Harlem's Twenty-Second District. In a fiercely fought campaign to win the African American vote, Reynolds argued that Powell had neglected the needs and interests of the constituents of the Harlem district.

As Powell had allegedly missed 68 percent of House sessions, Reynolds claimed he had thus failed to vote on decisions enormously important to blacks, like the anti-poll tax. In return, Powell accused Reynolds of allowing continuance of racial discrimination and segregation in prison as state commissioner of corrections. Although backed by Governor Dewey, who was well respected among black New Yorkers for his strong civil rights record, as well as the *New York Amsterdam News* and famous African American boxer Joe Louis, Reynolds ultimately lost to Powell.[3] He seemed to have replaced his fight for the integration of the armed forces with a political career that might give him more opportunities to make improvements for blacks, but Reynolds could never forget his time in the armed services and never gave up on his comrades or on the issue of military desegregation. His activism in the army and his revered status among black soldiers had always been a point of reference in the press when reporting on the congressional race.

The discussion over the end of segregation and discrimination in the military climaxed within the framework of the public discussion on selective service and universal military. The rise of the Cold War and the question to which extent the nation was prepared for an armed conflict with the Soviet Union further enforced the discussion on black military service and the necessity of military integration. The NAACP, the NUL, and newly founded liberal and interracial veterans' organizations intensified their activism.[4] The fight for military integration was one of the most prominent sites for the "convergence for foreign policy matters and domestic civil rights activities."[5] The avid debate on universal military training (UMT) and the draft became important platforms for this enforced activism, which exemplified the significance of manhood and masculinist rhetoric. Within this context, Grant Reynolds, along with A. Philip Randolph, was, for some time, in the midst of it all, challenging white as well as black concepts of citizenship's rights and obligations, civil rights activism, and masculinity.

The Problem with Universal Military Training

The debate on UMT was not a new one.[6] World War II had already produced an intense discussion in the public and press about the necessity and dangers of universal compulsory military training in times of peace. The specifics of UMT constantly changed, yet its basic concept was that young men of a certain age range had to serve in the armed services on a compulsory basis for a fixed period of time to ensure the nation's military preparedness. The victorious end of the war could not silence the voices demanding the continuance of a draft or compulsory military training, as the United States pondered its military response to growing tensions with the Soviet Union. A *Washington Post* editorial lauded it as a necessary measure to achieve long-term security through a well-prepared reserve.[7] Even before the war's end, President Roosevelt had launched a campaign to promote UMT as the only possible means to guarantee American security and military stability. After Roosevelt's death in April 1945, his successor Truman continued campaigning for UMT as a guarantee for national security and his staff began to push for it more vehemently.[8]

Army and air force advertising campaigns presented a military based on compulsory military training as unavoidable in the new postwar political climate and as a great opportunity for education, a good salary, and a promising career.[9] In December 1946, Truman established the President's Advisory Commission on Universal Military Training meant to undertake an independent study of UMT.[10] The president hoped the study's findings and recommendations would support his plans, and refute the fears raised by opponents who expected a "bad effect on the education and the morals of American youth."[11] Vigorous and costly campaigning for UMT followed. In 1947, the House Committee on Expenditures in the Executive Departments closely scrutinized the War Department for allegedly using public funds for UMT publicity. The investigations in the Subcommittee on Publicity and Propaganda of the Committee on Expenditures in the Executive Departments offered another opportunity for the opposing parties to state their respective cases.[12] Ultimately, even the President's Advisory Commission hesitated to fully embrace the UMT bill and called for its amendment with an eight-point security plan.[13]

The mainstream press and interest groups were deeply invested in discussing the consequences of UMT in a world increasingly dominated by the Cold War and its looming threat of war. Congressional hearings became special sites for heated discussions on the benefits and dangers of compulsory conscription. In particular, larger national newspapers published countless editorials, opinion pieces, and articles on UMT and the draft in general. The editors were swamped with letters from regular people whose opinions were as diverse as they were emotionally charged. Supporters of the bill considered UMT and conscription to be, for the most part, the most efficient and promising means to build and maintain a strong and reliable fighting force. The alternatively exclusive reliance on technologically advanced weapons and the atomic bomb could and would eventually have detrimental consequences for the nation.[14] Powerful groups, like active military officials, the American Legion, or the American Veterans of Foreign Wars, endorsed the call for universal military training. The Gallup poll also recorded continuously growing support for the UMT legislation.[15] According to the sample, only 66 percent of the respondents supported UMT in December 1942, while the figure rose to 77 percent by April 1948.[16]

Despite these seemingly strong indications of support for UMT, critics vehemently campaigned against UMT right from the start, calling it a "way to war."[17] Although the majority of military officers supported UMT, some former military personnel expressed doubts about UMT and its possible consequences. They did not consider it an appropriate means of reacting to the newly emerging threats and conflicts in the atomic age. Rather than preventing it, they predicted that UMT would eventually lead to war.[18] While traditionally pacifist and leftist groups, which did not have much backing in the general public, voiced their opposition to UMT most forcefully, renowned scholars and regular Americans from all social backgrounds also expressed their dissent.[19] They believed that the draft during peacetime would lead to a militarized society comparable to Nazi Germany and that the next war would primarily depend on atomic preparedness, and air and sea power, making increased ground troops unwarranted.[20]

One of the essential issues in the discussion of UMT in both factions of the debate was the question regarding the education of American youth, especially young men, in the spirit of American democracy.[21] Its supporters regarded UMT as a school of life that would turn boys into real men who would then devote themselves entirely to their nation and American values.[22] In contrast to UMT's opponents, they seemed unconcerned about a potential militarization of society, but perceived compulsory military training as promoting the equalization, democratization, and Americanization of the draftees.[23] At the head of the lobbying campaign, the American Legion alleged that UMT held indisputable advantages for all young men. They would become capable of confronting the new threats to the nation emanating from the rise of communism.[24] Opponents of compulsory military training, on the other hand, expressed fears over UMT's effects on the American youth.[25] They predicted an overpowering military presence in children's education, which would ultimately result in a militarized society. The devastating effects of conscription in Germany made compulsory military training in peacetime an especially sensitive issue. An article in *The Nation* by Harold Taylor, president of Sarah Lawrence College, exemplifies the importance of education in the opposition's consideration. UMT, Taylor argued, would lead young people "to give up rational and moral attitudes toward the solution of world conflicts." He avowed that military service and compulsory service had little to do with the successful education and acquisition of what were traditionally understood to be male virtues. "The need of the services in the last war was for boys who were healthy, strong, emotionally stable, intelligent, educable, and devoted to civic ideals. . . . The military had little to do with these virtues; . . . If a high quality of manhood is to be found in the America of the future, it will have to come from an expanded and improved educational system."[26] Despite predicting wide societal implications, neither opponents nor supporters usually considered issues of race and segregation in their debate on UMT. Predominantly white, they seemed to assume that recruits would be white.[27] The fact that the UMT training group established in Fort Knox, Kentucky, to test the system's usefulness and functionality did not allow black recruits failed to spark debates in mainstream discourse.[28] Questions of militarism or Americanism were the issues, not racism and racial inequality in the military.

To African Americans, however, UMT or any form of conscription was undoubtedly an issue of race. Blacks paid a great deal of attention to UMT, the draft, and military service in general, and racial segregation and racial inequality played a decisive role in their deliberations, as did manhood. The fact that the experimental universal military training unit at Fort Knox remained segregated indicated to blacks that the renewal of the draft plan or the introduction of UMT would permanently establish Jim Crowism in the armed forces.[29] Most interpreted this as an affront to African Americans who were prepared to serve and die for their country. This made it all the more important to fight for the inclusion of an integration clause in UMT that could not be conveniently circumvented by the armed forces.[30]

The African American community did not agree on the necessity of UMT or even the draft, however, the question regarding the appropriate education for the male youth prevailed in the black discussion as it did for whites. In June 1945, representative Arthur Capper presented the NAACP's initial opinion on compulsory and universal military training in Congress.

He quoted the NAACP's formal resolution, which opposed UMT on the grounds of its general unsoundness and its perpetuation of segregation and discrimination. "To many of us the entire plan of peacetime conscription seems unsound." [31] The militarization of society also mattered to some. In one of its editorials, the *Pittsburgh Courier*, for instance, based its opposition to UMT on the effect an enlargement of military power and influence of government would have on the American youth. Claiming it would "teach[ing] them blind obedience and dangerous State worship which can only result in goose-step psychology which has been the downfall of militaristic nations from the beginning of human history."[32] In its 1947 annual meeting with 800 delegates in attendance, the NAACP leadership declared its opposition to conscription in peacetime and spoke out in favor of voluntary military service.[33] Their steadfast opposition to UMT provoked criticism. Louis Lautier, a black news service columnist, criticized the NAACP for passing the resolution without having discussed it properly. "Colored people are divided in their thinking on this subject. Some are for it and some are against it. Why should not a ranking proponent and a ranking opponent of this subject have discussed it before the delegates?"[34] Although they disagreed on the necessity and usefulness of UMT, most blacks agreed on one thing: the necessity of an end to racial segregation in the military, with or without UMT or the draft.

The NUL had always supported African American involvement in the armed forces as a viable opportunity for advancement. In August 1945, it submitted a memorandum to President Truman that called for the end of segregation in military service and training. "We recommend that the Armed Services take or continue to take effective steps to abolish race segregation." They foremost argued for African American's protection from abuses and the morale boost integration would provide.[35] Despite its general opposition to UMT, the NAACP avowed, "that Negroes generally, and large numbers of white persons, believe it to be the responsibility of Congress to require in unequivocal language that in the Army and the Navy the selection of individuals for training, the determination of the type of training which an individual shall receive and the organization of units both for training and for service shall be accomplished without regard to or distinction on account of race."[36] Black commentators were interested in the racial setup of either system. The question was rarely whether UMT was to be introduced or the draft extended, but rather when and how blacks would be incorporated.

In an article for the *Negro Digest*, Roy Wilkins maintained that the continuation of segregation was the quintessential argument against conscription in all its possible forms. The possible indoctrination of white American males with segregation through compulsory training at their most "impressionable" age could only have negative effects on the status and progress of blacks in the United States. Raising and training young men under segregation and a system of discrimination, Wilkins reasoned, would result in black men being "crushed in spirit" and white men believing that "the proper way to handle Negroes is to jim crow them." They would consequently further implement this form of treatment in civilian life. Thereby, segregation would continue to be a fixture in "Negro housing, health, employment, recreation, education, travel, and all other facets of American life." The military would augment Jim Crow ideas and behavior.[37] An insignificant minority of African Americans backed segregation in the military. However, such opinions, which embraced the separate-but-equal paradigm to be both liberating and empowering, did not sit well with most blacks.

To most African Americans, the argument of racial pride through segregation did not hold water. They considered continued segregation in military training, whether within UMT, selective service, or the general daft, to be the greatest threat to their societal standing, the ideological outlook of America's youths, and the entire nation in the postwar world. Segregation and the pending dissemination of stereotypes through military training among young Americans highly susceptible and outside parental control gained importance. The *New York Amsterdam News* maintained that military training ought to be a multiplier of democracy and not a way to force racial stereotypes on impressionable youngsters. "The period of military training must not be a time for indoctrinating the entire young manhood of America with the anachronistic and neurotic race prejudices of the South."[38] Aligning Southern racism and segregation with Nazism, the *Pittsburgh Courier* joined in and maintained that conscription should only be installed if segregation was eliminated. The abolition of discrimination would ensure "that our young men won't think that freedom is a fraud, that there is mockery in democracy, or that the Declaration of Independence is just another scrap of paper. Millions of young Negroes who go through the conscript mill are not going to believe in the cause they are called upon to defend if they are grouped off to one side like pariahs."[39]

For the NAACP and other black opponents of compulsory conscription, fighting segregation was ultimately more important than fighting the UMT itself. While the NAACP gradually refrained from taking an official position on whether peacetime military training was a good idea, the organization remained firm that "we have expressed opposition to the segregated basis on which men are inducted and trained in the army and we have emphasized that if segregation is a part of compulsory military training we will oppose it without regard to the other features of the particular plan proposed."[40] Black newspapers supported them. In 1947, the *New York Amsterdam News* called on its readers to write protest letters to Truman K. Gibson or to the secretary of war directly.[41] As civilian aide to the secretary of war during the Second World War, Gibson had already lost the trust of many blacks. They still viewed him as a self-serving accomodationist and wanted to see him gone. Nevertheless, Gibson was now a member of the President's Advisory Commission on Universal Military Training. He fully supported UMT as a necessary tool in the growing conflict with the Soviet Union and as an opportunity for blacks to rise above and beyond their average opportunities.

In June 1947, the commission, to the surprise of Gibson's detractors, published a report expressing its opposition to racial segregation.

> Neither in the training itself, nor in the organization of any phase of this program, should there be discrimination for or against any person or group because of his race, class, national origin, or religion. Segregation or special privilege in any form should have no place in the program. To permit them would nullify the important living lesson in citizenship which such training can give. Nothing could be more tragic for the future attitude of our people, and for the unity of our nation, than a program in which our Federal Government forced our young manhood to live for a period of time in an atmosphere which emphasized or bred class or racial differences.[42]

The President's Advisory Commission propagated that, "Want, ill health, ignorance, race prejudice and slothful citizenship are enemies of America as truly as were Hitler and Mussolini and Tojo."[43] Its recommendation to loosen the existing segregation regulations seemed to answer the African American community's demands concerning military training or the draft.

Following the publication of the commission's report, Gibson stressed that there was virtually no disagreement among the commission's members with regard to issues of race. He called the report a "historic document" that "marks one of the few times that a commission composed of some of the best intellects in America has taken such a high moral position on this question and has made such forthright recommendations for the complete abolition of the archaic racial practices currently in vogue in this country."[44] The critics were right in their doubts. Despite the commission's recommendations, neither military leaders nor politicians pushed for a modification of the bill with respect to race. The UMT bill under consideration in Congress did not include an article on integration, nor was any reference made to this hot-button issue.

Although both powerful and smaller black organizations tried to raise awareness by publicizing the injustices of the existing UMT and the draft program, their activities had only limited success. Additionally, as important as amending any regulation on conscription was, it was only one of the many issues that the NAACP was handling and thus often seemed to have limited postwar priority.[45] Despite all obstacles, the looming Cold War enhanced the African Americans' drive for civil rights outside, but especially in, the American military and exerted more pressure on the government to make profound changes. Activism for a desegregated military peaked in the spring of 1948 with A. Philip Randolph's short-lived, but hotly debated, nonviolent civil disobedience campaign.

Joining Forces

Reynolds and Randolph were an unlikely pairing when they founded the Committee Against Jim Crow in the Military Service and Training in October 1947. A staunch Republican, the former had volunteered for military service during the Second World War. An influential, but often controversial labor leader with socialist roots, the latter had refused military service during the First World War for political reasons.[46] Reynolds supported peacetime conscription as essential for national security. Randolph remained skeptical at best. An article in the *Black Worker*, the official newspaper of Randolph's labor union, the Brotherhood of Sleeping Car Porters (BSCP), argued that UMT would not prevent war, but would perpetuate segregation and prove to be anti-labor by using "our youth on a mass basis . . . as a military strike-breaking, union-busting force."[47] Nevertheless, the fight against military segregation brought these two men together. Despite their differences, both had already drawn the ire of the War Department and at least two other administrations for their activism and fight for military integration.

While his March on Washington Movement had failed in bringing Roosevelt to order desegregation in the military and it ultimately fizzled out, Randolph had founded his next organization to fight Jim Crow in the armed forces in May 1945. The National Committee to Abolish Segregation in the Armed Services pledged to exert pressure on the president and Congress for a policy change. This small organization argued that the United States could not afford such inequalities in times of global conflict and democratization, while attempting to "maintain an unassailable position of world leadership in the fight for freedom."[48] The original committee did not stir much interest, but affirmed Randolph's belief in the absolute necessity of abolishing segregation and mobilizing more African Americans to fight for the cause.

In the summer 1947, William Worthy of the Fellowship of Reconciliation (FOR), a pacifist organization that wholeheartedly opposed UMT and military service in general, suggested the formation of a group to fight UMT and segregation to Randolph. Worthy hoped that the attachment of a desegregation amendment to UMT would make it so unfavorable to Southern senators that they would vote against it altogether.[49] Randolph agreed to join the "fragile coalition" and called on African American activists to establish the Committee Against Jim Crow in Military Service and Training, a bipartisan organization to end military segregation.[50] A number of important and influential individuals, like W. E. B. Du Bois, cofounder of the NAACP, Bishop William J. Walls of the African Methodist Episcopal Zion Church, who had recently visited the black troops in the European Army of Occupation as an official of the War Department, Dr. Channing H. Tobias, Horace R. Cayton, George Schuyler, a conservative columnist, and boxer Joe Louis, became some of the first members of the newly formed group.[51]

The committee's first press release challenged the official claim that UMT would contribute to "national unity by bringing together young men from all parts of the country to share a common experience." National unity could not be established based on racial segregation, and in fact, racial segregation and separation would be reinforced if "boys who have grown up in communities where racial segregation is not practiced would be

forced to accept the jimcrow pattern which would prevail under the proposed program." With this argument, they underscored that segregation
was an issue of national security and detrimental to "aspirations to moral
leadership in a chaotic world."[52] The committee's aim was "to insure
inclusion of equality amendments in pending legislation for universal
training."[53]

The diverse group initially used what could be called more traditional
routes of activism and thus did not especially distinguish itself from the
activities of other organizations. Reynolds and Randolph's organization
appeared to be just another pressure group among many. They protested
against the report of the President's Advisory Commission calling it a "lip
service to racial equality."[54] Moreover, Randolph solicited Gibson to refuse
to support the UMT bill without the attachment of antisegregation and
discrimination amendments.[55] In an attempt to sway Congress or President
Truman on the issue, Randolph and Reynolds sent out petitions, letters,
and requests for meetings.[56] Randolph also turned to Attorney General
Clark, criticizing that the pending UMT legislation "provides absolutely no
protection for Negro youth against racial segregation and discrimination"
and was therefore unlawful under federal government desegregation man-
dates. He asked the Department of Justice to take immediate action against
UMT in its current form.[57] However, their demands fell on deaf ears, while
their doubts and fears proved correct. The commission's recommendations
for racial change were not seriously considered in political discussion. In
fact, the eventual UMT bill while under consideration in Congress did not
include an article on integration, nor was any reference made to this hot-
button issue. Randolph later stated, "we have found our 'white friends'
silent, indifferent, or even hostile."[58] Moreover, although Truman spoke
out for civil rights more than most presidents, according to Randolph, "he
was not as accessible as President Johnson."[59]

Disillusioned by the ineffectiveness of their activism and the indifference they received, Randolph and Reynolds turned toward a new, more
radical and ultimately highly controversial approach in their struggle for
the abolition of military segregation. Their new course of action produced
a heated debate over appropriate civil rights activism with respect to the
integration of the American military in the immediate postwar period. Furthermore, it launched an animated discussion about African Americans'
obligation to military service and patriotism infused by issues and rhetoric

of manhood. With their plan, Randolph and Reynolds shocked white America and unsettled the majority of African Americans. The results of their work, if only for a short period, redefined black manhood and equality, still so deeply connected to military service.

A New Strategy

Since its founding in October 1947, the Committee Against Jim Crow in Military Service and Training had tried to secure a meeting with the president. Despite their pressing contentions, the president and his staff repeatedly deferred the delegation of black activists. On January 20, 1948, David K. Niles urged the president to meet with Randolph, as he was "an important Negro . . . and not a left-winger." The meeting, however, should happen after the president's planned civil rights message that would mention military segregation. Niles wanted to make sure that Randolph would "not be able to say that the message is a result of their visit."[60] Although President Truman repudiated Jim Crow in military service in the civil rights message he delivered on February 2, he did not order any changes with respect to segregation in the armed forces. While his speech aggravated white supremacists, it did not produce any presidential action.[61] As historian Paula Pfeffer has pointed out, Truman hoped that "the rhetoric alone would be sufficient to satisfy black demands and that his inaction would appease Southern Democrats."[62] Moreover, the White House did not grant Randolph and Reynolds an audience with Truman until the end of March.

In this meeting, which he later described as "perhaps the most explosive of any that we had had," Randolph boldly confronted President Truman, claiming that many African Americans hesitated to continue to serve in a segregated and unequal military.[63] "In my recent travels around the country I found Negroes not wanting to shoulder a gun to fight for democracy abroad unless they get democracy at home." This was, as Randolph later put it, "most unwelcome news to him [the president], as it was to me."[64] Surprised by their move, the president showed concern and made promises, but he took no immediate steps to improve black men's status in the military. For Randolph and Reynolds, backing out of their plan was no longer an option.

In mid-March 1948, the Senate Armed Services Committee again discussed the UMT bill. Proponents and opponents from all walks of life made their case to Chairman John Chan Gurney, South Dakota's Republican Senator, and his colleagues. Various black interest groups, like the NAACP or the NUL attended in order to speak out against segregation.[65] Similar in style, but different in tone and radicality, they agreed that if UMT were to pass and the military were to remain powerful in the future, then desegregation was an absolute necessity. They examined the inefficiency of segregation, presented the record of African American soldiers in America's wars, and pointed to the humiliating and racist treatment they had had to endure in a segregated setting. They furthermore demonstrated how it negatively affected both the morale and combat performance, not only of blacks, but also of the entire military. With their accounts of black soldiers, the speakers once again experienced the difficulty in highlighting the distinction of black troops, while explaining their apparent failures due to segregation. Low morale and the lack of incentives for performing well in segregated outfits proved a compelling and—at least according to testimonies of frustrated and disillusioned veterans—truthful argument. Again, blacks found themselves fending off allegations of inefficiency and unreliability. It was their task to prove that there was no such thing as an inherent, "Negro problem," but that segregation and discrimination lay at the root of all troubles. The witnesses, however, did not concur on the extent to which the system needed to be overhauled, or the speed with which to do it.

A recurring and powerful argument was that the continuance of segregation in the military would hurt the United States in its ideological and arms conflict with the Soviet Union.[66] Communist Russia, they warned, had a close eye on the United States and its race relations and its observations could ultimately only impede the nation in pursuing its worldwide interests. Pauline E. Myers succinctly formulated what most witnesses arguing in favor of an end to military Jim Crow believed: "There is urgent political necessity for the United States democracy to achieve the abolition of racial segregation. There is revolutionary dynamite inherent in a Jim Crow Army. Another war crisis can unite the 'world of color' in an anti-American crusade, a 'holy war' against the religion of white supremacy."[67] Potentially threatening scenarios and national security risks were presented as having their roots in the maintenance of segregation, against the backdrop of the global conflict against Communism. While originally demanding, the tone of these discussions ultimately turned rather conciliatory.

Truman K. Gibson, the only black member of the President's Advisory Commission, wholeheartedly made a case for UMT, while underlining the

Figure 2. African American leaders testify before Senate Armed Services Committee, calling for safeguards against racial discrimination in draft legislation. (R) A. Philip Randolph, National Treasurer for the Committee Against Jim Crow in Military Service and Training; (L) Grant Reynolds, New York State Commissioner of Correction. Washington, D.C., March 31, 1948, © Bettmann/CORBIS.

inefficiency of segregation. Military effectiveness and Russian propaganda, he argued, made the end of segregation advisable. He distanced himself and the African American community from the threats of resistance that Randolph had made during his meeting with Truman.[68] What would happen in the committee the next day left its members and the public worried, and threw the black community in a crisis of conscience for the next four months.

On March 31, well prepared, confident, and determined, Randolph and Reynolds appeared before the Senate Committee on Armed Services (Figure 2). News about their confrontational meeting with President Truman had already broken, but the threats of draft resistance were still not taken seriously. Reynolds spoke first. He represented the Committee Against Jim Crow in Military Service and Training. His testimony was a hard-hitting call for military integration that demanded seven attachments to the UMT bill ordering integration and protective measures for black soldiers. Reynolds closed ranks with Randolph and expressed in martial terminology his frustration and growing impatience with the system, a stance that stemmed from his experience in the army.[69] He made clear that the time of acquiescence and dependence on white benevolence had passed.

As aggressive and unyielding as it was, his statement did not compare with what would follow, when Randolph, Reynolds's collaborator, spoke again. Randolph clearly intended to push the envelope and shock his audience when he stated unequivocally, "Today I should like to make clear to the Senate Armed Services Committee and through you, to Congress and the American people that passage now of a Jim Crow draft may only result in a mass civil disobedience movement along the lines of the magnificent struggles of the people of India against British imperialism. . . . I personally will advise Negroes to refuse to fight as slaves for a democracy they cannot possess and cannot enjoy."[70] His call urged black and white youths to resist induction into military service if segregation and discrimination continued. His move was unprecedented, even radical. For generations, military service and equal rights were two sides of the same coin and African Americans were certain that their devoted military service would eventually lead to equality and recognition of an equal black manhood. However, although blacks served the nation and fulfilled their civil obligations, they did not receive the civil rights usually granted for military service.

Randolph's call to refuse to serve represented the dissolution of an already nonfunctional, male-focused social contract of citizenship. The civil disobedience campaign called into question the long-held idea that loyal military service would eventually lead to full civil rights. His call was also a clear claim to power and to full manhood. Patience and begging were no longer options. "I must emphasize that the current agitation for civil rights is no longer a mere expression of hope on the part of Negroes. On the one hand, it is a positive, resolute out-reading for full manhood. On the other hand, it is an equally determined will to stop acquiescing in anything less. Negroes demand full, unqualified, first-class citizenship."[71] As Randolph dared dissolve this link, if only for a short time, he questioned established concepts of manhood. Following the Gandhian model of nonviolent resistance seemed to contradict all conventions of gender, as, in the words of historian Timothy Stewart-Winter, "men who evaded the draft were the object of considerable scorn and stigma."[72] Randolph's movement reinterpreted traditional concepts of manhood and military service. The appeal to refuse to serve in the military called their manhood and patriotic dedication to the nation into question.

Randolph recognized the issues his call would create within the civil rights movement. Right from the start, he felt the need to rebut criticism from all sides. He countered the allegations that black men who refused to fight were "slackers," who lacked the "quintessential male" traits of bravery and patriotic loyalty. His rhetoric was filled with references to and claims of manhood. "I can only repeat that this time Negroes will not take a Jim Crow draft lying down. The conscience of the world will be shaken as by nothing else when thousands and thousands of second-class Americans choose imprisonment in preference to permanent military slavery."[73] Military service in a Jim Crow army thus became a betrayal of black manhood and, due to its interracial set-up, of manhood in general. Subjugation to white supremacy in the military would further deny black men their manhood. Draft resistance was not a sign of lacking manhood, but a sign of true masculinity. Resistance represented the path to civil rights and to black manhood that was equal, if not superior, to white manhood. Reynolds described black opponents to the civil disobedience campaign as effeminate "'Uncle Toms'" who were on "some governmental pay roll whose allegiance to a weekly pay check is greater than their devotion to justice." He only spoke for "Negroes with backbone."[74] The derogatory and gender-specific description denied full manhood to the opponents of the new movement who were comprised of unthreatening, submissive, and feeble personalities deprived of any traditional concept of masculinity. These alleged character flaws of African American males led them to collaborate with white hegemony instead of cultivating manly and virile open resistance, Reynolds insinuated.

The stigma of subservience was inherent in the epithets. By calling the opponents of civil disobedience "Uncle Toms," Reynolds, in return, denied them what the public considered the prerequisites of full manhood. According to Reynolds's rationale, obedient service in a segregated military turned black men into submissive servants of whites, whereas nonviolent resistance manifested their full and equal manhood. The main battle cry of the committee and their later partner organization, the League for Non-Violent Civil Disobedience Against Military Segregation illustrates the centrality of manhood in their fight: "If We Must Die, Let Us Die as Free Men Not Jim Crow Slaves." With Randolph and Reynolds's unprecedented declaration of nonviolent resistance, other speakers in support of an end to Jim Crow went virtually unnoticed.

A Tricky Cooperation

Randolph strengthened his campaign for civil disobedience, when he founded the League for Non-Violent Civil Disobedience Against Military Segregation in late June 1948.[75] The Committee Against Jim Crow in Military Service and Training's partner organization encouraged "all men of draft age to resist openly by failing to register or by refusing to be inducted. . . . The League will give legal support to any individual who follows a course he feels to more honorable than acceptance of segregation in the armed forces." The separation of the league from the committee was necessary, because not all the committee's members supported the civil disobedience campaign. Whereas the committee took charge of fighting military segregation in general by continuing to lobby congressmen and the president, the league was specifically responsible for the civil disobedience campaign. It was more involved in building grassroots activism vital to the success of the direct action approach, upon which the nonviolent civil disobedience campaign was built.[76] Ultimately, Randolph saw the two ongoing campaigns as "two aspects of a single movement" with "utmost cooperation for achievement of the common goal."[77]

The league's organizational staff, many of them white, consisted of members of organizations like the FOR, the National Council Against Conscription (NCAC), or the Congress of Racial Equality (CORE). Randolph had been on CORE's Advisory Committee since 1942.[78] The NCAC and FOR had always been opposed to conscription.[79] As early as December 1944, John M. Swomley, chairman of the NCAC and member of FOR, had attempted to convince the black press to publicly oppose peacetime conscription.[80] As a member of FOR and a steadfast conscientious objector, Bayard Rustin, who had closely worked with Randolph in the MOWM in 1941, solidified the link between the two organizations.

Even before the founding of the league, Rustin had acted as an activist and spokesperson for Randolph and Reynolds's committee. During a ceremony in April 1948 at which he received the Thomas Jefferson award for the advancement of democracy, Rustin made quite clear why civil disobedience was the only feasible means to fight segregation in the military. Not only would a continuation of military segregation in the UMT hurt young men at their "most impressionable age"—a common argument of the anti-conscription movement against UMT or the draft and, frequently against military service—but it would disseminate discrimination and segregation, that is, anti-democratic tendencies, to the rest of the world. He even compared civil disobedience with resistance against Nazism in Germany. Quoting justice Robert Jackson, chief U.S. prosecutor in the Nuremberg Trials, Rustin stated that "individual resistance to undemocratic laws" would have helped bring about the end of Nazi Germany and could play a considerable role in transforming the U.S. government for the better, since it was too "poorly organized to achieve democracy."[81]

This cooperation merged two strands of thinking that eventually proved difficult to unite. The position on military service was at the center of the problem. The profoundly pacifist background of the FOR members, in particular, caused tension between the league and the committee. Although Randolph had taken a pacifist stance during the First World War, by 1948 neither Randolph nor Reynolds believed that pacifism was the only way to counter security threats.[82] As they were neither pacifists nor conscientious objectors, their position on the draft was not based on full-fledged opposition to war and military service in general. The ultimate goal was the opportunity to serve in an equal, desegregated, and nondiscriminatory setting. Randolph and Reynolds considered military service necessary but only under democratic and fair circumstances. The FOR and its members, including Rustin and A. J. Muste, who now worked for the newly founded league, represented the pacifist tradition that rejected military service altogether. Although often opposed to Jim Crowism in the armed forces, these "traditional" pacifists thought that the "worst thing about the army is not Jim Crow but that it is the army."[83] For Rustin, this opposition had a deeply religious foundation, whereas in the case of Randolph draft resistance was for purely secular reasons.[84] During the war, Rustin had spent three years in jail for draft resistance, an experience that fortified his rejection of military service. Muste was a member of the Society of Friends and the executive director of FOR from 1940 to 1953, where he appointed Rustin to FOR's youth organization in summer 1941.[85]

The cooperation between the divergent groups caused frictions early on. Tense relationships between Rustin and Worthy, journalist and action director of CORE, and between Rustin and Reynolds were additional reasons for the organizational and financial separation of the committee and the league. They could not cooperate. Muste insinuated that Worthy, who now acted as executive secretary of the committee, was awarding himself an unreasonably high paycheck and possibly even held back funds.[86] The ubiquitous frictions were eventually the predominant cause for the fallout between the organizations' leading figures, especially Rustin and Reynolds, and the dissolution of the league. Reynolds distrusted Rustin and suspected him of planning to gradually take over the league and replace Randolph and other nonpacifists.[87] Pacifist conscientious objectors could also not agree with Randolph and Reynolds's concept of the masculine draft resister who would serve loyally in the military if segregation was abolished, a concept upon which the call for civil disobedience was built.

Although the league's priorities and tasks differed to some extent from those of the committee's, the organizations' actual differences and the division of tasks often overlapped. Randolph played a dominant and formative role in both organizations. He was their driving force, the most charismatic and outspoken personality, and the most publicly present. Both organizations considered grassroots activism the key to success. "One more word of warning: be sure the final committee isn't a 'big deal' set-up. We want 'big-names' but this is first and foremost a movement of *the people*. The men who will refuse to serve in segregated armed forces must have a say in all important decisions" (emphasis original).[88] As much as he needed the support of the black and white political elite, Randolph depended on the activism of regular people to make his two organizations and their campaigns operate successfully and foster the intended momentum.[89]

Based in New York City, both the committee and the league sought to gain a foothold across the country, and leaders urged their members and partners to form local chapters in order to successfully fight against military segregation.[90] Furthermore, they sought to make a shift from a movement rooted in intellectual circles to a mass movement.[91] Through campaigns, networking, flyers, and interviews in radio shows, the committee and the league attempted to recruit activists. The BSCP was a major site of recruiting, but not all members of Randolph's union were willing to join and some demanded that Randolph renounce his civil disobedience campaign.[92] Members of other existing networks like the NAACP, the NUL, the Young Men's Christian Association (YMCA), or the Young Women's Christian

Association (YWCA) also represented possible supporters of their campaign. Randolph's rather aggressive and pushy recruiting style begs the question of how successful the committee and league actually were in enlisting new activists. A labor activist who was unsure about whether to join the committee commented on Randolph's attempts to engage supporters and collect money, describing himself as "being bombarded."[93] Although no actual numbers are available, it is safe to say that both organizations had serious trouble securing active and paying members. The NAACP, for instance, meant to prevent its branches from joining the civil disobedience campaign by introducing a national policy forbidding it, although some branches did not keep to the official guidelines.[94] The unstable financial situation, which accelerated the collapse of the league, is a strong indicator for its lack of success in gaining active members.[95]

Although women had served in the U.S. Navy Women Accepted for Volunteer Emergency Service (WAVES), Women's Air Force Service Pilots (WASPs), or Women's Army Corps (WAC), the nonviolent civil disobedience movement focused on male personnel in their struggle to achieve military integration.[96] The integration of the nurse corps, for instance, which had been a fervent discussion during the Second World War, was not on the committee's agenda.[97] Nevertheless, the movement was not gender-exclusive and assigned an integral role to women in its efforts to push for the integration of the military. The committee called on women to join the protest against a segregated military, which confined their husbands, brothers, or sons to subservient positions in a country that prided itself in being democratic. Women should take part in the protest marches and support draft resisters unconditionally.[98] Randolph and his supporters considered women essential to the movement and praised them for the active role they took, for example, distributing flyers, buttons, writing to politicians on behalf of the cause, and so on, the league's action program even explicitly called for "poster walks by young women stating that they support civil disobedience."[99] Women organized local chapters for the League for Non-Violent Civil Disobedience Against Military Segregation. They cooperated closely with Rustin. Their grassroots activism seems to have been essential for the expansion and awareness of the two organizations' cause among the public.[100]

Randolph successfully solicited financial support from female followers. The Ladies Auxiliary to the BSCP in various cities donated money to what one organizer of the St. Louis Division called "such a worthy cause."[101]

Women took part in the struggle for military integration, but in general did not publicly voice their opinions on the issue as strongly as men did. Columnist Marjorie McKenzie, Charlotta Bass, editor and owner of the left-leaning *California Eagle*, and civil rights activist Mary McLeod Bethune were the most outspoken females concerning military integration. The public discourse and the image of military service therein remained largely male-focused. Moreover, the majority of reporters, commentators, writers of letters to newspaper editors or to Randolph, and witnesses in congressional hearings were male.[102] There was no reform or revolution of gender relations intended in the movement for military integration; instead, it was a confirmation of black male patriarchy.[103]

Proper American Behavior

The call for civil disobedience put forward by Randolph and Reynolds shocked the members of the Senate Committee and the hearing's audience.[104] Senator Wayne Morse, a Republican member of the Senate Committee from Oregon and a long-time white member of the NAACP board, made it clear that refusal to register for the draft would be considered an act of treason and result in the imprisonment of draft resisters.[105] Two weeks later, on April 12, 1948, Senator Morse brought the issue before the Senate and voiced serious concern. Although he expressed his sympathy for the African Americans' dissatisfaction regarding their status in the armed services, the senator insisted that the civil disobedience movement "would constitute conspiracy in aiding and abetting an enemy" and was convinced that the majority of African Americans would not follow their path, but fulfill "their patriotic duty in time of emergency or war."[106] Morse's threat, however, seems not to have left much of an impression on the two activists.

Already during the Senate committee hearings, Randolph and Reynolds asserted vehemently that they were prepared to face the consequences that might result from their nonviolent resistance. "In other words, if there are sacrifices and sufferings, terrorism, concentration camps, whatever they may be, if that is the only way by which Negroes can get their democratic rights, I unhesitatingly say that we have to face it."[107] In accordance with Randolph's belief, black males' national identity no longer required obedient military service to demonstrate their Americanness or their manhood: the real black American man openly resisted oppression. Self-abasement and compliance with a segregated military, even in times of national crisis, was not acceptable to a responsible and manly black American.

Although theirs was an activism based on nonviolence, Randolph and Reynolds's call for nonviolent civil disobedience was influenced by the contemporary (Cold) war terminology, in which warfare was a constant oxymoronic companion to notions of freedom or peace. "We shall wage a relentless warfare against Jim Crow without hate or revenge for the moral and spiritual progress and safety of our country, world peace, and freedom."[108] The use of the language of war underlined the embrace of the symbolic masculine warrior fighting against the internal enemies of democracy and equal rights, which endangered the well-being of the nation. Like the March on Washington seven years earlier, the civil disobedience campaign "carefully balanced gendered images of aggression and restraint."[109] Reynolds repeatedly underscored his rejection of self-abasement and humiliation in his testimony before the House Armed Services Committee maintaining "that a slave cannot fight for freedom, and my party loyalty [to the Republican Party], as you can see, ends, when human rights are in jeopardy." He argued that the army's attempt to permanently establish "Herr Jim Crow"[110]—alluding to the similarity between Jim Crow and Nazi ideology—"was the last straw which has ignited within us the spark of revolt that sets men free."[111] The activists were, in the words of historian Michael Geyer, "definitely the opposite of passivity."[112] They demanded civil rights and equality and refused to wait for "either a liberal or revolutionary platform" to grant it to them.[113]

Randolph's modus operandi corresponded with white middle-class concepts of decent male (and female) behavior. However, black men resisting military service should not act against other male ideals. Under no circumstances should supporters demonstrate resistance by inventing "false dependents, feigning illness, and resorting to any subterfuge to avoid service" as the FBI claimed many had done.[114] Such strategies were considered unmanly behavior and "fraudulent means." Randolph clearly stated that "the strength of our movement lies in truth and in those men who openly will inform the government that they are violating an unjust law."[115] Moreover, the league advised draft resisters on how to behave in case of an arrest: "We are depending on the goodwill that we can express to win not only freedom and liberty, but important to win over to our aide as many people as we can. We want to win the officials (including the police) to the belief that our cause is just. Behave in such a fine, dignified manner that the police officers become ashamed to arrest anyone who behaves so well."[116] The behavior of protesters should in no way go against dominant mores. The campaign hoped to raise awareness and gain white supporters, not create more opposition toward African Americans. In no way should it risk the confirmation of stereotypical black unreliability, violent tendencies, and unruliness.

In August 1946, the *Black Worker* had already designated African American men who did not "resort to violence" against mob attacks as displaying the highest form of courage. Nonviolence did not constitute cowardice, but superiority. White Klansmen who hid under their white hoods or white mobs that attacked unarmed blacks were considered the "cowards," as they resorted to unhampered violence in a country that claimed to be symbolic of democracy.[117] Under all circumstances and despite the language of war, it was necessary for civil disobedience activism to remain free of violence. "Your attitude must be one of absolute non-violence [emphasis in original]. . . . A part of that price is to accept suffering without anger, bitterness, or hatred. . . . Under no circumstances be mean, or curse, or look angry or strike back, even if *you* are struck."[118] The new movement took up these convictions. So as to not offend the dominant white culture, activists' behavior and appearance in the civil disobedience campaign corresponded with white, middle-class ideals of decent and acceptable behavior and dress codes. Thereby the activists were also to counter stereotypes of blacks as being "immoral, lazy, violent, and mentally deficient, along with being sexual superstuds, athletes, and rapacious criminals"[119] that had been deeply ingrained in American culture for decades.

Randolph referred to Mahatma Gandhi as his main inspiration for the civil disobedience campaign.[120] He drew parallels between the status of African Americans and the colonial oppression of Indians, emphasizing the success of civil disobedience in bringing about freedom for India. The movement of civil disobedience in the United States also reflected, and, according to the organizers, would help the worldwide struggle of the oppressed. "In refusing to accept compulsory military segregation, Negro youth will be serving their fellow men throughout the world."[121] Disapproval outside but also within the black community increased, as critics asserted that Randolph's approach was un-American and his claims did not apply to the situation in the United States. While Randolph never denied Gandhi's influence on his movement, he also stressed the American tradition to which the committee and its followers were devoted. Randolph and

Reynolds argued that the committee's civil disobedience campaign followed in the footsteps of the American Founding Fathers, who fought against the oppression of the British crown. Randolph asserted, "The colonists argued 'no taxation without representation.' Today Negroes and white people who love freedom say, 'no first-class dying for second-class citizenship; no service without equality for all.'" He highlighted the quintessential American character of civil disobedience. "Many of the contemporaries of these men [colonists opposing taxation without representation] called them 'agitators' and 'traitors'; but today our history books describe them as 'defenders of liberty' and 'true patriots.'"[122] In his eyes, the committee thus stood in the tradition of what was the most American and most masculine of all, the Founding Fathers. "When black Americans and their allies protested against racial injustice, they invoked Enlightenment-inspired ideals of freedom and equality, making their claims all the more compelling for being in the familiar national tongue of liberty and natural rights."[123] The League for Non-Violent Civil Disobedience Against Military Segregation later claimed that Gandhi derived his ideas from America, from Henry David Thoreau and Abraham Lincoln, who were forerunners of civil disobedience and simultaneously representatives of quintessential American manhood. The bulletin further quoted Donald Harrington, the assistant minister at New York's Community Church: "there are laws which it is man's duty to break." To be a true American and a real man in the American tradition, one had to break laws that undermined one's civil rights and manhood.[124]

This emphasis on the American character of the campaign was also necessary in light of allegations of anti-American tendencies and affiliation with communism. Such accusations discredited civil rights activists, in particular, as damaging the nation with their demands and playing into the hands of the communist enemy. Randolph and Reynolds were both staunch and outspoken anticommunists. The former maintained early on that communists "are not really interested in civil rights. They are interested in utilizing civil rights for their own purposes."[125] Nevertheless, numerous white critics blamed them for helping the Soviet cause of spreading Communism around the world by blemishing the reputation of the United States.

At a hearing of the House of Representatives Committee on Armed Services on April 19, 1948, Felix Hébert, Democratic member of the House of Representatives, maintained "I make this further observation, that if an advance copy of these two statements have [sic] been sent already to the Kremlin I am sure there is great joy in Russia today."[126] A tense exchange

of words and accusations between the representatives present followed
Reynolds's statement. Representative Charles Henry Elston, a Republican
from Ohio, in particular, alleged that the civil disobedience campaign supported Soviet Russia.[127] The FBI had always had a keen interest in Randolph's activities and his early allegiance to socialism made him suspicious.
Since his draft resistance during the First World War and his labor union
activism, they monitored his civil disobedience campaign closely for any
alleged un- or anti-American activism and possible communist background
or infiltration. The FBI collected newspaper articles on his activism and
tracked the reactions to Randolph and Reynolds's activities in the communist publication *The Daily Worker.* The FBI sent undercover agents to the
meetings of the committee and the league, who reported to the assistant
attorney general and J. Edgar Hoover.[128] Not only whites suspected Randolph and Reynolds of possible affiliations with Communism; some African
Americans were also concerned that a communist agenda lurked behind
the civil disobedience campaign. In a letter to Hoover, a Los Angeles resi-
dent with West Indian roots demanded life imprisonment or death for
"virus X A. Philip Randolph together with his socialistic communistic traitors to our government."[129]

Randolph and Reynolds opposed Communism and attempted to
counter communist allegations with rhetoric and argumentation, which
was anticommunist in both content and style. They argued that supporters
of draft resistance were not committing treason or threatening the American nation. In fact, those who perpetuated segregation in the armed forces
put America's national security at risk and undermined the American Constitution and democracy. Reynolds reciprocated the attacks on the civil disobedience campaign and accused Southern white supremacists and Senator
Morse of treason. Moreover, he stressed that during the Second World War,
Senator Eastland had claimed that he preferred "Nazis to Negroes" and had
not been tried for treason.[130]

Randolph and Reynolds used the acceleration of the Cold War to reinforce their demands and force the president and Congress to enforce military integration.[131] They underlined the potentially damaging effect that the
lack of civil rights in the United States would have in the worldwide struggle
against communist expansion and for the spread of American-style democracy and peace. While requesting a meeting in January 1948, Randolph
wrote to Truman maintaining "Might I remind you, on the other hand,
that the success of many internal and foreign programs finally depends on

a healthy state of the body politic. Such a state requires the elimination of, rather than the extension of, segregation and discrimination in military training and the armed forces."[132] Patriotism, democratic convictions, and national security considerations demanded that the call for civil disobedience be answered. Randolph and Reynolds thought that only a measure as radical and as assertive, albeit nonviolent, as resistance, could bring about change and a democratization of the United States. The threat of the Cold War helped bolster their argumentation by regularly pointing to the perpetual weakening of the American military and its moral strength in the face of this looming worldwide conflict. They hoped it would be an effective means to advance their demands, arguing that only a country deeply ingrained in democracy could survive and ultimately defeat Communism.

Against this background, Randolph, Reynolds, their supporters, and even many skeptics tried to counter any allegations of communist infiltration in their movement, an accusation that was often fatal to demands for social change. Columnist Earl Brown stressed more than once that neither of the two men could be mistaken for a communist, rather describing them as trustworthy black representatives of superior American character. He described Randolph as highly respected among blacks and as being known as a "courageous and honest fighter." His characterization of Randolph underscored his manly character traits. Brown claimed, "a man, white or black, cannot fight for his country with any heart or courage unless he knows he has the respect of his country." Furthermore, only a country that truly implemented democracy in everyday life could serve as a role model for Europe and the rest of the world. In spite of his admiration for Randolph and Reynolds, he made clear that the refusal to serve in the military was treason and further advanced the spread of Communism. However, he also stressed that Randolph and Reynolds were not responsible for the military's negative image. The only way to gain the support of colored citizens was "by demonstrating their ability to practice democracy by abolishing Jim Crow and discrimination."[133]

Even Schuyler, leading columnist for the *Pittsburgh Courier*, who was known for his adamant anti-Communism, his conservatism, and criticism of radical approaches to gaining civil rights, initially lauded Randolph and Reynolds stating that he was "proud to belong to" the Committee Against Jim Crow in Military Service and Training. He further argued that such a campaign would "prove terribly embarrassing at a time when our Government is beaming to all countries, especially Russia, loud self-serving praise of the freedom and justice enjoyed under the Stars and Stripes." He predicted that if segregation in the military were outlawed even "most Southern white boys would serve alongside Southern colored boys and there would be extremely little friction." To prevent Jim Crow conscription, he further demanded that African American campaigns enlighten whites on the important role black soldiers had played in all of America's wars. He called on African Americans to "appeal to the spirit of justice, honor, fair play and freedom of the American people, and ask not for money but for moral support and for political pressure on Congress to kill armed forces jim crow."[134]

Although many individuals refuted the communist allegations thrown at Randolph and Reynolds and defended the two men vigorously, no agreement on their "new and untried . . . and radical"[135] strategy could be reached. For over four months, their Gandhian inspired civil disobedience campaign against serving in a segregated military divided the African American community. Most African Americans admired Gandhi's fight against British colonial rule in India, but doubted and even dreaded its application in the United States. An intense debate on rights and responsibilities of black men ensued. Ultimately, Randolph and Reynolds's move put established civil rights organizations and their leaders on the defensive and put innovative civil rights strategies, which could eventually no longer be ignored, on the map.

Chapter 4

Mass Civil Disobedience

People all across the nation tried to make sense of the new and radical approach to integration. The call for disobedience made it into the pages of major national newspapers, when news on black issues rarely appeared in white publications.[1] The civil disobedience campaign was a serious enough issue that reflections on its implication for the country and national security were considered necessary. Even Southern papers reported on Randolph's radical step in the quest for full civil rights.[2] *Newsweek* published a three-page article on the issue, expressing understanding for the impatience and frustration Randolph and Reynolds experienced. It reasoned that Randolph's radical attitude resulted from the humiliation and denial of manhood that African American males had suffered from due to white treatment for so long. "A large mass of Negro veterans of the recent war, with their scars and humiliations still fresh upon them, regard it even more as a matter of outraged manhood and self-respect."[3] Clearly differentiating between Walter White's NAACP, and Randolph's more radical approach to civil rights, *Newsweek* described White's method as "careful and cautious." White was so incensed by the characterization that he wrote to the editors of *Newsweek*, keen on bolstering his self-proclaimed status as a "dangerous radical."[4] He considered it necessary to justify his objection to civil disobedience in order to dissuade the impression of 'having gone soft' in comparison to Randolph. The NAACP and he, White emphasized, had not stopped their fight against military segregation, but there was "no obligation on my part to accept unquestionably that proposal."[5]

While White felt that the article questioned his dedication to civil rights, Reynolds thanked *Newsweek* for its "fair and objective" reporting and further noted that, "the daily press" had otherwise "failed to grasp the significance of this movement and has little conception of the widespread bitterness which makes Negroes determined never again to submit to a jimcrow draft." According to Reynolds, the public had to be more thoroughly informed by more articles similar to the one published in *Newsweek*, in order to make them aware of the "explosive issue on its doorsteps."[6] *Newsweek* might have defended Randolph and Reynolds's stance on civil disobedience to a certain degree, but most other white publications did not show much sympathy and dismissed their move as endangering national security and racial tolerance. Although many papers criticized segregation or at least its rigidity, they still maintained that civil rights demands ought not to hamper the passage of UMT, the draft, or military service in general, which was considered essential for the nation's survival. A *New York Times* editorial described racial segregation and UMT as "separate problems"[7] that, for the sake of the nation's security, should not be mixed. The military was, according to the *Washington Post*, not a place for "social experimentation," although the paper described segregation as "a wasteful procedure that does not make the most efficient use of manpower." The paper further noted that the call for civil disobedience represented an "essentially cheap appeal" and noted that most blacks were loyal to the United States.[8] Occasional criticism from readers existed, but most white papers and their readers agreed that blacks' denial of military service could not wipe out discrimination; only dedicated military service would ultimately lead to equality.[9] Even if they claimed to understand African Americans' impatience about the refusal to desegregate the military, white newspapers and commentators tried to disassociate Randolph and Reynolds from the African American community and turn them into a minority within an otherwise patriotic black community. White's concern over the militancy of Randolph's efforts was an increasingly popular stance in the press and Congress.

Deeply invested and concerned blacks and whites, civil disobedience supporters and opponents sent letters to Randolph and Reynolds. A number of segregationists directly addressed Randolph, repudiating his actions. A white woman from Bethpage, New York, who, fearing reprimands from the "Society of the Advancement of Colored People [sic]," wrote under the alias Ellen Hunt, expressed what many other white people most likely felt. She claimed that blacks should "take pride in their outfits" and stay among themselves instead of tearing down the morale of everybody else. Accusing blacks of a serious lack of racial pride was a common and hurtful allegation on the part of white segregationists. The seeming omnipresence of black protest made them feel uncomfortable and question their own position in society. In her support for segregation, Hunt stated, "I have always felt good-will toward Colored people, but recently I find that kind of feeling is beginning to wane because of your insistence in making life miserable for everybody. . . . Just because you 'fought and died' in this last war does not mean that we have to take you into our homes and coddle you."[10]

Many whites, even liberals, were uneasy with respect to African American civil rights activism, especially if it was considered radical. Recognizing black military service was one thing, but for many, granting social equality remained unthinkable. They dreaded the intrusion of blacks into the most intimate and private spaces of white society. Ultimately, this could only lead to miscegenation and intermarriage.[11] They also feared an infringement on their own rights. African Americans' unrelenting efforts to achieve civil rights unsettled whites, since they contradicted the idea of content blacks who were satisfied living in the segregated state that many whites in the North and South still found agreeable. Emotions ran high. African American protest movements and, in particular, the possibility of an integration of the armed forces, raised white anxieties over their own status and reinvigorated stereotypes of African Americans who would negatively affect white people's lives in an integrated environment.

"Negro Opinion Is About as Split as It Very Well Can Be"

Randolph's call for civil disobedience was "something of a minor sensation in the Negro circles," as it broke with "the philosophy of agitation within bounds that are acceptable to white leadership."[12] Black newspapers widely debated the unconventional campaign. Where would African Americans stand on a move that seemed to go against every concept of male citizenship and patriotism? How should they position themselves and the whole community in what could lead to either a great civil rights gain or an enormous backlash? There was no agreement on the course of the struggle for civil rights and more equality. Ultimately, in the words of columnist Marjorie McKenzie, "Negro opinion is about as split as it very well can be." What was the right method to fight segregation and finally end Jim Crow in the military specifically and society in general? The civil disobedience campaign showed "that Negroes are worlds apart" on the strategies of activism and the process of desegregation.[13] African Americans proved unsure of how to react to this challenge to military service, which had traditionally been their most potent claim to equal rights.

More traditional strategies of civil rights activism came under closer scrutiny. It seemed as if the radical step and the unforgiving and, to many, militant language Randolph and Reynolds used, awoke the African American community. Newspapers printed a plethora of editorials and letters from readers reacting to the call for civil disobedience. The NAACP headquarters in Washington also received a large amount of mail from its branches, members, and individuals on the subject.[14] It was time to take a clear and unambiguous stance. *Pittsburgh Courier* columnist Marjorie McKenzie, for instance, complained that the approaches the civil rights movement had, until now, followed in its fight for military integration had only resulted in promises, and never led to tangible changes that would actually abolish military segregation once and for all. She applauded Randolph and Reynolds for their unorthodox approach, a necessary effort in order to finally bring about a change in the military system. She asserted that common men backed the movement and made it a force to be reckoned with, and that Randolph and Reynolds guided the civil rights movement in a more radical and unapologetic direction.[15]

Supporters and opponents of the call for civil disobedience used masculinist rhetoric to make their case, reflecting on what an appropriate black male identity in the United States entailed. Reflections on black manhood infused their discussion of civil disobedience and military service in all their forms. Issues of true patriotism and manhood, as well as the rights and duties of citizenship, dominated the discussion. It was understood that the fight over segregation was a conflict over manhood and equal rights as men, which in turn subverted white male dominance.

Like Randolph and Reynolds, followers of the campaign fended off allegations of lack of patriotism and manliness and felt the need to defend their stance by deeming their actions essentially patriotic. For Randolph and Reynolds's supporters, draft resistance "on grounds of racial injustice" was the only acceptable behavior of a genuine black American (male) citizen and soldier.[16] They emulated the rhetoric of the civil disobedience movement and underscored its patriotic foundation and male character. The threat was blatant. Numerous parishes and individuals like Adam Clayton Powell, black representative from New York, or Joe Louis, the black boxer, who had already joined their committee in October 1947, supported the call for civil disobedience. Keeping to this argumentation and tone, Powell claimed, "There aren't enough jails in America to hold the Negro people who will refuse to bear arms in a Jim Crow army." Based on historical record, the loyalty of blacks to the nation could not be called into question. Powell further argued that they were the better American men, "manly" and American enough to stand up against the leaders who "whitewash [their] un-Americanism." The real traitors were not draft resisters but the white mainstream that was unwilling to grant civil rights to African Americans and other minorities.[17] Black veterans seemed especially prone to be attracted to a direct-action approach that challenged the oppressive system straightforwardly. They returned to the United States often proud that they had helped defeat "fascism abroad," but they were also especially incensed that homegrown fascism—white supremacy—had survived the end of the war and now denied them the freedom they had fought for.[18] Many grew convinced it needed more than legal action purported by the NAACP. To numerous veterans, Randolph's civil disobedience campaign was an answer, as "instead of being subservient to meaningless lip service handed out by some leaders in this country we need to get busy and do something that will be felt."[19]

The *Sun*, an African American newspaper from San Francisco, wrote, "Have we the guts of our forbearers to take this power in hand and mold the democratic future of America and the world? ARE WE MEN OR MICE?"[20] A reader of the *Chicago Defender* acknowledged the notion that Randolph and Reynolds represented masculine characteristics with their radical civil disobedience campaign, asserting that men should take "some action to do something to cure this monstrous evil, and stop trying to throw a block in the way of the man who has the courage to act."[21] In the eyes of the reader, all previous campaigns did not go far enough to end military segregation. George McCray, a columnist on labor issues for the ANP, lauded Randolph and his campaign, underlining the activist's labor background as the cradle for his manly courage. "And frankly it is—indeed surprising to many that a Negro would dare speak so brazenly. But it must be kept in mind that the men who elbow their way to the top in the labor movement are strong and brazen men." He elaborated that African Americans were no longer willing to accept the rule of the "former master," but had developed their own self-respect and courage to challenge white male dominance.[22] Joe Louis built on this call to manhood when he argued in a letter to the Senate Committee on Armed Services, "This [Jim Crow in the armed forces] is more than men with spines will endure."[23] It was hard to accuse Joe Louis of lacking manhood for supporting the civil disobedience campaign. Louis was "a powerful symbol, appearing in most media of war propaganda and representing heroism, patriotic values, and black military significance [and he] became the quintessential symbol of Americanness" during the Second World War.[24] The opponents of civil disobedience, on the other hand, represented the "'old Uncle Toms'" who were "the 'yes, massa' type of the old slave plantation" who "might at least have kept their mouths shut but they didn't agree and show the white folks they're the real leaders."[25] In the supporters' rhetoric, these opponents of the movement lacked the manly character the new objectors of segregated military service held.

The fervor and rebelliousness of the movement impressed many commentators and newspapers. The vehemence of the criticism of or opposition to civil disobedience varied greatly within the black community. Critics and opponents of the campaign cared about patriotism and manhood, as did its supporters. Horace R. Cayton, initially a member of the Committee Against Jim Crow in Military Service and Training and a columnist for the *Pittsburgh Courier*, wrote, "You can like Mr. Randolph or you can dislike him, but the man has simple, unadulterated guts. . . . I don't know how many big-shot leaders will bring up Randolph's stand, but from my observation about fourteen million little Negroes will say 'Amen'." Cayton described Randolph's statement to the Senate Armed Services Committee as a boxing match between Randolph and Truman, in which Truman, though noble in his efforts with his civil rights program, was "pinned . . . to the ropes." This metaphorical description of Randolph's activism underlines the importance of manly strength and valor, which, in Cayton's eyes, Randolph had demonstrated.[26]

Commentators were unsure and often anxious as to what would be the outcome of the movement, even if it was only a threat and would not actually lead to draft resistance and law breaking. Many feared allegations of and ultimately trials for treason, and remained convinced that the fight against segregation and discrimination had to stay "loyal and patriotic."[27] Whether they were careful critics or full-fledged opponents, commentators largely agreed that resisting military service would send the wrong signal in the struggle for civil rights. Observers often lauded Randolph and Reynolds for their fight against military segregation, but did not embrace their course of action or their reinterpretation of black manhood; rather they affirmed more traditional ideas of masculinity. They hoped it to be a "'bluff tactic' to disconcert and throw the enemy off balance" and open the eyes of the white majority to the advantages a desegregated military would offer in facing the nation's new challenges in the Cold War.[28]

In his column "Seeing and Saying" dated April 4, 1948, the African American William A. Fowlkes expressed understanding for Randolph and Reynolds's position; however, he doubted that their strategy would be successful. He expected white Southerners would take advantage of such action to denounce the rights of African Americans even further. African Americans' military service was "a glorious page in American history," and Fowlkes stressed the importance for this group, "to exhibit their manhood with all its implications" and to no longer allow that they be treated like children. Only groups that demanded their rights without betraying the nation and going against its foundation were to be "first-class American citizens deservant of the benefits and treatment of American citizens, they must act the part and demand the part. Such a spirit must infiltrate their being and environs."[29] Lem Graves, a reporter and columnist for the *Pittsburgh Courier*, ran an extensive exposé on Randolph that elaborated on his manliness and composure in the Senate hearing. Although he worried about the effects of a campaign as radical as civil disobedience and resistance to military service, Graves was nevertheless impressed by Randolph's "dramatic, coldly calculated move." The article on Randolph's strong and persistent stance on military segregation demonstrated the inherent admiration of male qualities that Graves saw in Randolph's call to action. The severity of the action, worrisome as it was, could also turn out to be an excellent tool to exert pressure on and to end segregation in the armed forces once and for all.[30]

The NAACP and its position epitomized an ambiguous and cautious understanding of the new civil rights strategy:

> While practically all Negroes agree 100 per cent with Randolph on the evils, there is no indication as yet how many agree that civil disobedience is the way to meet the situation.
>
> The NAACP has never counseled American Negroes to refuse to serve their country in time of danger. . . . It does not believe at the present time that any section of the population is justified in refusing to bear arms in time of national peril except the religious conscientious objectors. This is the Negro's country. Whatever its shortcomings, he has no other.[31]

In their activities to end segregation in the armed forces, the NAACP kept to traditional courses of activism and concepts of military service as a national patriotic duty and the ultimate path to full citizenship. Consequently, with refusing to serve, the black man would "sacrifice[s] his right to demand the abolition of the evils that keep him a second-class citizen."[32] Aware that many considered Randolph exceptionally daring and potent, the NAACP saw it necessary to underline its own radicality in the fight against military segregation. "But we cannot refuse to serve if, despite our protestations, the detested jim crow remains. Our protest has been too clear and sharp and unanimous for any to think that our service marks our acquiescence to the system."[33] The NAACP leaders certainly did not want to appear appeasing in the light of the new strategy. They respected Randolph, but they also saw him as competition stealing their thunder.[34]

The organization sent out questionnaires to 13,000 black male college students to determine their stance on civil disobedience; an astonishing 73 percent of the respondents supported Randolph's call, while only 15 percent opposed it. It was clearly only a "sampling of opinion of young college men" and did not poll less educated men of the same age, but it was widely noted and interpreted as a sign of the serious impatience young men felt regarding the civil rights movement's lack of progress.[35] It became clear that a growing number of especially younger African Americans grew increasingly weary of the lobbying and legal strategies the NAACP pursued. They turned to a more direct action approach that promised to put more immediate pressure on local as well as national decision-makers. A new and younger generation of activists in the civil rights movement, among them Bayard Rustin, seemed to be on the horizon, which challenged, whether knowingly or inadvertently, the NAACP's predominance.[36] Thirteen presidents of black colleges, on the other hand, clearly opposed the civil disobedience endeavor. While pursuing an increase in the number of Reserve Officers Training Corps (ROTC) programs at black colleges, the presidents pledged their unrelenting loyalty and willingness to fight in the armed forces in spite of continued segregation.[37]

Despite rejecting civil disobedience as a strategy to attain military integration "for very practical reasons," the NAACP expressed their utmost understanding for Randolph and Reynolds's impatience in their demand for an end to segregation. Walter White, the executive secretary of the NAACP, admitted in a letter to a labor activist that he was "glad that Philip Randolph focused nation-wide attention on the evils of segregation in the armed services in such a dramatic fashion."[38] He underlined that there was "sympathy in many hearts for the Randolph point of view."[39] White even promised that the NAACP would grant legal support to young men who refused military service on the grounds of military segregation. Nevertheless, civil disobedience was not an option for White. Over recent years, he had grown increasingly suspicious of grassroots activism and generally more radical methodologies. White, and with him the NAACP as a whole, continued to rely on lobbying and a legal approach in their fight for rights but always feared a shift in the public's attention in favor of the more direct action tactic.[40]

Some members of the NAACP were also worried about the negative effects any association with Randolph or the civil disobedience campaign might have on their organization. In a letter to White, the Illinois Branch in Decatur, for instance, wrote, "those hysterical people in Washington . . . want something like this to discredit the Association."[41] Their fear was not unfounded. As they were dependent on white support, especially in Congress, an association with such radical approaches could have detrimental consequences for the interracial civil rights group. After Randolph and Reynolds's appearance before the Senate Armed Services Committee, Senator Morse, a long-time member of the NAACP and supporter of civil rights, threatened to quit the organization and no longer speak on behalf of civil rights if the NAACP did not distance itself more vehemently from Randolph's plan for action. White exchanged letters with him following his threat stating that although a "good friend of minority groups and supporter of civil rights legislation, but it apparently is not possible for you to realize how bitterly Negro Americans feel about Jim Crow in the armed forces." Morse argued in favor of a much more gradual, slower course to attain civil rights and equality, predicting that any support for Randolph's approach would set civil rights efforts back several years.[42] He further elaborated on his fear that the civil disobedience campaign would hurt any legislative civil rights efforts in Congress: "Randolph's proposal for a program of civil disobedience is being used by many Republicans and, of course, by many Democrats too for an excuse for nonaction on civil rights. . . . Furthermore, I don't like to see those of us in the Congress who have been fighting for civil rights legislation confronted with another barrier to surmount, particularly when it is a barrier which didn't need to be placed in our path." His take on the right path to full civil rights became more obvious when he equated Randolph's strategy with that of the opponents of civil rights and called the strategy a series of "intolerant actions which are used, only in a different form." The only way to enhance civil rights was clearly the legislative path taken by civil rights supporters in Congress, who were primarily familiar with the procedures of politics. At one point, Morse even went so far as to compare Randolph's civil disobedience campaign to mob action.[43] Nonetheless, White managed to calm Morse down and convinced him to stay in the NAACP and advance civil rights in Congress. However, this continued mollycoddling of the senator from Oregon did not sit well with all NAACP members. In a letter to White, W. W. Law, the National Youth Chairman of the NAACP, opposed "making any concessions to Senator Wayne Morse" who he considered a "congenial next door neighbor" to Southern white supremacists.[44]

Despite the NAACP's, in particular White's, attempts to appease liberal white congressmen like Morse, the organization simultaneously used Randolph's radical campaign to exert pressure on and scare white politicians and citizens. While repeatedly distancing the organization from the call for civil disobedience, White emphasized that Randolph was not a "self-seeking opportunist" and reminded Morse that Randolph's "opinion carries weight among them [numerous blacks]."[45] The civil disobedience campaign underlined the urgency of the cause for military integration, and even for those activists who opposed it; it represented a useful tool in the fight for more equality. Its quality as an instrument of coercion within the context of the fight for military integration and civil rights was undeniable. White especially directed his criticism toward the Republican Party of which Morse was a member. Unlike Truman and liberal Democrats like Senator Hubert Humphrey, Republicans had seldom exhibited investment in civil rights and had been unwilling to counter Southern Democrats like Senator Richard B. Russell from Georgia, a steadfast segregationist. Most Republicans stalled or overtly opposed military integration. White exchanged a large number of letters and telegrams with Morse, discussing and trying to explain Randolph's efforts. The partial publication of the correspondence in both African American and white newspapers demonstrated the significance of the issue for blacks and whites alike.[46]

White used the opportunity to openly scold the reluctance to support civil rights as the "cheapest of politics is played with even a minimum civil rights program." It was used as a lesson that needed to be taught to the white majority so that they may begin to fathom the degrading experiences of soldiers in the Second World War, who after serving in the military, had hoped that the government would "keep at least some of its promises to make democracy more of a reality."[47] In the ongoing fight between the political parties for African American voters, White used the black vote as an incentive for politicians to earnestly support military integration and civil rights. With the threat of civil disobedience, the Cold War, and the watchful eyes of a world audience, military integration and civil rights became increasingly important issues. White and his fellow NAACP members were willing to use the strategy of civil disobedience as leverage for their own good.

In his weekly column "The Watchtower," Roy Wilkins, NAACP assistant secretary, lauded Randolph for his "blunt and brave testimony" that used "no weasel words" but "brave words in a great cause." However, he withheld his support for the movement itself, maintaining that as citizens blacks had an obligation to fight for their country no matter what. Randolph's strategy was a "puny weapon" in the fight against racial oppression and not applicable in the minority's fight against a majority.[48] According to Wilkins and others, only by serving the nation in the military would African Americans attain equality and full civil rights. Swaying from the path of activism within the framework of white concepts of respectable male behavior and displays of patriotism was not yet an option for many African Americans. It was not the time, and military service was certainly not the place for this challenging strategy. Wilkins privately worried about the possibility of a serious shift of interest toward Randolph resulting in a loss of influence of the NAACP. Contemplating on organizing a demonstration of veterans against military segregation, he stated that such a move "would give some punch to our protest—a punch that was lacking in the testimony of Jesse Dedmon which was smothered by Randolph's dramatic declaration."[49] For many of Randolph and Reynolds's critics, staying within what were understood to be the legal, rightful, and American boundaries of protest, was the most effective means to successfully achieve full civil rights.

Clear-cut opponents of resistance against military service were more vehement and unforgiving in their rejection of the civil disobedience strategy than the NAACP and other critics. They believed that only full-fledged avowals of loyalty and patriotism could eventually bring about the implementation of full civil rights—and what better way to prove this than unconditional military service. Civil disobedience would only tarnish the record of African Americans' unconditional loyalty to the American nation and endanger any progress already achieved or yet to be achieved. They considered the move "drastic," even "extremist," and predicted that it could prove "extremely dangerous and perhaps catastrophic" for African Americans and national defense.[50] The *Evening Star* went so far as to claim that Randolph and Reynolds's course of action had done more damage "in a single day to the Negro than discrimination could do for years."[51] Opponents feverishly tried to extinguish all doubts that blacks would resist to fight for the American nation, despite its flaws. In their view, military service would allow them to criticize the United States, while effectively putting pressure on the government to gain their full civil rights. Allegations that the civil disobedience campaign was an un-American, if not anti-American act quickly established themselves within and outside of the African American community.

In accordance with Morse's contention with the civil disobedience campaign, opposition papers and commentators were convinced that all acts along the lines of Randolph and Reynolds's strategy were treason. Therefore, they were not only reprehensible but dangerous for the well-being and progress of the race, and eventually detrimental for the nation. They claimed that African Americans had made a great deal of progress and segregation was gradually weakening, otherwise Randolph would not have had the chance to speak his mind unpunished before the Senate Armed Services Committee. For many critics and opponents, gradualism and compliance with white norms and expectations was the key to the progress of the race. "However much we hate a second-class status, and all Negroes do hate it, we must eliminate it by ways that are legal and patriotic." African Americans would never commit treason. The fear of being identified as "fifth columnists" of Communism also lingered as a factor preventing more outright forms of protest.[52] Such opponents held the view that the only way to gain full civil rights was to serve in the armed forces and prove one's dedication to the nation. The path of civil disobedience was too radical and daring to be a viable option and strategy for change.[53] Criticism of America's treatment of blacks was strong, but a departure from what was understood to be American behavior was not an option for most critics of American society.[54] Randolph's opponents found a prominent voice in Truman Gibson, a member of the advising committee on UMT and avid advocate.

Gibson, who many perceived to represent the military establishment and who was viewed with open suspicion even by some of Randolph's critics, reacted with "shock and dismay" to Randolph's call. In a letter to

President Truman immediately following reports on Randolph and Reynolds's meeting with the president, in which they first postulated civil disobedience, Gibson was adamant that they did not speak for the African American community. He argued that their campaign "exist[ed] principally for newspaper purposes." Furthermore, he insisted that they "seized the emotional issue of army segregation" to defeat UMT as a whole.[55] Gibson did not support segregation, but argued in favor of the efficient use of black soldiers based on their individual ability. Especially in times of crisis, a man could only demonstrate his patriotism through absolute loyalty to the nation, despite its flaws. More than the NAACP, Gibson remained within the confines of traditional concepts of loyalty to the nation and patriotic black masculinity: "Patriotism is not the subject of cynical bargaining. Negroes have participated in the military history of this country to the fullest extent allowed in the past. They certainly will do so in the future. To express sentiments to the contrary is unfair to the millions of loyal citizens who know only this country and who do not look to any foreign ideology to correct the plaguing domestic evils that concern us."[56]

For Gibson and others, including *New York Amsterdam News* editor C. B. Powell, civil disobedience attacked the American system and implied support for the Soviet Union. Although Gibson backed the end of segregation in the military, he did not believe in coercing desegregation under all circumstances, since that would threaten American national security. He believed attainment of full civil rights and equality had to be subordinate to national security concerns. A man's national and military duty was a priority, despite any injustice. African American men were not to endanger the strength and prowess of the military and the nation by defying the draft. For Powell, civil disobedience was a sign of a lack of patriotism, Americanness, and manhood.[57] In his nationally syndicated column "Between the Lines," printed in the *Los Angeles Sentinel* and *Birmingham World*, among others, Gordon B. Hancock agreed with Gibson's views on the integration of the military, based on the belief that change would be generated through education.[58] Hancock pointed to the dangers of antigradualism as well as the limits of black patience with respect to civil rights, but he vigorously maintained that the best path to full civil rights was black participation in the armed forces and a stellar record in case of war. "The valor of Negro soldiers has disarmed too many foes of Negro advance, to have the Negro's loyalty questioned today. Say what we will the willingness of Negroes to bear arms for a country that refused them full manhood rights has armed his friends and disarmed his foes." Military service would be an enormous "moral leverage" in the hands of blacks, and was not to be surrendered to follow Randolph's dangerous path, a path supported only by a minority.[59]

Gibson's statement in the Senate hearing garnered accolades from many whites. Senator Morse called it "one of the finest defenses of the Negro race in regard to civil rights that it has been my pleasure to read." He asserted that the majority of African Americans would firmly support Gibson.[60] In a White House memorandum, David K. Niles called Gibson's testimony a way "to counteract the bad impression created by Randolph."[61] In the white mainstream, statements like Gibson's were met with relief, as they defused the urgency and impatience felt by many African Americans with regard to military service and segregation. Supporters of the civil disobedience campaign, on the other hand, publicly scolded Gibson for his stance and rhetorically called his manhood into question. They referred to his service as the civilian aide to the secretary of war during the Second World War, during which he had already earned the reputation of not doing enough for African Americans in the services.[62]

Just as he had three years prior, during the dispute over the performance of black soldiers, Reynolds attacked Gibson. He called him "the twentieth century Uncle Tom whose recent testimony [before the Senate Armed Services Committee] ranked him conclusively, in my opinion, as the No. 1 Quisling among Negroes."[63] The term "Uncle Tom" again implied that Gibson lacked manhood. His critics argued that instead of standing up against white oppression, he subordinated himself and followed orders. He thereby not only denigrated his own manhood, but also prevented the entire race from advancing and gaining their rightful place, which black soldiers had heroically fought and also died for. Moreover, Reynolds alleged that Gibson, like Quisling, collaborated with an overtly oppressive system. His speech before the Senate Committee seemed to elucidate once more that working within the system represented a roadblock to profound change and profited only a handful African Americans. Reynolds admonished that Gibson focused on self-advancement instead of working for the progress and equality of all blacks in general and black soldiers in particular. Ultimately, the former civilian aide, according to Reynolds, betrayed African Americans by acquiescing to the rules of the military establishment instead of fighting them openly. Their divergent viewpoints nearly led to a fistfight outside the Senate hearing room.[64] The episode further adulterated Reynolds's troubled relationship with Gibson, whom he had always suspected of harming all blacks and him personally, when he had been thwarted in his attempts to remain in the armed forces. The two did not publicly cross paths again. Reynolds continued to work with the Committee against Jim Crow in Military Service and Training,[65] while Gibson, on the other hand, left his work with the armed forces behind, and began a career as a professional boxing promoter.[66]

The White South Fights Back

Richard B. Russell was the highest-ranking member of the Senate Armed Services Committee and present when Randolph and Reynolds made their statement.[67] The senator from Georgia remained silent while the two men spoke, but left the room twice during their presentation.[68] Earlier in the Senate, he had praised Gibson for what he called a "fine statement of Americanism."[69] He stylized Gibson's argumentation as the only proper form of African American national identity, silencing any critical aspect the former civilian aide's statement might have contained. At the end of the session with Randolph and Reynolds, Russell turned to the press calling the civil disobedience campaign an act of treason. He could not stand any civil rights advocacy and an end to Jim Crow was not an option for the senator from Georgia. Since Russell believed that blacks were not equal to whites, he seriously questioned why they should be granted equal rights. To him, black soldiers performed poorly in the military, and were the greatest disgrace to the armed forces. Integrating them with white soldiers who he thought fought so valiantly not only dishonored white soldiers, but also ultimately threatened national security. Russell's argumentation against racial progress and integration in the draft and military service was based on the destruction of positive images of the African American soldier.

On April 3, 1948, General Dwight D. Eisenhower took the stand to comment on UMT. While questioning the general, Russell hoped to find ways to undermine not only the civil disobedience campaign, but to force Eisenhower to speak out in favor of segregation. The destruction of the image of the African American soldier was also at the center of Russell's argumentation against racial progress. Other committee members, knowingly or not, provided Russell with the necessary argumentative grounds in his pursuit. Senator Leverett Saltonstall, a Republican from Massachusetts, asked Eisenhower what he thought of the mandatory separation of black from white soldiers. Eisenhower asserted:

> In general the Negro is less well educated than his brother citizen that is white, and if you make a complete amalgamation what you are going to have is in every company the Negro is going to be relegated to the minor jobs, and he is never going to get his promotion to such grades as technical sergeant, master sergeant, and so on, because the competition is too tough.
>
> If, on the other hand, he is in smaller units of his own, he can go up to that rate, and I believe he is entitled to the chance to show his own wares.[70]

According to the highly respected general, the likelihood of African American soldiers to advance in a segregated environment was greater than in an integrated one. Blacks, he argued, would not have a reasonable opportunity to be successful in an integrated setting. Although Eisenhower claimed that he was no longer fully convinced of the validity of "this extreme segregation," he supported its continuation in the armed services as long as the human race did not "grow up" and end race prejudice and segregation. His statement seemed not to be blatantly racist, but rather cautiously reflective and well meaning. In his column "The Watchtower," Roy Wilkins of the NAACP maintained that although not as "vicious" as Russell's, Eisenhower's "testimony is bad to those like this writer who believe that segregation should be abolished, but it is not as bad as it was reported in the newspapers."[71] Nonetheless, a patriarchal and racist benevolence informed Eisenhower's stance. Furthermore, similar to Southern states' rights claims, he made unmistakably clear that as federal regulations and laws would not change attitudes and feelings, they were not an appropriate means to deal with the issue.[72]

Russell poked and prodded the general to take a more determined stand on segregation. His questioning attacked the character and performance of black soldiers in previous wars. Based on questionable data, he asserted that rates of crime and venereal disease were extremely high among blacks serving in the military. Compared to white soldiers, black soldiers allegedly lacked character, were less trustworthy, and posed an imminent danger to both white women and men. In response to Russell's charge, Eisenhower admitted that data indeed indicated that a higher crime and venereal disease rate existed among black recruits; however, he tried to put it into perspective, suggesting that the lower educational and social standards prevailing among blacks were responsible for these high numbers.[73] While Eisenhower maintained unambiguously that education could resolve these differences between blacks and whites, Russell held fast to his belief that the data was a clear sign of blacks' deficient character and innate inferiority to whites. Eisenhower did not support this overwhelmingly negative assessment of black soldiers as much as Russell would have liked. Nevertheless, the general did not wholeheartedly dismiss Russell's allegations and the continuation of segregation. His testimony made Eisenhower an unviable candidate for presidency for most African Americans.[74]

Russell had three primary objectives in mind when he posed his questions to Eisenhower. First, he wanted to underline the necessity of UMT. Second, it was an opportunity to defend white supremacy and segregation by championing individual and states' rights. Third, he was able to degrade black soldiers with respect to their morale, discipline, and health. His approach struck the core of black male identity, since soldiers' honor and valor had a decisive status in the African Americans' self-worth and identity formation. Russell used these three strands of argumentation extensively throughout his long-lasting campaign against military integration. To Russell, all three were reason enough to preclude integration in the armed forces.

Under Pressure

President Truman felt the pressure to initiate political change. African American activism for military integration had been insistent in soliciting him since he became president, but the radicality of Randolph and Reynolds's call for civil disobedience and its unknown consequences were a different matter. As the Cold War grew in intensity, and minority rights became more and more important on an international stage in an election year, segregation proved hard to defend. The president drastically increased the pledges he made to African American activists in 1948, but he still shied away from passing any clear and binding civil rights legislation. He feared creating a split within the Democratic Party, which had drifted apart because of his civil rights rhetoric.[75] Losing support of Southern Democrats completely was simply not an option in a presidential election year. Early in 1948, Senator Russell warned that Southern states would go Republican if the Democratic president continued his support for civil rights.[76] Truman found himself trapped between appeasing both white Southerners and black voters, who were no longer willing to accept empty promises.

A conference of leading African American civil rights activists and military officials at the end of April 1948, shortly after the launch of the civil disobedience campaign, only increased the pressure. Its planners, Secretary of Defense James Forrestal, and Lester Granger, his long-time confidant, and executive secretary of the National Urban League, agreed to organize a conference on discrimination and segregation in the armed forces with representatives of all military branches. Granger was one of the black civil rights and labor activists highly committed to pushing for stronger African American involvement in the armed forces, more specifically in the navy. In early 1945, he had been offered the position as civilian aide to the secretary of the navy. Although rejecting the offer, he worked closely with the navy, inspecting and advising on its racial policy.[77] For Granger, the "role of the Negro in military service [was] perhaps the primary issue before American Negroes" and the candidates' position on this would decide the vote of blacks in the next presidential election. All civil rights activists, he maintained, worked especially hard at "breaking down the uneconomic, pernicious and anti-democratic system of segregation in the armed services."[78] Forrestal and Granger ultimately wanted to see an advisory committee formed to provide "constructive recommendations for improvement in the defense policies—immediately and on a long-time basis."[79]

In charge of the list of participants, Granger summoned civil rights activists from all walks of life, but left out Randolph. Walter White, one of those invited, asked Granger more than once to add the famous labor leader to the list of participants. Although not fully agreeing with Randolph's approach, White argued it would "be difficult to explain ignoring him to the large public which trusts him."[80] Granger worried that the civil disobedience campaign could have negative repercussions for blacks' demands at the conference and refused to invite either Randolph or Reynolds to attend. He interpreted Randolph's statement before the Senate committee as having been a "dramatic expression of resentment, rather than advice to the Department."[81] Granger felt cornered by Randolph's radical statement and thought that the army would block any of his more moderate proposals for change because of Randolph's activism.[82] While his refusal to invite Randolph was most likely based on his fear of losing the fight for racial integration, it was also spurred by his bruised ego and the feeling that Randolph had taken over the lead in a struggle Granger considered his own.

Although Randolph would not participate, and most of the conference's participants did, albeit not openly, support his radical approach, his campaign and the impatience it expressed were omnipresent. In general, the civil disobedience campaign "made it easy for 'more conservative' leaders . . . to reject emphatically any concept of segregated military service."[83] The atmosphere was tense and the black representatives were unwilling to compromise. Shortly before the meeting, the otherwise often assuaging White straightforwardly pressed the issue. His tone resembled the impatient rhetoric of Randolph and Reynolds when he stated, "there is no thought of compromise in my mind, and as far as I know in the minds of the others invited." Again, issues of male prowess and opposition were both overtly and covertly ingrained in the discussion, when Benjamin McLauren of the BSCP commented on the conference and its participants: "If a compromise is proposed in the Forrestal conference we will take on all corners including weak-kneed Negro leaders who do not back up their own convictions but give support to their good white friends in order to keep their support."[84]

Even Granger, whose dislike of Randolph's activities was well known, confirmed the "intense resentment and moral indignation which prompted Randolph's statement."[85] The participants of the conference capitalized on its shock effect. Granger's later report on the conference referred to the civil disobedience campaign as "emphatic evidence of the need for immediate steps by all branches of the armed services to correct any remaining policies which are demonstrably undemocratic in nature, and, in so doing, to square the official practices of our federal government with this nation's ideals and principles as set forth in our constitution."[86] Granger admonished that the armed forces, foremost the army, held on to its "stubborn conviction that its civilian officials, its general staff, and its white officers, on down to second lieutenants, 'know Negroes.'" Moreover, they would not even consider their excellent war record.[87] Such insults aimed at black men ran deep. Charles Houston, dean of Howard Law School and conference participant, struck a rather aggressive note when he warned that integration was the only option available. During the conference, Houston maintained that, despite his reluctance to support Randolph's radical path, he was glad Randolph had proposed it publicly, as his move underlined the urgency of the issue.[88] But despite all impatient demeanor and argumentation, no agreement could be reached between the opposing groups. The attending black delegates left the conference dissatisfied with its course and outcome, as segregation in the military remained untouched. Subsequently they collectively refused to work as advisors to the armed forces should segregation continue.[89]

The African American press clearly remarked on the connection between Randolph's campaign and the newfound resolve demonstrated at the meeting organized by Forrestal. Charley Cherokee, commentator at the *Chicago Defender*, noted, "Phil's ghost was there, chum, standing behind every chair. . . . It's a showdown and Phil's ghost still prowls the Pentagon."[90] The *New York Amsterdam News* congratulated the black conference participants on their "courageous stand and forthright expression of the attitude of the Negro population on Jim Crow in the Army, Air Force and Marines." The newspaper aligned segregation and discrimination with the reign of totalitarianism in the United States, which an African American citizen would not relent to fight "until he is, in theory and practice, a first class citizen."[91] The paper's editorial cartoon dated May 1, 1948, emphasized the masculinization of the African American civil rights activist in the struggle for military integration (Figure 3). Whereas Forrestal was represented as an effeminate man wearing an apron and a skirt, a black man, representing the "16 Negro Leaders," towers over him freeing himself of the Jim Crow system of the armed forces. Agency was clearly with the black male, whereas the army was reduced to a weak, effeminate position. The gendered discourse was undeniable.

The tone of the debates on Randolph's civil disobedience campaign was, whether one supported the move or not, one of increased impatience, putting pressure on the Pentagon and the president. The possible loss of black votes in the upcoming election loomed powerfully over the White House. Backing down on the issue of abolishing military segregation seemed not to be an option for most African Americans, whether they supported Randolph's campaign or rejected it. Randolph's committee and league were the most disconcerting and publicly discussed of the civil rights organizations. The committee and league increased their public presence and activism. Members who supported the civil disobedience campaign organized picket lines at the GOP and the Democratic National Conventions (both in Philadelphia), where the two parties were choosing their presidential candidates

Figure 3. "Cutting Himself from the Apron Strings." Cartoon, *New York Amsterdam News*, May 1, 1948, 10. Reproduced by permission of copyright holder; further reproduction prohibited without permission.

(Figure 4). The days-long picketing, involving protesters walking up and down the street with signs expressing unwillingness to serve in a segregated military, did not go unnoticed, and when Randolph attended, the press certainly paid attention.[92]

With their civil disobedience campaign underway, Randolph and Reynolds continued sending letters to the president, pushing for military integration and ratification of an executive order.[93] The situation gained in intensity within and especially outside of the African American community. Certainly, Randolph and Reynolds were not the only ones to bombard Truman with letters in their quest for military integration. The NAACP also

Figure 4. Picketers outside Democratic National Convention, Philadelphia, July 12, demanding equal rights for Negoes and Anti-Jim Crow plank in the Party platform. Leading the pickets is A. Philip Randolph (L), president of the Board of Sleeping Car Porters and chairman of the League for Non-Violent Civil Disobedience against Military Segregation. © Bettmann/CORBIS.

continued to write to him demanding change. Yet, no one else exerted an equally intense pressure on the president as they did by relentlessly repeating their plan to go through with resistance to military service and reminding him of the support they claimed they had among blacks and whites alike.

A Dubious Ally and an Old Enemy

Although Truman and his advertising apparatus intensely pushed for it, the UMT bill failed to make it through Congress. The draft, however, remained up for discussion and as of May 1948, Congress considered a draft bill, which, however, did not contain any racial equality regulations. While civil disobedience was one path they used, Randolph and Reynolds also followed the more traditional route of lobbying. They hoped that the shock effect of resistance would make politicians across the aisle listen to their demands. They saw the need to complement their militant activism with the solicitation of congressmen in order to push for civil rights amendments to the draft bill. They sought people in the Senate and House willing to make the case against military segregation and publicly reveal its shameful hypocrisies. After many disappointments, they found a supporter in Senator William Langer from North Dakota—a staunch opponent of the draft with a somewhat questionable civil rights record. More than most other members of the Senate, Langer supported black equality, but he had repeatedly used the addition of civil rights amendments to kill bills that he opposed.[94] His ulterior motives and his use of civil rights as a means to an end notwithstanding, Randolph had no reservations cooperating with him. The black labor leader was impressed that a senator from North Dakota, "where the colored vote is negligible," intended to support the committee in its fight to end segregation in the draft and military.[95] More important, Randolph and Reynolds did not have many alternative candidates who would support their cause and speak for them in the Senate. Langer was, as the *Afro-American* later said, "as liberal a man as there is in the Senate" and thus one of the only members to which the activists could turn.[96] His intention to kill the draft altogether made him readily willing to attach civil rights amendments to the draft bill, which he knew the Southern senators would then be compelled to oppose.

Southern senators were outraged over Randolph's civil disobedience campaign and Langer's civil rights amendments and promptly made their countering move. Senator Russell led the opposition and butted heads with Langer on the issue. Although Russell might never have quite emulated the extreme and "inflammatory language" of senator Theodore G. Bilbo of Mississippi, one of the most infamous Southern white supremacist demagogues, he believed in the inferiority of blacks and the validity and necessity of racial segregation.[97] His opposition to military desegregation was part of a larger agenda of upholding white supremacy in the South, thereby ultimately defending "a social system that was indefensible."[98] As polished and covert as his language may have appeared, it produced humiliating attacks on African Americans and revealed his paternalistic racism. In his argumentation for voluntary segregation, he questioned African Americans' patriotism and worthiness of equal rights in the military and society in general. Russell based his campaign against military integration on the notion that segregation was innately American, rather than Southern, thereby catering to a wider audience across the nation.[99] The control over the image of the African American soldier—the slurring of his efforts and character in the public mind—proved a cornerstone of Russell's fight against military integration. Following the call for civil disobedience by Randolph and Reynolds, and the submission of the civil rights amendments to the draft bill by Senator Langer, Russell intensified his efforts to preserve military segregation.

When Langer submitted Randolph and Reynolds's seven amendments to the Senate for consideration, Russell had another chance to present his anti-civil rights position with reference to the draft bill. In early May, Langer had promised Randolph he would fight against a Jim Crow draft and "introduce an amendment to bar all forms of racial segregation under any draft and I shall fight vigorously for its adoption."[100] The amendments demanded integration of the draft and various protective measures for black soldiers.[101] Randolph and Reynolds provided soldiers' memoirs, facts, and figures so that Langer would be able make a strong case outlining the trials, tribulations, and needs of black soldiers in and outside the armed forces.

In June 1948, Langer stood before the Senate to voice his support of the civil rights amendments. Only a few people were present when "Wild Bill," a name other senators had given the North Dakota native for his unpredictable ways in Congress, commenced his speech.[102] He spoke fervently as he asked, "Who can expect our millions of Negro citizens to be willing to fight to the death, if need be, for a system which oppresses them, in an army which itself subjects them to discrimination and segregation based solely upon the color of their skin?" [103] He followed the argumentation of the African American community, who had first raised the question why they should serve a country that refused to grant them equal rights.[104] However, his motive of preventing the draft altogether often got the better of him.

Langer linked the Cold War threat with the quest for civil rights, a line of reasoning that was not new. African Americans, like A. Philip Randolph and the committee that issued the report *To Secure These Rights*, had used this argument against segregation and discrimination for some time. The senator from North Dakota asserted that the mistreatment of minorities in the United States would negatively affect efforts in foreign, nonwhite countries all across the world. "If we have nothing better to offer the peoples of the world than a type of bias and exploitation of the rights of our colored citizens simply because they happened to be born dark, then no one will believe us when we claim that we are fighting for freedom and decency and individual rights against the dark evil of totalitarian Communist doctrine."[105] Accusing Truman of failing to eliminate Jim Crow, Langer claimed his amendments finally lived up to what the president, the president's committee, and his own party had formerly promised. "The parties of Lincoln and Jefferson must together remove from America now the irony of a segregated Army which in World War II brought grief, humiliation and tragedy to hundred [sic] of thousands of Negro GI's."[106]

Although Langer tried to make a strong case for his civil rights amendments, his reasons for opposing the draft often overshadowed his argumentation. He often directed his arguments in such a way as to explain why the draft in and of itself was entirely superfluous and a threat to the American nation.[107] This left the discomfited impression that his primary focus was the draft, rather than the lack of civil rights or racial equality regulations in the bill. He even remained vague on whether he himself would vote in favor of a draft bill that contained his civil rights amendments.[108] Constituents who wrote to Langer in the wake of his argumentation fully supported and admired him for his—in their eyes—genuine position. Numerous politicians and newspapers across party lines, on the other hand, presented a more critical assessment of Langer's civil rights efforts.

Supporters of the draft saw a great threat in Langer's attempts to incorporate civil rights amendments into the draft bill. They thought the amendments could delay or even prevent the passage of the draft they believed was indispensable for the security and, indeed, survival of the nation. Langer did not find many supporters for his plan in the Senate. Even advocates of civil rights legislation were expected to oppose his proposals, since the draft had a "'must' status" in Congress and needed to be passed.[109] During the June 7 session, Senator Wayne Morse interrupted Langer's speech and explicitly rejected his amendment proposal, arguing that the United States needed the draft, but was not yet ready to abolish segregation in the armed forces. John C. Gurney, Republican from South Dakota, chairman of the Senate Armed Services Committee, noted that a "defense measure is no vehicle for use in fighting out the civil rights question."[110] If the draft failed to pass in the legislature, he argued, the nation was "foolishly gambling with the future safety and wellbeing of its people and its way living."[111] He maintained that such a move would result in a deadly filibuster by Southern senators and gloomily predicted the end of the United States as a free nation.[112] In accordance with Gurney, Langer's own party felt that the draft was not the proper vehicle to instigate social reform and scorned his campaign.[113] As predicted by civil rights supporters, Southern senators were outraged during the long, drawn-out discussion on the amendments.

As Langer spoke lengthily on African American military service, Senator Russell made every effort to disrupt and discredit his civil rights advocacy. Following Langer's account on Crispus Attucks, the first man to die in the American Revolution in protection of the soon-to-be independent nation and who happened to be black, Russell posed his first question meant to invalidate or, at very least, to question the event's significance. The story of Attucks's death held special meaning for the African American community and was often cited to highlight the long history and significance of their dedication to their country.[114] The senator from Georgia began to undermine the service of all African Americans to the nation, when he pointed out that Attucks was not alone in his death that day in Boston, claiming that six or seven others, presumably white, also lost their lives, yet nobody remembered them. "It always seemed to me to be a bit unfair that all the others have been forgotten and are never mentioned, although Attucks, who, of course, was one of the heroes of the Revolution is mentioned time and again in all discussions of matters of this nature. . . . I say to the Senator, since he is speaking of discrimination, that I think it is discriminatory against the others."[115] He downplayed discrimination of blacks, while he highlighted the alleged collective oblivion to white war heroes and indirectly contended an exaggeration of blacks' fighting efforts. Russell's argumentation inverted the system of discrimination, making whites victims while placing blacks into a position of power, thus implying that they did not require further empowerment.

To counter the virulent civil rights efforts and at least make the voice of segregation heard, Russell and his collaborator Senator Burnet Maybank, a Democrat from South Carolina, proposed their own plan to deal with blacks in the draft. On June 8, 1948, they presented their amendment to the Senate. It ensured that soldiers of all races had the option between training and serving with their own race only or in desegregated units. Race classification would to be based on the system the Bureau of the Census had used in 1940, which stipulated that a "person of mixed White and Negro blood was to be returned as Negro, no matter how small the percentage of Negro blood."[116] Only people from racial minorities that comprised less than 1 percent of the population would be allowed to serve with the majority, if organizing separate units proved otherwise impractical. Russell and Maybank claimed that their amendment did not intend to reinforce segregation, but the individual's freedom of choice, a quintessential American right.[117]

Senators Russell and Maybank's speeches were laced with paternalistic racism. Emphasizing the goodwill and honest intentions in which the proposition was rooted, Russell claimed that, since he came from Georgia, a state with a large black population, he was more interested in the "equal treatment of Negroes drafted" than any other person. The two senators tried to appear as if it was benevolence toward blacks, who would lose opportunities in the army and society if they served alongside whites, that was their primary motivation for promoting the amendment. Their argumentation invoked the myth of the Old South and slaveholders' goodwill toward their slaves, which claimed that enslavement as well as white guidance and control had ensured the happiness and well-being of all blacks. According to their line of reasoning, neither whites nor most blacks wanted social equality or even miscegenation. Russell maintained that blacks were as unwilling to serve in integrated units as whites were, "I also in the amendment demand for my Negro constituents the right to claim the privilege of serving in units composed of members of their own races. There is little doubt in my mind that a majority of them will affirmatively request service with their own race."[118]

Protecting freedom of choice, Russell purported, proved beneficial to whites as well as African Americans who already enjoyed the same rights and opportunities as whites, as long as they remained in separate spheres. Truly, the amendment called for the continuation of segregation and white supremacy. Yet as its primary proponent, Russell maintained that the continuance of this alleged freedom of choice was the best option for the nation and all its races. Russell stylized himself in the tradition of paternalistic white Southerners, who did not only mean well but also spoke for and represented African Americans, who had chosen them as their representatives in good knowledge and trust. According to the senator from Georgia, he and those like him in the South but also in the rest of the country, rightfully and adequately represented the black masses. He asserted that a vocal minority of blacks were on the wrong path in a quest for something they would already have if they just let themselves be guided by the well-meaning white Southerners who knew what was best for them.

Similar to Eastland's comments three years earlier, Russell's discussion on his amendment also applied familiar rhetoric and methods: discrediting and humiliating black soldiers, their character, and their performance. Russell contended that he could not support compulsory military service if there was no "freedom of choice in the individual as to the race of the military unit in which he is forced to serve," and further maintained that the "morale and health of the men is sure to be adversely affected."[119] Although he refrained from the verbal expletives Bilbo, Eastland, and other segregationists applied, Russell forcefully put into question the qualities of blacks, insinuating that they could not be good American citizens and soldiers. By presenting questionable data and statistics, he made the case that African American soldiers were more prone to crime and venereal diseases. Thus, Russell invoked long-held stereotypes of African American males as sexual predators and threats to white women, and represented them as unreliable and deficient fighters who could not live up to the standard of white males, but instead threatened their lives in any number of ways. Russell's claims outlined the fear that white manhood would be degraded, if white men were forced into close contact with black men in the military—a place where men were imagined to be made, not weakened. Desegregation of the military, according to Russell, would result in the degradation and humiliation of the allegedly superior white race as well as that of blacks.[120]

Russell turned desegregation on its head, picking up on the tricky link in the African American argumentation for integration, which claimed that the morale of black soldiers was low because of segregation. Rather than purport that segregation negatively affected African Americans' will to serve, he called segregation an empowering experience that some blacks were just too weak to see. "Mr. President, I would that I could inspire the members of the Negro race in this Union with the same pride of race that I feel in mine."[121] Russell insinuated that that those African Americans who fought for desegregation ultimately lacked racial pride. Whereas the Japanese immigrant soldiers fought valorously for their country in their separate units without complaining, black soldiers were convinced of their unfair treatment.

According to Russell, Nisei, second generation Japanese in the United States, understood that those Japanese who served in segregated military units were not seen or treated as inferiors, but were equal to whites. The Nisei used the opportunity to show their patriotism and racial pride by serving only with their own race. The senator reasoned that instead of celebrating their racial pride in segregated units, African Americans only complained to cover up their own incompetence. Furthermore, he nurtured persistent stereotypes of blacks in American military history, which struck the core of virile and strong masculinity: showing weakness in the face of the enemy. "It is a great pity that other minority groups do not emulate their example instead of fading in the face of enemy action or refusing to serve at all in defense of their country unless they can dictate all of the terms of their service even though such terms may be violative of the rights of other American citizens."[122] It was not the minorities who suffered from racial segregation; rather whites suffered and were endangered by blacks' lack of racial pride, a characteristic Russell claimed to have identified. Senator Maybank chimed, "The wars of this country have been won by white soldiers. . . . Certainly there are some Negro soldiers and some Negro units which have demonstrated a certain degree of effectiveness on the battlefield; but by and large, Negro soldiers have rendered their greatest service as cooks, drivers, maintenance men, mechanics, and such positions, for which they are well qualified."[123] A nationwide change of course in the military set-up could only be utterly destructive to the nation and its people.[124]

Russell's proposal caused a great stir. Mainstream papers repeated their opposition to mixing selective service and national security with civil rights, which would be "a poor service to either cause."[125] The senate discussion also resulted in often emotional reactions, ranging from utter disgust to sincere support from whites who feared the distortion of their lives by the integration of varying races in one of America's most essential institutions. This fear of losing power and supremacy was omnipresent in the great deal of letters Russell received from citizens across the country. Opponents to his plan were in the minority and his white constituents saw their way of life and their very survival as being endangered by this—in their eyes—outrageous and appalling civil rights movement. They demanded that politicians "put them [blacks] in their place."[126] A "real Southerner" expressed his fear of loss of control and of an increase in the power of African Americans with the ratification of military desegregation, by stating, "If this bill is passed, I think we are letting the Negro tell us what he is going to do and not giving the white people a chance to say what they want."[127] In their reasoning, whites were the victims of the African American threat and a persecuted rightful majority in dire need of protection.

While Congress had declined to pass the UMT bill, it, after long discussions, eventually enacted the Selective Service Act of 1948, which lacked a provision that ruled out segregation and implemented equality of all races in the draft and armed services. Truman did not see a reason to order an end to Jim Crow and signed the law on June 24, 1948. The presidential approval of the draft law without an integration amendment was a blow to blacks and white liberals. The civil disobedience campaign, the letter campaigns to the president, and the protest movement were not abandoned. In a letter dated June 29, 1948, Reynolds and Randolph plainly stated, "that it is our belief that the President, as Commander-in-Chief, is morally obligated to issue such an order [ending segregation in the military] now." They were determined to progress with their civil disobedience plan if Truman was not willing to comply with their demands.[128]

While the struggle had been going on for decades, the renewed debates on UMT and the draft after the Second World War considerably spurred the African American fight for desegregation in the military. African Americans fought hard for their ultimate goal. Randolph and Reynolds's civil disobedience campaign was exceptional in its radicality. It upset many in the African American community who responded by eagerly pledging their allegiance to their country and their willingness to serve. At the same time, the campaign emboldened blacks to act and argue more forcefully when pushing for military desegregation. Unwilling to back down, they made clear-cut demands that left many whites worried and put enormous pressure on them, especially on the president. While the African American community might have been divided on how to achieve military integration, they agreed on the essential nature of the cause. Ending segregation in the military represented a powerful gateway to achieving integration in society as a whole, as full civil rights remained deeply connected to military service.

In the wake of the 1948 presidential election and the growing importance of the black vote, President Truman was forced to address questions of civil rights more directly than ever before. It became increasingly clear that mere promises of change as made in Truman's speech on civil rights in February 1948 would not suffice. African Americans made unmistakably clear that their patience was running out.

Chapter 5

Truman's Order

The pressure on the president to make decisive changes mounted, as the chances of winning over the increasingly important black vote in the upcoming presidential election became more difficult. At the end of June 1948, an anonymous White House memorandum recommended that Truman "support the introduction of moderate [civil rights] legislation beating the Republicans to the punch" and garner "credit."[1] The president felt it necessary to act, but followed a slightly different route. On July 26, he issued Executive Order 9981, which called for the "equality of treatment and opportunity for all persons in the Armed Services without regard to race, color, religion, or national origin."[2] Since executive orders do not require the approval of the House or Senate, Truman circumvented painstaking discussions and the likely rejection of any such civil rights legislation in Congress.[3] Contrary to numerous accounts and after-the-fact interpretations, the presidential order did not officially demand the immediate and complete desegregation or integration of the military. Instead, it established the President's Committee on Equality of Treatment and Opportunity in the Armed Services, later known as the Fahy Committee, to ensure the order's implementation and to force the armed services to change.[4]

Clark Clifford, special counsel to the president, maintained that the decision to issue an order had been a primarily moral issue with only, "some political flavor to the timing of those two events." He claimed that Truman felt "it was outrageous that men could be asked to die for their country but not be allowed to fight in same units because of their color."[5] It is certainly true that the executive order moved the armed forces and the country as a whole toward military desegregation, but Truman never unambiguously "ordered his military leaders . . . immediately to begin to integrate all service branches."[6] Although he certainly proved to be more open to the black quest for civil rights than any president before him, the decision involved a great deal of political calculation.

Philleo Nash, special assistant to the president for minority problems from 1946 to 1952, had a more pragmatic explanation. In an interview years later, Nash reflected on the importance of the order as a symbolic act. "What means something to the voter is something he can see and handle, such as an Executive order, even if the Executive order doesn't change anything, the mere fact that it is an Executive order and is presidential, it gets it out where he can see it. Then he says, 'Well, he does mean business after all.'"[7] Historian Brenda Gayle Plummer calls Truman's move a "prompt, election-year action" that "earned him substantial Afro-American support for administration policies generally."[8] Truman intended to lure African Americans away from supporting his opponent, Thomas E. Dewey, who many blacks believed had a strong civil rights record as New York governor. Former vice president Henry Wallace, the candidate of the newly founded Progressive Party, also challenged Truman with respect to civil rights.[9] Additionally, it was a smart move in the ideological conflict with Soviet Russia, in which America's flawed race relations played an essential role. The claim that the order eventually intended to desegregate the military was to help not only Truman nationally, but internationally as well.[10]

At no point did the executive order mention the words "segregation," "desegregation," or "integration." Rather, it remained vague and refrained from giving clear instructions that would enforce immediate desegregation. Furthermore, it did not give a deadline for when the Committee on Equality and the armed forces would have to complete this process. The fear of completely putting off the Southern bloc and the segregationists also played a role in the cautious wording of the order. It was, after all, an election year; and despite the importance of the black vote, Truman could not afford and did not want an ultimate split in the Democratic Party and risk the loss of the undecided white citizen's vote.[11] Truman came under fire from all sides for the initiation of racial change, the vague wording of the order, as well as his failure to mention integration explicitly. At a press conference three days after passing the order, Truman "categorically" assured the audience that its purpose was to eliminate segregation in the armed forces.[12] Ultimately, however, the end of segregation was not inevitable or guaranteed, as the armed forces, especially the army, were not willing to give up old structures easily.

Army officials pointed out that integration did not have to be implemented, since the order did not specifically demand it. An immediate or even speedy course toward desegregation was not in store. The Southern bloc agreed with the rejection of integration or any modifications on issues of race in the military.[13] They were appalled and considered the orders "articles of unconditional surrender to the Wallace convention and to the treasonable civil disobedience campaign" that grew "out of political fears that such action [prosecution of draft resisters] would alienate the few Negroes who remain loyal to him [Truman] in the present political campaign."[14] The order and Truman's subsequent assurance that it indeed signified the end of military segregation spurred Southern opposition. For Southerners, Truman's move was an unmistakable sign that he had given in to the pressure of an unreasonable black minority, which tried to dominate a silent majority. With Republican support, Southern congressmen continued to introduce amendments of voluntary segregation to the draft act for the next few years.[15]

Rejecting any idea of change in race relations, army chief of staff general Omar Bradley asserted: "The Army is not out to make any social reforms. The Army will put men of different races in different companies. It will change that policy when the nation as a whole changes it."[16] Although Bradley later apologized for his remarks to Truman, his statements reflected the general mood in the U.S. army.[17] The NAACP was, according to its press release, "deeply shocked at General Bradley's statement" and demanded repudiation.[18] Bradley, however, found an influential supporter in Hanson W. Baldwin, *New York Times* military expert, who applauded the general for his "straightforward and courageous statement" that did not "represent 'white supremacy' dogma, or the illiberal mouthings of a professional race-hater."[19] His article received attention from all sides. Southern Senator Richard B. Russell personally thanked Baldwin for his "objectivity with which you discuss this very important matter."[20] Walter White sent irritated letters to the editor of the *New York Times* lambasting Baldwin's conclusions. White's impatient rhetoric was still eerily reminiscent of A. Philip Randolph's, as he arduously maintained that the "Negro today is fed up with the patent hypocrisy of the army policy of segregation and the resultant limitation of opportunity. . . . He has no desire to make sacrifices for ideals and rights which are denied him."[21] The NAACP was ready to take on all obstacles in the fight for military integration. According to Roy Wilkins, NAACP assistant secretary, a "new day" and "a new kind of Negro" had evolved, and African Americans no longer waited but demanded their "reward" for decades of devoted service.[22]

Randolph and Grant Reynolds initially demurred to the order and saw no reason to end their civil disobedience campaign. Randolph called the order "unsatisfactory in that it does not outlaw segregation in the armed forces"[23] and "a misleading move, obviously made for political purposes and deliberately calculated to obscure the issue of segregation and to confuse the people at home and abroad." To them, although it was the result of their "vigorous campaign of civil disobedience that we have waged and that has become an international issue," the order did not go far enough. Bayard Rustin made clear that "passivity" was not an option and stated that their fight was not over until an executive order or legislation was passed that explicitly abolished segregation in the armed forces, "even though thousands may be arrested and jailed. Freedom is at stake."[24] They contacted the president's office to determine the true intentions behind Truman's order. In a memorandum to Rhode Island senator James Howard McGrath, who acted as the chairman of the National Democratic Committee and organizer of President Truman's 1948 election campaign, Reynolds forthrightly demanded a meeting to clarify the details of the executive order. He pushed hard to ensure that the order's ultimate goal was the end of segregation in the armed forces and the draft. He even threatened to publish the letter filled with sharp questions, to embarrass the president's civil rights intentions by calling them untrustworthy.[25] Although Randolph still expressed his ambivalence toward the order, calling it not "wholly satisfactory," he ultimately conceded, believing it to be a "victory" that bound him "morally" to give up the civil disobedience campaign.[26]

Overall, African Americans were divided in their reaction to Truman's order. They discussed the meaning and credibility of Truman's action extensively, always infusing the national and international implications of the order into the debate. White was one of the first to assess the order positively, maintaining that it "envisions abolition of segregation" and "help[s] to restore faith in the democratic process at home and rebuild American prestige abroad."[27] White's statement caused internal troubles in the NAACP. A member of the New Rochelle branch reprimanded White's stance, claiming, "Truman very carefully evaded the question of segregation." Therefore, praise for Truman was premature as well as politically charged; it could be interpreted as a pre-election endorsement for the president. This, however, would go against the NAACP official pledge of neutrality on partisan politics. External critics later scolded the NAACP for taking sides in a presidential election.[28] With the election three months away, the *Chicago Defender* wired Truman its endorsement. The paper expected the order to set in motion "the machinery for the abolition of segregation which will eventually destroy Jim Crowism in all aspects our national life" and that it would enhance and protect the American way of life.[29] The paper campaigned for Truman's reelection. However, not everyone was as convinced of Truman's intentions.

Most African Americans joined Randolph in his initial uncertainty about the order. The degree of their dissatisfaction varied.[30] Editorials in the *Pittsburgh Courier* were especially critical. One of its first headlines in reaction to Executive Order 9981 was "The Order Mr. Truman Did Not Issue," pointing to its vague deficiencies.[31] In his nationally syndicated column "Tips for Veterans," James L. Hicks alluded to an assumed lack of male assertiveness, noting that "the order is more becoming to the corporal of a squad who is not sure just how to handle some of the unruly members of his squad but who realizes that he must 'do something—even if it's wrong.'" Instead of advocating a middle ground and thereby instigating criticism from blacks, liberal whites, and white conservatives, Truman should have ended segregation in the armed forces, Hicks asserted, thereby capitalizing on the worldwide attention Jim Crow was receiving, and making a positive difference in the global standing of the United States.[32]

Despite Senator McGrath's assurance that integration of the armed forces remained the president's ultimate objective and would be realized one way or the other, some commentators remained relatively cynical about the possible motivations behind Truman's move. The *Black Dispatch* from Oklahoma expected the order "to appease Negroes past the November ballot," implying that it was more about the black vote in the upcoming presidential election than anything else. Although hopeful that Truman was honest about his civil rights plans, columnist Arthur P. Davis also pointed to the potential political considerations. Winning over "the Negro man-in-the-street" to whom "Truman is beginning to look like another Lincoln" seemed to have been rather successful. Despite his cynicism and his reflections on whether the incumbent was a "humanitarian or a shrewd office-seeker," he believed that Truman provided "his country a great service." Raising awareness on the civil rights issue, he maintained, was nonetheless a great victory for minorities.[33] The majority of the black press did not endorse Truman in the election even though they were pleased with his support of civil rights. They felt that his Southern roots, concessions to

Southern Democrats, and recurring inaction on civil rights warranted black voters to support his opponents.[34] They knew there was a long road ahead to finally reach integration in the armed forces.

"Fairyland of Civil Disobedience"

To the disappointment of some and the relief of many, Randolph and Reynolds called off their civil disobedience campaign in mid-August 1948. In a press release, they explained that the termination of their campaign was "to prevent any American youth from languishing in jail." They argued that Truman's order had reduced the number of young men prepared to sacrifice their freedom.[35] In an attempt to amend the divergences and fallouts within the African American community and among liberals resulting from their radical strategy, Randolph and Reynolds thanked "Negro leaders and liberal Americans who have fought segregation in the manner best known to them although they felt unable to subscribe to the principle of civil disobedience."[36] However, Randolph was convinced that his "intense 9-months campaign" was largely responsible for initiating "action" on military segregation.[37] Nonviolent civil disobedience was a radical approach that promised to work.

In an article in the *Nation*, Reynolds elaborated on the success of the civil disobedience campaign for the black cause in the United States. He argued that traditional forms of civil rights activism "couched in familiar legal and Constitutional terms" left the Senate committee unimpressed and caused representatives of the black civil rights movements, like the NAACP, to be subject to "cool and indifferent treatment." However, Randolph and Reynolds's call for civil disobedience shook up the "Senators across the table, including Senator Wayne Morse of Oregon, [who] came to life and seemed to realize that here was something new to contend with." Reynolds claimed that African Americans had shown that they were "now ready, in 1948, to go beyond the discussion, petition and protest stage." Although it was tabled for a time, he predicted that the use of civil disobedience and direct action would and had to recur in the future to enhance civil rights and end segregation. "Agitation for racial justice broke out of traditionally respectable bounds on 31 March, and I, for one, do not believe that Negroes will ever again be satisfied with the mere issuance of educational and propaganda material or with the hat-in-hand approach to members of legislative bodies or to the White House itself."[38] He saw a relentless power and prowess in the African Americans' fight for equal rights that was far from the stereotype of the submissive "Negro" or the "Negro brute." The claim for manhood, although not plainly stated, was intrinsic in the powerful language and contentions made by Reynolds.

The two founders dissolved the League for Non-Violent Civil Disobedience against Military Segregation and distanced themselves from any continued campaign of open resistance against military service.[39] Its dissolution did not sit well with its more radical members, who mostly belonged to CORE or FOR. To them, the order misled the public. Those who continued to support a campaign of civil disobedience were "cynical" about Truman's order and did not want to let down young men who had signed up for civil disobedience and refused to register in a still segregated military.[40] Bayard Rustin, with the help of FOR staffers in the league, continued with civil disobedience activism after Randolph and Reynolds had left, but did not receive much attention within or outside of the African American community. With respect to Rustin and the civil disobedience movement that continued after August 1948, Randolph said, "While I think they are wrong, I cannot stop them."[41] The rift between Randolph and Rustin began to deepen.

On October 11, 1948, Randolph and Reynolds issued a joint press release in which they tried to elucidate their decision to disband their civil disobedience campaign. Oscillating between admitting to serious financial troubles due to lack of support and claiming to have maintained a large group of activists, the statement spoke of the campaign's contrived nature. In their statement, they harshly accused Rustin and the "religious pacifist nucleus within the League" of using it "as a front for ulterior purposes" and blamed them for applying "unethical tactics." The cooperation with pacifists was an "internal weakness of the League" and led to the release of unauthorized statements that "blasted President Truman's executive order even after he announced that under it he contemplated the eventual abolition of segregation and after Sen. J. Howard McGrath, chief spokesman for the President, had personally re-affirmed to us this interpretation of the executive order." They emphatically underscored that they did not oppose conscription or military service. Moreover, the statement emphasized that they did not abandon the movement out of fear of imprisonment, attempting to counter all allegations otherwise, which often put the activists' manhood in question.[42] Ultimately, the end of the civil disobedience campaign meant a return to the well-accepted link between military service and civil rights. Although never having given up the link completely, the campaign had questioned it by aligning black manhood and patriotism with draft resistance, rather than with obedient service despite lack of equality and fairness.[43]

When Randolph and Reynolds discontinued their campaign, even papers that had not fully opposed the strategy endorsed their step. The *Chicago Defender* maintained that it was better that the movement be abandoned for the sake of the advancement of the African American community and the nation in general. What had worked in India, a country of "people whose traditions are far different from our own," most likely would not have worked in America.[44] Earlier critics of civil disobedience and its radicalism greeted Randolph and Reynolds's abandonment of the campaign with relief and enthusiasm, congratulating them on finally returning to the only appropriate course of action to achieve full civil rights: adherence to the rules and demonstrating one's unhampered national loyalty and patriotism. Always opposed to their radical ideas, the *Pittsburgh Courier* sardonically commented, "Well, we all live and learn . . . , we are willing to acknowledge his [Randolph's] superior vision and his recently acquired discretion. . . . If we have helped in the education of one of our greatest leaders, we are certainly gratified, although we would be the last to minimize the imminence of draft registration day as an influence of telling importance."[45] The campaign's method had put everything into question regarding considerations of appropriate behavior for an American male citizen, and now, discarding the movement represented the only option in the fight for desegregation and equality.

George Schuyler immersed himself in self-righteousness. His postmortem analysis of the campaign was scornful and distanced from his initial assessment of the possibly positive effects of the civil disobedience campaign. He now claimed that he had always been opposed to their strategy for its un-American character and criticized them for the manner of their withdrawal: "Why not honestly come out and say, 'Listen kids! This racket is getting dangerous so we're cutting out. If any of you goofs want to go to jail, that is your little red wagon. We choose freedom!'"[46] For him, those who practiced civil disobedience lacked manhood, but he also attacked Randolph and Reynolds for not being brave enough to carry through. Columnist Willard Townsend, who had opposed civil disobedience all along, now derided Randolph and Reynolds for abandoning the "fairyland of civil disobedience," and "nine day wonder, which was expected to shake the very foundations of our Negro-white social relations in the armed forces." He predicted the "casualties" of the anticlimactic end of the campaign to be "the sincere and morally conscious Negro and white boys who enthusiastically joined in." Townsend alleged that the campaign had never been more than a media stunt. At the same time, he encouraged young men not to give up on civil disobedience and live up to the "fine type of manhood" that he felt Randolph and Reynolds, in the end, had failed. He further elaborated on his doubts over the manhood and leadership potential of Randolph and Reynolds who never would go beyond "paper and pamphlet status" with their movement, calling for young, new leaders to replace the old guard. He expressed his fear that young followers would lose their "desire to achieve a decent America, free from social and economic discrimination," because they had been let down by their leaders. Moreover, he applauded, among others, Bayard Rustin, George Houser, and Bill Sutherland who continued the civil disobedience campaign and the league under a new name. "To me these three kids represent the finest type of young manhood in American [sic]."[47]

At the end of the civil disobedience campaign, activists from all backgrounds claimed that it had been their own protest methods that had pushed Truman to a clearer commitment to military integration. The rifts and competitions over leadership in the civil rights movement persisted. Lester Granger maintained that the conference with Forrestal in April 1948 was the ultimate incentive for Truman to issue his order, pointing to the contested nature of responsibility for the president's move.[48] The competition between different civil rights organizations and their strategies became ever more evident. Granger's aversion to Randolph continued even after the latter walked away from the civil disobedience campaign. In private correspondence, Granger expressed dislike and mistrust for Randolph and his cause. In a letter exchange with Loren Miller, civil right activist, lawyer, and later California superior court justice, who said Randolph "never finishes any job he undertakes," Granger deprecatingly called Randolph a "queer bird" and put into question his role as a leading figure in the civil rights movement. "I still don't know the inside of Randolph's change-of-pace, whether it was because he decided that prison bars didn't look so pretty from the inside, after all; or whether he realized that the colored brother, young or old wasn't going to accompany him in his prison march. But whatever the reason, it has cooled off any future chance of playing the

Mahatma role." Granger was eager to deconstruct Randolph's influence among blacks in general.[49] He wrote a short note, however, to Randolph in which he congratulated him and Reynolds on their public dismissal of Rustin's civil disobedience campaign, which though it had not necessarily worried him, had left him uneasy.[50]

Roy Wilkins of the NAACP praised Randolph and Reynolds's positive effect on civil rights in that they had managed to raise awareness of the impatience and grievances of blacks in the United States and "put all of them [white Americans] on the defensive." Their actions were indispensable in initiating change and the issuance of the executive order.[51] Although many concurred, they did not yet consider civil disobedience "an effective weapon in our fight."[52] Another seven years and a bus boycott were necessary to have civil disobedience accepted as a truly powerful method. In the case of military service, however, especially in times of national crisis, many did not consider it an option. Attainment of civil rights was too closely linked to the figure of the black soldier proving himself as a man in battle as to question or abandon black military service.

With Executive Order 9981, Truman ultimately took the wind out of the sails of the opposing presidential candidates with respect to civil rights. The *Chicago Defender* noted that the tides were turning in favor of Truman even before the executive order. John H. Young, the paper's correspondent on Truman's campaign train from Washington to Berkeley, noted that black people had changed their attitude. Whereas the majority of press reports portrayed the black public as having a negative stance on Truman, the author claimed that people increasingly supported him because they began to perceive him as a "fighting President" for civil rights.[53] Even if Eisenhower ran for office, he had disqualified himself as a viable candidate in the eyes of blacks due to his earlier statement before the senate committee in June.[54] Dewey and Wallace had good chances among African American voters because of their strong civil rights records and rhetoric. However, Dewey's reputation as a supporter of civil rights was limited to the East Coast and it declined over the course of the campaign.[55] Wallace, although favored by many black leftists, did not have a real chance of becoming president due to his political leanings that many interpreted as being socialist, and some even called communist.[56] Executive Order 9981 played a major role in the increasing African American support of Truman. In the words of the *Black Dispatch*, the "Negro vote, which the South a long time ago cast aside, has now become the head of the corner.[57] Moreover, the presidential directive was so inoffensive and vague in its wording that Truman did not lose all his support from Southern Democrats.

To the surprise of many Americans, Truman won the election. Whether or not they had supported Truman, most black papers expected an immediate turn for the better and improvements for African Americans, within and outside the military.[58] The *Atlanta Daily World* called the victory "unexpected and startling," but "a victory for the masses of people of this nation and, perhaps, the world."[59] The *Chicago Defender* confidently assured its readers that during Truman's second period in office, "Negroes shall achieve full citizenship in our democracy and that civil rights represent the bedrock upon which our republic rests."[60]

The end of Randolph and Reynolds's campaign did not signify an end to black activism against military segregation and reflections on African American military service in times of peace and war. African Americans saw it essential to remain vigilant, especially as the army's reluctance to change remained strong. In April 1949, Marcus H. Ray, the Advisor on Negro Affairs of the United States European Command (EUCOM), wrote in a letter to White, "From my restricted corner, the Army appears to be tugging hard to move toward reaction and the pre-war status quo. Reasons for restricted opportunities to Negro soldiers still revolve around the bromide that they are not yet ready and that integration would only result in a sifting through of all Negroes to the least important assignments."[61] The army continued to assert that it was not a place for "social reform," and that it would only change its course of action if society as a whole changed. Although black papers and commentators predominantly interpreted Truman's mandate as calling for the immediate and full integration of the armed forces, the actual realization of the order was not guaranteed.[62] A cartoon in the *New York Amsterdam News* picked up on the army's reluctance and Truman's wavering stance on ending Jim Crow in the army (see Figure 5). The executive order Truman had passed pointed in the right direction, but military reality spoke a different language. Kenneth Royall, secretary of the army, reconfirmed Omar Bradley's earlier rejection of military integration. While Royall had stated he would resign before ordering desegregation in May 1948, he now assured that the order did not directly request integration, and therefore, the pursuance of equality could take place in a segregated setting.[63] The Fahy Committee's members continuously had to disperse fears that the order was a mere "publicity stunt" intended to circumvent the issue of "segregation."[64]

Figure 5. "Adding Insult." *New York Amsterdam News*, October 8, 1949, 12. Reproduced by permission of copyright holder; further reproduction prohibited without permission.

Ultimately, the prospects of ending segregation depended on the committee, its authority and cooperation with the military branches, and its own perspective on segregation and equality, which could hardly be predicted.[65] Beginning in January 1949, the Fahy Committee summoned and interviewed witnesses on the conditions, possible changes, and underlying objectives of race relations in the armed services. The committee regularly met or communicated with President Truman, providing him with status and progress reports for all three military branches. Representatives from all military branches testified, justifying and elaborating on the modifications they planned to make in order to comply with the new demands. African Americans' testimonies of their situation in the armed services and in the preceding wars became important. Over the next couple of years, Charles Fahy, the committee chairman, and his colleagues tried to push the military branches, especially the reluctant army, to reevaluate and modernize their racial practices. Many army officials opposed civilian interference in the armed forces and desegregation in particular. A speedy course toward integration remained improbable because of the broad and indecisive order whose many loopholes allowed the army, with its high number of black recruits, to resist reform and maintain racial hierarchies.[66]

Although they trusted Truman's assurances that the order's goal was to eliminate Jim Crow in the armed forces, Randolph and Reynolds felt it would not "automatically change the long-established pattern of military segregation." The public needed to be aware of the fact that it was important to maintain pressure on politics and society. Furthermore, Randolph felt that the civil rights forces "can use to advantage the sudden renaissance of the liberal spirit, educating and arousing the nation to action." He considered the end of military segregation to be "the basic key to smashing all discrimination."[67]

The committee acted as a "watchdog" of the integration process and wanted to draw on the impetus for change and garner as much support as possible within and outside the African American community. Complementing the official hearings by the Fahy Committee, Randolph's committee organized hearings in major U.S. cities, including St. Louis, Washington, D.C., and Los Angeles. The inquiries brought together black veterans, military officials, and politicians who reported on their situations and the progress of military desegregation. The purpose of these hearings was to prevent the public from being "lolled into a false feeling that everything has been solved by the issuance of the Order."[68] The organizers submitted the transcripts of the hearings to the Fahy Committee as serious evidence for the faults, failures, and damages that segregation in the armed forces had caused and would continue to cause not only for African Americans, but also for the American nation in its conflict with Communism.[69] The Fahy Committee invited Reynolds to an audience. Together with representatives from the AVC, the NUL, and the American Civil Liberties Union (ACLU), he testified in April 1949 on behalf of military integration.[70]

Reynolds tried to put the civil disobedience campaign behind him. In the Fahy Committee hearing in Washington, D.C., on April 25, 1949, Reynolds stated that despite holding on to the demands made in the speeches before the Senate committee the previous year, the Committee against Jim Crow in Military Service and Training had given up its radical path of civil disobedience. "If any reference is made to that [statements dated March 31, 1948], I beg your grace to eliminate any threats that were then included in that testimony. We felt, at the time, that it was necessary to do that, as embarrassing as it was to us and to the country, it has had some beneficial results."[71] Reynolds distanced the committee and its leaders from earlier strategies of activism and returned to methods that were more traditional. Although he confirmed the committee's abandonment of civil disobedience and its determination to adopt traditional methods of activism and pledges of patriotic allegiance, the criticism of segregation and discrimination in the armed forces stayed strong. He intrinsically constructed race and civil rights as a domestic as well as international problem, warning that, "you cannot lose sight of the impact of this responsibility on our foreign relations. In your hands lies the opportunity to enhance the prestige of American democratic idealism throughout the world."[72] The struggle had to continue, but civil disobedience against military segregation and resisting participation in the next war were no longer an option. Distancing the organization from draft resistance and civil disobedience was essential for garnering support.[73] The fear of failure or public contempt by association with an almost revolutionary concept that questioned the very nature of patriotism and male civil obligations continued to trouble African American civil rights activists, as well as their white supporters. Moreover, it took yet another conflict with numerous casualties before Jim Crow's abolishment in the armed forces.

At the end of April 1949, however, another prominent African American pushed civil disobedience and the issue of refusing to fight for the United States to the forefront. At an international peace conference in Paris, Paul Robeson, the acclaimed African American singer with alleged connections to the Communist Party, was quoted stating that African Americans would not be willing to pick up guns for Americans "who have oppressed us for generations" and use them against the Soviet Union, "which in one generation has raised our people to the full dignity of mankind."[74] In response, the black community immediately, and yet again, felt forced to take a clear stance in reassuring the public that black America would always take up arms for the United States. The response to Robeson was not nearly as intense as it had been when Randolph issued his call for civil disobedience, but the incident launched a debate on who represented and spoke for the African American community.

The reactions to Robeson's statements ranged from scathing dismissals to reflections on freedom of speech. Most claimed, "Paul Robeson does not represent any American Negroes. . . . So Mr. Robeson has none but sentimental roots among American Negroes. He is one of them, but not with them."[75] The singer's communist affiliation was at the center of attention during the scandal, and the African American community felt obliged to prove its patriotism and willingness to fight. Moreover, white Americans expected blacks to rid themselves of any possible communist affiliations, which could seriously damage the civil rights cause. The black press adamantly rejected the claim that African Americans would no longer be willing to fight for the United States in the event of a war with the Soviet Union.[76] *Pittsburgh Courier* columnist Schuyler referred to Robeson's alleged comment as a "smearing of 14,000,000 Negroes as potential traitors" without having "any mandate to speak for colored Americans."[77] The avowal of being true and full American citizens was the most used form of rejection to Robeson's claims. The preparedness to serve as a soldier implied inclusion in the national body and the race, thus simultaneously precluding exclusion.[78]

Still, African Americans did not write off Robeson as virulently as depicted by the white press, in which readers were assured that the overwhelming majority of African Americans denounced Robeson and his controversial statement to the fullest.[79] The support for black military service did not result in full condemnation of left-leaning radical critics in the black community like Robeson.[80] Although African Americans disassociated Robeson from the larger African American community, there existed a clear tendency to empathize with Robeson's frustration.[81] Contextualizing and justifying the singer's statement, most black commentators affirmed the right to freedom of speech for Robeson and all critics.[82] His controversial announcement provided room for the criticism of America's racial hierarchies. The overwhelming majority of black commentators expressed at least some degree of understanding for his views.

Although Randolph himself had initiated the discussion on the objection of military service on racial grounds a year earlier, he now attacked Robeson claiming that, "anyone who says the American Negro would not fight for the United States in a war with Russia simply does not know the Negro."[83] His fervent rejection of Robeson's stance notwithstanding, Randolph never denied him the right to express his opinion, but merely asserted that Robeson could not claim to speak for blacks as a group. Most other members of the black elite and press argued along the same lines and used this opportunity to condemn race relations and racism in the United States. NAACP executive secretary White maintained that, "until the United States cleanses itself of its own racial sins, it will not have the right to criticize without hypocrisy such statements as those of Mr. Robeson in Paris."[84] Black papers followed a similar path, lauding Robeson for his unswerving fearlessness and insistence on free speech, and admonishing critics for denying him the right to free speech in the midst of the anticommunist frenzy.[85] The *Oklahoma City Black Dispatch* described Robeson's statement as "careless." However, it pushed for black male agency in the struggle for civil rights, maintaining that "There is too much virtue in Robeson, as he fights for social justice for us to lose step with him entirely simply because he was for a moment faulty in his thinking." The paper expressed the wish more men "had the forthright manhood and courage of Paul Robeson" to pressure politicians and society forcefully to finally attain black equality.[86]

As a response to Robeson's statement, the House Committee on Un-American Activities scheduled hearings to investigate Robeson and African Americans' loyalty to the United States in general. The NAACP, among others, was outraged by the hearings and protested on the grounds that "There has never been any question of the loyalty of the Negro to the United States of America." The organization saw no reason for holding hearings to prove a well-known point.[87] The frustration among African Americans grew further when a performance by Robeson in Peekskill, New York, was followed by riots. They believed that people had the right to protest against Robeson, but called the subsequent violent unrest a "persecution" and "lynching," although no one was killed. Columnist Gordon Hancock understood that the assault on Robeson was an attack on the African American community as a whole, and predicted that similar reactions to other free-speaking blacks could ultimately result in a spread of Communism among African Americans.[88]

The reaction to the 1949 Robeson case points toward the growing mainstream African American rhetoric on civil rights in the years to come. For the most part, the rhetoric was not radical; rather it distanced itself from approaches that most civil rights activists and the black press imagined to be damaging to black progress and the movement's success. African American civil rights movements immersed themselves in patriotic and Cold War rhetoric. However, despite the limitations that were often self-imposed, civil rights activism did not cave in completely and could not be silenced by the increasingly conservative climate of the times. While playing up patriotic and masculinist rhetoric, black activists continued to pursue military integration, equality, and civil rights for blacks and criticized the United States extensively, presenting its undeniable faults and failures to an international audience in the sensitive climate of the Cold War. Most blacks considered freedom of speech essential, even if they disliked the content of the comments in question. The new war on the horizon would not put an end to this trend.

When on June 26, 1950, Kim Il-sung, the leader of Communist North Korea, launched an attack on the American-advised South, Robeson blatantly denounced the subsequent American intervention in the Far East. In a speech in New York two days later, he advised African Americans not to join the war effort, but support the Korean fight for independence from Western oppression and for their own freedom at home.[89] His glorification of Communist Russia overshadowed his justly critical position on American race relations and forced the black community to take a stance. The grand majority of blacks rejected Robeson's call for resistance and supported the American mission in Korea. Nevertheless, when the State Department withdrew Robeson's passport, many black commentators yet again demanded freedom of speech and expression for all.[90]

As the majority of African Americans pledged their loyalty and willingness to fight for the United States, black men of draft age continued to join the military and subsequently embarked on a journey to a war they did not know much, if anything, about. However, blacks did not join the war effort uncritically. They used it as an opportunity to decry publicly and forcefully the "insults and ostracism," violence, and injustices that African Americans and African American soldiers in particular, had to endure.[91] The fight for an end to segregation and establishment of equality during the war may have "played it safe." In the climate of growing anticommunist frenzy in the United States, black organizations, foremost the NAACP, did not cooperate with and often excluded leftist and communist groups from their ranks.[92] The African American reaction to the war itself often proved emulative of white discourse. Yet, their fight was provocative in its own right. Civil rights activism took many shapes and did not relent in its attempts to improve African Americans' social status and public image.

One major goal for activists remained the desegregation of the armed forces, especially the army, which had left for Korea in a mostly segregated state. African American soldiers faced the same discriminatory treatment in the Korean War as in previous conflicts. For the first year, they remained segregated; their fighting ability was doubted and their reputation slandered. However, while the war in Asia raged, African Americans did not relent in pushing the military to finally abandon its ossified and discriminatory setup. The army's willingness to change remained limited. Moreover, Southern politicians did everything in their power to block black equality and desegregation. Days before the war's onset, Russell had resubmitted his amendment to ensure "voluntary segregation" in the Selective Service Bill.[93] The ensuing troubled course of the Korean War, however, forced the American military and especially the army to thoroughly reconsider their policy of racial segregation. The army continued to stall its progress, but its fighting strength suffered from the lack of replacements. While black units received an abundance of new soldiers, white ones failed to fill their ranks. Desegregation became a necessity in the long, but ultimately unsuccessful, struggle for victory and Korean unification.

Chapter 6

A Country They Never Knew

Korea was at "its modern nadir"[1] when a new war began in the Far East country at the end of June 1950. Rural and scarred by an economic depression, war, and Japanese repression, Korea remained poverty-ridden and its people mostly illiterate. Its economy was deeply grounded in labor-intensive rice agriculture and technological advances remained scarce. In Korea, American soldiers faced an uninviting topography and climate. Often scorching hot and humid in the summer and freezing cold in winter, the rugged mountains and valleys drained soldiers and civilians alike. The dirt roads made advances difficult and slow. Against this background, feelings of senselessness and frustration ran high. Most Americans did not know much, if anything, about the country or the conflict. As one soldier put it: "I am here because the goddam president of the United States would put me in jail if I didn't report for duty." Yet the question remained, "What the hell am I doing here?"[2]

On Japan's surrender in August 1945, which ended forty years of Japanese occupation,[3] the Soviet Union and the United States agreed on forming a trusteeship and arbitrarily divided the small country along the 38th parallel. Three years later, the Republic of Korea under American purview and the Democratic People's Republic of Korea under Soviet purview were founded in the South and North respectively. The situation had been tense in the Asian peninsula since the Second World War ended, as often violent altercations flared up between the country's divided parts. It reached a breaking point, however, when North Korean troops crossed the 38th parallel and quickly invaded their Southern neighbor on June 25, 1950. The invasion of South Korea startled the United States and left it concerned about the possibility of a third world war. Most Americans suspected that the Soviet Union stood behind this invasion, a link that made the threat of another world war even more likely.[4]

Before the attack on South Korea, the United States had drastically reduced military presence and weapons support for the peninsula. Earlier warnings notwithstanding, the invasion was surprising, as most Americans had expected West Germany to be next on the list of Russia's conquests. Korea, according to chief of staff of the army Omar Bradley, "had no appeal" and "would certainly be bypassed" in the event of military operations in Asia.[5] Although the small country in the Far East bordered Russia in the North and China in the West, it initially held no special position in the growing U.S. global plan to contain Communism. Neither South Korea nor the American troops stationed there were prepared for the major military blow with which the well-equipped and well-trained North Koreans hit them.[6] Washington looked for support in its mission to halt the dreaded spread of Communism. It gathered its allies under the UN flag, closely cooperating with countries that intended to keep their colonial possessions and uphold racial oppression.[7]

Although the powers in Washington did not believe direct Russian interference in the war was imminent, they believed that the Soviet Union was responsible for the North Korean invasion.[8] Truman and his advisors were convinced of and propagated a monolithic view that a communist movement originating in Moscow was prepared to take over the world. In a radio and television speech on July 19, 1950, Truman declared: "The attack has made it clear, beyond all doubt, that the international Communist movement is willing to use armed invasion to conquer independent nations. An act of aggression such as this creates a very real danger to the security of all free nations."[9] For Washington, North Korea's attack completed Stalin's intentions and was the beginning of worldwide Soviet aggression. Therefore, the hostilities became a war of international dimensions with unpredictable repercussions for the Western world. With an atomic threat looming, the spread of war to the West and even to the United States was, in the eyes of many contemporaries, very likely, if the North Koreans and Soviets could not be contained in Korea. Consequently, the United States entered the Korean conflict without officially declaring war.[10]

Initially, the general American press and public supported the U.S. involvement in a war Truman diminutively called, throughout its three-year course, a "police action." Americans agreed it was indispensable for the nation and the freedom of the world to contain the spread of communism. In early July 1950, a Gallup poll showed that 77 percent of the American population favored the decision to enter the war in Korea.[11] Following the president's reasoning, Americans primarily viewed the Korean War as resulting from a vicious act of Soviet imperialist aggression.[12] The *New York Times* called it "Russian-sponsored."[13] The *Washington Post* left no doubt that "the invasion of Southern Korea is of Soviet origin" and saw it as a security and moral necessity for America to defend South Korea against this aggression.[14] Even publications that were more left leaning and critical followed this argumentation. The *New Republic* stated affirmatively that Russia was "*behind the assault.*"[15] In the *Nation*, Willard Shelton described the incident as a "sudden attack of Russian-backed North Koreans" that reflected the "Russian determination to expel American influence from any important advance post on the Asiatic mainland."[16] The war's long background and civil war quality all too often did not find a place in the public discourse.[17] When China entered the war in November 1950, 81 percent of people questioned in a Gallup poll believed Russia had instigated this intervention as well.[18] An initial call for full-fledged and unconditional unity swept the nation.[19]

Support for the United States war effort might have been initially strong, when the air force and navy started their mission in Korea at the end of June and the first ground troops arrived in early July. But skepticism and criticism rose when the UN allies fared unsuccessfully, demonstrating their unpreparedness and lack of sufficient weaponry. In the first few months of the war, when the United States, precipitately and poorly prepared, entered Korea under the UN flag, victories against the North Koreans remained rare. Initially, General Douglas MacArthur, the UN commander, promised presumptuously to push back the North Korean troops "in the shortest possible time."[20] However, the reality of war turned out to be quite different. The expected superiority of American troops and equipment did not manifest itself, and as the news from the war zone grew shockingly negative, the American public began wondering whether the intervention in this distant Asian country was as easy a task as military officials and politicians had predicted.[21] Despite Americans' presence on the Korean peninsula and their combat efforts, they were unable to stop the North Korean advance until September 1950. Since late June, North Korean troops had held Seoul, the South Korean capital, and pushed American and UN troops back into the small southeastern corner of the country. American wins were sporadic at best. Along the newly established Pusan Perimeter, the UN troops under American leadership had serious difficulties defending their footing on the peninsula against constant North Korean assaults.

American troops, in particular those stationed in Japan, lacked the training and readiness for ground combat with an unexpectedly well-trained and well-positioned enemy. The territory, climate, and North Korean fighting tactics overwhelmed the American troops and often proved very different from the experiences of World War II. Frequently relying on guerrilla warfare that took American troops by surprise, the North Korean enemy outnumbered and often overpowered them. The UN troops were "absurdly pressed to find the resources with which to fight a limited war in Asia."[22] Shortly into the war, the *New York Times* had to admit grudgingly that substantial numbers of trained soldiers proved to be necessary to fight "the well-prepared and well-directed Communist attack from the North . . . which gives a new meaning to the term 'police action'."[23] Since World War II, and despite the continuation of the draft, the American military had downsized considerably in both manpower and weaponry.[24] Owing to the units' lack of preparedness, equipment, and tactics, the first two months of the war proved an almost complete failure.[25]

Moreover, the U.S. military and political decision makers approached the hostilities in Korea with deep-seated "cultural and racial arrogance."[26] A *Washington Post* article assessing combat performance is exemplary for the underlying racist attitude toward Koreans both north and south of the 38th parallel. According to the article, military leaders had expected the North Koreans to flee the front lines as their South Korean counterparts allegedly did when they "began to get hit a bit." However, they "stood up like veteran soldiers, and even when tanks were knocked out their crews refused to come out and surrender."[27] Despite the almost devastating experience with the Japanese military during World War II, many could not imagine an Asian people prepared to fight against a presumably superior nation like the United States, victor in two world wars. As the troops under MacArthur struggled, public opinion oscillated as much as the UN troops' performance did between success and failure in their endeavor to defeat the seemingly weak foe from North Korea.

Black Calls for Unity

When the first American soldiers were sent to stop the North Korean invasion, segregation and discrimination remained the norm in the armed forces. All-black units were among the first troops to embark to Korea. Nonetheless, the air force and navy had made progress integrating, which supported African American claims that racial integration did not destroy military morale or efficiency. While it was both a victory and leverage in the black fight for civil rights, the army, in which the majority of black soldiers served, continued to resist real change. At the beginning of the Korean War, "the Army possessed almost exactly the same racially segregated organizational structure that had existed in World War II."[28] Nevertheless, while the army showed no interest in changing its racial setup, many leaders in the African American community reasoned that the war in Korea would be the one that would finally lead to full equality for blacks and disprove long-standing stereotypes. The major organizations and leaders of the African American community joined the general call for national unity in times of crisis. The Colored War Veterans of America pledged they would return to the service.[29] African American civil rights activists and organizations, in particular, weighed in on the developments in Asia. The NAACP and the NUL, the two biggest civil rights organizations, fervently and without question backed the call to arms.[30] Both organizations supported the entry into the Korean War and joined in the anticommunist discourse. A. Philip Randolph, who only two years earlier had made an all-out call for draft resistance, championed the war effort wholeheartedly as well.

By 1950, Randolph had turned his back on civil disobedience against military service in times of peace and war. In order to preserve freedom and protect the nation, Randolph pledged his utmost support to President Truman for the cause in Korea and the general struggle against Communism.[31] He openly and ardently opposed any display of sympathy for Communism or the representation of Russia as peace-loving and even slightly helpful to the black cause. Randolph claimed "this wise act of statesmanship on the part of President Truman for the United States and the United Nations may serve to halt the mad march of Communism across the world and give new strength, spirit and hope to democracy, the only salvation of minorities and labor, and hence should receive the united support of all Americans regardless of race, color, religion, national origin or ancestry."[32] He denounced the Soviets for their allegedly "phony peace petition offensive and civil rights hypocrisy."[33] In his eyes, blacks could only lose by affiliating themselves with communists in their struggle for civil rights,[34] and he called on African Americans for national unity in both military and employment. To him, America's entry into the Korean War was a necessary step to fight off Communist Russia in the struggle over world domination, since North Korea was a mere "puppet of Soviet Russia." Letting them have their unrestrained way would endanger democracy and have detrimental effects on peace and prosperity in the United States and around the world.[35] Randolph was thoroughly convinced that it was necessary to counter any communist advance at home and abroad "with a big stick"[36] for the sake of African Americans, the nation, and the world's freedom.

From the onset of American involvement in Korea in July 1950, most African Americans closely followed the military's progress. Black papers filled their front pages and editorial sections with articles and commentaries on the developments of the war in Korea.[37] The black community and press reacted diversely to the war. Some conservatives as well as leftists put forth calls of anti-interventionism. George Schuyler opposed the war efforts in Korea because he considered the fight against Communism at home to be more important than the one abroad.[38] The left-leaning *California Eagle* and communist-oriented Paul Robeson and W. E. B. Du Bois referred to the American presence in Korea as an imperialist endeavor and demonstrated support for the Soviet Union.[39] Between these two anti-interventionist extremes, however, an overwhelming number of more mainstream and seemingly more conformist arguments supported the war effort.[40] Although far from unified in political orientation, most African Americans rejected ideas of anti-interventionism, and agreed on the necessity of a quick intervention against what they considered the violent and detrimental spread of Communism.[41] Conservative as well as liberal voices in the African American community were immersed in Cold War rhetoric.

The most virulent call for national unity against communist aggression came from the *Los Angeles Sentinel* on July 13, 1950. Under the caption "United Front on Korea," it stated, "No one knows what the Korean situation will lead to—no one, that is, but the Moscow leaders. . . . By leaping in now with both fists we may make a lasting impression on the Kremlin and thus prevent a full scale conflict later."[42] The *Sentinel* later assured its readers that whatever the cost and deficiencies of democracy in the United States, the fight of black soldiers in Korea, like in any other war, was "worth it."[43] The *Norfolk Journal and Guide* agreed and noted: "The Communists are on the march" declaring that "Nothing can stop this force now but a demonstration of superior force. Stalin and his legions do not listen to reason."[44] The less conservative *Chicago Defender* also left no doubt in its belief that war was a Russian-inspired attack on South Korea, pointing to the Russian war equipment allegedly being used by the North Koreans as evidence. It pledged wholehearted support for Truman and the UN course in halting the spread of Communism and thus preventing a third world war, which loomed due to North Korean-Russian aggression.[45]

Others were more cautious in their reaction to the outbreak of the war. They did not use hyperbolic and anticommunist language as extensively as other newspapers. In its first editorial, the *Pittsburgh Courier* called the Korean War a "civil war" and expressed its uncertainty as to where it was going to take the United States and the world in the long term. Ultimately, the paper applauded Truman for his decision to call on the UN and trust the organization in countering the "aggression against the southern Korean republic."[46] The *Afro-American* argued that the South Koreans did not "have their hearts in the struggle," since the United States failed to prepare and equip them appropriately, whereas Russia backed North Korea to the fullest.[47] The paper foremost directed its criticism at the United States for having focused too much on "ferreting out a few Communists in the U.S." instead of preventing "millions of persons in foreign lands" to be drawn to communism.[48] It scolded what it considered the shortsighted strategic decisions of the American government, which, according to the paper, had failed to prepare Korea to protect itself in its own right, and now had to use America's "best troops in an effort to restore order." All criticism not-withstanding, both papers supported the decision to join and lead the fight against North Korea.[49]

Given the controversies of the previous few years, many African Americans felt obliged to publicly pledge their patriotism and support. The *Chicago Defender* made sure to point out that "The Negro has rallied to the defense of the American flag in every crisis in the nation's history. . . . The record of our race for loyalty cannot be questioned and there will be no cause to questions [sic] it in the future. . . . Whatever the future holds, we shall stand together in solid opposition to the Russian menace."[50]

Pledging patriotism and dedication to the national cause in Korea was an important element in the black press and black public discourse. Equally important, however, was the expressed black uncertainty about the willingness of many whites to remove the racist obstructions to unity in order to face and defeat communist aggression.[51] Whether it was the editors of the *Black Dispatch*, columnist Gordon B. Hancock, or the otherwise often blatantly patriotic *Los Angeles Sentinel,* the black press found it necessary to point out that white supremacists and the lack of civil rights hampered the unity of the nation.[52] They believed that this prevented, if not destroyed, alliances with people around the world, especially with peoples of color, in the first months of the war. Despite apparent similarities to white press reports on the surface, African Americans often added new aspects to the war dialogue that the general public did not take into consideration.

The majority of black newspapers and many of their active readers believed that civil rights in the United States were an international issue that stood at the crossroads of failure or success in Korea and in the general fight against worldwide Communism. As long as white America remained unwilling to close ranks and foster national unity, there was only a slight chance that the "hell of a mess" in Korea, as the *Sentinel* called it, could be resolved favorably for the United States.[53] In an attempt to free African Americans from sweeping accusations of communist affiliation that usually ensued in lieu of all civil rights demands, many black commentators inverted the allegations and accused white "Jim-Crowers" of disloyalty. They maintained that white segregationists were "really supporting it [communism] by creating sympathy for it."

The continuance of racial oppression in the United States could only further communist ideology, which had allegedly long parted ways with racism and racial exclusion. The success and failure of democracy in the world therefore eventually depended on the judgment of the "darker humanity."[54] Despite the recurring pledges of patriotism and loyalty, blacks' criticism of the war and American action was more frequent than previous research has admitted.

"A War of Color"?

Domestic and international issues of race fused, as people attempted to make sense of and explain the war on the Asian peninsula. Columnists and civil rights activists lambasted the United States for its covert and overt allegiance to white supremacy, considering it detrimental to the efforts in Korea. The link between the international crisis in Korea and the domestic situation of minorities was clear. "Koreans are definitely non-white," the *Pittsburgh Courier* noted early in the war.[55] African Americans widely discussed the question whether the Korean conflict was a "race war."[56] The question many blacks contemplated was whether Russian propaganda made the war out to be racially biased to convince colonized peoples of the merits of the ideology, or whether it was American inaction with respect to civil rights at home and freedom of colonial people abroad that ran the risk of doing so. It was a dangerous terrain for blacks to navigate. Communists had long capitalized on the hypocrisy and bigotry inherent in American race relations and democracy. Their charge that the United States claimed to be a haven of democracy, but oppressed, discriminated, and segregated its minority populations further increased with the onset of the Korean War. Propagandizing these apparent and devastating faults of American democracy was a promising method to attract more support among peoples of color for the conflict with the Western world. Russia was quick to point out that American intervention in Korea indicated that the war was one between the races, one of imperialism versus freedom from racial oppression and discrimination.[57]

Blacks knew of the dangers, and many feared the suggestion of procommunist leanings should they criticize the United States. Roy Wilkins of the NAACP agreed with Thurgood Marshall that it was essential to make clear that communists were "our enemy." He maintained, "this is not a race war, but a war between Communists and the Western world. . . . Negroes are not Communists and never have been as their record in America shows, and that the Communist armies opposing us are killing Negro Americans right and left."[58] Not all agreed with this interpretation. The *Black Dispatch* from Oklahoma maintained that the "struggle just ahead will be a race war. It is going to be between the dark and white races and it should be our strategy at the outset to get some of the dark races to fight on our side."[59] The paper blatantly condemned the American government for playing into the hands of the communist enemy with its continuance of racial segregation and oppression of black people on the home front and in the world as a whole. In an angry letter to Frank Pace, Jr., secretary of the army, in July 1950, Roy Wilkins avowed that sending blacks in segregated units to Asia could not "disabuse the minds of the Koreans and others that this is a racial war."[60] The black press and civil rights activists relentlessly demanded change and warned that only definite action could result in transforming the thinking in the colored world. The blunt article did not go uncommented on in the black press. In its October 1950 edition, *Ebony* castigated the article for feeding into communist propaganda and endangering national security as well as the freedom of Korea and the world.[61] The magazine, as many times before and thereafter, feared that these statements would raise doubts about African American patriotism and allegiance to the American cause.

Still, although many papers dismissed the race war hypothesis as a mere tool of Russian propaganda, their reflections still left much space for criticism, as, according to the overly patriotic *Los Angeles Sentinel*, it remained an "undeniable fact that racial discrimination does exist in the western world which is the stronghold of democracy." [62] According to many commentators, black soldiers on the Korean front who were willing to give their lives for the nation "were putting color into what otherwise would be a war of whites against colored, which wouldn't sit too well on the stomachs of the South Koreans themselves."[63] Inherent in these assessments were strong claims of black agency and power in world affairs. They insinuated that the American endeavors against Communism could fail if blacks withheld their support. African Americans imagined themselves as a force to be reckoned with in world affairs, a position that would also manifest itself on the domestic level. Nevertheless, even if African American soldiers could help better America's position in the world, the country would still need to take serious steps to improve blacks' lot. Many black papers openly raised the question whether it was a coincidence that the first troops that had been sent to Korea were all-black. The *Afro-American* affirmed this assumption by quoting an army officer who asserted that the use of blacks in battle was a strategy to "help forestall Communist propaganda that the fight in Korea is between white and colored men."[64] However, these charades could not end doubts over America's racial position. Ultimately, racial discrimination had to be eliminated in order to win the "ultimate victory." The United States had to change and improve its domestic race situation; otherwise, it would lose the support of the colored peoples of the world who made "their choice on the basis of what we do."[65] Although pledges of patriotism were essential, harsher criticism could not be silenced, at least at the beginning of the war.

The majority of the black press pointed unremittingly to the great propaganda opportunity the communist forces had in Asia because of the continued disenfranchisement and oppression of African Americans in their homeland, not only at the hands of radical groups like the Ku Klux Klan, but also due to the inaction of the American government. "Well over a billion darker peoples—three-fourths of the earth's population—in Asia, Africa, North and South America have their eyes on Korea and on America," *Our World* blatantly warned. The paper claimed that "slowly but surely, the current of events is forcing the moulders of American policy— both in domestic and foreign matters—to recognize the rights of colored peoples all over the world. And the American Negro should benefit from this enlightened view."[66] In an editorial distributed by the ANP, A. J. Siggins suggested that the war was more than a limited conflict in Asia: it provided communists the argumentative foundation "to declare that U.S. white imperialists have supplanted the British and French counterparts in Asia to force colored Asians to submit to the rule of their puppets." The article highlighted the tarnished image of the United States in Korea and Asia in general; an image engendered by the country's racist actions and racial arrogance that it claimed was exemplified by the dropping of two atomic bombs on "colored Asians."[67]

Black commentators linked the troubled course of the American intervention in Korea to white racial arrogance and ideas of white supremacy. Hancock, writer of the syndicated column "Between the Lines," sardonically commented on this racial arrogance as "boastfulness" shown by the United States, especially since Pearl Harbor, and called it a sign of American "unpreparedness" in Korea. The article maintained that the failures in Korea were undoubtedly rooted in "race hate and race vilification" on the home front.[68] The home front thus disabled the war front in Korea. Instead of gearing up against the threat of communists abroad, the United States aimed to continue subordinating blacks, thereby sacrificing "our poorly armed boys" in Korea. According to Hancock, Communism's best allies were white supremacists. Their "color contempt,"[69] as the *Chicago Defender* called it, was detrimental to the war effort and the building of an ally system beyond white peoples "as we try to conquer Negroes first and the foreign foe secondly."[70] One month into the Korean War, an African American columnist sarcastically declared, "Big Uncle Sam kicked in his teeth by 'gooks'—as the white folks choose to call colored folks—and needing anallout, up-in-the billions drive to stop a tiny nation which has never figured in ANY military strength." The columnist pointed to the fact that the segregation and discrimination of African Americans in the United Sates did not go unnoticed among the "'colored' folks fighting 'white' folks." The author blatantly maintained that they were "well aware of the way Unc has treated his 'colored' folks over here" and did not "have any faith in Unc," for they feared American dominance in Asia.[71] Black papers condemned what Michael Sherry has called the "cultural and racial arrogance"[72] shown toward Koreans before and during the war.[73] They argued that it was not only military unpreparedness that prevented American troops from advancing successfully in the war, but also a profound underestimation of the Asian enemy based on concepts of the racial inferiority of nonwhite peoples. The serious problems American troops faced in Korea had special "symbolic aspects for blacks,"[74] as they belied white supremacy and superiority over nonwhite peoples. This allowed African Americans to expand their criticism of racial hierarchies at home and abroad, and to further pressure the U.S. government for change.

An editorial in *The Crisis* openly reprimanded white politicians for using racial epithets. Listing terms like "'menacing hordes of Asia'" used for the Chinese, or "'gooks'" for Koreans, the author of the editorial expressed his belief that the fight for freedom and unity of all peoples was seriously endangered, since politicians insisted on the notion that "civilization [is] the permanent monopoly of one small section of mankind—European whites."[75] The *Afro-American* also pointed to the damaging effect of derogatory terms like "gook," used so casually in the white press and by white soldiers in Korea. The mere use of the word negated American attempts to "prove that there is nothing racial about the present war." Although the term was mostly used to describe the North Korean enemy, the editorial argued that South Koreans would be just as offended by its use. For dramatization's sake, the paper aligned the term with the use of the word "niggers" during the Civil War by Union soldiers, although blacks were fighting on the side of the Union.[76] The paper, like many others, maintained that the use of racial epithets in war was the most damaging factor in the war effort and America's standing in the world. An extension of friendship to nonwhite peoples was futile if white America continued to use "disparaging names" that were testament to the American "sense of superiority."[77] Even the least interested paper could not fully evade the issues involved. After China entered the war and seriously damaged the already worn-out American units in Korea, the *New York Amsterdam News* published an article on the misconception of the Chinese soldier at U.S. and UN headquarters. Contrary to general belief, Chinese soldiers "prove[d] they're tough men" with superior tactical training and knowledge of the area. Although the UN had more weapons and air control, the Chinese enemy was able to ambush and take UN troops by surprise, thus decimating their numbers and equipment. The "American soldier" being "humiliated by the defeats in northern Korea" disproved the xenophobic "calculation of many Americans—that one good GI is equal to 10 Asians." Even though the article's author did not explicitly name racism and concepts of white supremacy as at the root of the problem, it represented an explanation for the Chinese strength and capability that ridiculed white America and its concepts of racial hierarchy.[78]

Marjorie McKenzie, the *Courier*'s only regular female commentator, followed a similar line of argument when she claimed that Korea revealed the "rising importance of Asia in world affairs," which the United States, to the delight of Communist Russia, had ignored because of its focus on Europe. She blamed the loss of Asia to Communism on America's neglect of people of color whom it considered "different and 'backward.'" McKenzie was not shy to call out the "racial arrogance" America had shown peoples of color and to point to the possibly fatal path the Western world would take, if it did not veer away from its racist attitudes and concepts of Western superiority. She also warned that the Western world was in serious danger if Asia fell to Communism. Only by abandoning racism could the West prevent its own extinction, since "beyond the North Atlantic circle, the world is mostly yellow, brown and black."[79] In the same issue of the *Courier*, columnist Horace Cayton also harshly criticized the shortsightedness and indifference of the United States to oppressed peoples all around the world and its inability to find a proper way of dealing with their problems and needs. A defeat of Communism, he maintained, was only possible if the United States would empower peoples of color and "develop a dream of hope which will include the peoples of the world, the yellow people, the brown people, the black people and the white people." A "One World" concept represented the only way to freedom and peace and was more powerful than "guns and bullets."[80] As long as the "dirty colored linens" of the United States hung for the world to see, an American victory was not possible.[81] The African American press pointed out the embarrassment in this dangerous discrepancy. Despite the growing threat of McCarthyism, closing ranks in times of war did not trump the criticism of American race relations. The Korean War, whose failed course put into question notions of American and white superiority, was a medium that could be used to exert pressure on the achievement of equal rights. Not without some degree of satisfaction did the papers report on how the American soldier had to acquire "a new respect for Asia's fighting-men."[82] America's fate and standing in the world was indivisible from the struggle for success of colonial peoples.

The Strange Case of Racial Sensitivity

One of the symptoms of American "racial arrogance" was the widespread use of stereotypes in depicting Asians. The white press along with white politicians often evoked the same stereotypes that had been used for Asians during World War II.[83] The image of Asians as wild beasts, as brutal and reckless in their fighting was revived on a grand scale. The *Los Angeles Times* printed a row of cartoons from three American newspapers that were reminiscent of cartoons of Japanese soldiers during World War II, depicting them as apes and lesser men.[84] They reflected the idea of barbarism and purported a strong dehumanization of the enemy by playing on the facial features of the Chinese and Korean enemies. American press reports from the front lines conveyed the impression not only that North Korean war tactics were unfair and deceitful, but that the "enemy follow no rules of international warfare known to us."[85] The press constructed a savage enemy to which American soldiers, who allegedly only applied fair and humane methods of warfare, were exposed and fighting. When they initially overran the American troops, North Koreans and later Chinese surpassed American expectations and uncovered the U.S. troops' utter unpreparedness and lack of experience and training. Their fighting style not only halted Americans in their efforts to defeat the enemy, resulting in catastrophic casualty numbers and human suffering, but also dealt a serious blow to the American ego and feeling of superiority. The overpowering strength of the enemy was usually not accredited to good preparation and training, but to the savagery and inhumanity allegedly shown. This alleviated, at least for the public, the pressure of an in-depth investigation into the real reasons for the tribulations of the American troops against a supposedly inferior enemy.

In contrast to African American allegations of a predominant lack of racial perceptiveness,[86] the white national press was not entirely unaware of the negative effects racial stereotypes had on the Korean War effort. The *Chicago Daily Tribune* maintained, "American soldiers have alienated the native population by invariably referring to Koreans as 'gooks.'" The article reflected on the serious problems ensuing from an administration that did not teach its soldiers respect and empathy for the people for whom they were fighting and risking their lives.[87] Hanson W. Baldwin, the *New York Times* war correspondent, admitted to the negative effects of the racist attitudes with which Americans went into Korea. "We tended prior to Korea, despite the hard lessons taught us by the Japanese in World War II, to look down upon the Koreans as an inferior race. It was with this attitude of patronizing contempt that we went into action in Korea."[88] For reasons of maintaining positive relations with Asian allies, even the armed forces started to worry about the effect racial intolerance could have on the course of the war and the success of the mission. The army even distributed a pamphlet to soldiers on how not to treat and address Asians.

The African American press self-assuredly weighed white racial arrogance and racist/racial stereotyping against the alleged racial sensitivity of blacks. Their experience as an oppressed minority, the press boldly claimed, made blacks more aware of guilt by racial association and thus receptive to the needs and characteristics of Koreans. The NAACP directed its accusations at whites and their belief in white supremacy, thereby also assuming an African American aloofness to racial exclusion and dominance. Like many African American newspapers, the NAACP asserted the existence of a certain racial sensitivity of blacks toward Asians. Black papers even claimed that "the word 'gook,' a derogatory term for Orientals, is not a part of the average Negro GI's vocabulary; he knows almost too well how offensive pet racial names can be."[89] They furthered the idea that blacks were more perceptive to cultural and racial differences and, therefore, less prone to stereotyping and demeaning behavior toward other minorities, which would damage American efforts against Communism. The fact that the term "Oriental" itself was quite dubious and mainly associated with stereotypes, however, was not widely reflected upon. Many reporters believed that their stories from Korea, a country entirely foreign to the people at home and soldiers alike, would "narrow the barriers between us and contribute toward better understanding and lead toward peace."[90] The black press understood itself and black soldiers to be trailblazers of interracial understanding and peacemaking.

In December 1950, when the situation of the UN troops in Korea, in light of the Chinese intervention, seemed bleaker than ever, Harold E. Stassen, president of the University of Pennsylvania and former delegate to the UN San Francisco Conference, suggested that Ralph Bunche, African American Nobel Peace Prize winner for his mediation in Palestine, should lead mediation in the Korean conflict. [91] The *Chicago Defender* wholeheartedly supported this proposal. In one editorial, the paper argued that

Bunche's experience in the Middle East and his racial background would make him the most fitting candidate to bring all sides to the table to resolve the conflict. Alluding to the alleged superior usability of African Americans in foreign missions, the newspaper maintained that Asians would trust an African American more than they would a white mediator. In the wake of the call for Bunche as the chief negotiator to the conflict, the *Chicago Defender* explained that the "whole conflict in Asia today can be traced directly to the doctrine of 'white supremacy.'" According to the paper, Russia was able to lure Asians "by their phony show of friendship" and their repudiation of white supremacy, while they learned to "hate the white world and all it stands for." Understanding white supremacy better than anyone else might have, Bunche could more aptly tackle the "Korean problem" if the Western powers were finally willing to "utterly" destroy white supremacy.[92] According to this reasoning, an African American could foresee the troubles ahead since he understood the situation of a racial minority. As early as July 1950, the *Chicago Defender* had campaigned for Bunche, arguing that he would "strengthen the hand of the forces of freedom and further enhance the moral integrity of the position of the United Nations forces in Korea."[93] For many blacks, he may very well have been America's only hope for ending the war without much more bloodshed. Bunche simultaneously symbolized black usefulness and dedication to the national cause, while representing a criticism of white supremacy and a symbol of black superiority on the international stage.

Moreover, the press turned African American soldiers in Korea into symbols of racial respect and a reason for Asians' admiration and love for the United States, thus balancing the bad reputation of white American arrogance. Milton A. Smith, the war correspondent who replaced L. Alex Wilson in Korea in November 1950, called black soldiers "good will ambassadors." The correspondent claimed that Koreans, who allegedly applied names to all ethnic groups they came in contact with, did not have an abusive name for blacks, claiming that white soldiers were said to be "rougher than Negro soldiers." African Americans, the article maintained, were kinder and treated Koreans with respect. Due to Koreans' awareness of Jim Crow in the United States, Koreans "tend[ed] to identify themselves with Negro soldiers."[94] Superior to white Americans and less receptive to their damaging stereotypes, blacks and black soldiers in particular, as described in many articles, safeguarded the nation's reputation across the world. A cartoon in the *Afro-American* at the beginning of the war reflected

It Seems Like Only Yesterday When He Went Away

Figure 6. "It Seems Like Only Yesterday When He Went Away." Cartoon, *Afro-American*, July 15, 1950, 4. Reproduced by permission of copyright holder; further reproduction prohibited without permission.

the allegedly good relations between black and South Korean soldiers, as well as blacks' willingness to fight for a country most of them knew nothing about (Figure 6). Their color and status as an oppressed minority that was gradually freeing itself from its bonds was turned into an undeniable asset. Once their demands for equality and civil rights were met, it was believed blacks had the potential to advance democracy and American victory over communism in Korea and around the world. The key to establishing trust and reaching success in Korea, and ultimately securing the survival of the nation, was consequently the fair treatment of blacks and the application of their skills.

The *Chicago Defender*, underlining the presumed racial sensitivity of African Americans, directly addressed the incompetence of intelligence services and white generals. The paper saw a remedy for the many defeats the American troops suffered in the "help and counseling of qualified Negroes. Such integration might go far to save the lives of many American boys in the days ahead." Reflecting on the failures in war and intelligence strategy in Korea, the *Chicago Defender* candidly claimed that the use of blacks ought to take place on larger scale in the war effort since they had "no racial misconceptions" and would therefore be a great asset in the fight against North Koreans and Chinese. According to the editorial, whites were so blindly guided by their belief in the "alleged inferiority of non-white peoples that they underestimate the foe."[95] Not only did the article deride general assumptions of white superiority, it also insinuated black superiority in terms of the war and cultural exchange. Although the article avoided this phraseology, the idea of a war between the races was not a far-fetched one, as the war in Korea was understood to be a competition between the various races that subverted the long-held idea of white supremacy. Always considered intellectually inferior and in need of education from whites, African Americans were now assigned an educator's role that could ultimately save the American nation from defeat by a race mistaken for being inferior.[96]

As Washington repeatedly contemplated dropping the atomic bomb to bring the enemy to his knees, many black commentators considered the issue a question more of race than of military success and failure. Hancock was convinced that "high-strung southerners" pressured Truman to use the atomic bomb in Asia.[97] In its column "National Grapevine," the *Defender* warned the U.S. administration that dropping an atomic bomb would only lead to more mistrust and suspicion among the "three-fourths colored population," who already felt contempt for the United States due to its "day-by-day race performance."[98] The use of the atomic bomb in Asia would clearly prove the persistence of racism. Alvin E. White of the ANP foresaw "an immediate protest and possible uprising from the darker people of the world" if the atomic bomb was dropped in Asia once again, especially in light of the fact that Germany had been spared a similar fate during the Second World War.[99] At the end of the war in Korea, Langston Hughes, the renowned African American poet and columnist, stated that

the bomb would be a "great mistake for the white world" that would neither end the war nor the racial conflict, but aggravate both.[100]

Although many civil rights activists reasoned that there was a connection between the Asian, in this case Korean, struggle for independence and
the African American fight for civil rights, this imagined interracial association often did not replicate itself on the Korean front or in the black
press.[101] While decrying the white press and politicians for using derogatory
language and racial epithets, accounts based on the experience of black war
correspondents and soldiers in Korea did not differ considerably in this
regard from those of whites. African American papers often showed racial
insensitivity when reporting from Korea. Neither reporters nor soldiers
seemed to draw many parallels between their experience as oppressed people, and the Korean struggle for independence. They highlighted and
aligned themselves with the worldwide protest against American race relations, nevertheless they all too often did not show much interest in real
cooperation.

Many reports from Korea disprove the claim that African Americans
had a special understanding for and trust in Asians. Although many
claimed to act as negotiators between the different races and cultures, they
ultimately drew a clear racial and cultural line between African Americans
and Koreans, friend and foe alike.[102] This did not have so much to do with
Koreans' possible communist tendencies or affiliation, but was rather based
on their perceived cultural and racial difference. Black war correspondent
L. Alex Wilson commented in a less than culturally and racially sensitive
manner on the nature of Koreans, assessing them as "semi-primitive."
According to another correspondent, Koreans were in a "near primitive
state," dirty and lazy, but most shockingly "immature economically, politically and their educational status is far from what could be termed standard." While blacks fought for the foreign country, they wanted "to get out
of the pig's sty, as soon as possible."[103] Correspondent James Hicks called
Korea the "most dirty, the most stinking, the most filthy place on God's
earth."[104] Ralph Matthews bluntly described the war-ridden country as a
"god-forsaken dismal place, the misery of which I can find no words to
describe."[105] Worst of all for the correspondents and seemingly indicative
of the inhabitants' mental and cultural backwardness, Koreans seemed to
be satisfied with their state of existence. An article in the *Chicago Defender*
maintained that the "average Korean has demonstrated in more ways than
one he is contented with his way of life; that he wants to tend his rice

paddies and live in peace in his huts. Many have made clear they want the 'foreigners' out of their country."[106] War correspondent Milton Smith reported on Koreans' indifference to fellow human beings and their suffering. Reflecting on the similarity between "the problems of colored Americans and Koreans," Milton maintained that "every GI I questioned said, in effect: 'I'd rather be a colored man in Alabama than a Korean anywhere over here'."[107] A commentator for the *Afro-American* condescendingly claimed that Korea was not ready for a modern war and ultimately unwilling as well as unable to advance.[108]

Presenting Korea as a backward country was an apt method in painting African Americans as superior, if good-willed agents in helping the people achieve a better life. The white press liked to print stories of American soldiers taking care of Korean children and introducing American life to them, which was understood to be far superior to life in Korea. African American papers also ran such stories, outlining the immense generosity of black soldiers in comparison to whites.[109] The *Chicago Defender* argued that the Korean youth were the only hope the country had to rid itself of poverty and elevate to maturity. With their recent exposure to UN riches and cultivation, they could strive for a better life.[110] Matthews, one of the more sensitive war correspondents, frequently described the despair and destruction in Korea from a more sympathetic perspective. In one article, he even freely admitted to a "feeling of guilt" since "much of the power and steel which caused this havoc came from [our] native land." Despite all sympathies for the "innocent victims" in Korea,[111] however, his articles still displayed the belief that Koreans were a people stuck in past centuries. After a rather sensitive presentation of the devastating losses of lives and resources in Korea, Matthews concluded that building up Korea was an almost impossible task and a waste of time. Using their heating system as an example, he concluded his article by stating, "these are ancient feats of engineering foreign to our modern mechanical genius."[112] The superiority of the Western world toward Asian "primitives" was omnipresent in his articles despite some apparent sympathies for the country. The same held true for Matthews's account of the tragic fate of Korean children, in which the American soldiers were presented in exaggerated terms as good Samaritans aiding impoverished and starving creatures. A pictorial rendition of the idea of the American soldier (Figure 7) as a savior supplemented his point.[113] He reasoned in the end, however, that not even the children could be trusted. Inspired by his experience of being robbed by Korean children, Matthews

Figure 7. Ralph
Matthews, "GIs Have
Big Hearts." Cartoon,
*New York Amsterdam
News*, September 8,
1951, 7.

admitted he had joined what he insultingly called the "I Hate Koreans Cult"
so very prominent among American soldiers, both white and black.[114]

The lack of racial sensitivity that African American soldiers displayed
and the black press commented on came through in their indiscriminate
use of racial slurs to describe Koreans. African American soldiers used the
term "gooks" for North as well as South Koreans. An African American
Korean War soldier decorated for his heroism was quoted in an article
having stated, "I got it in the left hip, but not before I inflicted a little
damage on a few 'Gooks' (North Koreans) myself." The *Chicago Defender*,
in which the article was printed, did not seem to consider the term problematic, since the author merely added "North Koreans" in parentheses to
explain its usage to the unknowing reader without referring to its demeaning quality.[115] Many reports on African American exploits on the war front
or in supply lines quoted the term, "gook," as being used by African American soldiers, who did not show any sensitivity with regard to the term or
its derogatory meaning.[116] The reports on the alleged heroic feats of African
American soldiers, which were so essential for the claim to equality and
civil rights, seem to have trumped racial sensitivities. The African American
press often used descriptions of North Korean and Chinese soldiers and
fighting similar to those in the mainstream press.[117]

The *Courier* called North Koreans and Chinese "Communist-dragooned
. . . hordes,"[118] denying them any humanity and individuality. The paper's
war correspondent, Bradford Laws, proudly reported on an African American soldier who had managed to "mow . . . down 30 Reds in one day." The

killing spree was a sign of virility and combat ability, and did not spur a critical inquiry into the deadliness of combat. A direct quote from the soldier underlines the dehumanizing concept of the racially "othered" enemy: "Fighting those guys [North Koreans] is like fighting armed mountain goats."[119] Furthermore, blacks reported the difficulties in telling enemy and ally apart. According to L. Alex Wilson, "the average GI cannot tell the difference between a South Korean and a North Korean."[120] Black and white soldiers tended to mistrust all Asians in the conflict. African American papers, the statements of soldiers, and soldiers' memoirs are testaments to the negative perceptions many African Americans had of North Koreans and later of the Chinese. In these documents, enemies are often dehumanized and perceived as racial others who allegedly had no respect for other humans. Although American soldiers often showed respect for the enemies' tenacity, they interpreted their combat strategy and fighting style as evidence for their ruthlessness and barbarity. While usually not explicitly stating it, the articles insinuated a correlation between the allegedly unprecedented brutality of combat in Korea and the race of the enemy.

Believing in their superiority as fighters, many African American soldiers might have been certain that their mission in Korea would end quickly. As is evidenced by a variety of sources, they underestimated and disliked Koreans as much as their white counterparts did.[121] Yet, the reality of the war belied their feeling of superiority in combat. The unconventional fighting methods of the enemy were, without a doubt, as disturbing to black soldiers as they were to whites. The vigor and nearly unprecedented nature of the attacks led to a racist bluntness that further dehumanized the enemy. The *Defender*'s war correspondent, Wilson, called the suicide attacks used by North Koreans, "one of the most barbarous inventions of human warfare."[122] Reports from the front, especially from Wilson, who covered the first year of the war meticulously, emulated mainstream discourse and were filled with dehumanizing phrases and racial epithets. "Joe-Koats," a term used for North Koreans, was associated with claimed acts of savagery and deceit that were seemingly unknown to American soldiers. With their "Indian tactics against our modern warfare"[123] and mastery "at camouflaging the exact shades of the landscape,"[124] their unpredictability invoked ideas of savagery, primitivism, and barbarism. Though not creating his own term for the enemy, correspondent Hicks followed a similar line of reasoning in his description of the character of Asians. He noted, "Oriental peoples generally do not play about war. They fight or they don't fight—and right now they are engaged in war. To them, the enemy is an enemy, and they treat him accordingly, indifferent to the nice conventions with which Western peoples are familiar."[125] Koreans, whether from North or South, were perceived as culturally and mentally different from civilized peoples. Stories from Korea seemed to corroborate the dehumanized image of the enemy who outnumbered American troops. Black correspondents reported that Koreans used civilians as shields against American attacks. This type of reporting was reminiscent of the racist discourse on the Japanese and Chinese during the Second World War.[126] A reported case of North Koreans who had painted their faces black and tried to break African American defense lines further increased black mistrust and frustration with the North Korean tactics.[127] Soldiers often expressed suspicion toward South Koreans and maintained that telling them apart was almost impossible. Even behind American lines, danger lurked.[128] During the Korean War, Asians and African Americans mostly did not appear as allies in their struggle for freedom.

The differences identified as existing between (black) America and Korea were presented as almost insurmountable, thereby also belying stereotypes of black inferiority and backwardness and creating a "black modern subjects capable of being incorporated into a narrative of Western historical progress."[129] Many articles on black soldiers and their experience in Korea testified to their racial indifference and suspicions, if not outright antipathy, toward Koreans. Rather than bring Koreans and African Americans closer together and toward a better understanding of each other, the reports reveal an " "imperial gaze"[130] and "did much to alienate a homefront audience from enemy and ally alike."[131] African American reporters in Korea emphasized the differences between blacks and Asians, ultimately asserting black's racial superiority, rather than fostering an understanding for cultural differences. By distancing African Americans from another oppressed racial minority, they established black's allegiance to whites, rather than to Asians.[132] The racial sensitivity of blacks toward Asians and the interracial solidarity or even alliance against white supremacy, which had been put forward by the black elite, did not survive the realities of the war. Although some might have related to the enemy, many war correspondents and soldiers maintained an African American version of "orientalism" that often placed African Americans in opposition to Asians and in line with Western feelings of superiority.[133] This "black orientalism" was in part their claim to Americanness, and their inclusion in the American nation.[134] Articles on and interviews with black soldiers on the front were filled with racial slurs and references to the alleged underdeveloped state of Korea and its inhabitants. The commonality of racial difference did not lead to mutual respect or understanding. It was, after all, a war situation. Correspondents built rifts between African Americans and Koreans with their demeaning reports on the life and people of the peninsula.

A Man's World

The representation of Korean and Japanese women in African American papers was especially problematic,[135] as reports on Asia in general objectified women, thereby confirming "black men's status as deserving patriarchs."[136] The images of Asian women produced in these articles are evidence of the racial and cultural condescension that existed among African Americans in the war zone. The "good-will ambassador" status many correspondents claimed for black soldiers was absent, especially in their discussion of Korean women.[137] The war and occupation brought with it a major increase in the use and abuse of local women. For many women, prostitution was the only way to alleviate the dire poverty in which they lived. Whether it was in Korea or in Japan, where many soldiers went on a five-day leave, American men, black or white, made ample use of their fiscal power to pay for sex. For many African American soldiers, like for many whites, their time in Japan and Korea represented a rite of passage, to which sexual experiences belonged. The majority of servicemen were under twenty-three, and many had their first real sexual encounters during their time in Asia.[138]

According to reports in black papers, men on the front lines preferred the company of Asian women to female servicepersons because the Asian women treated the soldiers as men ought to be treated, submissively and with respect.[139] Women served as nurses and in service staff in the Women's Army Corps (WAC) or the Department of Army Civilians (DAC), but they had a tainted reputation. Soldiers described them as unattractive and frigid, and suspected them of lesbianism.[140] Soldiers judged women by their looks, alleged characteristics, and availability.[141] Matthews even complained that the "total absence of sex life can be as demoralizing to an occupation army as overindulgence." He cited the scarcity of sexual intercourse with Korean women as being at least partly responsible for the army's "flop in Korea."[142]

The availability of women as sexual outlets was considered a prerequisite for successful completion of a war mission. Most relationships with Asian women rendered them objects rather than human beings. The relationship was a transaction based on availability of females. "Abuses of power in the name of military interest"[143] were accepted. Their legality or morality was rarely questioned, but prostitution and the inherent female use and abuse was taken for granted and considered a male right as well as a military need.[144] Ultimately, relationships with these women were nothing to worry about, Matthews claimed.[145]

Reports described Japanese women as beautiful or delicate. In a two-page article with extensive pictures celebrating the beauty of Japanese women, L. Alex Wilson explained why black men liked these women, propagating long-standing stereotypes of Japanese women. Wilson quoted Ethel Payne, director of an Army Service Club in Yokohama, who stated, "by tradition, the Japanese woman is submissive." Another female interviewee argued that the Japanese woman did not talk back and obediently supported and pampered her mate, while additional statements from African American soldiers corroborated the image of the subservient Japanese woman. Some reporters called on African American women at home to limit their outspokenness to be able to win back African American males returning from Asia.[146] James Hicks affirmed this by reporting that African American men wanted women who acknowledged the "man as Head of the House." The alleged docility of Japanese women dominated the black press. Soldiers' experience presumably showed that "docile Japanese women [were] an 'ideal mate' for men who 'like to be the boss in the family.'"[147] Wilson was sure many of the unions between blacks and Asians were meant to survive the soldiers' return to the States.

Some African American women seemed to feel intimidated and threatened by these interracial relationships between Asian women and black men. In her own article on Japanese women published in the *Chicago Defender* a week after Wilson's, Ethel Payne condemned Asian women by using racial slurs and insinuating that Asian women were inferior to American ones. Payne mocked the stature of Asian women as well as their, in her opinion, embarrassing attempts to master Western cultural norms and dress codes. If anything, she claimed condescendingly, the arrival of soldiers in Japan had managed to emancipate the Japanese woman "who, even at best, had been virtually a slave." However, Japanese women were quick to learn the power of their presumed "helplessness" to exploit their "Chocolate Joes." Payne asserted that "Nipponese girls are playing GI's for suckers." African American men were clearly also responsible for these developments, since Japanese girls who had been submissive and controlled prior to the Americans' arrival, now sought to take advantage of the "gallant boys." The demeaning portrayals of Asian women sought to trigger fear among female readers that they were losing their soldiers.[148] A gendered hierarchy of the races existed, as well as hierarchies of female behavior in which African American women were morally superior in their presumed struggle to regain the black men they had lost to Japanese women.

In November 1950, interracial marriage between Japanese women and black men moved the *Courier* to launch a poll among its female readers. The paper claimed that "most American women say: 'Let GIs wed Japanese girls,'" even though they were "taking away the scarcest commodity in the U.S. market, MEN." The individual reactions listed, however, somewhat belied the article's title. Although the majority of women interviewed stated that marriages with Japanese should be allowed and could even help solve the race question, they viewed marriage between Japanese women and black men with suspicion. According to the poll, many doubted the black GIs really fell in love, claiming that they were merely "lonely and in a strange country" and should be "granted their desires."[149] There was also a certain sense of envy and rivalry in the comments.[150]

According to a columnist and colleague at the *Chicago Defender*, war correspondent Wilson received a number of letters from women who expressed their outrage over the report on African American men and Asian women. One letter was especially vehemently opposed to Wilson, and compelled him to issue a public reply. A woman scolded the author for his article, which she considered an advertisement for cross-racial relationships and for the advantages of Asian women over African American females waiting at home. Using explicitly racist terms, she maintained that Wilson "'encourage[d]' Colored Yanks to desert their Colored mates left here in America and 'git one' a them fine, pretty Oriental chicks.'" In her interpretation of Wilson's article, she claimed that he had further denigrated African American women and elevated Asian women, whom she angrily—and lacking any sensitivity to racial difference—described as having "a big 'pie-face'" with hair "which doesn't have to be pressed." She also alluded to the strengthening of black manhood, which she suspected black men felt they had gained by dating "an other race in the world beside 'his own.'" For the female writer, and perhaps for many more African American women, interracial relationships would further destabilize the African American community and lead to the humiliation and identity crisis of black women.

Wilson replied to the furious letter. He claimed that his assailant misrepresented the facts he had previously presented merely to inform the home front, and argued that only a small number of blacks were with Asian women. However, these cases revealed that black soldiers preferred an Asian woman because black American women treated African American men with contempt. He stated. "American women, some of them have serious faults. Those faults are responsible for our boys, so many of them turning to the Japanese girls. When the first civilian Negro girls went to Japan they shunned some of our boys. Some of them, matter of fact the very first one, got herself a white man. Tan GIs haven't forgot that, nor other things that happened in America."[151] The contention between Wilson and the female readers revealed the gendered nature of Japan's occupation and the problematic relations between the sexes.

The *Afro-American* argued along the same the lines. Matthews reported that the African American WACs felt rejected by black GIs who preferred Japanese girls. According to the author, a clear competition between the races for the African American male existed, as well as a "war between the sexes." According to the article, black women were furious over the men's choice and alleged that the "little straight-haired girl[s] fawning all over them" were "mostly professional prostitutes" or "from the poorest families," therefore mostly interested in the men for the money. The reason for the men's choice was the sexual availability of "Japanese girls," the interviewed women claimed, all the while they themselves were looking for a real relationship. The male soldiers interviewed for the article described the WACs in derogatory terms, insinuating that WAC members had only joined the armed forces because they could not find a partner at home. Japanese girls, on the other hand, were beautiful and easily available. "With the native girls you play a lone hand and just keep looking until you find something that looks good, make a fast play and you are all right." [152] The objectification of women, especially Japanese women, and an inherent sexism underscore statements like this one.

African American male and female interviewees clearly looked down on Japanese women, distancing and elevating their own national and cultural background above that of the Asian "other," despite men's preference for the committed and submissive Japanese women abroad. The short article accompanying a drawing on male-female relations (Figure 8) stated that most black soldiers would not be able to stay with their Japanese lovers. "But the Wacs always get the last laugh when the troops transport pulls out, leaving the heartbroken girl to be comforted by her poor old Mamma-San with often a little brown baby to rear. All GI's promise faithfully they're coming back, but they seldom do."[153] The few articles on interracial relationships between Japanese and Americans refer to Japanese women as "girls." American females, on the other hand, were described as full-grown women, thereby creating a rhetorical hierarchy between black women and females of "the other race." Not only were Japanese women deprived of any agency in these allegedly fact-based, objective reports—if they had any agency, they executed it on a merely sexual level, luring men into relationships—but they were ridiculed, with the ultimate power seen as being in the hands of the Americans. Many reports insinuated that American culture and traditions were superior.

According to many articles, Korean women lacked the female virtue assigned to Japanese women. One soldier said, "I have found them to be the only women in any country uglier than the men."[154] War correspondent Wilson elaborated on the alleged dirtiness and lack of hygiene of Korean women, claiming that women at home would not have to worry about their men cheating on them. Japanese women, on the other hand were serious competition, owing to their fine features and submissiveness. Wilson claimed that ordinary Korean women were dirty and their living quarters "stinking straw-thatched, flea-ridden hovels." The only exceptions in Korea were "comforters," or prostitutes in a "Special Service Center for UN Forces." It was the sexual availability and attractiveness of women that Wilson took into account in order to judge the character and the cultural and developmental status of Korea as a nation. The female body represented the underdeveloped status of the nation that needed the guiding hand of the Western world. Constructing American troops as a liberating and superior force in their coverage of the Korean War, Wilson and many other black correspondents emulated the discourse of oppression.[155] Correspondents Matthews and Milton A. Smith furthered the negative image of Korean women. Smith corroborated Wilson's stories, reporting the lack of hygiene and high venereal disease rate among them. In an article on why black women did not have to worry about losing their partners to Korean women, he primarily described most soldiers in Korea as devoted husbands and boyfriends. However, as he listed more reasons for their abstinence,

Figure 8. "Battle Between Wac's and Native Girls Rages in Japan." Cartoon, *Afro-American*, September 22, 1951, 8. Reproduced by permission of copyright holder; further reproduction prohibited without permission.

the author referred to the high venereal disease rate among Korean women, as well as their alleged filthiness and bad odor. In the eyes of the interviewed soldiers and the reporter, Korean women clearly did not match Western standards, even if they tried to "westernize."[156] Cpl. Charles W. of Brooklyn, whom Milton described as a "devoted hubby," was quoted stating that "I would not kiss one of these dirty mouthed women." Another soldier reportedly asserted, "There's nothing these dames can do for me. I don't like the way they look and I hate the way they smell."[157] Matthews added another aspect that led to the condescension toward Korean women. Their treatment of their children, he claimed, was one of regular physical violence, which explained why Japanese women were preferred to Korean ones.[158]

A year after the end of the war, the *Afro-American* reflected somewhat more positively on Korean women and interracial unions. In an article on African American soldiers marrying Korean women, the paper presented the latter in a more favorable light. Pictures of good-looking Korean women accompanied the article to explain and justify their appeal to the black soldier. Despite presenting marriage to Korean women as an option, the article was convinced that "with no one to shoot at and nobody shooting at them, the men find more time to play, and to think of the girl and marriage." The paper maintained that American men considered Korean women to be a second choice after American women, noting, "the longer they stay away from the American women, the better the Korean girls look to them." The article did not openly slur Korean women or the possibility of interracial marriage; however, it downplayed the intentions of American soldiers with them. In this way, the article covertly addressed the precariousness of interracial marriage in an Asian setting.[159]

Integrating Asians

The proclaimed special understanding of African Americans for the Korean allies due to their shared experience of racial oppression had its limits in another respect. African American newspapers fervently debated the presence of African American soldiers in segregated units at the Korean front, while actual integration of blacks in the army was progressing slowly. In compliance with the UN character of the war effort, however, the army admitted South Korean soldiers into its all-white combat outfits. It praised their fighting ability and the cooperation of white and Asian soldiers. South Koreans served, housed, and ate together with white soldiers; they wore American GI uniforms and received the same treatment as American soldiers. The *Washington Post* reported extensively on the alleged smoothness of the integration of Asians with white Americans. Language and culture seemed to be no barrier in the attempt to strengthen the forces. The newspaper even recounted, "Americans no longer call them Gooks." Apparently, all prejudices could be overcome by a simple move toward integration. The article quoted a U.S. sergeant whose statement seemed to stand as a testament to the equalizing effect of the move: "How in heck can you call a guy a foreigner when he's shared your foxhole, split your shift on guard and helped you fight off a night attack?"[160] In contrast to black soldiers, South Koreans' reputation seemed strong in integrated military units. According to the *New York Times*, American soldiers and officers described them as "intelligent," "courageous," willing to fight, and not fleeing front lines.[161] MacArthur felt that integration of Korean soldiers was true to the UN war effort and was furthermore necessary to counter communist propaganda.

Black papers took special offense at the American army, as they had integrated non-English-speaking Asians into their white outfits as equals but continued to exclude African American soldiers. The fact that blacks, although they were American citizens remained excluded, whereas Koreans without citizenship enjoyed preferential treatment and could serve in integrated outfits, stirred a deep sense of injustice within the African American community.[162] It dishonored black soldiers as soldiers and as men. Shortly after the reports on the alleged Asian American harmony in otherwise all-white outfits, the *Pittsburgh Courier* published an editorial titled "An Insult in Korea." The integration of "alien Koreans" into the "citizen Army of the United States" was a pure "insult which burns deep into the soul of every black American." The army seemed to consider all other races "good enough to fight alongside the American white man except the black American citizen. He is the outcast, the pariah, the untouchable." Not only were Asians, whom Americans usually considered inferior, allowed to serve alongside whites and prove their masculinity on equal grounds, they were also generally applauded for their combat fitness; a front even more hurtful for blacks as they struggled with the racial slurring of their own combat readiness. The editorial saw it as an additional perversion of the concept of American citizenship. It referred to the alleged mutual dislike between Koreans and Americans that would reveal this attempt to continue racial and international harmony as a farce. Asians and people of other races, the paper claimed, would see right through this flawed attempt at convincing others of American racial inclusiveness and the end of segregation. The continued existence of segregated black units would trump and tarnish this positive image integration of Koreans had achieved. The editorial ended with a frank plea to President Truman to end segregation in the armed forces once and for all with a second executive order, thus indirectly pointing to the limits and failures of Executive Order 9981. A new order would "make our democratic claims ring true."[163]

The *Afro-American* called it a "discouraging fact that South Korean soldiers were being treated better than they [blacks] and were accepted early as equals in our lily-white units."[164] Blacks were appalled that although they were citizens, they had once again been reduced to second-class citizenship. In the *Pittsburgh Courier*, Horace Cayton expressed blacks' incomprehension and feeling of humiliation that the continued segregation brought with it. He denounced the hypocrisy the United States maintained and outlined the dangers it brought for the American public image and reputation. The Cold War threat to American national security and dominance loomed strongly in discussions on the continued segregation in the armed forces. "In this war we are daily losing to the enemy. And we are losing because it is clear for the world to see that democracy here does not include people whose color is not white."[165] Their claim to racial equality and fair treatment, however, did not contain much interracial solidarity, which many commentators claimed African Americans had had toward Asians. The admittance of South Koreans to white American units again undermined the link between military service and full citizenship and thus fueled the African American struggle for desegregation even further.

When war came in the Far East only five years after the end of the Second World War, most African Americans, like the general public, supported the mission. However, they did not hold back their criticism. The Korean War presented another chance to put pressure on the American government and demand civil rights. As black soldiers fought and died in Korea, civil rights activists and the black press launched another "Double V" campaign pointing to the hypocrisy of American democracy. They vehemently pushed Truman and Congress to enact another FEPC, so blacks would finally have a fair chance on the job market, not only in the trenches.

Despite allegations of communist affiliation, the black community also criticized American foreign policy, accusing it of short-sightedness and racism. The war against another oppressed race offered a platform for severe condemnation of the U.S. system of white supremacy that blacks effectively helped to drag into the international spotlight. African Americans presented equality and integration as an undeniable asset in gaining the trust of Koreans and other minorities worldwide. Moreover, vocal parts of the black elite claimed that blacks had a better understanding of and connection with Koreans. This, they argued, could prove essential for winning the war in Korea and the wider war against Communism. Nevertheless, the special bond of "peoples of color" against white oppression often did not come to fruition, especially on the Korean front. As the army continued to segregate, black soldiers and correspondents not only fought a relentless enemy, but they faced persistent racial segregation and discrimination in the field.

Chapter 7

Black Men at War

Right from the start of the Korean War, African American newspapers and their war correspondents attempted to emphasize the necessity and advantages of integration. Black soldiers sent to war in integrated outfits would be the ultimate validation of their previous efforts in all wars. In the *Courier*, columnist Marjorie McKenzie wrote: "They [the headlines in black newspapers] were a proud boast of the non-segregated participation of Negro airmen and naval personnel in South Korea's defense. Almost nothing could give Negroes a greater sense of belonging to this nation than the right to die for it on a basis of equality and dignity. To be permitted less is to feel less."[1] The story of ensign Jesse L. Brown, in particular, contained everything the leaders of the black community, the black press, and its readership could long for in the midst of war.

Ensign Brown's time in Korea was as memorable as it was short. As part of an integrated outfit that flew bombing missions near the Chosin Reservoir, the black officer's plane was shot down and subsequently crashed in enemy territory. Jammed in the plane, he could not free himself. His white comrade, "who knew no barriers of race," made an emergency landing. "Without regard for his personal safety," Lt. Thomas J. Hudner[2] attempted to free Brown from the plane in vain. Brown died in the burning jet, less than three months after he arrived in Korea in September 1950.[3] Both the black and white press picked up the story—it was too good a tale of heroism and sacrifice to ignore.[4] Furthermore, black papers capitalized on the story to foster racial pride and antidiscrimination.

Brown epitomized everything the black community hoped a black soldier would be. He had one of the most dangerous jobs in the war. According to reports, his record was flawless and only death could stop him from fighting the enemy, while he "spread . . . terror among Korean Reds." Reports on Brown made him a symbol of American masculinity that belied long-standing racial stereotypes.[5] He was the poster boy for black success in an integrated military, for the breakdown of racial barriers, and for African American advancement in the navy.[6] Roy Wilkins wrote in his column, "Jesse Brown never believed he could not do what other fellows could do, no matter what their color. . . . Jesse Brown is proof that things are happening, that progress is being made."[7] In the black press, his life had been a story of black heroism and success; his death was a tale of interracial camaraderie and black men's sacrifices for the nation. Both epitomized the success and necessity of integration and racial brotherhood, especially in the midst of war. Many in the African American community considered Brown's tragic death of great strategic use in their fight for integration.

The incident, heartrending as it was, fed all the needs of the African Americans' discourse on war and race. It built racial pride—black male pride in particular—and validated integration. Constructed as an African American male war hero, Ensign Brown had defied all racial barriers in his home state of Mississippi in order to join one of the most respected fighter units in the American armed forces. His story was one of dedication to his race and nation. He had succeeded in a segregated environment and then excelled in an integrated one. Brown became a representative of African American male prowess and heroism that equaled, if not exceeded, white men's war performance. His white carrier commander called him "one of the best pilots in the air group and this was borne out by today's performance."[8] The press made Ensign Brown into the ultimate embodiment of the black citizen soldier.[9] His life encapsulated the American dream of working hard and being successful against all odds.

According to the *Norfolk Journal and Guide*, Brown was "a typical Negro farm boy, performing the usual chores of chopping wood, plowing and hoeing. This practice of working hard won him second honor in high school and a good scholastic record."[10] Hard work would prove all stereotypes of black inferiority wrong. African American men should be willing to emulate Brown's overcoming of racial barriers and claiming of the role of a citizen soldier. He had to battle the enemy abroad and the enemy at home. In black press reports, agency was clearly with Brown as a representative of African American males. His success in his integrated environment came not through white charity, but from hard work and infallible patriotism through military service. These were American values, virtues through which an African American male could claim his equal position in American society. His familial situation and religious background furthered the idea of an "all-American man" who happened to be black, and complemented the strong component of a black identity in the construction of his persona. Many reports mentioned his nuclear family and his apparently deep belief in God. His wife, a young African American, was presented as a committed spouse and mother of the young daughter to whom Brown had, in addition to his love for his country, dedicated his life.[11] As a family, they corresponded with traditional gender norms and middle-class respectability. Nothing about them could offend anyone.

Brown's fate was foremost a story of interracial cooperation and camaraderie. An article in the *Norfolk Journal and Guide* called it a "lesson in brotherhood of man,"[12] claiming that it could belie all domestic allegations that integration was not effective, as well as put an end to Russian propaganda allegations that the United States could not mend racial differences, which were a denunciation of humanity. With respect to this propaganda, the paper maintained in another article, "Ensign Brown was a Negro. His shipmates are white. According to the latest Russian reports, America is so torn and bitter over racial strife and discord that there is no possibility of its two major races fighting effectively together or living in harmony."[13] The life and death of Ensign Brown seemed to prove these stories wrong. Integration, the articles implied, made better soldiers out of both races. Combat and the threats involved in it, were commonly shared by Americans of all races, and could be better dealt with in racial union. The *Afro-American* maintained that Brown's death was an "example of true Americanism, demonstrating that true democracy knows no color line."[14] Albert Barnett in the *Chicago Defender* argued that no one, "no matter what their race, color, or religion," could ever forget the heroism and interracial dedication shown by Brown's death.[15]

Following his death, Brown's comrades collected $2,700 and established a college fund for Brown's little daughter. Thus, the lesson seemed to be that military integration abroad could bring about change on the home front. Mary Whittaker, a reader of the *Chicago Defender*, maintained that Hudner would not have tried to save Brown if it had not been for the respect the black man had garnered among his white comrades. The physical closeness of military living conditions and the emotional closeness that combat begat, made it possible for them to get to "know Jesse Brown as an individual not as a Negro" and establish a "brotherhood" never previously experienced. The reader figured that Brown's death was not in vain, but "was given to cause which will win out in the end—the cause of freedom."[16]

Other articles on Korea tried to underline interracial male bonding through the progress of integration. In a time of crisis, it was performance, not skin color, that counted. "The color of a man's skin does not determine his acceptance. Rather he must have ability, training, and experience that can be used in the battalion."[17] Even Southerners accepted African Americans once they had seen them performing as efficiently as they had seen whites perform. The white endorsement of African Americans as equals proved important as evidence for the functionality of integration. Black papers ran a story of a white Mississippian who had been captured by North Koreans and saved by African American soldiers. This, the articles claimed, confirmed that there was "no place in democracy for racial bias."[18] The immediacy of the perils of war and male courage were the unifying factors for the two races, normally in conflict with one another in society. The combat experience was a rite of passage for the establishment of national unity, full civil rights, and manhood.

Progress?

While reports showed that desegregation progressed rather successfully in the air force and navy, as both branches adhered for the most part willingly to the recommendations of the Fahy Committee, it was less successful in the army.[19] *Freedom to Serve*, the Fahy Committee report on integration efforts, recommendations, and the resulting changes in armed forces policy published in June 1950, deemed integration a success.[20] Somewhat disappointed, Lester Granger of the NUL noted that the report "constituted a minimum rather than a maximum plan of action."[21] More optimistic, the NAACP stated that "victory was in sight."[22] Korea seemed to be the proving ground, as soldiers fighting in the field could not afford to uphold segregation or racial animosities.[23] To survive, the black press reasoned, one had to fight beyond color lines. African Americans were certain that the army brass in particular obstructed integration as well as racial harmony and understanding.

The overwhelming majority of blacks, however, still served in the army, which remained as segregated as it had been during World War II.[24] In his 2007 memoir, Charles Rangel, a U.S. Representative from Harlem and black

Korean War veteran, noted "If that was so [integration of the military with Truman's Executive Order 9981], what was my black ass doing in an all-black outfit—besides the commissioned officers—in 1950?"[25] Integration in the army had not been actualized to the degree that many had hoped. Although he periodically praised black soldiers for their combat record, General MacArthur eschewed ending racial segregation in the army.[26] Even the Red Cross continued to uphold its segregation of blood at the beginning of the war.[27] In 1951, reports of the public display of the confederate flag in Korea enraged the black home front.[28] The war was full of setbacks that left African Americans in limbo, continuously struggling with their status and image.

As blacks were among the first soldiers shipped to Korea and sent into battle,[29] the *New York Amsterdam News* noted, "The American Negro soldier is playing his part in the fight for democracy and a free world on the battlefronts of Korea."[30] While their families and communities were most likely unhappy about their departure and having to risk their lives, those on the home front also seemed proud that black soldiers were going to the war as one of the first troops. After all, valorous military service, they thought, could only help the black cause and the community's claim to civil rights and equality.[31] Yet, few could overlook the tragic irony of the situation. A cartoon in the *Courier* in September 1950 (Figure 9) poignantly captured the underlying bigotry and frustration. It displayed two war-weary African American soldiers on the front in Korea, talking about the fact that this was the first time they were not being threatened for "settin' right up front." African Americans across the nation, whether direct victims of Jim Crow or not, understood the reference to Jim Crow public transportation regulations that ordered all blacks to sit in the back of the bus. In the South, African Americans who dared sit at the front of a bus still frequently catalyzed violent racial clashes between whites and blacks, both on and off the base.

Nevertheless, blacks joined the military and embarked for Korea. Many had to; the draft remained in effect, and the number of deferments especially among African Americans, remained low.[32] Of the roughly 1.5 million men inducted during the Korean War; about 25 percent of them were African Americans; of these, 13.5 percent were drafted, and 13.4 percent joined voluntarily. Some returned to military duty after having served in World War II and others enlisted for the first time. Despite the army's attempts to limit the number of black recruits by upholding the quota system after the

DARK LAUGHTER
By OLLIE HARRINGTON

"Say, cousin, it sure is grand being way out here in front ain't it? This is the first time in my life they ain't wanted to lock me up or beat my brains out for settin' right up n front!"

Figure 9.   Ollie Harrington, "Dark Laughter." Cartoon, *Courier*, September 9, 1950, 14. Reproduced by permission of copyright holder; further reproduction prohibited without permission.

Second World War, African Americans joined in large numbers.[33] They signed up for many reasons. While some hoped to prove themselves to the white world, most went to make better lives for themselves and their families, since discrimination and segregation seriously limited their chances in the thriving postwar economy. For many, military service was their only chance to escape poverty and support their families.[34]

Reporting from Korea

L. Alex Wilson, a black war correspondent, embarked on a dangerous mission when he left for Korea in July 1950.[35] His colleague, Albert L. Hinton, associate editor of the *Norfolk Journal and Guide*, died in a plane crash July 27, 1950, even before filing his first report from the front lines.[36] Wilson had served in World War II and had experienced military segregation and discrimination. He and his colleagues, most notably Frank Whisonant of the *Pittsburgh Courier* and James Hicks of the *Afro-American*, knew that their mission was a dangerous and difficult one. The rugged terrain and the weather extremes typical for Korea made fighting even more arduous. It also made reporting much more physically demanding and hazardous.[37]

Little had changed for black war correspondents since World War II. They received broad-spectrum news on Korea from mainstream news services, but information on black soldiers should come from their own inside sources. The largest African American weeklies sent their own war correspondents to the Korean front: "Our Negro newspapers here again demonstrate that they are a fortress in a world where white is white and black is black. To black America and the world they pledged to give the unbiased truth to that, we here at home supported by facts could be a bulwark of protection for our soldiers . . . for other wars have been used to damage and dishonor the loyalty of Negro soldiers and civilians alike."[38] Black papers wanted to fall back on black correspondents and news agencies to report on stories of the war from a black perspective, which white papers excluded. The African American press was invested in complementing what they perceived as a whitewashed presentation of the war and its soldiers. Most papers covered the early phase of the war meticulously.[39]

When the United States sent the first black soldiers to Korea in July 1950, black newspapers all across the country filled their front pages with reports on the black units.[40] The *Chicago Defender* noted on its front page that it had made "arrangements for exclusive week-to-week coverage of Negro army, navy and air corpsmen in the Korean operation."[41] These papers reported on the American military performance in general and African American soldiers' situation in particular. Black war correspondents told of the successes and often-tragic fates of the black draftees and the growing number of black volunteers.[42] They reported on their defeats and celebrated the first American victory African American soldiers achieved in late July 1950. They praised the success of integration,[43] but they also pointed to the soldiers' daily struggles with continued segregation and discrimination.[44] Most black war correspondents, like their white counterparts, had actively served in World War II and were thus familiar with the procedures of the armed forces.[45] Soldiers related to and accepted the man with the typewriter as one of their own. These correspondents linked the home front to Korea, and soldiers to home.

Newspapers assigned a special role to women at home. Soldiers wrote to newspapers asking for female pen pals to ease their feelings of "loneliness, [and] the aloneness."[46] Throughout the war, newspapers and soldiers urged women to do their share in the war effort by lovingly and emotionally supporting the young soldiers, who were willing to sacrifice their lives for their country and protect security at home. A soldier in Korea stated in a letter to the editor of the *Courier*, "To one who's away from home, one of the daily calls that we go to with great expectations is 'mail call,' hoping to hear from mom, dad, sis, wife, or sweetheart. . . . I've often wondered if the people there at home ever realized how much pleasure they can bring into our lives by just taking a few moments out of each week to write a letter?"[47] The *Afro-American* even gave instructions on what "girls back home" should write to the "lonesome lads" in Korea, going so far as to ask women at home to send their measurements and, if willing, pin-up pictures to please the young soldiers on the front.[48]

This request was not a new one. During the Second World War, pin-up girls were an essential part of wartime culture. According to historian Robert B. Westbrook, women in general, and pin-ups in particular, were "icons of male obligation . . . for which men would fight."[49] African American pin-up girls, however, were rare. A group of soldiers went so far as to ask the NAACP for help "to give us our own beauties to admire."[50] The contact between soldiers and their female pen pals at home was an asexual one that confirmed conventional gender norms.[51] Whereas African American women at home had to remain pure and respectable, soldiers could satisfy their sexual desires in fleeting encounters with Asian women.[52] According to war correspondents, this kept their will to fight alive, and its extramarital occurrence could be overlooked in times of war and in light of its alleged importance for military effectiveness. All that women on the home front could do was to help "keep our soldiers fighting and winning" by writing letters and assuring them they had not been forgotten at home.[53] There was a "feminine world beyond the battlefield" that "sustain[ed] hope of reintegration with peacetime society." When men returned home, women should help their providers and protectors transition back to this world of "civilian masculinity."[54] Ultimately, sexual relationships with women in Asia, as long as they remained in the past, confirmed the image of a virile soldier, as well as marriage, as the foundations of the American nation. The heterosexual relationships upheld traditional gender roles. Men were in control of women abroad and at home.

Black newspapers covered all black personnel in the war effort, from combat troops, to service troops, to medics, describing them with pride using heroic rhetoric.[55] Service troops were as essential as combat outfits for fighting back the "Red attack on the South."[56] Hundreds of pictures of African Americans in combat gear holding guns of all kinds, black men in control of captured enemy soldiers, black marines, most accompanied by subtitles of their gallant deeds and stalwart efforts for an American victory, splashed the front pages of black papers all across the country for months. Involved in all aspects of a war, blacks were on a dangerous mission with many casualties and not many victories, but according to the press, black soldiers fought valiantly against all odds, whether in all-black or in integrated outfits.

The reports from the war oscillated widely between celebrating all-black units, while lamenting their understandable lack of morale due to racism, and lauding the efficiency of integrated outfits. Integration and an end to second-class citizenship remained the African American community's main goal, but the reputation of black soldiers should not suffer from their path of argumentation.[57] African Americans longed for the end of segregation in the armed forces, but they were also proud of the success of all-black units. Proving one's equality in these units was essential for bolstering the demand for speedy desegregation. Even the *California Eagle*, one of the few black newspapers fully opposed to the war and African American involvement in it, commented on the valor of back soldiers.[58] Whether in a segregated or integrated outfit, black soldiers' manhood manifest in the combat record should not be questioned. Black newspapers reporting from war walked a fine line between helping and hurting their cause. Overstating the efficiency of all-black outfits affirmed segregationists, who asked why blacks longed for integration if they were so successful without it. Underlining the lack of morale argument would bolster white stereotypes in their belief in black inability and inferiority.[59] At the same time, emphasizing blacks' invigorated performance in integrated outfits could lead to whites arguing that blacks only performed well with white guidance and expertise. The reputation and honor of the black soldier mattered as much as integration itself, since it was the foundation for claiming equal rights and full citizenship. The image of black soldiers and the whole race was at stake when stories of poor performance in battle by blacks surfaced. Salvaging the allegedly stellar reputation of all-black units was as essential as arguing against the all-black unit itself.[60] The discussion over the path toward military integration heated during the course of the Korean War, and the military masculinity of black soldiers always played a crucial role in the discourse.

The content of war reports itself had changed since the Second World War. The press were considerably freer to write what they felt reflected the war's realities, as censorship remained voluntary until December 1950.[61] Whether white or black, newspapers attempted to paint a picture that was as realistic as possible. They tended to not withhold the grim reality of the war from their readership back home. The press made the utter brutality of the war and the suffering of American soldiers on the front lines visible. Explicit pictures papers published often portrayed the badly wounded young soldiers. As historian Andrew Huebner has shown, fatigue and grief became major components of stories from Korea. Soldiers freely spoke of the grievances and troubles with the enemy, but also of the deficiency and failures of American military leadership. The reports lacked the "roseate warrior image" of World War II, which according to Huebner, had already developed some "cracks" during its last phase.[62] The shocking pictures of pain and suffering notwithstanding, the articles and captions satisfied the readers' underlying need for stories of war heroes who confronted their fate and withstood the enemy valorously.[63] Despite the relatively unrestricted portrayal of soldiers' despair and the general American military failure, the press stayed true to the image of the heroic American soldier, troubled, but unwavering in his willingness to fight for his country and democracy. An article in *Time* magazine titled "The Ugly War" set out to elaborate on the "ugly story of an ugly war," but not without maintaining:

> The American effort and the American soldiers are magnificent. . . .
> They were scared at first. In some places, they abandoned positions that seasoned troops might have held. But in a land and among a people that most of them dislike, in a war that all too few of them understand and none of them want, they became strong men and good soldiers—fast. . . . I have seen boys who by rights should have

been freshmen in college transformed by a week of battle into men
wise in the terrible ways of this especially terrible war.[64]

The message was clear: despite setbacks, American soldiers rose to the challenge and grew up quickly in order to embody those concepts of American
manhood that were undoubtedly superior to those of any other people.

The press toned down the reports on the failure of American soldiers
and focused on their heroism and the actions they performed under the
extraordinary circumstances and dangers they faced in Korea. The *New
York Times* reported: "It [the balance of the war] can tell of great heroism
and many deeds on the part of all United Nations forces, and in particular
the outnumbered ground troops who are bearing the brunt of the war."[65]
The articles described soldiering with all its flaws, failures, and doubts. The
fighting, although often unsuccessful and bearing great loss, was even more
valorous considering the conditions with which they struggled. The young
age of the average soldier made the stories of their fate in Korea even more
heart wrenching. The explanations generated in the press turned American
soldiers into suffering, circumstantial victims. Press reports predominantly
remained within the confines of the construction of American superiority
in the combat field. Heroism was essentially an American character trait,
though it could, at times, also be applied to American allies. Although the
North Korean high level of training and organization was undeniable, articles emphasized the staggering number of enemy soldiers that a small number of presumably brave, but underequipped soldiers had to withstand,
rather than the enemies' actual combat capacity. The press did not shy away
from displaying the American soldiers' despondency and fear. The image
of a vulnerable, yet masculine American soldier was common. According
to Huebner, the press was caught between the iconography of World War
II that had mostly boasted of American heroism, and the human tragedy
and suffering of American soldiers in Korea.[66]

For its part, the black press also increasingly presented the downsides
and hazards involved in war.[67] A simple heroic presentation of soldiers was
no longer possible in the papers. Articles on atrocities, pictures of dead,
and fearful black soldiers could also be heroic displays of manhood. Tales
of death walks, grief, and the suffering of young men, who often had just
left school, emerged. In December 1950, *Our World* ran a story entitled
"Death in Korea" that exemplified the changing tone of war reports.[68] The
articles portrayed the problems American troops faced on the front quite

honestly. The obvious flaws in strategy and troop strength resulted in criticism of American war efforts and the nation's unpreparedness. The stories told often left the impression that the soldiers, black or white, had to fight not only the enemy and the harsh conditions in Korea, but also the military's inability to lead and prepare them for battle. Early in the war, the black and white press asked accusingly where the equipment and the much-needed replacements for the exhausted and overly strained soldiers were. They reported on starving soldiers, as the American food supply did not operate adequately.[69] Two months into the war, L. Alex Wilson noted that many reinforcements were needed to stop the enemy from advancing. He stated, "I put it mildly when I say that the 24th heartily welcomes the new recruits. Not only that outfit but every one here."[70] Wilson made clear that while all of the outfits suffered from the terrible conditions caused by a lack of soldiers and equipment, African Americans seemed to suffer disproportionately more than others.[71] The lags and failures of military leadership especially afflicted black soldiers, while discrimination and segregation further aggravated the situation.[72]

The euphemistic terminology that reduced the war to a police action was countered with these crude stories of male suffering and death. In reference to the everyday experience of soldiers—regardless of color—war correspondent Wilson stated harshly "One doesn't set up grave markers week after week over the dead bodies of American soldiers and call same 'police action.' One doesn't haul train loads of wounded men to the hospital from the front lines and call the fighting 'police action."[73] The military's unpreparedness and the severity of fighting with heavy casualties could not be ignored. Soldiers of all races suffered from fatigue and exhaustion, and were overwhelmed by an overpowering enemy. Nevertheless, war was still understood as a rite of passage to manhood. In his report on a long-drawn-out battle in September 1950, Hicks noted, "Watch those MEN come down. The MEN who had gone up there a few hours earlier as green boys."[74] The reports from the front lines focused on black units and individuals' alleged successes, and countered the general neglect or slurring of black soldiers, thus providing a foundation for the quest for integration and equality. "Interesting" stories "of courage and bravery" in which the life of the Korean enemy did not count for much, but was often a mere number to brag about, were constantly printed on the front pages of black newspapers in order to bolster African American racial pride and national belonging in times of crisis.[75]

In comparison to that of African American soldiers, the assessment of white soldiers in the mainstream press never included a racial component. White soldiers were considered to be the norm and, thus, failure was not a question of race. The press judged whites' performance on a much more personal basis, citing lack of training, poor leadership, or an overpowering and menacing enemy force to explain poor performance. Based on the alleged superiority of the white race, whiteness was not a category for evaluation and of influence.[76] This understanding of performance presented itself much differently when it came to commenting on black soldiers, which, although it occurred seldom, did occur. The reasoning in the mainstream press followed in the footsteps of many military officials, who used race and alleged racial characteristics—mostly stereotypes rooted in concepts of black inferiority—as explanations for the struggles and failures of black troops. They overtly or covertly asserted that African Americans were as a race per se, subpar, whereas failures by white troops were explained by bad training, weather conditions, and equipment.

The First Victory in Korea

At the end of 1950, an all-black unit won the first victory in the Korean War. Years later, official military histories would deny that any real fighting took place, claiming that North Koreans fled before it came to a serious exchange of fire.[77] However, when news of the first win broke, these suspicions were not yet an issue, and the African American press lauded the victorious all-black troops on all their front pages for days on end. There were clear reasons to feature the success of a segregated unit; it bolstered racial pride by stressing the male heroics of these African American men, and disputed the allegations of black soldiers' cowardice. It furthermore provided evidence for the allegiance blacks felt to the nation and its mission.[78] Black America considered the power of African American soldiers as symbols and agents in the fight against white supremacy and humiliation as overwhelming. "It [the victory] squelched any doubt that colored Americans were not first class soldiers on the field of combat. The victory made a farce of crazy-quilt American traditions of racial inferiority."[79]

The *Chicago Defender* noted the "biggest victory to date for American democracy in the Korean war, it can now be revealed, is the victory over the racial theories of some of the most important brass hats. Negro G.I.s in daring exploits . . . have stunned the white-supremacists in the military establishment."[80] The victory of the 24th Infantry Regiment at the end of July 1950 was considered proof that blacks were willing to fight for the United States. Furthermore, it seemed to indicate that African American soldiers did as well, if not better, than white soldiers, who, up to that point, seemed to have been unable to hold ground against the frequently, but wrongfully underestimated North Korean troops. The *Pittsburgh Courier* jubilantly noted that "The victory at Yechon thus became the symbol of the real strength of Uncle Sam's ground forces, and it was these Negro soldiers who made it that way. These men of the Twenty-fourth Regiment came from every sector of the United States."[81] African Americans had proved not only their combat readiness, but also their entitlement to the full rights of an American citizen and American identity. Numerous stories of African American soldiers' heroism overtly and covertly countered decades of belittling assessments of black war performance, manhood, and racial and national identity, which had ultimately been used to confirm established racial hierarchies. For a brief moment in summer 1950, the enfeebling and disempowering effects of the decades-long discriminatory experience in and outside the military seem to vanish. The reports from the front deflated common accusations of cowardice, unreliability, and the lack of dedication of black soldiers: "their prowess and manhood are the equal of any of America's sons."[82]

Not only did African American soldiers prove their equal manhood, they even exceeded that of whites by taking a hill that other troops—white troops—had been unable to hold against a large number of the enemy. These men were the first to win a victory against such poor odds, all the while carrying the additional burdens of discrimination and the humiliation of racism. White men now had to undertake tremendous efforts in order to live up to and match the successful record of African American soldiers. Moreover, Lucius C. Harper abrasively maintained that white Georgians tried to evade military service by "climbing out the back windows of the Georgia Armory." Whereas African Americans served and died valiantly, white men who otherwise decried African Americans as inferior allegedly showed their lack of manhood through cowardice, thus destroying all notions of white supremacy. Black papers depicted African Americans as displaying traits of hypermasculinity, thus clearly defeating whites in the ongoing competition over manhood.[83] The stories were meant to build racial pride, but they also fostered national belonging. The successful black soldier embodied and bestowed black (male) agency.

Celebratory reports on the presence and success of all-black troops on the front lines in the black press might seem to be in contradiction to the ultimate African American goal of integration.[84] Yet these successes were the foundation for their argumentation. The *Chicago Defender* straightforwardly stated that the victory "was an eloquent plea for full integration into American life," by taking the demand for desegregation beyond the military and into the civilian world.[85] African Americans agreed that first-class citizenship for blacks had to follow the victory of the "first-class fighters."[86] The *Afro-American* printed a letter from an African American GI in Korea who forcefully demanded that the United States provide full democracy to all Americans regardless of race, creed, or color. The letter exemplifies how deeply military service and combat performance were still linked to the advancement of the entire race on the home front. Finishing the "small police job" in Korea would be followed by the spread of democracy and equality at home. Sacrifices on the Korean front were to be rewarded.[87]

As black papers celebrated the braveness and performance of African American soldiers on the Korean front, they also underlined the possibly negative repercussions this publicity could have on the worldwide conflict with Communism. They warned that Russia could easily make a case by pointing out the very existence of segregated troops on the front. The reintroduction of Russell's idea of voluntary segregation in the military in Congress aggravated America's position even more. Harlem's Representative Adam Clayton Powell called it a "tragic backward step" that would help the "Soviet completely undermine our fighting machine and destroy, even before peace, all hope of a victory of democracy."[88] The proposed amendments would provide Soviet Russia ammunition for their fight against the United States.

"Dark peoples" inhabited the majority of the world, as well as Korea. The *Black Dispatch* raised the argument that segregated black troops, even if they were successful, would eventually "sow seeds of racial strife in Asia which need not have occurred." The paper capitalized on American politicians' and military officials' fear of feeding into Russian propaganda and offending African and Asian peoples. A *New York Amsterdam News* cartoon in October 1950 reflected on this continuance of segregation in the army (Figure 10). By maintaining a segregated force, the United States deterred these foreign peoples from joining up in the fight against the worldwide spread of communism. "A jim crow army is certainly not the best symbol of democracy and freedom. It represents repression, restriction and confinement, principles in government having nothing to do with liberty,

Figure 10. "Exposed." Cartoon, *New York Amsterdam News*, October 28, 1950, 8. Reproduced by permission of copyright holder; further reproduction prohibited without permission.

democracy and freedom. . . . The white man must make open confession regarding some of his sins before he can hope to form genuine new alliances in world society."[89]

Although blacks used the victorious segregated outfit as proof of African American fighting ability and patriotism, they considered the very existence of segregated units to be one of the war effort's most humiliating and damaging elements.[90] Black newspapers and with them civil rights activists were convinced that the United States could only successfully counter Soviet propaganda if they honored blacks and ended segregation. An underlying assumption was that the public recognition of African American successes in battle would finally improve America's standing in the world. The black soldier was an indispensable asset to the war effort and should thus be given his due acknowledgment both in and outside of the U.S. military.[91]

"U.S. Hails Tan Warriors"

U.S. troops had desperately needed a success in July 1950. Since their arrival in Korea, they had been seriously struggling with the unexpected strength of the enemy, the terrain, and the difficult supply situation. The black troops had proven that they could beat the odds.[92] For a short time, the relieved and grateful nation showered the African American community with praise. The *Defender* even printed a collage of white newspapers' front pages that hailed the African American victory in Korea. For the first time in a long time, African American soldiers made it into numerous white newspapers and magazines with favorable stories.[93] James Hicks reported on the positive effects these articles, which endorsed black soldiers' performance in the white and black press alike, had on the African American combatants in Korea. According to him, morale increased significantly with the knowledge of public appreciation.[94]

Mainstream papers often expressed their accolades in a somewhat patronizing fashion, unable to hide their surprise at the fighting power of black soldiers. Blacks had now proven their value to the nation.[95] Even Southern papers could not evade reporting the victory black soldiers had achieved, though their excitement was restrained. The *Fort Worth Star-Telegram* praised the work of African American soldiers at length and alluded to the misconception of many who had underestimated and degraded African American fighting power. Even North Koreans, the paper maintained, had "expected to find a soft spot in the American lines. They were badly fooled." Congratulating the black 24th Infantry Regiment for its "splendid work," The *North Carolinian Gastonia Gazette* reasoned that this "may help forestall Communist propaganda that the fight in Korea is between white men and colored."[96] Public praise for black soldiers on the front lines also added strength to the American side of the ideological conflict with communism. John M. Hightower, a correspondent for the Associated Press (AP), maintained that black soldiers were "helping to win more than strategic hilltops in the struggle with communism. . . . They are dramatic proof that the war to smash Red aggression in Korea is not a 'white man's war.'"[97] Allegations that Korea was a race war could be detrimental and needed to be disproved. Blacks on the front line seemed a perfect tool to do just that, providing a convenient opportunity to prove America's dedication to minority rights and entice minority groups all around the world into trusting the United States. How could a country not be trusted whose African American minority, whose racial "other," was willing—and in fact had always been willing—to fight and die for it?

Congress also recognized the exemplary performance of black soldiers at Yech'on. Their success promised a propaganda opportunity too important to forego in the Cold War ideological struggle. In the early months of the Korean War, Frances Bolton, a representative from Ohio, for instance, claimed self-reassuringly that Russian propaganda distorted the "Negro existence in America" to such an extent that it created a stereotype that was "grotesque as to be at once amusing and deplorable." The progress in race relations, especially in the armed forces, the representative maintained, had been so immense since the Civil War that there was no truth to the "propaganda from totalitarian slave states."[98] Massachusetts Democratic Representative Thomas J. Lane took it upon himself to make the case for black soldiers in the House, only three days after news had broken of their victory in Korea. The *Atlanta Daily World* reprinted his speech on its front page, as praise for African Americans in Congress was rare.[99] His speech called for an improvement of the status of blacks in the United States. The physical presence of black soldiers in combat and their victory against the odds supported the fight for integration, and provided evidence against Soviet propaganda. With the figure of the victorious black soldier, Lane underlined African American patriotism and listed the impressive record of African American soldiers as proof for their right to equality and for the immediate integration of the troops. On the other hand, he used it to rebut Soviet propaganda that had continuously made use of the racial inequality of blacks in the ideological conflict between Communism and American democracy: "Communist propaganda took it on the chin at Yechon when the Korean Reds were blasted by American Negro troops who believed not only in the United States as it is, but in the better nation that it will become when intolerance is also defeated. They fought and won for all of us. . . . Segregation is on the way out in this world, and we are in this fight, among other things, to hasten its departure."[100] In his argumentation, African

Americans had, beyond a doubt, proved their right to integration, as well as its necessity, and were able to live up to the challenge of leading the way in battle. According to Lane, the successful black soldier who was willing to sacrifice his life for a still imperfect, but rapidly improving nation, countered any allegations of his lack of patriotism. Across party lines, congressmen underlined that black soldiers on the fronts disproved the notion that the Korean War was a race war.[101]

The highest validation of African American soldiers came when President Truman congratulated the victorious black soldiers on their success in Korea. His message sent to the annual convention of the Brotherhood of Sleeping Car Porters assigned a special role to African American soldiers in the fight against communist aggression and propaganda. He called their role in the "struggle for the minds, hearts and loyalties of millions of human beings," "historic" and commended their "valorous performance . . . in Korea." Furthermore, Truman praised their "courage and skill and high morale" and used their physical presence in the war and their willingness to fight as proof of the fact that the U.S. military and society were the "most democratic in the world."[102] Truman joined the many commentators and congressmen who did not miss the opportunity to try to gain control over the damaging allegations of racial oppression by commenting on black fighters' successes.[103]

The black press understood the propaganda opportunity that the events in Korea provided the American nation bolstering its standing in the world. Nevertheless, its focus often lay on capitalizing on African Americans' war record to demand integration, as well as on the symbolic importance of blacks' status for American foreign policy.[104] It was the foundation for making their demands more urgent. Columnist Gordon B. Hancock put into words what most blacks felt: "Negroes cannot live by praise alone. The Negro wants full rights and responsibilities that should be the reward of the valour being praised. Negroes have been praised before but this praise has been accompanied with a stern determination to bar the Negro from the gates of the paradise of full-fledged citizenship, vouchsafed freely to every other group, even the enemy groups."[105] There was no way this opportunity for societal advancement would be taken away from them. The Korean War and the acclaimed black record of support and sacrifice ought finally to lead to the equality of blacks, the fulfillment of their long-standing demands, and their rightful entitlements. The link between combat performance and the advancement of the entire race on the home front remained strong. That is, African Americans thought, or at least hoped that this was the case. The victory at Yech'on was great, both for the military and especially for the nation in its war against what was understood to be the communist plan to spread across the world. The black soldier had proven himself beyond any doubt. Nevertheless, many warned that the positive record of an all-black unit could hamper integration in the military. A reader of the *Afro-American* expressed his reluctance to trust whites who "play[ed] up the exploits of 'colored' troops, who upon their return to the States no doubt will be accorded the same treatment they have been receiving all the time."[106] Opponents of integration could use the events to argue that segregation affected neither the black soldier nor his performance negatively. Abolishment of segregation would therefore not be necessary.

Integration was not a foregone conclusion. The *Dallas News*, for instance, followed a strategy of benevolent paternalism. Commenting on the success of the all-black outfit, the paper underlined the frequent advantages of segregation for blacks and their social recognition: "If it had been a mixed outfit, the Negroes in it would not have got the credit. But because it was a Negro division the credit goes to their race. This does not prove that segregation is always right. But it does suggest that there are sometimes advantages to the Negro race in working (and fighting) alongside picked men of their own color."[107]

These arguments proved harder to contest than any open racial slur and defamation. The record of the 24th Infantry Regiment could be used as grounds for the continuation of military segregation. However, for the black press or the NAACP, it was essential that the success of segregated units not be interpreted as proof of segregation's effectiveness and reason for its continuance.[108] Once again, black troops had proven their equal value; integration and full civil rights had to follow.

White segregationists still fought this possible move toward integration relentlessly. Georgia senator Richard B. Russell received a considerable amount of mail from his constituents who overwhelmingly and viciously protested the armed forces' move toward integration and equality. Their disgust over white soldiers serving with African Americans, let alone under their command, was deep-seated. Nothing, most argued, could force white men to give up their integrity and manhood by serving with blacks whom they considered inherently inferior. The integration of "negroes" and whites, they predicted, was destined to end in a military defeat in the "present crisis" in Korea. The black soldier allegedly embodied "cowardice and unfitness" that would be detrimental for the whole nation if trying to "mend their uncivilized, barbaric ways" by forcing them to fight with allegedly superior whites.[109] A reservist from Georgia argued that serving in a mixed outfit would lower the white soldiers' fighting ability and willingness to fight. He warned that rebellion and resistance would ensue "even though our country is passing through dark days." White Southerners could simply not accept cohabiting and serving with blacks.[110] Another correspondent stated that serving with "half savage worthless niggers" was a "humiliating situation" that would most likely cause "mental breakdowns" among white servicemen. Most writers covertly established a link between the serious troubles the American troops faced in Korea and forced integration. Because the "burden of victory" lay with whites who could not fight valorously when forced to fight together with blacks, the military situation in Korea would deteriorate further.[111]

In their uncompromising attempt to uphold segregation and white supremacy within and outside the military, white supremacists had to rely on contradictory strands of argumentation. They temporarily praised the successful performance of all-black units, often alleging that blacks had no racial pride if they pursued integration. Moreover, they argued that black soldier's victories in Korea justified and necessitated the continuance of segregation. Concurrently, white supremacists continued to deny blacks any fighting ability in order to uphold the idea of white superiority and supremacy. They resorted to discrediting African American soldiers on a larger scale. Instead of simply misusing the acclaimed record of black soldiers to argue for segregation, reactionary responses were also marked by a return to the neglect and even "smearing" of African American soldiers in the mainstream press that had prevailed in the past.

Reviving the "Double V" Campaign

While African American soldiers risked their lives on the Korean front lines in still mostly segregated outfits, black newspapers and civil rights leaders fought to improve the long-term opportunities of blacks on the home front. Hoping that black soldiers' presence on the battlefields of Korea would help in the fight against discrimination and segregation at home, which had been experiencing a renewed increase, they revived the World War II "Double V" campaign, which called for the defeat of the enemy abroad and at home.

Advances at home became as important as those on the Korean front. For most African Americans, the war and the fight for civil rights were two sides of the same coin. The war in Korea was a reason to push more fervently for change, economic justice, and upward mobility. In his column "Seeing and Saying," which was syndicated nationwide, William A. Fowlkes stated, "minority Americans today find themselves again forced to fight for victory at home and abroad." He maintained that, in their "two-front battle," blacks had to fight "legal, state and national demagogues" and, all the while battling "Red propaganda which uses pictures of lynched and segregated Negroes saying 'this is the way they do it in America—this is their way of life, come over with us and we will give you land and freedom.'"[112] Columnist Hancock called on his readers and the whole nation to end the hypocrisy in race relations. For the sake of the oppressed, and the nation as a whole, the war should be seen not as a reason to silence the protest, but rather to expand it. "War must not muffle the voice that tells the nation of its sins."[113] The public scolding of Americans' faults and a fervent call for change were implicit in African American commentaries on the war that went beyond purely accommodationist rhetoric.

The presence of black soldiers on the front and serious restrictions on African Americans' jobs in the armed forces in Korea and at home made the hypocrisy of American democracy all the more striking. African Americans openly reflected on how the U.S. government could so easily send black soldiers as cannon fodder to the Korean front, when white employers were allowed to refuse them work based on color and race. The fact that African American soldiers fought in Korea, but lacked fair employment in the United States, was the Achilles heel of American democracy.[114] To blacks, military service in war should clearly result in rewards in the society they protected, but civilian life still did not provide all people regardless of race, creed, or color, the right to work.[115]

Early in the war, the argumentation that a lack of civil rights was detrimental to the war effort became an article of faith for many African American activists, especially labor leaders like A. Philip Randolph, Roy Wilkins of the NAACP, Lester Granger of the NUL, and their followers.[116] They argued that, the "war in Korea serves to highlight the necessity for equality in employment of opportunity for minorities in our democracy."[117] The campaign for democracy "would be much easier, and much more productive if the American government, here and now, took a forthright stand against racial and religious discrimination in employment practices."[118]

Winning over the minds of the people all around the world was as essential as winning the military conflict and would only speed up the progress of the war. Furthermore, they predicted that America's curtailed use of manpower would seriously hamper the war effort and limit morale in the trenches of Korea, and thus, on the home front.

Civil rights activists were well aware of the possibly powerful effects of using an international crisis for the expansion of civil rights and fair employment, something which they were explicitly willing to do. They surely hoped to benefit domestically from their renewed "Double V Campaign."[119] Korea and the international image of the United States were a constant point of reference in African Americans' struggle for a permanent implementation of the courage and skill and high moral FEPC, which Roosevelt had first passed during World War II, but whose efficiency had dwindled and eventually expired. The increased public exposure of America's racial flaws through the Korean War, and the presence of still segregated troops on the front who were ultimately fighting for a racially oppressive and exclusive American democracy, fired up and rhetorically informed the African American demands for a permanent and federal legislation to guarantee equality in employment.

The reinstatement of the FEPC had been under consideration since the end of World War II. In early 1950, a conglomeration of southern Democrats and Republicans continuously filibustered the bill in the Senate. Senator Russell, who still tried to block all changes in race relations and equality in both the civilian and military realm, headed this opposition. In the Senate in May 1950, he spoke out against the pending bill, arguing that a federal FEPC would enhance communist leanings among citizens in the United States who would then plan to subvert the nation and its social foundation with civil rights legislation. His anticommunist stance was effective in discrediting the civil rights bill among numerous conservative congressmen.[120]

Civil rights activists planned to destabilize Russell's commanding argument; the onset of the Korean War and the subsequent manpower needed to fight it seemed a valuable, albeit terrible, opportunity to do so.[121] On July 9, 1950, one day before the Senate decision on the FEPC, Walter White wired Russell, urging him to drop his filibuster and finally allow the much-needed use of full manpower in a time of national and international crisis. The Korean conflict, White reasoned, ought to quickly lead to "justice and equal rights for all" on the home front. It would not only allow full and efficient use of America's manpower, but would boost the morale "of every serviceman and industrial worker." Walter White claimed that calling an end to the stall of the FEPC would be an "expression of patriotism" and "a major contribution not only to national unity but also to national well-being and national productivity in a period of grave crisis."[122] A continued filibuster of the FEPC, however, represented a "disastrous luxury" that would "further jeopardize America's fate in Korea."[123] Nobody seriously expected Russell to submit to White's demands. As steadfast white suprem-acists, Russell and his followers would not swerve from their reactionary politics even in times of crisis. Nevertheless, as maintained by the *Courier*, White's attempts at communication were a "clever" propaganda device to embarrass "Southern solons" in the fight for civil rights and fair employ-ment, and rally more African Americans to the vote.[124]

On July 10, 1950, immediately following the onset of the American intervention in Korea, Senate Majority Leader Scott Lucas from Illinois spoke in favor of the FEPC bill, filing a petition to cloture.[125] Like African American advocates, he drew a clear link between the success of the fight in Korea and the passage of the FEPC in the American Senate. Lucas argued that the war in Korea made the passage of an FEPC necessary, as the United States needed to "prove itself to men of all races and creeds who are fighting and dying in this far off land." Racial advancement would strengthen America's standing among all peoples, especially among those of different racial backgrounds who were fundamentally important in the fight against worldwide communism. Despite Lucas's argumenta-tion and African American lobbying, the FEPC did not manage to pass the Senate vote, but was rejected to limit the time of its discussion and break the Southern filibuster.[126]

Following the FEPC defeat in the Senate, the *Afro-American* warned gloomily that its failure would feed the growth of Communism, damage American prestige, and cost "possibly more American lives" in Korea where "Uncle Sam finds himself out on a limb alone."[127]African Americans con-sidered a federal FEPC to be an absolute necessity in the wake of a new war and to bolster national unity.[128] In a political cartoon in the *Afro-American* (Figure 11), a broken oar symbolized the self-destructiveness of American domestic policy. Languishing in the dangerous waters of the Korean crisis, the United States had deprived itself of the chance to achieve full manpower use by voting against the federal FEPC. This was not only considered detri-mental in regards to manpower on the war front however, as blacks were excluded from fair employment and equality at the workplace, the move

Figure 11. "That Broken Oar Really Slows Him Down." Cartoon, *Afro-American*, July 22, 1950, 4. Reproduced by permission of copyright holder; further reproduction prohibited without permission.

also cost the nation the use of its full manpower resources for wartime preparation at home. Furthermore, white prejudice and privilege barred blacks from training for more skilled jobs, which led to manpower shortages in specialized areas much needed for the war effort.[129] African Americans clearly understood the FEPC to be a domestic issue of racial equality with detrimental repercussions for the United States on an international level. In July 1950, Alice Dunnigan, the first black female White House correspondent, prognosticated solemnly that the defeat of the FEPC

AN FEPC WOULD HALT THIS SUBVERSIVE ACT

Figure 12. "An FEPC Would Halt This Subversive Act." Cartoon, *Afro-American*, October 21, 1950, 4. Reproduced by permission of copyright holder; further reproduction prohibited without permission.

would be "a grave injury to U.S. prestige" in the world and symbolized a lack of national unity that could be detrimental to the outcome of the war.[130]

A later cartoon in the *Afro-American* (Figure 12) represented this damaging exclusion and segregation of "Negro manpower." In the cartoon, a well-prepared African American worker is ostracized from a job of preparing and equipping the nation in an already ongoing war. Similar to the argumentation in Randolph's civil disobedience campaign in 1948, the act of treason the cartoon alluded to was not the black call for equality or the full use of black manpower, but the killing of the FEPC and the halting of social change. The greater good of the nation was not the reactionaries' priority, but rather the futile continuance of racial segregation.

Walter White, A. Philip Randolph, and Lester Granger continued to lobby the president for an FEPC. Activists kept on linking the Korean War and its special requirements to the necessity of fair and equal employment of African Americans and other minorities in American plants and industries. The campaign for the FEPC, however, also had the tendency to reveal the increasing fragmentation and conflicts of interest and competences within the civil rights movement. Antagonisms reappeared. Whereas White and Randolph joined forces to talk to W. Stuart Symington, the National Security Resources Board chairman, about a permanent FEPC and fair employment in wartime, Granger did the same on his own. White and Randolph sent a short message to Truman, requesting immediate action on behalf of African Americans' labor opportunities. Granger's six-page outline followed only a day later. Since the end of the civil disobedience campaign, the difficult relationship between Granger and Randolph in particular had not been resolved but had instead further deteriorated. Despite their shared interest in an FEPC and equal inclusion of blacks in wartime production, the two sides were apparently unable to find common ground.[131]

Korea and white opposition to federal legislation enhanced blacks' fight for a permanent FEPC. For them, a seemingly national issue became an internationally meaningful weapon against oppression and the exclusion of blacks. Black activists hoped that the physical presence of black soldiers on the Korean front could act as a powerful weapon and indicator for the necessity of the legislation. Black columnist William Gordon raised the question of how it could be possible that white reactionaries celebrated the defeat of the FEPC, when black soldiers won the first victory in the war in Korea and thus ought to be celebrated and rewarded. Comparing this circumstance to blacks' willingness to fight despite their underprivileged position in American society and their "unselfish contribution for the preservation of democracy [that] will go down in the annuals of history completely unchallenged," Gordon claimed that whites who opposed the FEPC were "far less democratic and loyal than the very least among us who claims citizenship rights in America." He thereby turned around the Southern argument that activists for racial equality undermined the much needed national unity and military effort.[132] The black war record and military service in Korea became the ultimate tool to pressure for fairness and equality in the job market at home, and the FEPC became an international issue for its propaganda value in the struggle for the hearts and minds of minorities around the world. Despite serious setbacks for the civil rights movement in the fight for equality in employment, black activists continued to demand an FEPC and the end of discrimination and segregation in the workforce.

The link between civil rights on the domestic front and the international crisis in Korea underlined the necessity for change and the advancement of racial equality. Walter White claimed that thousands of American boys were being or would be killed in Korea because of the "flaming resentment of non-white peoples all over the world against racial bigotry here in the United States and in places like Asia and Africa. Bloody chickens are coming home to roost on the stars and stripes."[133] The insinuation of a race war against the United States amidst the communist threat was clear. Southern resistance to the FEPC, he claimed, was at the center of the self-induced crisis of trust and support. The combination of the American upholding of colonialism abroad and the domestic racial oppression of African Americans had, and would continue to have, major repercussions for America's position in the world and the Korean crises. Only Pakistan and India's support of the UN mission had "minimize[ed] the racial angle in the present imbroglio."[134] The blame for the war was with reactionary Southerners who frequently constructed themselves as guardians of American democracy and its values, which they understood as inherently Southern. It is curious that White refrained from mentioning anticommunism in his menacing vision of the future of the United States. Statements like these were typically accompanied by a anticommunist tirade to fend off allegations of communist sympathizing. It seems the situation in Korea was already too grave and African American soldiers too deeply involved in the actual fighting.

Political positions and decisions on civil rights were now judged with respect to "such critical days America faced when the war began."[135] Southern Democrats and their Republican supporters were not the only ones who were directly and publicly confronted with the threat of an intensification and expansion of the Korean War if long-overdue civil rights programs were not implemented. Randolph, other civil rights activists, and large parts of the press grew increasingly convinced that Truman was dragging his feet on the FEPC instead of simply authorizing another executive order to counter Russian propaganda.[136] In search of an effective strategy to force the passage of the FEPC, columnist M. Moran Weston of the *New York Amsterdam News* suggested that Randolph organize and this time execute a march on Washington similar to the one organized in 1941 in response to President Roosevelt's reluctance to enforce fair employment to fill the nation's manpower needs. In his reasoning, the FEPC would have such a positive effect on the war effort—or even eventually lead to the end of the Korean War—that "one less division would be needed in Korea if the right to work were given everybody here at home. One wise guy put it this way: a Negro soldier is safer in Korea than in Georgia, or Alabama or Mississippi or Washington, D.C."[137] In December 1950, Wilkins once again voiced doubts over President Truman's civil rights program despite his seeming personal investment in civil rights. Wilkins was upset that two Southerners received high-ranking positions in the administration.[138]

Many African Americans questioned how Truman could not honor the valiant service of blacks in Korea by issuing an executive order on the FEPC. Their service on the Korean front, which was so desperately needed, ought to be rewarded on the home front by providing the entire African American (male) community with fair and equal employment. Deeply suspicious of Truman's civil rights agenda which he called a "fraud," the conservative commentator Joseph Bibb noted that "not even the gallantly [sic] and hero- ics of colored fighters in Korea have moved the Democratic administration to fulfill its solemn pledges made to America's colored citizens . . . The President promised to lead the fight against segregation and discrimination. . . . He has done nothing but fumble and fidget around."[139] The American Council on Human Rights (ACHR), an organization that had been estab- lished by all-black fraternities and sororities in 1946,[140] argued that it was only "simple justice" that black soldiers' "fathers and brothers at home [are] permitted to help produce the planes and guns they use so effec- tively." The African American soldier and his willingness to fight and die for the United States were seen as a powerful element in bringing about social change on the home front. Pointing to a guilty conscience, African Americans turned fair employment regulations not only into a question of efficiency, war preparedness, and national security, but also into a question of morality.[141] The black soldier's unwavering loyalty to his country and oftentimes his injuries or even death should neither be in vain nor unrecog- nized and uncompensated for. A group of activists in Wisconsin demanded the issuance of a wartime FEPC under the same premise. They believed that the federal government should provide blacks at home with the opportunity to serve in plants and industries, but more important, they demanded that black soldiers be able to come back home "to jobs and not be forced to walk the streets hungry, looking for work which they will be denied because of the color of their skin."[142]

In a later article, the *Chicago Defender* expressed the frustration with Truman that many blacks felt. The paper blatantly criticized Truman for being willing to offend Republicans and Southerners when rightfully ousting General MacArthur, yet seemingly unwilling to upset opponents when it came to civil rights and the FEPC. In light of African American soldiers' heroism on the Korean War front, Truman should have declared "D-Day on racial discrimination in defense employment. It would have been an additional assurance to all Jesse Browns who willingly risk their lives in the defense of democracy. It would have crowned Lt. Hudner's bravery in a manner befitting his sacrificial efforts to save a comrade and a brother."[143] Military service in Korea proved African American eligibility for equality in employment. Combat in war was still considered the ultimate ticket to equality, which politicians could hardly deny. The evocation of male camaraderie and sacrifice was a powerful sign for the success of racial integration that should and could be transferred to the civilian world.

Truman's reluctance to rise to the occasion and pass an insurmountable executive order in wartime led African American civil rights leaders to push more vehemently than before for a meeting with the president in January 1951. In light of the troubled course of the war in Korea, it seemed even more important than during World War II to ensure the full use of manpower.[144] The group of black activists meeting with the president wanted "to discuss certain policies of our government to adopt in this war crisis which we consider of vast and vital importance to the unity and strength of the nation." They argued assertively that not many appointments the president had scheduled were "as important to the national security and unity of our country as the requested conference for Negro leaders."[145] In February 1951, the NAACP's *The Crisis* demanded not only an executive order that instituted fair employment, but "federal fair employment legislation with teeth in it." The editorial assured its readers that minorities could not give their best for the nation and its national emergency efforts if they were not treated equally and were "confined to the unskilled categories" of labor. The article insinuated that minority workers would be as greatly affected by "low morale" as black soldiers if segregation and discrimination continued.[146] The warning that the war effort might further sputter if minorities were not treated according to the "preachments" of democracy and freedom was clearly implied. Black frustration and impatience with the community's progress in and due to the war were tangible.

On February 2, 1951, President Truman issued Executive Order 10210 declaring that "there shall be no discrimination in any act performed hereunder against any person on the ground of race, creed, color or national origin, and all contracts hereunder shall contain a provision that the contractor and any subcontractors thereunder shall not so discriminate."[147] As Order 10210 did not include an enforcement clause, it was ultimately "meaningless"[148] and thus African Americans protested. In view of the upcoming election and the growing importance of the black vote, Randolph and other civil rights activists, among them Mary McLeod Bethune, managed to garner a meeting with the president. On February 28, 1951, they again turned the Korean War into a platform for social change and civil rights. In their eyes, the international crisis forbade any leniency when it came to issues that hampered national unity, which was so decisive for the success of the mission on and off the battlefield. They clearly asserted that blacks were willing to "play, in this crisis, our full role as American citizens, unhampered and unfettered by those forces which weaken our democracy in the eyes of the world and which all too frequently give our enemies a justifiable reason to spread dangerous propaganda against us." They pointed out that national unity, security, and war preparedness were not endangered by claims to civil rights and racial equality as white segregationists argued; rather, white reactionaries themselves, who prevented the maximization of the black workforce, constantly endangered the war effort. The nation, black activists argued, needed to be making "fullest use of the services of the Negro citizens in this hour of national emergency" in order to win the war and have an effective tool against communism, as well as to win over Asians and Africans, who were increasingly doubtful of the sincerity of white Americans.[149] The defense needs were too pressing for the United States to take any chances. A year into the war, the situation looked bleak, as did the image of the American nation among peoples of color around the world. The precarious situation in Korea required that the United States gain all the support it possibly could and emphasized the necessity to not only "talk" about, but also "practice" democracy.[150]

As had been the case in all previous wars, this hypocritical discrepancy wore on black morale. The events developing on the home front often strained African Americans' willingness to fight. Not only did the demeaning representation of black soldiers, Southern filibusters, or Truman's reluctance to pass an executive order for a federal FEPC have negative effects on the soldiers, news of racial violence at home regularly reached the black soldiers on the Korean front.[151] After a white mob attacked a black veteran and his family for moving into a white neighborhood in Cicero, Illinois, a black soldier writing from Korea warned it would be impossible to prove that America's "form of government is the best for them [peoples in Asia and Africa] when American citizens participate in such riots." The riots had a "deadlier effect on my morale and on (that of) hundreds of other colored Americans than any Communist bullets."[152]

A Mixed Army

Although black soldiers achieved the first victory in Yech'on, the situation of the UN troops in Korea remained unstable. American troops and their allies continued to struggle in Korea's rugged terrain against the North Korean fighting ability and high stamina. In early September 1950, the loss of Battle Mountain, a hill the opposing sides had long fought over, made the front pages. North Korean troops had broken through American lines. All units on the battlefront were struggling and the North Korean troops again proved superior to Americans, white and black alike.[1] Yet it was, once more, black soldiers who came under particular scrutiny and were publicly blamed for general failures and the commanding officers' weak strategy. With the retreat from Battle Mountain, questions whether blacks made good enough soldiers to fight reemerged.[2] With every negative report, the prospect that the recognition of black soldiers' valiant military service would finally help expand civil rights of African Americans faded.

The army contemplated breaking up the famed all-black 24th Infantry Regiment following black soldiers' allegedly abysmal failure, and even considered converting it from a combat to a labor unit.[3] This possible downgrade and exclusion from combat was considered an "embarrassment" to black soldiers.[4] The change would have meant that "the right to fight" of African Americans in the most renowned all-black outfit, a right for which they had struggled for so long, would be renounced. The *Pittsburgh Courier*, among many others, read it as an "attempt afoot to discredit the marvelous fighting record compiled by the unit during the forty-five terrifying, bloody days of bitter battle."[5] The charges against black soldiers and their performance in the defense of their positions at Battle Mountain were grave: according to many army reports and the white press, African American soldiers ran from the scene, froze, and generally did not act like soldiers, like real men. Major General William Kean, commander of the 25th Infantry Division, contended that the 24th Infantry Regiment, the African American community's pride and joy, had proved itself to be "untrustworthy and incapable of carrying out mission expected of an infantry regiment" and ultimately jeopardized the United States War effort in Korea.[6] Assessments like these often shaped white ideas of black performance.[7]

The African American press felt obliged to forcefully counter these allegations, and told a different story of combat on Battle Mountain. Numerous articles and editorials contested that the all-black unit had fled from the enemy. No doubt, black outfits had shown serious weaknesses, a fact most commentators did not deny,[8] but it was the way military leaders and the press represented blacks' troubles that incensed black commentators the most. An editorial in the *Courier* maintained that while black troops were publicly criticized for allegedly "bugging out," the same move was referred to as a regular "retreat" when it involved whites. War correspondent Frank Whisonant maintained that white troops' inability to hold off the North Korean troops was an enemy "infiltration," while in the case of blacks it was a "breakthrough," borne out of weakness and lack of effort on the part of black soldiers. African American soldiers suspected that they were intentionally left undermanned and underequipped for the sake of putting them under strain and blaming them for military failures.[9] Indeed, few black commentators failed to notice this and argued that black soldiers were thus blamed for white officers' inefficiency and fear in battle. This treatment, they claimed, undermined the morale of black soldiers and weakened their dedication to the cause of the war.[10] For many African Americans, this made blacks a scapegoat for failure, a setup that discredited all-black units in light of their previous success, which, they believed, had unmistakably proved their equality and was grounds enough for integration and full citizenship. Many whites, on the other hand, seemed to be willing to go to great lengths to prevent integration by demeaning blacks and attempting "to cover up their [own] weaknesses."[11] Blacks suspected that the prevention of integration was as much an aim of such criticism as was the dissolution of black combat outfits whose solid war record could most effectively raise doubts over white superiority and the rightfulness of white supremacy.

Three months into the war, the outlook of UN troops under American leadership became more promising. On September 15, 1950, UN troops landed at Inchon in an amphibious counterattack devised by General Mac-Arthur. Their updated strategy and increased military clout paid off. The UN forces managed to push back North Korean troops and, after crossing the 38th parallel, made their way deep into North Korean territory. After a string of victories, an overall UN triumph over North Korea seemed imminent in early November 1950. MacArthur boldly predicted that the troops would be home by Christmas that year. Korea, he claimed, would be united under Western auspices and peace reestablished. While American troops steadily progressed, pushing back North Korean troops, reports on the rising number of courts-martial against black soldiers for misbehavior in battle swept the United States. These punishments reaffirmed the deeply ingrained stereotypes of black cowardice and unreliability that continuously undermined black soldiers' standing. The acclaimed bravery of black men and the patriotism of the entire race came into question, as negative reports on black soldiers, their performance in combat, and subsequent courts-martial, which the *Courier* called a "GI smear" and "propaganda for Negro-phobes," surfaced.[12]

Gilbert's Case

No other case stirred as much interest and turmoil in the African American community as the case of lieutenant Leon A. Gilbert, in charge of Company A in the 24th Infantry Regiment.[13] Gilbert was thirty-two years old when he was sentenced to death in a swift court-martial on the Korean front lines. He had refused to lead a group of black soldiers into a most likely futile mission into combat on July 31, 1950, and thus failed to follow the orders of his superiors. Only days after the first victory of the all-black unit of which Gilbert was a member, his commanding officer reported that the lieutenant had "refused to return to his post during the fighting, explaining that he had 'a wife and children to consider.'"[14] During the court-martial hearing, the superior officer claimed that Gilbert had stated that "he was scared" and would therefore not follow the official order. These widely reported allegations of cowardice and disobedience fed off and seemed to confirm long-standing stereotypes of the black American soldier and his supposedly inferior fighting ability, which in turn put his manhood and claim to full civil rights into question. Because of the essential role the figure of the black soldier had maintained, many blacks felt that the African

American community as a whole was on trial. His fate, blacks feared, seriously damaged "the social prestige which Negro soldiers and the Negro people as a whole have earned through generations of earnest plodding on American soil."[15]

All in all, a disproportionate number of blacks were court-martialed. According to an NAACP investigation, only two white soldiers were punished, while thirty of the thirty-two African Americans charged received sentences, ranging from life in prison to five or twenty years of hard labor.[16] Punishments for black soldiers in general proved unusually harsh, especially in comparison to sentences for similar crimes committed by white soldiers. The softest court-martial sentence for an African American soldier was five years, which was simultaneously the longest sentence for any white soldier who had committed comparable offenses in Korea.[17] This asymmetry left the African American community fuming over the apparent race prejudice of the army's court-martial system. Even African American commentators, who believed that Gilbert deserved punishment for his alleged disobedience, argued that he was singled out for his action because he was black.[18]

Blacks in battle seemed to be well aware of the dangers that courts-martial could present to them. This knowledge prompted them to take control of their fate. In his memoirs, Charles M. Bussey, a Tuskegee airman during World War II, recalled an incident in Korea in which a black soldier in his unit shot an elderly Korean civilian. As the perpetrator's commander, Bussey was obliged to report the event to his superiors, which would have led to a court-martial. However, Bussey consciously decided against reporting the incident, fearing an unfair trial due to the soldier's race. "Duty demanded that I do what was legally, morally, and religiously right, but I could see the press and the holier-than-thou rear-echelon officers browbeating another 'nigrah soljuh' and smearing this crime on every other Negro in the theatre of operations."[19] Bussey feared a collective indictment and condemnation of black soldiers, a development familiar to many blacks. One black man's crime would become indicative of an inherent character trait that was applied to the entire race. The prejudiced justice system in and outside the armed forces usually aggravated the prospects of the accused black soldier, with repercussions for the whole black community.[20] The incident is testament to the inherently difficult struggle for control and power in a system of white dominance.

The courts-martial of Gilbert and his fellow soldiers received a great deal of coverage in the press. Indeed, blacks could get the impression that courts-martial of blacks were almost the only reports on African Americans in Korea that managed to make it into white newspapers, an indication that blacks were unfairly singled out not only by the armed forces, but by the press as well. Nevertheless, for many white commentators, the reasons for Gilbert's failure to obey and subsequent sentence were simple and unrelated to race. Most mainstream papers argued that Gilbert had "cracked up," and was mentally incapable to fight or think properly. They highlighted this mental instability as reason for his alleged disobedience and hardly ever raised the question whether his race or racism played a role in this conviction or the large number of blacks being court-martialed in general.[21] The *Washington Post* was an exception, and introduced race to the discussion. Ultimately, however, the paper made unmistakably clear that neither the court-martial proceedings nor the sentence had anything to do with race, claiming that such allegations were made by "certain elements, abetted by the Communists."[22] Most white papers considered death too harsh a punishment in this case, especially when compared to previous capital punishment verdicts in court-martial cases. In spite of their sympathy for Gilbert, however, they mostly advocated that the military had to safeguard discipline to be able to operate successfully.[23]

As Gilbert's case captivated the minds of the public and the front and editorial pages of the black press, African Americans tried to find explanations for circumstances that might have led to a court-martial. They hoped to clear the court-martialed soldiers of their alleged crimes and, by extension, free the whole race from accusations of cowardice. Citizens from all across the nation flooded President Truman with letters protesting Gilbert's sentence. Many were convinced that his case was a "frame-up" that had more to do with the color of his skin than his alleged misconduct.[24] One letter claimed that, "Mr. Gilberts' was delt [sic] the same kind of justice dealt out to a Negro in the South."[25] Black journalists developed their own theories as to why African Americans were court-martialed so frequently in the army. For them, Gilbert's case epitomized the persistence of racial bias and white supremacy and ultimately boiled down to the white need to keep African American men in a subordinate position in military and society.

According to black papers, a "sudden change" had occurred in the assessment of the 24th Infantry Regiment, which had not all too long ago been highly acclaimed by the general public. For such papers, this suggested a deliberate persecution of black soldiers in Korea. Containing emotional stories of male pride and honor lost in the midst of army racism and

Are We to Believe His Crime Greater Than Theirs?

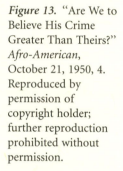

Figure 13. "Are We to Believe His Crime Greater Than Theirs?" *Afro-American,* October 21, 1950, 4. Reproduced by permission of copyright holder; further reproduction prohibited without permission.

discrimination, the *New York Amsterdam News* purported that the "ARMY VICTIMIZES TAN GI'S."[26] Blacks suspected that the military, in a desperate attempt to explain the generally poor performance of most troops in Korea, blamed failures on blacks by invoking a connection between cowardice and race.[27] A cartoon in the *Afro-American* in October 1950 (Figure 13) showed MacArthur watching a group of "Japanese war criminals" leaving prison, whereas Lt. Gilbert remains locked up in the neighboring cell. A black raven asks, "Why not open the other one too?" The cartoon relied on racial stereotyping by juxtaposing the "good" African American against the "bad" racial other who was drawn as caricaturized Asians reminiscent of World War II propaganda posters. The cartoon alleged that the United States was willing to free Japanese sentenced for crimes against humanity, whereas a racist system confined an innocent African American to prison. For most blacks there was no doubt that a racist system had brought about the harsh sentence. In an interview, Gilbert supported this assessment and placed blame on the white officers who, he alleged, used black soldiers as scapegoats "for their mistakes."[28] African Americans suspected that a vendetta against black soldiers and blacks' fight for civil rights manifested itself in the court-martial. Moreover, according to *Afro-American* and many others, the army in "its resistance to full integration" had been "making an issue of the valor of colored troops in an attempt to smear them as unworthy."[29]

Amid all allegations and debates, the black press helped Gilbert invoke a masculinist rhetoric in his defense. Initially not altogether different from the white press in its assessment of the case, the black press explained his disobedience by citing his troubled mental state. Gilbert himself claimed that, although he had tried, he was unable to go into battle. In a letter to his father reprinted in various black newspapers Gilbert wrote: "Dad, I told him [his superior] I would go, and I meant to with all my heart but when I tried to move, I couldn't, and I began to shake all over, uncontrollably." He initially disclosed having suffered a mental breakdown.[30] The mental breakdown argument was increasingly complemented, at times even fully replaced, with one of heroic resistance against the poor and deadly decisions of white superiors. In the following months, it became more and more important to the black press and Gilbert himself to paint a virile picture of him in order to counter explanations of mental instability and weakness—traits traditionally perceived as unmanly. Newspapers quoted Gilbert widely in October 1950 as stating that "he did not refuse to obey the order given to him by Colonel White. '. . . I am not a coward, and I was not afraid at the time. I would walk back to combat now if they would let me.'"[31] In the revised version of events, Gilbert evolved into a war hero manhandled by white prejudices, participating in a war fought not for his own freedom but for that of another people.

Similar to A. Philip Randolph's civil disobedience rhetoric, Gilbert's supporters tried to fend off all probable allegations of cowardice and lack of manhood by creating a new concept of the black man, whose masculinity was based on the open defiance of oppressive rules. Fulfilling all expectations of a respectable middle-class persona, Gilbert was happily married and soon to be a father of three. More importantly, he was a World War II veteran with a spotless record who reenlisted before the Korean War had broken out. In the African American press and in his own testimonies, Gilbert constructed himself as a heroic and fearless soldier protective of his family and his unit. His parents, his wife, and his two children functioned as important agents in the attempts to alter his fate and rectify his image. Not only did they speak of his courage in his long and successful military career, but they also affirmed his stable background and dedication to his family, that in turn fulfilled a white middle-class ideal of the male protector and provider of his family and his nation.[32]

The discourse on masculinity that underlined the unfairness of the trial and the alleged culprit's valorous endurance went hand in hand with and often even overshadowed emotional pleas for help and calls for Gilbert's pardon. Following this interpretation, articles pointed out that Gilbert was "not afraid to die," rather he now fought for his good name, his reinstatement in the armed forces, and all blacks.[33] In general, the story now told was overwhelmingly one of resistance against the questionable and deadly decisions of white commanding officers who sent their units on fatal and futile missions. Moreover, they put Gilbert and his comrades on trial under the worst and most unjust circumstances while putting the blame for their failures and deficiencies on black soldiers. He and his penalized comrades functioned as figures around which the African American community could rally in their continuing struggle to establish a "raceless democracy."[34]

Many of the court-martialed soldiers contacted the NAACP for help in getting their sentences revoked. The NAACP made the legal defense of these convicted black soldiers its top priority. Amid the mounting pressure, President Truman commuted Gilbert's sentence from death to twenty years hard labor in November 1950.[35] Nevertheless, the NAACP did not stop its investigation, but planned to send Thurgood Marshall to Korea. Marshall was head of the NAACP legal department[36] and was already working on *Brown v. Board of Education of Topeka*, the lawsuit that would change America's school system. The stakes were high, especially in consideration of the national and international significance of the allegations against both black soldiers and the army itself. The *Courier* described Marshall's mission as "what may well be the most difficult assignment in his distinguished career."[37] Marshall himself called it "the most important job I have done," as he went against the "masters at obfuscation" to save court-martialed soldiers and clear their names.[38] His work in Korea prepared him well for the *Brown* case.

MacArthur initially refused to allow a black lawyer to investigate the army and its court-martial system, a move many blacks understood as "an almost obvious slap at Negro servicemen."[39] Only after immense pressure from the NAACP, which warned that a denial of access to the court-martialed soldiers would feed "inevitable communist propaganda throughout Asia," did MacArthur allow Marshall to probe the cases and talk with the defendants, their superiors, and him. In a telegram from his headquarters in Japan, MacArthur emphatically maintained that all soldiers in the army, black or white, were treated and tried equally. "No evidence at this headquarters of injustices alleged . . . no slightest bias in this command as every soldier is measured on a completely uniform basis." He claimed that although there was no reason for Marshall's investigation, there was also no reason to object to it.

Marshall started his one-month tour of Korea and Japan in January 1951.[40] African Americans expected a "sympathetic study" that would disprove what they considered faulty statements made by racist witnesses about their "Negro boys." It would show that "those noble sons of black mothers" were not cowards, but willing to give their lives in Korea for a nation that did not allow them full civil rights. Furthermore, Marshall's observations would prove that black soldiers had to endure not only horrific warfare, but also racist "Southern customs" that weakened the troops and thereby helped communist forces.[41] Black critics were well aware of the potentially embarrassing information on American democracy that would result from these investigations, and were willing to use it in their struggle to end segregation in society and the armed forces.[42] The black community was on a mission to claim its rights and rightful position in the nation as well as instate a powerful and masculine image of the black soldier.

Before the publication of his findings, Marshall and Roy Wilkins discussed how best to use the report in their argumentation. Wilkins suggested making use of the demonstrated American weakness and elaborated on the possibilities. "I think, also, that it would be a good tactic to point out that the treatment of the Negro soldiers by their own High Command and government will be used by the Communists in this country as an argument to weaken resistance to Communist armies." Both were aware of the pitfalls and dangers of alleging that there was a deeper racial element in the war and in the use of African Americans in the war, as such argumentation was often associated with communist rhetoric. Wilkins also advised Marshall on how to make use of the powerful argument without leaving the impression that blacks were unpatriotic or sympathetic to Communism. Marshall was to make perfectly clear that blacks were resistant to communist propaganda.[43]

In May 1951, the NAACP published the results of Marshall's investigation in its monthly journal *The Crisis*. In his report, Marshall revealed that army segregation produced low morale among black soldiers and negatively affected their efficiency, which in return resulted in unfair and humiliating treatment that lowered morale even further.[44] Discrimination, segregation, and racist officers who were unwilling to lead blacks into battle took a toll on black troops who, like whites, already had to struggle enough with the overwhelming number of enemy forces and the general conditions in Korea. Ultimately, Marshall concluded that African American soldiers were victims of discrimination, segregation, and an unfair court-martial system. Their rushed hearings often took no longer than fifty minutes and no witnesses for the defense were present. Suffering from a lack of replacements and sleep deprivation due to long hours of combat, the soldiers were strained beyond imagination. Another curiosity, if not insult, according to Marshall, was that black troops had to serve under white officers who more frequently criticized them and made official complaints about their alleged cowardly behavior. Marshall pointed to the fact that although the navy and the air force drew "men from the same forces as the Army, frequently from the same families," they rarely reported similar problems with black cowardice or disobedience. This comparison ultimately confirmed previous explanations that segregation in the army was not only at the root of the unfair courts-martial, but in fact, at the root of all problems.[45] Marshall's findings and his success in reducing thirty court-martial sentences in Korea may very well have further spurred hope for his later efforts in *Brown v. Board of Education*. Gaining a legal victory in the ossified structures of the military and its court-martial system made the possibility of change on the home front feasible.

While Marshall published his findings, the belittling of black soldiers at home continued. In an interview with the *New Yorker*, President Truman commented disparagingly on Lieutenant Gilbert, referring to him as "the colored officer in Korea who ran away in the face of the enemy." He maintained that such behavior was a serious offense and "if I'd been this fellow's commanding officer, we wouldn't have needed any trial at all; we would have handled it in our own way. That's a serious thing, to run away in the face of your country's enemy."[46] These comments from the president denied Gilbert any manly valor and, ultimately, did not factor in or question underlying issues of racism. They caused Walter White to send a long letter to the president complaining openly about the "disturbing" comments that were not "justified by the facts." He included Marshall's reports from Korea and Japan and urged Truman to read them and rethink his position. White eagerly defended Gilbert's character and military record as he sought to prove that, "Lt. Gilbert is no coward." Gilbert's sentence, White maintained, was an attack against the record of all black soldiers meant "to offset the nation-wide praise of Negro troops after the 24th Infantry Regiment won the first major victory in the Korean conflict on July 28, 1950." White's plea to Truman to "correct this unfortunate statement," affirms that, with Gilbert's fate and unjustifiably tarnished image, the reputation of all African Americans was at stake. White ended his letter expressing his concern that a presidential affirmation of slurs against black soldiers, "could go down in history to make the lot of the Negro more difficult."[47] Gilbert's fate became all the more incomprehensible and repugnant, as other acts of disobedience went unpunished.

At the beginning of November 1951, while Gilbert still fought for his life and reputation, China entered the war. The Chinese intervention in the Korean War marked a serious blow to UN war successes and public support of the war. In a Gallup poll in January 1951, 66 percent of respondents wanted the United States to withdraw and 49 percent were convinced it was a mistake to have intervened in the first place.[48] The enormity of China's fighting force at times overwhelmed the UN allies and shocked the American public. UN troops were pushed back across the 38th parallel once more. In March 1951, the retreat culminated in a stalemate along the 38th parallel. The war's generally unsuccessful course and long deadlock without a clear victory spurred increased frustration with a war that seemed so far removed from America's immediate problems. In the midst of the quickly deteriorating UN outlook, MacArthur stipulated the use of Nationalist Chinese forces led by Chiang Kai-shek, which had retreated to Formosa to cross the Chinese border, and threatened to bomb China. MacArthur thereby not only angered but also embarrassed Truman; as a result, his relationship with the president worsened. On April 11, 1951, a furious president dismissed MacArthur as commander of the UN troops in Korea for insubordination.

Most black newspapers and civil rights activists rejoiced over the firing of a man who many considered, despite his celebrated strategic and military brilliance, a white supremacist with dictatorial tendencies.[49] They perceived MacArthur's ouster to be just payback for his refusal to desegregate the army, which had made "Tokyo look[s] like Mississippi so far as racial signs are concerned."[50] Many African Americans saw a racist double standard in the fact that Gilbert received the death sentence for an alleged case of minor disobedience, whereas MacArthur, a white general who repeatedly and deliberately disobeyed the commander-in-chief, was merely relieved of his duties and received a hero's welcome in the United States.[51] A year later, a case of clear insubordination proved to them yet again that a racist court-martial system had unjustly convicted Gilbert. A group of air force reservists refused to fly their assigned mission in Korea. The armed forces and the American public reacted with leniency to their "stay down" protest.[52] Yet many African Americans were appalled by what they considered an obvious double standard. Based on this incident, Marshall once again pushed for Gilbert's immediate release.[53] Yet it would take another three years before Gilbert gained his freedom. Ultimately serving five years, he returned to civilian life with a dishonorable discharge that scarred him for the rest of his life. A few years before his death, Gilbert again attempted to clear his name with the help of a lawyer, but remained unsuccessful.[54]

The Gilbert case epitomized the precarious position African Americans held in the American military. Throughout the war, African American soldiers were closely scrutinized with respect to their performance on the front lines, while integration in the army was growing slowly. African Americans longed for integration, but many struggled with and contested the reasons for the fundamental changes propagated by white armed forces officials and the press, which invoked the rhetoric of benevolent white paternalism. Agency, control over integration, and the stories that accompanied them, remained with whites.

How Do Our Negro Troops Measure Up?

"How Do Our Negro Troops Measure Up?" journalist Harold Martin asked in the *Saturday Evening Post* a year into the Korean War. The article set out to embrace African American war performance and emphasize the positive effects of integration on blacks. Its seeming benevolence, however, was disturbingly patronizing. The title itself was indicative of the article's underlying premise. In a condescending style, Martin's piece ultimately confirmed long-held, degrading stereotypes of black soldiers that denied them proper male characteristics and gave them instead a childlike quality. The allegations were still familiar to and accepted by many white readers, whether from the South or the North. For instance, the article quoted a white officer who stated, "You'd be fighting like hell, and suddenly you'd find yourself alone. . . . They'd just fade off into the brush. God knows where they went."[55] The article maintained that blacks often fell asleep on duty and were afraid of the dark, making them hazards in nighttime battle.[56] It further insinuated that African Americans could only perform well in the company of white soldiers.

Martin supported integration, but his argumentation for it was problematic at best. "Given the great morale boost that comes from being accepted as an American soldier on equal footing with every other American soldier, given the steadying influence of white men around him, given the chance to rise in rank as far as his talents will permit, he will fight as well as any man."[57] The notion that the black soldier was in need of white guidance in order to reach his potential and combat effectiveness, underscored Martin's perception of the issue. Although he spoke out in favor of integration, Martin's piece seemed to prove black inferiority by suggesting that only white command could uphold order. In response to the article, an enraged Southerner wrote to the *Saturday Evening Post*, Martin "says [Negroes] won't fight as a unit, etc., but will fight when integrated with white troops. If this is true, it is because the whites along side of him make him fight, just like we make them work down here."[58] The system of the South that the army embraced should not be disrupted, since it replicated the natural order of things. While it was not as blatantly racist as Theodore Bilbo's assessments, many of the article's conclusions were nonetheless rooted in stereotypes and a covert belief in white superiority and rightful paternalism.[59] The construction of white soldiers as a formative and educative element in making blacks good soldiers under integration degraded black manhood and combat readiness.[60] It not only eliminated any black agency from the process of integration, but also managed to turn integration into a question of white dominance and proof of white superiority.[61]

The *Saturday Evening Post* article and the ensuing discussion in the African American press recalled the debate on the 92nd Division and its disputed combat record in Europe at the end of World War II. The problematic image of African American soldiers was still too widely disseminated to ignore. Martin's article became one of the most discussed press pieces on African American soldiers in the Korean War. Within a month, all major African American newspapers had commented on the article in some form, though they did not agree on a uniform way to react to it.

They were confronted with the complicated task of adequately handling a vigorous endorsement of integration that concurrently demeaned black soldiers. Some praised the report as an example for why integration ought to be enforced nationwide, and chose to neglect the underlying racist assumptions. Walter White, as head of the NAACP, acted apologetically on the author's behalf when he stated, "Mr. Martin, a Post war correspondent now in Korea, is consciously guilty of no racial bias and that he had done everything possible to tell the truth as he sees it." He was less enraged by its basic tone and allegations than one might have expected from the leader of the biggest civil rights organization in the United States. His main contention was the author's limited perspective, as Martin lacked a comparative approach to the problem by excluding white troops and their performance from his scrutiny. White demanded that the article be mandatory reading for military officials, so they may finally understand the necessity of integration. [62] Well aware of the article's racist premise, P. L. Prattis, a *Courier* columnist, also chose to favor integration over the negative imagery: "It is more important that we should recognize the virtues of integration as stressed by Mr. Martin than that we should get all huffed up because he wrote that sometimes, in the heat of battle, we had not shown sufficient interest in our job."[63]

Others, however, condemned it as "bad press" that subtly but efficiently degraded African American soldiers.[64] Martin's reasons for integration came under attack because of their bias, as he stereotyped and blamed black soldiers where white officers should have been made accountable. Whisonant, the Korean War correspondent for the *Courier*, rejected the article's underlying assumptions that African America soldiers were ultimately bad soldiers in segregated units. Instead of critically assessing the white officers' arguments, he maintained that Martin "unwittingly accepted a great deal of the white man's love for exaggeration of the Negro as truth." Following a similar strand of argumentation, L. Alex Wilson blamed any regiment's failure on white officers in charge, who he considered either "inexperienced," "rank hunters," or "psychologically unfit" to lead. Worst of all, according to Wilson, were the racist stereotypes and negative assumptions that the white leadership brought with them, which debilitated the morale and battle readiness of the African American soldiers under their command. He maintained, "one can't continue to cram insults down the throats of soldiers on the battlefield and the same second-class citizens in civilian life, [and] then expect them to grin and bear it." Refuting the idea of race as an explanation for combat failure, an editorial in the *Chicago Defender* argued that African Americans' possible deficiencies in combat performance could be explained by their being "set apart and ostracized" under segregation. The editorial even went so far as to question the status of white men, when it noted that segregation led to "false notions regarding their own merit."[65] An editorial in *Ebony* attacked the *Saturday Evening Post* piece and slammed the criticism of almost all other commentators as not going far enough. "Written ostensibly as a plea for integration of Negro and white troops in the Army, the Post piece is as trumped-up and perfidious an indictment of Negro soldiers as has appeared in public print in years." Moreover, the *Post* piece maintained that African Americans "feel racial discrimination in the U.S. does not give them anything worth fighting for."[66] *Ebony* considered this questioning of the patriotism of African American soldiers and the use of their lack of civil rights as an explanation for their alleged poor fighting record as the most deprecating of theories presented by Martin.

The diverse reactions to the *Post* article are proof of the difficult situation in which African American integrationists continued to find themselves when discussing black soldiers' performance and the need for integration. All African American newspapers agreed that integration in Korea and on military bases was the only viable option, yet the black community was split on whether the way to integration was as essential as integration itself, or whether the end would justify the means. It was a question of how much failure in combat one could admit to, without providing the nigh on inevitable fuel for white paternalism and white stereotypes of black men. A neutral assessment of black performance was not possible. African Americans were still not in control of their image and story. All attempts notwithstanding, they had failed to cut the link between poor performance in battle and skin color. The troubled course of the Korean War certainly did not make their task any easier. All troops, whether white, black, or integrated, struggled, but the weakness of white soldiers was never understood to be the result of their failure as a race; if anything, their failures were excused as being rooted in individual shortcomings.[67] Martin's article yet again augmented attempts to exonerate black soldiers in which counter-allegations against whites asserted black manhood and questioned white military masculinity.

While the black press was still struggling with Martin's article, word on the ultimate dissolution of the 24th Infantry Regiment surfaced in the summer of 1951, a few months before its official deactivation on October 1, 1951.[68] It was a bittersweet moment for many African Americans. Mary McLeod Bethune expressed her joy in a letter to James C. Evans, civilian assistant to the secretary of defense: "It is glorious history to know that the 24th Infantry Regiment dating from 1869 now comes to a close and we have one Army under our great Government."[69] Others feared, however, that with its dissolution, "people [would] forget the sacrifices made by so many who gave their lives over here."[70] The news of the disbandment of the regiment filled the front pages and editorial sections of black newspapers as they fought false assumptions on why the unit was being disbanded.

Most white newspapers reported that the army "said that Negro soldiers serve better in mixed units."[71] This reasoning left a bitter aftertaste with many African Americans, as they worried that the regiment's termination would buttress once again the notion that black soldiers needed white guidance in order to serve valorously. In an attempt to counter allegations that termination of the "Glorious 24th" was the result of poor performance and blacks' need for white men's guidance, the regiment's impending disbandment warranted a look back at its "stellar" record. All major black papers partook in the glorification and mystification of the unit. Although "nostalgia" and "sentimental" feelings were certainly in order, integration was the right and only step that "should have happened years ago."[72] Papers adamantly discarded lingering assumptions that blacks fought better under and with white soldiers, arguing vehemently, in the words of the *Courier*, "we believe the case for integration should be argued and won on its merits and not with any insulting and invidious implications which only give a new slant to the old pernicious philosophy of Negro inferiority."[73] The motivation behind integration proved to be of essential importance to many blacks. They asked themselves how one could accept integration if it was based on the same notions of black inferiority with which white supremacists had previously justified the continuance and necessity of segregation in the armed forces. These degrading concepts had to be defeated just as much as segregation itself, since real equality could not be achieved with these images lurking beneath the surface of a collective understanding of race.

In February 1953, the *Courier* published an editorial under the headline, "They Also Ran," that embodied blacks' frustration with the fact that African American soldiers were singled out for poor combat performance, while white troops' "bugging out" was not castigated. The editorial tried to eliminate the link between race and poor combat performance that had denigrated and tarnished the reputation of African American soldiers over the course of the Korean War and in previous wars. The *Courier* vehemently rejected the idea that "these men defected because they were in all-Negro units and not mixed units. "Cowardice and panic," the editorial assured, were not the result of race, but "personal reactions which anyone may experience regardless of color, no matter who is beside him on the firing line." Statements like these continued to necessitate explicit pledges in support of integration. A defense of all-black units too often still resulted in the white mainstream's questioning of the necessity of integration. In an attempt to counter this, the *Courier* noted, "We took this position because racial segregation anywhere and anytime is a vicious and unsound policy, and not because we felt that fighting beside a white soldier would make a black soldier braver, or vice versa."[74] African Americans perceived the argument of "white guidance" as almost as disempowering as segregation itself, as it reaffirmed the myth of black cowardice and inferiority. Integration was without a doubt the ultimate goal, but the reasons put forward to a national and international audience should not regurgitate derogatory comments about black soldiers that were deeply rooted in the belief of the innate inferiority of blacks. Integration should not follow allegations of a lack of black combat performance, since the defamed minority's acceptance on equal footing would then be impossible. The image and progress of black soldiers and the whole race was at stake with the dissemination of these questionable reasons for integration. For the African American community, the story of the path to integration was as essential as integration itself.[75]

Loss of Interest

In April 1951, General Matthew B. Ridgway replaced MacArthur as commander of the UN forces in Korea, but despite these radical changes in military leadership, the course of the war and the troops' outlook did not improve. The number of articles and editorials on the war in white and black media outlets decreased noticeably. The absence of a quick victory, the rather high death toll of American soldiers, and the drawn-out truce talks, which started in July 1951 and lasted for two years, made the war and Truman unpopular.[76] In 1952, Eisenhower called for an end to the war in Korea. His speech, "I shall go to Korea," greatly influenced his winning the presidential election.[77] For the next two years, the opposing forces remained entrenched in a stalemate. There were no quick solutions for this underestimated conflict. American military leaders used strategic bombing in their futile attempts to defeat the North Korean enemy supported by the Chinese and Soviets. They failed to cut supply lines of troops and weapons. Truce talks spread over a period of two years and were interspersed with costly fighting, and psychological and propaganda warfare.[78]

Many African Americans continued to hope that taking on the obligations of citizenship would bring about change at home and increase their civil rights. With reference to the black soldiers' performance, they continued to fight for racial equality on the job market at home. Aiming at improving the "Means for Obtaining Compliance with the Nondiscrimination Provisions of Federal Contracts," blacks hoped that Executive Order 10308, issued December 3, 1951, would be a step in the right direction.[79] Philleo Nash, however, adamantly emphasized that the executive order did not create a fair employment practice commission. Nevertheless, Channing Tobias advised Truman to publicize the order internationally and use it in the worldwide propaganda war with Russia. Again, most African Americans were disappointed with the limitation of the order. *Courier* columnist Bibb called it an "emasculated, watered-down edict" that not even liberal Democrats could take seriously.[80] In his eyes, parts of the order even suggested that it was a preemptive push to win over the black vote in the upcoming elections, rather than a serious measure toward civil rights.[81] Despite the war in Korea and the fact that nonwhite peoples of the world were growing increasingly distrustful of the racial outlook of the American government and people, essential progress on civil rights since the onset of violence in Korea had not and could not be made.

Southern politicians still held on to their purviews of power and acted as efficient roadblocks to change.[82] While opinions on black soldiers in Korea changed among their white comrades, many white Southerners at home continued to adamantly reject integration, especially in the military.[83] Throughout the war, Senator Richard B. Russell and his supporters resubmitted their amendment to base the draft on what they euphemistically called "freedom of choice."[84] Positive reports on black soldiers' performance in the military and on the rather smooth progress of integration appeared to be mostly ineffective in eradicating white supremacy. The federal government often proved unwilling to make fundamental changes despite serious efforts by civil rights activists. The Korean crisis had seemed to provide convenient leverage in the domestic fight for civil rights and African American rhetoric on the home front. However, its effectiveness remained limited and with the war's increasingly troubled course, references to it in the African American civil rights movement decreased. As early as December 1950, columnist Marjorie McKenzie noted that the possibility of achieving full civil rights had "risen and fallen with the changing fortunes of the Korean war."[85] The Korean War and its results also unveiled the limits war placed on the civil rights movement.[86] Ultimately, the renewed "Double V" campaign at home faltered and African Americans failed to take full control over the image and reputation of their soldiers. But although the war and the soldiers' war efforts seemed to have lost their domestic usability, attempts did not disappear completely.

Uncertainty persisted as to when the conflict would finally end and the troops return home. As the stalemate continued, the option of ending the war by returning to the prewar status quo at the 38th parallel became increasingly popular. In April 1953, 84 percent of respondents in a Gallup poll wanted a peace settlement, while 56 percent even approved of giving in to certain demands if it meant that the fighting would stop.[87] The public increasingly lost interest in the war and focused its attention on domestic issues.[88] Most African Americans also grew oblivious to the developments in Korea.

While the truce talks made it to the front pages of some black newspapers from time to time, coverage of the war certainly did not dominate the news, as it had during the early months of the war. Reports on the later battles of the war also became rare. The *Atlanta Daily World*, the only black daily, reported most actively on the difficult truce talks. Their articles predominantly relied on mainstream news services, which did not pay much attention to the race issues that many blacks still considered being deeply entrenched in the war in Asia.[89] Black soldiers named for their bravery and heroism made headlines, but the stories increasingly faded away. What still made the front pages of papers, black as well as white, was the prisoners of war (POW) issue. The truce talks dragged on with the status and fate of POWs at the center of the discussion and scrutiny. The issue even outlasted the official end of the war: an armistice in summer 1953.

And Three Stayed Behind

Throughout the war, POWs had played an essential role in the propaganda war between the United States and Russia. According to the Geneva Conventions agreed on in 1949, governments were to exchange their POWs in full. However, a new directive in the truce between the UN and the North Koreans and Chinese permitted voluntary repatriation. It allowed POWs on both sides to decide against returning to their home country and instead to remain with their captors. Roughly 47,000 North Koreans and Chinese made use of the repatriation clause.[90] This staggering number of alleged communists fleeing the regime should have been a propaganda victory for the United States. However, when twenty-one Americans decided to remain in Asia, the national uproar and alarm was tremendous and the propaganda value of the American defectors for communists was enormous.

Papers investigated the twenty-one defectors' motivations for staying behind and sought explanations in psychology and social sciences to make sense of the perceived character flaws of the former POWs. They often found reasons originating from a broken home, a lack of focus, education, religious training, and weak American values. In an article on them, the *Washington Post*, representative for the ongoing public discourse, elaborated on the social, educational, and mental predisposition of the POWs unwilling to return. The paper claimed that the men were social outsiders lacking "intellectual capacity—or parental urging."[91] *Newsweek* went so far as to describe the twenty-one so-called "turncoats" as "a sorry bunch of losers and misfits" who were "bound together more by homosexuality than Communism."[92] These stories seemed to confirm what Senator Joseph McCarthy had suspected all along: a large-scale communist subversion of American citizens.[93] Moreover, the alleged homosexual tendencies among soldiers who stayed behind corroborated contemporary ideas of sexual deviation and lack of manhood and vice versa. The scenario was even worse considering that it was American soldiers, the embodiment of national strength, who seemed to be susceptible to the "brainwashing" techniques that could ultimately immobilize if not destroy the whole American nation. The unsuccessful course of the war and its outcome in the status quo ante raised doubts over the mental and physical preparedness of American males. The American military reacted by frantically launching investigations into the characters and political orientation of its returning soldiers. The public was disturbed and suspected many returning soldiers of communist infiltration.[94]

When news broke that three African Americans were among the defectors, the POW issue catalyzed a resurgence of the discourse on race that had troubled blacks and whites, especially at the beginning of the war.[95] Books and articles seemed intent to disperse any looming fears that African

YBP Library Services

KNAUER, CHRISTINE.

LET US FIGHT AS FREE MEN: BLACK SOLDIERS AND
CIVIL RIGHTS.
                              Cloth   341 P.
PHILADELPHIA: UNIV OF PENNSYLVANIA PR, 2014
SER: POLITICS AND CULTURE IN MODERN AMERICA.

EXAMINES PERSISTENT EFFORTS OF ACTIVISTS TO FULLY
INTEGRATE THE MILITARY AFTER WW II.
LCCN 2013046747
  ISBN 0812245970   **Library PO#** FIRM ORDERS

	List	49.95	USD
8395 NATIONAL UNIVERSITY LIBRAR	**Disc**	14.0%	
App. Date 1/07/15 COLS 8214-08	**Net**	42.96	USD

SUBJ: AFRICAN AMERICAN SOLDIERS--HIST.--20TH CENT.

CLASS E185.63   DEWEY# 355.00899607 LEVEL GEN-AC

- -

YBP Library Services

KNAUER, CHRISTINE.

LET US FIGHT AS FREE MEN: BLACK SOLDIERS AND
CIVIL RIGHTS.
                              Cloth   341 P.
PHILADELPHIA: UNIV OF PENNSYLVANIA PR, 2014
SER: POLITICS AND CULTURE IN MODERN AMERICA.

EXAMINES PERSISTENT EFFORTS OF ACTIVISTS TO FULLY
INTEGRATE THE MILITARY AFTER WW II.
  LCCN 2013046747
  ISBN 0812245970   **Library PO#** FIRM ORDERS

	List	49.95	USD
8395 NATIONAL UNIVERSITY LIBRAR	**Disc**	14.0%	
App. Date 1/07/15 COLS 8214-08	**Net**	42.96	USD

SUBJ: AFRICAN AMERICAN SOLDIERS--HIST.--20TH CENT.

CLASS E185.63   DEWEY# 355.00899607 LEVEL GEN-AC

Americans would fall for communist propaganda more easily than would whites. The *Washington Post* quickly clarified that only three of the twenty-one defectors were black, "just about corresponding to the percentage of Negroes in the United States."[96] The expression of this fact most likely meant to reassure readers that race was not an issue, but that the defectors, at least in their social and racial background, represented American society. As reports indicated that African Americans prisoners of war were singled out to make public pro-communist statements their captors hoped would "grow into a crescendo that would reverberate throughout Asia and Africa,"[97] white fears of "angry black men with guns" needed soothing.

Thus, most white papers reassured their readers that blacks were not prone to turning against whites, but valorously withstood communist indoctrination, although communists considered black American soldiers their "most important captives," expecting them to be "disgruntled and rebellious."[98] The *Los Angeles Times* guaranteed its readers that there was "no racial friction" between the POWs in captivity, despite captors' attempts to incite racial conflicts for their propaganda against the United States.[99] There was also no preferential treatment of African American POWs; they were as badly treated as whites.[100] Virginia Pasley, author of the book *21 Stayed*, covered the reasons why the three black defectors stayed behind. Although referring to their experiences of racial discrimination and segregation, she concluded that these experiences ultimately had nothing to do with their decision to defect. Quoting one of the defectors' teachers she noted: "The average colored boy faces up to the segregation and accepts it and goes on about his business." Instead, the decisive point that had made them susceptible to communist propaganda was their troubled social background and lack of profound education. Admitting to widespread and devastating racism and considering race a factor in the soldiers' decision-making process seemed to be a step that was simply too upsetting to white Americans to take.[101]

These argumentations not only demonized Communism, but also purported an image of a unity of races as blacks and whites suffering together in captivity alleged that the color line was being overcome. Furthermore, the accounts confirmed African American allegiance to the United States. The fear that because of a lack of acknowledgment of racism, segregation, and discrimination, a minority would turn against the United States was very real and a concern that had to be eradicated. Articles on black POWs created a sense of racial harmony and brotherhood as they tried to silence any justified criticism that communist propaganda allegedly raised. White discourse meant to create a sense of security in the American public and to renounce the idea that dissatisfaction, let alone militancy, could exist among African American soldiers or civilians. Instead, the articles and books often left the impression that African Americans were content with the status quo.

The African American press also covered the POW issue extensively as well. Black papers meticulously investigated why Clarence Adams, the young black corporal from Memphis, Tennessee, and two other African Americans, private first class William White from Plumerville, Arkansas, and sergeant Clarence B. Sullivan from Santa Barbara, California, left the United States behind. Although Sullivan's father claimed his "boy was never subjected to harsh treatment or segregation," all three had certainly experienced prejudice and racial discrimination on a daily basis in the United States.[102] The NAACP tried anxiously to convince the three defectors to return to the fight for full civil rights in the United States. According to White of the NAACP, the situation was improving so fast that although full freedom and equality had not yet been achieved, it was now only a question of time.[103] The black press went on a mission to investigate and explain the life of POWs and the refused repatriation.

African American papers from the *Birmingham World* to the *Los Angeles Sentinel* all reported on the horrific treatment of POWs, interviewed returning prisoners and their families, and looked into the course of their lives during and after captivity. They reported in detail the racial outline of the prison camps. According to stories from returning black GIs, North Koreans and Chinese separated African Americans from their white comrades. Supposedly, their captors argued that separation would benefit the soldiers' study of Communism. Even stories of intentionally instigated race hatred and riots were reported. Public displays of black aversion and resistance to Communism dominated many of the articles. In light of the anticommunist frenzy in the United States that especially affected minority groups in their fight for equality, distancing oneself from Communism remained of great importance.[104]

Most papers and articles praised the valiant resistance to communist indoctrination that African Americans had shown under what a reporter for the *Chicago Defender* called "Red Slavery."[105] Only a small minority had broken under the pressure of communist indoctrination and only three blacks stayed behind, the papers emphasized. More important, "colored American soldiers were more resistant to Communist propaganda than the whites."[106]

The African American press painted this resistance as a sign of male heroism and a testament to black men's superior manhood and black America's unflagging loyalty. Black soldiers were made out to be savvy in circumventing attempts to brainwash them. According to *Afro-American*'s William Worthy, African Americans used "passive resistance to disrupt the regimen in the name of 'Big Chairman Mao'," which included "playing dumb," "laughing," and "ridiculing." Their techniques were reminiscent of methods used during slavery and segregation.[107] According to an article in the *Philadelphia Tribune*, these were "defense mechanisms" that were "useful to less favorably placed individuals, often because of their color, in American society."[108] A prominent argument was that the communist countries had nothing tangible to offer them. Many of those interviewed claimed that they were Americans, and despite discrimination, they were better off in America than anywhere in the world, especially under Communism.[109]

The truthfulness of many aspects of Soviet racial propaganda could not, however, be denied. "At the heart of many of the men's confidential comments was the recurrent theme that a good bit of the wearisome Communist propaganda in the camps was true when it dealt with the American race problem."[110] Every article or column reporting on the racial propaganda of Communism, even if they denied it any substance, continued to reiterate the topic in public discourse and thereby made it discernible for the world to see. The predominant message in black papers was clearly as much a pledge of allegiance as it was a critique of the United States: African American prisoners of war had experienced racism at home, but continued to fight for a flawed country. Moreover, black men resisted communist indoctrination even though they knew that "what they told you about your country and its treatment of the Negroes was true." While African American soldiers returned to the country as torchbearers demanding change, they had to realize that, "they [the conditions of blacks] had not changed."[111] Their fate at home was often presented as being not much different from, and at least as humiliating as, their fate in communist prison camps. Ultimately, the figure of the resistant African American POW represented patriotism and manly valor, but also reflected the flaws of American democracy to people at home and abroad.

Over the next few years, the African American press repeatedly commented on and tried to explain why three black soldiers had decided to defect.[112] They oscillated between various strands of rationalization and reasoning, never coming to a shared conclusion. Pledges of loyalty, a distancing from the three soldiers' decision and from Communism in general, and attacks on racism and segregation, were all part of the African American discussions on these "misguided three."[113] Journalists and newspapers kept the question of a race war and racial grievances circulating in the press and asserted that, "the racial facts would embarrass every white American."[114] Linking the spread of Communism to the persistence of racial inequality remained a weapon in the fight for black civil rights. It was a conscious decision for African Americans to apply this argument and thereby claim agency and empowerment. Moreover, for some, defection was not an embarrassment; rather it showed that a radicalization of blacks was taking place. Defection from democracy and America was surely not inherent in African Americans; rather, whites' humiliating treatment was the source of all evil. Columnists Gordon B. Hancock and J. A. Rogers predicted that a "New Negro" was on the rise who would no longer accept denigrating treatment. While they did not maintain that Communism trumped democracy, they seriously and openly questioned the American version of democracy.[115] Their warnings were a call to arms, a warning not only to white America, but also to black leaders who continued to pledge their unconditional loyalty to a country that persistently oppressed them.

An Uncertain End

The course of the war and the generally often troubled performance of American troops in Korea warranted analysis and explanation. However, instead of ending in the victory Americans had expected at the onset of the war and a definite peace agreement, the war resulted in a mere truce in July 1953. By the end of the war, an estimated 2.5 million Koreans and 36,940 American soldiers had lost their lives.[116] A three-year air war had destroyed large parts of North Korea and almost ended in the deployment of the atomic bomb to bring North Korean and Chinese troops to their knees. All sides committed atrocities.[117] Ultimately, the UN troops under American leadership did not win, as the 38th parallel still separated the Communist North from the South. The slow end to the fighting, and the truce, led many African American newspapers to reflect anew on the performance of black and white soldiers, segregation, and integration in the military, and its national as well as international ramifications.

When the war finally ended, African Americans, like the American public in general, were relieved. There was "no shouting in the streets"[118] and no "outward rejoicing among Negroes or whites . . . , however, many happy hearts."[119] Yet blacks were often split along partisan lines in their assessment of the war. Conservative voices like the *Los Angeles Sentinel* and the *Courier* chastised Truman for his intervention, maintaining that his tactics helped the Chinese and North Korean enemies. As early as mid-February 1953, they perceived a shift for the better in the fight against the "New Slavery of Communism" with Eisenhower's presidency.[120] Others were more lenient and, like the *Afro-American*, expressed content that "the killing of our soldiers" was over and a communist takeover of South Korea had been prevented.[121]

Nevertheless, the black press celebrated one aspect of the war as an undeniable victory: the integration of the military, and of the army in particular. Out of the spotlight and in war, military leadership under General Ridgway, who replaced MacArthur after his ouster, integrated the armed forces beginning in spring 1951. Personally convinced of the moral wrong in segregation, Ridgway also found efficiency and preparedness seriously lacking. Therefore, to ensure combat readiness, integration was essential. Finally, black and white soldiers fought, slept, and ate side by side, usually without much trouble.[122] The war had brought about the change in the military that blacks had hoped and fought for for over a century.

Blacks called the necessity of integration a "lesson of Korea" and expressed hope that more progress in democracy would be a "by-product of the Korean war" with "tremendous implications beyond the military realm."[123] Praising the heroism of black soldiers in the war, many maintained that their combat performance had disproved long-standing racial stereotypes of black men. In familiar masculinist rhetoric and emphasizing black men's mastery of the gun and the enemy, the *Afro-American* exclaimed, "these brave men taught the generals a lesson . . . that fighting men have no time to be concerned about color."[124] Over the three-year course of the war, in which ultimately 600,000 blacks served, integration had become a reality in one of the most important and undeniably most conservative of American institutions.[125] Although this often reluctant transformation did not happen for moral, but for pragmatic reasons, it was a remarkable moment: This change was unprecedented in any other societal realm.

Whereas the armed forces had ended Jim Crow, although not discrimination, the civilian world remained segregated. A cartoon in the *Afro-American* suggested that the continuance of a segregated home front had weakened American fighting power, represented by the weak right arm of the boxer, Uncle Sam. Integration had provided the troops with great strength, yet the segregated home front endangered the defense of the nation against outside attackers. While the cartoon did not directly refer to the Korean War, it was most likely read in reference to the ambiguous outcome in Korea. The end of the war was not a full-fledged defeat, but it was also not a victory. The home front, the cartoon suggested, had damaged and would further damage American preparedness for future conflicts if it held on to segregation.[126] (Figure 14) The connection between military service and equal rights and opportunity was loud and clear, and the end of segregation and discrimination in the armed forces was inexorably linked to the Korean War. Pictures of integrated troops were omnipresent in the papers (Figure 15). African American soldiers were seen as fighting and suffering symbols of patriotism and the need for the end of racial inequality and exclusion. America should be obliged to reciprocate the presumably undying patriotism and bravery of the black soldier by granting them the equal rights they deserved.

"A Korean War Hero"

Courtney L. Stanley became one of the last war heroes and the embodiment of what military service, and the black soldier in particular, still meant to a great majority of the African American community. Stanley was a nineteen-year-old black GI from Louisiana on his first assignment in Korea. In March 1953 he saved his white superior and singlehandedly fought off a Chinese attack until back-up arrived. The reports on his achievement made the front page of nearly every African American newspaper. Stanley's story and especially the way the press reported it united tales of combat heroism and courage, of democratic deficiencies and opportunities, and of racism and its defeat. It fulfilled America's, in particular black America's need, for an American hero who, driven by religious values, had acted beyond class and racial lines showing utmost devotion to his unit and his country when it was most in need. Stanley's performance was entitled to "warm praise," turning the "Negro youth from Louisiana," a state in which racial stereotypes of black inferiority and racial hierarchies continued to persist, into a man who had "won the admiration of the American people"[127] and, according to his white commander, was the "bravest man I've ever seen."[128]

He's Got A Good Left, But No Right

Figure 14. "He's Got a Good Left, But No Right." Cartoon, *Afro-American*, April 18, 1953, 4. Reproduced by permission of copyright holder; further reproduction prohibited without permission.

By saving his commander and fighting without an official order, Stanley embodied black male bravery and belied all stereotypes of black cowardice and the necessity of white guidance. Nevertheless, he also symbolized American hypocrisy. In an ironic twist of events, the superior Stanley saved was from Georgia, one of the most reactionary states, which, along with Louisiana, was led by political figures who vigorously opposed all civil rights efforts and drives for integration, military integration in particular.

Figure 15. Integrated Unit New Jersey. GIs from New Jersey share a feeling of glee on returning from the Korean War, April 2,——. As part of the 2,238 veterans brought into New York Harbor aboard the MSTS transports *General Weigel*, they were given a big welcome-home party aboard ship, with professional entertainers providing the music and laughs. Manhattan, New York City. © Bettmann/CORBIS.

Although well aware that nothing Stanley had done would ultimately change the racist thinking of people like Richard B. Russell of Georgia and Allen Ellender of Louisiana, he still was evidence that black men were equals, and willing to give their life for a country "which never has given him the same opportunities as those afforded other citizens."[129] Stanley's story perfectly bolstered the demand for black (male) equality, while feeding on masculinist and martial rhetoric, as well as underscoring the still ubiquitous link between civil rights and military service. Despite its limits, this link and the black soldier were still perceived to be the most powerful elements in the quest for equality and for disproving long-held stereotypes of blacks. Racial change was to follow the war. The *Chicago Defender* noted that the white soldiers saved by Stanley would finally have to judge African Americans not by race or the color of their skin, but on an individual basis, since there were "heels and heroes" in all races.[130] This "narrative of heroism, patriotism, and democracy"[131] portrayed war as an "equalizing moment at which racial and national identity were reconciled."[132] The democracy and equality black Americans were trying to install and protect was at work on the field in Korea. It was also proof that eventually something good, something equalizing, would come out of the war that ended so disappointingly and, for many, did not have a reason, higher calling, or meaning.

Whether military integration would translate to an integration of society in general was difficult to foresee. African Americans hoped that "it will influence the total race pattern of America."[133] Blacks intended to fight for their rights and equality after the Korean War, just as they had been willing to fight for the nation during the war. Many black Korean War veterans, who had experienced a greater degree of integration and equality than ever before, but also saw the limits of change, joined the civil rights movement. They were no longer willing to accept oppression and segregation as they might have before the war.[134] The military had shown that progress was possible, but pressure was necessary. White America's willingness to allow profound changes in the nation's racial power structure was limited. *Brown v. Board of Education of Topeka* in 1954 was promising, but its realization was often slow and deliberately hampered. However, black veterans and civilians were not willing to wait for change to happen. The resentful comment of a reader in reference to an article in the *Saturday Evening Post* titled, "For Negroes, It Is a New Army Now" is testimony to the growing impatience and dissatisfaction black Americans felt with white paternal benevolence: "Just think you wonderful white people have decided to give us poo lil' ol' Negroes a break and let us live with all of you wonderful white people in the Army. . . . And just think, maybe in another 150 years of American independence and freedom, you all will get around to deciding that maybe we ought to have jobs, decent housing, and equal educational facilities, too."[135]

On October 30, 1954, the Department of Defense released a report on integration in the U.S. armed forces. It boldly declared that all black units had been abolished ahead of schedule.[136] Yet the fight was far from over for many black soldiers and veterans. The struggle over black image and the memory of the Korean War continues today and speaks for the deep meaning with which military service is imbued for the African American community in its quest for equality.

Epilogue

Today, sixty years after the end of the Korean War in 1953, military integration has become a reality. African Americans can be found in all positions and ranks of the military.[1] In 1989, Colin Powell became the first black man to serve as chairman of the Joint Chiefs of Staff. When he joined the armed forces in 1958, five years after the stalemate in Korea, the military, according to his memoir, "was the only place . . . where a young black kid could now dream; the only place, where the color of your guts and the color of your blood was more important than the color of your skin."[2] The Korean War Veterans Memorial on the National Mall in Washington, D.C., manifests in granite and stainless steel this alleged fulfillment of racial diversity and equality in the military. With it, the Korean War shed its image as a "bitter war that Americans forgot,"[3] and was turned into the victorious beginning of the end of the Cold War. Moreover, the war was constructed as a success story not only with regard to the Cold War, but for race relations in the United States as well.[4]

Even though the memorial's design represents, in the words of art historian Kirk Savage, "no victory party," it displays America's (allegedly) successful acceptance of diversity.[5] At the memorial's dedication celebration in July 1995, President Bill Clinton stated, "In steel and granite, in water and earth, the creators of this memorial have brought to life the courage and sacrifice of those who served in all branches of the Armed Forces from every racial and ethnic group and background in America. They represent, once more, the enduring American truth: From many we are one."[6] The memorial affirmed the "the idealized self-image of a multiethnic, multiracial democracy, hospitable to difference but united by a common sense of national belonging."[7] At the opening of the nationwide anniversary celebrations in June 2000, President Clinton repeated this thought when he noted,

"Korea helped remind us . . . that our people and all our rich diversity are our greatest strength, that a fully integrated military is our surest hope for victory, that our freedom and security depends on the freedom and security of others, and that we can never, ever, pull away from the rest of the world."[8] Clinton and the other speakers at the events reminded their audiences that America should never forget how far the nation had come and how much it had to offer to the world. Official commemorations of military integration before and during the Korean War have all too often forgotten or rather ignored the long African American struggle for desegregation in the armed forces. Moreover, politicians and the press have embraced and replicated this inclusive and equal picture of American democracy and the Korean War, thus not only silencing the struggle of African Americans at the time, but also the continuing grievances and racial tensions in the United States.[9]

Like most Korean War veterans, African Americans were happy about a memorial erected on the Mall in their honor. Korean War veterans, regardless of race, had long complained about their societal lack of recognition and commemoration. Many felt that they had not received sufficient gratitude for the sacrifices they made for a foreign people and the American nation during a war that took place in a country that, in the end, nobody really seemed to know and care much about.[10] They had felt for all too long that they had been sandwiched between World War II's "Greatest Generation" and the tragic figures of the Vietnam War,[11] although they had also participated in a bloody and costly war. The memorial on the Mall managed to heal many old wounds, but for many black veterans the fight was still far from over. For African American veterans, the alleged lack of commemoration was hurtful. Even more painful, however, was that when the Korean War was remembered, their achievements were often left out or degraded. They felt that the rectification of and control over their image as soldiers in public memory and history was still outstanding. Segregation might have ended, but black soldiers' portrayal as failed combatants during the Korean War continued. The major history books on the Korean War reiterated the negative assessments of black soldiers that white officers had made during the war. Instead of fighting valorously, all-black units allegedly disrupted combat coherence, thus endangering the whole mission.[12]

Charles M. Bussey and David K. Carlisle,[13] two Korean War veterans, took it on themselves to fight this, in their eyes humiliating, portrayal of black soldiers in Korea. To them and their former comrades, the official history books were prime examples for the continued dissemination of lies about black soldiers and their combat valor. The rectification of negative representations of black Korean War soldiers became a key element of their activism to prove that "black Americans' achievements in combat have at least equaled other Americans'."[14] All their attempts continue to be deeply infused with masculinist rhetoric and claims to full manhood. In his autobiography published in 1991, Bussey, tried "to bring the noble efforts and sacrifices of the soldiers of the 24th Regimental Combat Team to the attention of the American people."[15] He wanted to present a "full and accurate picture of black men's failures *and successes* in the Korean War" (emphasis in original).[16]

Bussey and Carlisle first went against historian Roy Appleman's book, which was included in the military history series the United States Army Center of Military History published. Carlisle rejected Appleman's official account and accused it of having an "ulterior motive, like all other references to black combat units, [is] intended to denigrate the contributions that black fighting men have made for our country."[17] The Center of Military History felt forced by the veterans' virulent public outcry to order a new study with the goal of reexamining Appleman's findings. The results of the research were published in *Black Soldiers, White Army* in 1996. The way the book represented black soldiers and their performance, however, would still not satisfy the veterans. Carlisle stated, "The 24th Infantry performed as well as, and accomplished at least as many outstanding combat successes as, other U.S. regiments. Even in 1996, Army historians continue misleadingly and insultingly to characterize the regiment's combat performance."[18] Carlisle and Bussey were not alone in their fight against black Korean War soldiers' negative status in history and memory, but backed by their former comrades and renowned historians Gerald Horne and Clay Blair. [19] Veterans even planned to sue authors and publishers over the content of *Black Soldiers, White Army*.[20]

Curtis James Morrow was seventeen when he joined the military and when the Korean War began. In 1997, he published his version of the war's history in his book, *What's a Commie Ever Done to Black People*. He intended to set the record straight in accordance with his truth as an African American private during the Korean War. His memoir went beyond and against the interpretations of the official military history, as revisionist as they may have attempted to be. "And if things didn't work out for them [white officers] favorably, they could always blame it on the troops under their command (we blacks)," Morrow assailed.[21] According to many black veterans, not much had changed since Korea, as they remained scapegoats for an omnipresent incapable white leadership during the war. In their eyes and experience, official histories still presented a distorted and degrading picture of their participation in combat. To most black veterans, their reputation was still as important as racial equality through integration.

The emotions and frustrations continued to run high, as the African American veterans' struggle with their negative image and their desire to erase it transcended into the new millennium. In 2002, veterans of the 24th Infantry Regiment had their annual meeting in St. Louis. The *St. Louis Post-Dispatch* ran a long article on the reunion, capturing the frustration of the veterans with the continuously racist attitude toward black soldiers of the Korean War and any other war involving the United States. Their painful experience as well as their claimed heroism that, in their eyes, had been silenced for so long should not be forgotten but should be "a lesson to our nation."[22] A year later in 2003, the final year of the fiftieth anniversary celebrations of the war, a history conference on African American soldiers' participation in Korea at Morgan State University in Baltimore embarked on a similar mission.

Under the title, "No Longer Forgotten: Afro-Americans in the Korean War," the conference brought together historians and veterans to discuss the role of black soldiers in the war effort.[23] It was an emotional event, a reunion of former comrades and a reflection on their experiences as black men and women in Korea. Burney Hollis, the Dean of the College of Liberal Arts at Morgan State, opened the conference. His introductory comments underlined the importance of the event, and lay out the purpose of the conference. It was meant

to correct that wrong, to heal that painful wound, to correct that awful oversight, to raise the conscience of this nation once again to a level of appreciation for the unquestioned patriotism, the unrivaled courage, and inestimable sacrifice of those who served , those who were wounded and those who died in the Korean War, more specifically those African Americans whom this country never fully embraced when they returned from the battlefield and for whom this nation never realized or expressed its gratitude.

Panelists as well as the veterans in the audience expressed their abhorrence with segregation, which had left so many emotional scars. They conveyed, however, that its end should not be falsely explained with the bad perform-ance of segregated units. Integration was important and something they had longed for, but recognition of the successes all-black units had achieved in a discriminatory environment seemed even more important to the veter-ans present. They still struggled with the allegations of cowardice in the face of the enemy, a notion that many military historians seemed to dissem-inate, thus dominating public memory of all-black outfits. When the ses-sion focused on the 24th Infantry Regiment, the last all-black outfit of the Korean War, and its war record, its veterans in the audience as well as on the panels eagerly corrected its tainted reputation. Almost in tears, one of the veterans in the audience avowed, "But that [the success of segregated units] is our history. And don't ever distort my history. Because when you distort my history you make a liar out of me and all of the guys who went and gave their lives for this country." Thunderous applause followed his statement. Another veteran noted that the all-black 24th Infantry Regiment had been mistaken for the 24th Division in which no blacks had served. The all-black outfit, he claimed, did not fail in combat, but white soldiers did. "We took the blame by being the 24th Infantry Regiment. They didn't have any black troops in the 24th Division."[24] Furthermore, black units were often assigned to combat fields that were almost impossible to protect. According to a very enraged veteran, this was a tactic meant to humiliate blacks, and use them as scapegoats for the overall unpreparedness of the U.S. military. "They won't tell you that [the 24th Infantry Regiment's exploits in combat] because they put us in these positions for us to fail." The audience supported his contention with an "Amen!" It was the veter-ans' mission to introduce their history and their memory of the war into the official history of the Korean War, so as to once and for all be accepted as heroes and no longer described as cowards. African American soldiers were described as valorously fighting for equality, proving themselves as men on Korea's battlefields, especially in comparison to white men. They all suffered from and struggled with segregation and discrimination, but the story they told was one of survival, agency, and heroism. The confer-ence gave them a platform to take control of their history and rewrite it by introducing what they considered the truth. It is a prime example of a struggle with the "imperial gaze." In taking control over their history, the veterans were intent to destroy the subjugation and inherent denigration of their manhood. As Bob Fletcher, a veteran at one of the conference's panels, claimed, making their voice heard was about "proving our worth."

The conference in Baltimore represents yet another high point in the long struggle of black Korean War veterans against their negative representation in the public realm. The veterans' identity as black men has remained contested and challenged in a society that, despite all its advancements with respect to race relations, has clung to underlying racial stereotypes. Adding their experiences to the master narrative no longer seems to be the only goal, rather they seek to shift the dominant narrative of history and collective memory, by ensuring that their side of the (his)story and memory of the Korean War survives. Moreover, their drive has not simply centered on correcting the black image in the white mind; rather, they have sought to instill a sense of racial pride in and bolster the will of future generations to fight for their rights. According to the veterans, younger generations needed to know their history to be well prepared for their lives and struggles as blacks in a society that remains far from being postracial.[25]

When Bussey died in April 2004, the *San Francisco Chronicle* published a long obituary. The newspaper praised the military career of a "decorated World War II veteran of the famed Tuskegee Airmen and later a hero of the Korean War." The newspaper celebrated American patriotism by quoting one of the most conciliatory remarks from Bussey's book *Firefight at Yechon*: "I loved my country for what it could be, far beyond what it was." With his death, it seemed that the newspaper saw a chapter of American history being closed: military integration had been accomplished and the struggle of black Americans against their negative representation in public memory had come to an end. Shortly before his death, Bussey was awarded the Korean War Service Medal, Korea's official war medal. The *38th Parallel*, a paper published during the three-year long, fifty-year Korean War commemoration, reported on the award ceremony. In both cases, however, Bussey's fight against African American soldiers' misrepresentation in history and memory and the persistence of black inequality went virtually unmentioned. Even Bussey's personal fight for recognition and the Congressional Medal of Honor for his war achievements that had shaped most of his life since his service in Korea was ignored. Instead, national unity and patriotism across racial lines was emphasized.[26] The American public imagined the history of the Korean War as triggering and resulting in racial and national unification and healing. However, as conciliatory as Bussey and his comrades were with regard to the United States and their Korean War experience, what often shaped their military and postmilitary life was the struggle with continued racism, exclusion, and negative representation in Korean War history and memory, as well as in contemporary society. Their fight seems far from over.

Abbreviations and Acronyms

ACHR   American Council on Human Rights
ACLU   American Civil Liberties Union
ANP   Associated Negro Press
AP   Associated Press
AVC   American Veterans Committee
BSCP   Brotherhood of Sleeping Car Porters
CORE   Congress of Racial Equality
DAC   Department of Army Civilians
DSM   Distinguished Service Medal
EUCOM   United States European Command
FDR   Franklin Delano Roosevelt
FBI   Federal Bureau of Investigation
FOR   Fellowship of Reconciliation
FEPC   Fair Employment Practice Committee
MOWM   March on Washington Movement
NAACP   National Association for the Advancement of Colored People
NCAC   National Council Against Conscription
NUL   National Urban League
POW   Prisoner of War
ROTC   Reserve Officers Training Corps
UMT   Universal Military Training
WAC   Women's Army Corps
WASP   Women's Air Force Service Pilot
WAVES   Women Accepted for Volunteer Emergency Service
YMCA   Young Men's Christian Association
YWCA   Young Women's Christian Association

ACLU Records. American Civil Liberties Union Records, MC#001 Box 1100 Folder 4, Segregation in the Armed Forces. Information on ACLU and Fahy Committee; Public Policy Papers, Department of Rare Books and Special Collections, Princeton University Library, Princeton, New Jersey.

Barnett Papers. Claude A. Barnett Papers: Associated Negro Press News Releases, 1928–1964, Part III: Subject File on Black Americans, 1918–1967. Chicago History Museum.

CORE Papers. The Papers of the Congress of Racial Equality, 1941–1967, Bethesda, Md., Microfilming Corporation of America, 1980.

FOR Records. Fellowship of Reconciliation Records (DG013), Bayard Rustin Files Series D, Campaign to Resist Military Segregation: Press Clippings. Swarthmore College Peace Collection, Swarthmore College, Swarthmore, Pennsylvania.

Gibson Papers. Truman K. Gibson Papers, Library of Congress Manuscript Division, Washington, D.C.

HR Hearings 1948. Grant Reynolds, Hearings before the House Committee on Armed Services, 80th Cong., 2nd sess., H.R. 6274 and H.R. 6401: An Act to Provide for the Common Defense by Increasing the Strength of the Armed Forces of the United States, and for Other Purposes, 12–23 April and 3 May 1948, 6422–32.

Langer Papers. William Langer Papers, Orin G. Libby Manuscript Collection, University of North Dakota, Grand Forks.

League Papers. League for Non-Violent Civil Disobedience Against Military Segregation December 1941–June 1948, CDGA Collective Box, Swarthmore College Peace Collection, Swarthmore College, Swarthmore, Pennsylvania.

NAACP Papers MF. Papers of the NAACP Microfilm Edition.

NAACP Records. National Association for the Advancement of Colored People Records, Library of Congress Manuscript Division, Washington, D.C.

NARA. National Archives and Record Administration, College Park, Maryland

Nash Papers. Philleo Nash Papers, Harry S. Truman Papers, Harry S. Truman Library, Independence, Missouri.

NCAC Papers. National Council against Conscription Papers, Swarthmore College Peace Collection, Swarthmore College, Swarthmore, Pennsylvania.

NUL Records. Records of the National Urban League, 1900–1988. Library of Congress Manuscript Division, Washington D.C.

Randolph FBI. Assistant Attorney General T. Vincent Quinn, Criminal Division, Director, FBI, A. Philip Randolph, Treason, July 7, 1948, A. Philip Randolph FBI File, microfilm, Princeton University Library, Princeton, New Jersey.

Randolph LBJ Interview. A. Philip Randolph Oral History Interview I, October 29, 1969, interview by Thomas H. Baker, Internet Copy, Lyndon B, Johnson Library, http://www.lbjlib.utexas.edu

Randolph Papares MF. Papers of A. Philip Randolph Microfilm Edition, ed. John H. Bracey and August Meier. Bethesda, Md.: University Publications of America, 1990.

Russell Papers. Richard B. Russell, Jr., Collection, Series 2 Civil Rights IA, Box 30, Folder 8, Richard B. Russell Library for Political Research and Studies. University of Georgia, Athens, Georgia.

Truman Papers. Papers of Harry S. Truman, Harry S. Truman Library, Independence, Missouri.

Wilkins Papers. Papers of Roy Wilkins, Library of Congress Manuscript Division, Washington D.C.

Introduction

1. Christine Knauer, "Grant Reynolds," in *African American National Biography*, vol. 6, ed. Henry Louis Gates, Jr., and Evelyn Brooks Higginbotham (Oxford: Oxford University Press, 2007).

2. Quoted from Diagnosis of Grant Reynolds made by Anthony E. Coletta, Captain, Medical Corps, U.S. Army, National Association for the Advancement of Colored People Records, Library of Congress Manuscript Division, Washington, D.C. (hereafter NAACP Records), Part II, General Office File, 1940–1956, Box A 503, Folder 1943–1950.

3. See letter exchange between Truman K. Gibson and Walter White, NAACP Records.

4. Resignation Letter Reynolds to Walter White, September 28, 1944, NAACP Records.

5. In his later testimony, Reynolds underlined his unwillingness to leave the armed services: "I was put out of the Army because the Army said I had migraine headaches. Yes, I did have them and still have them but I begged to stay in the Army because my services were needed and my report will show it." Universal Military Training: Hearings Before Senate Committee on Armed Services, 80th Cong. 2nd sess., 686 (March 31, 1948) (hereafter Senate Committee Hearings 1948).

6. Grant Reynolds, "What the Negro Soldier Thinks," *The Crisis*, November 1944, 352–53, 357. Reynolds went so far as to compare the armed forces to the "plantation system." "What the Negro Soldier Thinks About the War Department," *The Crisis*, October 1944, 316–18, 328.

7. Reynolds, "What the Negro Soldier Thinks About This War," *The Crisis*, September 1944, 291.

8. Reynolds, "What the Negro Soldier Thinks About the War Department."

9. See, e.g., Jennifer E. Brooks, *Defining the Peace: World War Veterans, Race, and the Remaking of Southern Political Tradition* (Chapel Hill: University of North Carolina Press, 2004), esp. 13–36.

10. On white supremacy and its defenders: Jason Morgan Ward, *Defending White Democracy: The Making of a Segregationist Movement and the Remaking of Racial Politics, 1936–1965* (Chapel Hill: University of North Carolina Press, 2011); George Lewis, *Massive Resistance: The White Response to the Civil Rights Movement* (London: Hodder Arnold, 2006); Kari Frederickson, *The Dixiecrat Revolt and End of the Solid South* (Chapel Hill: University of North Carolina Press, 2001); Keith M. Finley, *Delaying the Dream: Southern Senators and the Fight Against Civil Rights, 1938–1965* (Baton Rouge: Louisiana State University Press, 2008); Jason Sokol, *There Goes My Everything: White Southerners in the Age of Civil Rights, 1945–1975* (New York: Vintage, 2006).

11. "It's Later Than They Think," *Los Angeles Sentinel*, April 29, 1948, Editorial Page.

12. Usually the terms "Jim Crow" and "Jim Crowism" are capitalized. When quoting sources, the spelling in the sources is reflected.

13. There have been a number of books on A. Philip Randolph's activism: Jervis Anderson, *A. Philip Randolph: A Biographical Portrait* (Berkeley: University of California Press, 1986); Paula F. Pfeffer, *A. Philip Randolph, Pioneer of the Civil Rights Movement* (Baton Rouge: Louisiana State University Press, 1990); Cornelius L. Bynum, *A. Philip Randolph and the Struggle of Civil Rights* (Urbana: University of Illinois Press, 2010). Pfeffer provides detailed information on Randolph's civil disobedience, but she does not consider questions of gender. Bynum's study covers civil disobedience only in his epilogue. Historian Eric Arnesen is currently writing a biography of Randolph.

14. John D'Emilio, *The Lost Prophet: The Life and Times of Bayard Rustin* (Chicago: University of Chicago Press, 2003), 150.

15. Randolph's protest for the integration of the military was a movement in the broadest sense of the word.

16. On diverse takes on Truman and civil rights in general: William C. Berman, *The Politics of Civil Rights in the Truman Administration* (Columbus: Ohio State University Press, 1970); Donald R. McCoy and Richard T. Ruetten, *Quest and Response: Minority Rights in the Truman Administration* (Lawrence: University Press of Kansas, 1973); Michael R. Gardner, *Harry Truman and Civil Rights: Moral Courage and Political Risks* (Carbondale: Southern Illinois University Press, 2002). See also Monroe Billington, "Civil Rights, President Truman and the South," *Journal of Negro History* 58, 2 (April 1973): 127–39; Barton J. Bernstein, "The Ambiguous Legacy: The Truman Administration and Civil Rights," in *Politics and Policies of the Truman Administration*, ed. Barton J. Bernstein (Chicago: Quadrangle, 1970), 269–314. In her challenging reevaluation of Truman, Carol Anderson questions the baseline on which Truman's civil rights record is assessed. Although a look at Executive Order 9981 supports her argument, Anderson fails to consider this important but neglected episode in Truman's presidency. Anderson, "Clutching at Civil Rights Straws: A Reappraisal of the Truman Years and the Struggle for African American Citizenship," in *Harry's Farewell: Interpreting and Teaching the Truman Presidency*, ed. Richard Stewart Kirkendall (Columbia: University of Missouri Press, 2004), 75–104. Jon E. Taylor has published

a book on Truman and Executive Order 9981 in the Routledge Series Critical Moments in American History that provides students "a window into the historian's craft through concise, readable books." His study could not be considered in this publication. Taylor, *Freedom to Serve: Truman, Civil Rights, and Executive Order 9981* (New York: Routledge, 2013).

17. First paragraph of Executive Order 9981, *Harry S. Truman Library*, http://www.trumanlibrary.org.

18. Morris J. MacGregor, Jr., *Integration of the Armed Forces, 1940–1965* (Washington D.C.: Center of Military History of the United States Army, 1985), http://www.history.army.mil; Sherie Mershon and Steven Schlossman, *Foxholes and Color Lines: Desegregating the U.S. Armed Forces* (Baltimore: Johns Hopkins University Press, 1998); detected only recently: Rawn James, Jr., *The Double V: How Wars, Protest, and Harry Truman Desegregated America's Military* (New York: Bloomsbury Press, 2013).

19. Alex Lubin, *Romance and Rights: The Politics of Interracial Intimacy 1945–1954* (Jackson: University Press of Mississippi, 2005), 2.

20. Lee Nichols, *Breakthrough on the Color Front* (New York: Random House, 1954).

21. See, e.g., James Foreel, "Military Set Example for Civilian Life," *Philadelphia Tribune*, April 3, 1954, 4.

22. Richard M. Dalfiume, *Desegregation of the U.S. Armed Forces: Fighting on Two Fronts, 1939–1953* (Columbia: University of Missouri Press, 1969), 219.

23. Quote in George C. Reinhardt, "No Segregation in Foxholes," *The Crisis*, October 1953, 457; J. F. Marszalek, Jr., "The Black Man in Military History," *Negro History Bulletin* 36, 6 (1973): 125.

24. See Harvard Sitkoff, *The Struggle for Black Equality, 1954–1980* (New York: Farrar Straus & Giroux, 1993); C. Vann Woodward, *The Strange Career of Jim Crow*, 3rd ed. (New York: Oxford University Press, 2001).

25. Michael J. Klarman, "Rethinking the Civil Rights and Civil Liberties Revolutions," *Virginia Law Review* 82, 1 (February 1996): 8.

26. Glenn Feldman, ed., *Before Brown: Civil Rights and White Backlash in the Modern South* (Tuscaloosa: University of Alabama Press, 2004), 1.

27. Jacquelyn Dowd Hall, "The Long Civil Rights Movement and the Political Uses of the Past," *Journal of American History* 91, 4 (March 2005): 1233–63. But Hall does not even mention the integration of the American military as an important but neglected issue that ought to be covered in historical research to better understand questions of race and national identity, gender, and civil rights in the early Cold War period. Steven Lawson and Eric Arnesen, among others, challenge the idea of a "long civil rights movement." Lawson argues for the "long origins of the short civil rights movement," for a long black freedom struggle, of which the traditional civil rights movement was a "bref durée." Steven F. Lawson, "The Long Origins of the Short Civil Rights Movement, 1954–1968," in *Freedom Rights: New Perspectives on the Civil Rights*

Movement, ed. Danielle L. McGuire and John Dittmer (Lexington: University Press of Kentucky, 2011), 9–38, 28.

28. To name only a few: Glenda Gilmore, *Defying Dixie: The Radical Roots of Civil Rights, 1919–1950* (New York: Norton, 2009); Thomas J. Sugrue, *Sweet Land of Liberty: The Forgotten Struggle for Civil Rights in the North* (New York: Random House, 2008); Brenda Gayle Plummer, *Rising Wind: Black Americans and U.S. Foreign Affairs, 1935– 1960* (Chapel Hill: University of North Carolina Press, 1996); Martha Biondi, *To Stand and Fight: The Struggle for Civil Rights in Postwar New York City* (Cambridge, Mass.: Harvard University Press, 2003); Mary L. Dudziak, *Cold War Civil Rights: Race and the Image of American Democracy* (Princeton, N.J.: Princeton University Press, 2000); Glenn T. Eskew, *But for Birmingham: Local and National Movements in the Civil Rights Struggle* (Chapel Hill: University of North Carolina Press, 1997); John Egerton, *Speak Now Against the Day: The Generation Before the Civil Rights Movement in the South* (New York: Knopf, 1994). None of these studies cover Korea in detail.

29. Desmond King, "The Longest Road to Equality: The Politics of Institutional Desegregation Under Truman," *Journal of Historical Sociology* 6, 2 (1993): 119–63; Dalfiume, *Desegregation of the U.S. Armed Forces*, 219; MacGregor, *Integration of the Armed Forces*; Mershon and Schlossman, *Foxholes and Color Lines*. Most studies on military desegregation take a sociological or political approach. For example, the most important study on military desegregation is Leo Bogart, ed., *Project Clear: Social Research and the Desegregation of the United States Army* (New Brunswick, N.J.: Transaction, 1992), which today can be considered an excellent contemporary source; John Sibley Butler, *Inequality in the Military: The Black Experience* (Saratoga, Calif.: Century 21, 1980); Charles Moskos and John Sibley Butler, *All That We Can Be: Black Leadership and Racial Integration the Army Way* (New York: Basic Books, 1996); Nichols, *Breakthrough on the Color Front*.

30. One of the few historians merging cultural and military history on the Korean War is Andrew Huebner, *The American Warrior Image: Soldiers in American Culture from the Second World War to the Vietnam Era* (Chapel Hill: University of North Carolina Press, 2008). See also his article "Kilroy Is Back: Images of American Soldiers," *American Studies* 45, 1 (Spring 2004): 103–29. A recent detailed study on American soldiers' experiences in the Korean War is Melinda Pash, *Standing in the Shadow of the Greatest Generation: The Americans Who Fought the Korean War* (New York: New York University Press, 2012). On blacks and Korea, Selika M. Ducksworth, "What Hour of the Night: Black Enlisted Men's Experiences and the Desegregation of the Army During the Korean War, 1950–51" (Ph.D. dissertation, Ohio State University, 1994). Kimberley Phillips's book *War!* contains an important chapter on African Americans in Korea. *War! What Is It Good for? Black Freedom Struggles and the U.S. Military from World War II to Iraq* (Chapel Hill: University of North Carolina Press, 2012); Kimberley Phillips, " 'Did the Battlefield Kill Jim Crow?' The Cold War Military, Civil Rights, and Black Freedom Struggles," in *Fog of War: The Second World War and the Civil Rights Movement*, ed. Kevin M. Kruse and Stephen Tuck (Oxford: Oxford

University Press, 2012), 208–29. The only book-length study on blacks in the Asian Pacific before Vietnam, especially Korea, is Michael C. Green, *Black Yanks in the Pacific: Race in the Making of American Military Empire After World War II* (Ithaca, N.Y.: Cornell University Press, 2010). David Widener has published an article on the topic, "Seoul City Sue and the Bugout Blues: Black American Narratives of the Forgotten War," in *Afro Asia: Revolutionary Political and Cultural Connections Between African Americans and Asians*, ed. Fred Ho and Bill V. Mullen (Durham, N.C.: Duke University Press, 2008), 55–87. A short chapter in John Fousek, *To Lead the Free World: American Nationalism and the Cultural Roots of the Cold War* (Chapel Hill: University of North Carolina Press, 2000).

31. See, e.g., L. D. Reddick, "What Should the American Negro Reasonably Expect as the Outcome of a Real Peace," *Journal of Negro Education* 12, 3 (Summer 1943): 568–78; Dalfiume, *Desegregation of the U.S. Armed Forces*; MacGregor, *Integration of the Armed Forces.*

32. Kenneth L. Karst, "The Pursuit of Manhood and the Desegregation of the Armed Forces," *UCLA Law Review* 38, 3 (1990/1991): 499–581.

33. Frederick Douglass quoted in Gail Buckley, *American Patriots: The Story of Blacks in the Military from the Revolution to Desert Storm* (New York: Random House, 2001), 56.

34. W. E. B. Du Bois, *Black Reconstruction in America: An Essay Toward a History of the Part Which Black Folk Played in the Attempt to Reconstruct Democracy in America, 1860–1880* (New York: Russel & Russel, 1935), 104.

35. Arthur W. Little quoted in Peter S. Kindsvatter, *American Soldiers: Ground Combat in the World Wars, Korea, and Vietnam* (Lawrence: University Press of Kansas, 2003), 268.

36. Timothy Stewart-Winter, "'Not a Soldier, Not a Slacker': Conscientious Objectors and Male Citizenship in the United States During the Second World War," *Gender & History* 19, 3 (November 2007): 543.

37. Steve Estes, *I Am a Man! Race, Manhood, and the Civil Rights Movement* (Chapel Hill: University of North Carolina Press, 2005); Steve Estes, "A Question of Honor: Masculinity and Massive Resistance to Integration," in *White Masculinity in the Recent South*, ed. Trent Watts (Baton Rouge: Louisiana State University Press, 2008); Christina S. Jarvis, *The Male Body at War: American Masculinity During World War II* (DeKalb: Northern Illinois University Press, 2004); Graham Herman, III, *The Brothers' Vietnam War: Black Power, Manhood and the Military Experience* (Gainesville: University Press of Florida, 2003); Chad Williams, *Torchbearers of Democracy: African American Soldiers in the World War I Era* (Chapel Hill: University of North Carolina Press, 2010); Chad Williams, "Vanguards of the New Negro: African American Veterans and Post-World War I Racial Militancy," *Journal of African American History* 92, 3 (Summer 2007): 347–70; Adriane Lentz-Smith, *Freedom Struggles: African Americans and World War I* (Cambridge, Mass.: Harvard University Press, 2009). Law historian Kenneth Karst remained, for a long time, one of the few historians who studied the

military desegregation in the immediate postwar period and its link to issues of manhood. His 1991 article provides first insights into the connections between military integration and the African American pursuit of manhood, without, however, going into greater detail. He essentially neglected the civil rights movement and its perceptions of the developments and the Korean War. Karst, "The Pursuit of Manhood."

38. See Michael Geyer, "War in the Context of General History in an Age of Total War: Comment on Peter Paret, 'Justifying the Obligation of Military Service'" and Michael Howard, "World War One: The Crisis in European History," *Journal of Military History* 57, 5 (October 1993): 154–55.

39. R. W. Connell, *Masculinities*, 2nd ed. (Berkeley: University of California Press, 2005), 181. In his critical reevaluation of the term, Connell states: "Hegemonic masculinity was not assumed to be normal in the statistical sense; only a minority of men might enact it. But it was certainly normative. It embodied the currently most honored way of being a man, it required all other men to position themselves in relation to it, and it ideologically legitimated the global subordination of women to men." R. W. Connell and James W. Messerschmidt, "Hegemonic Masculinity: Rethinking the Concept," *Gender and Society* 18, 6 (June 2005): 82.

40. Steve Estes, one of the leading historians of African American manhood studies, provides substantial insights into the gendered language of African Americans in their quest for equality during and after the Second World War. His first chapter deals with the fate and fight of African American and white soldiers during the war and the masculinist rhetoric involved. However, he concludes his analysis of the intersections of manhood, masculinist rhetoric, military service, and citizenship at the end of the war and resumes his research with *Brown v. Board of Education of Topeka*. Although his aim is not to conduct a comprehensive study of the civil rights movement or the significance of the language of masculinity for African Americans, especially for soldiers and veterans, he selects specific chapters in history and excludes immediate postwar developments with respect to military integration and the Korean War in which, as will be shown here, manhood played such an important role. Estes, *I Am a Man!*, chap. 1.

41. Charissa Threat, "'The Hands That Might Save Them': Gender, Race, and the Politics of Nursing in the United States During the Second World War," *Gender & History* 24, 2 (August 2012): 468.

42. Brooks, *Defining the Peace*, esp. 16.

43. See, e.g., George M. Fredrickson, *The Black Image in the White Mind: The Debate on Afro-American Character and Destiny, 1817–1914* (Middletown, Conn.: Wesleyan University Press, 1987).

44. bell hooks points out that "white supremacists have recognized that control over images is central to the maintenance of any system of racial domination." bell hooks, *Black Looks: Race and Representation* (Boston: South End Press, 1992), 2.

45. Robert O'Meally and Geneviève Fabre, "Introduction," in *History and Memory in African-American Culture*, ed. Geneviève Fabre (New York: Oxford University

Press, 1994), 3–4. Stephen Tuck has argued along the same lines: "The question of the black image was not a sideshow to the main story of wartime protest. It was integral to the main story, taking its place alongside campaigns for black inclusion in the war effort and for black rewards because of their contribution to the war effort." Tuck, however, focuses on popular culture, especially movies, thereby mostly neglecting the press as well as history and memory in general. "You Can Sing and Punch . . . But You Can't Be a Soldier or a Man: African American Struggles for a New Place in Popular Culture," in *Fog of War*, ed. Kruse and Tuck, 101–26, 103; cf. Justin T. Lorts, "Hollywood, the NAACP, and the Cultural Politics of the Early Civil Rights Movement," in *Freedom Rights*, ed. McGuire and Dittmer, 39–69.

46. hooks, *Black Looks*, 7.

47. "The reports of integration and segregation at the same time resulted in a confused reaction in the Negro press. The *Pittsburgh Courier* claimed that the Twenty-Fourth Infantry was being 'framed' and used as a 'scapegoat' and called for an immediate end to segregation. In the very same issue, the *Courier* praised the integration in Army combat units in Korea. The NAACP charged that discrimination was evident in courts-martial of black soldiers in Korea. Thurgood Marshall, the chief lawyer for the NAACP, went to Korea to investigate. Negro leaders called upon the President to end segregation in the Army at once. Negroes were obviously not aware of the extent of the revolution occurring within the Army in Korea." Dalfiume, *Desegregation of the U.S. Armed Forces*, 206–7. The *Pittsburgh Courier* temporarily changed its name to *Courier* in September 1950. Some of the papers had additional regional issues; if not otherwise noted, however, the study quotes from the national edition of all publications.

Chapter 1. Fighting for Respect

1. A. Philip Randolph, "'Defense Rotten'—Randolph: Let's March on Capital, 10,000 Strong, Urges Leader Porters," *Pittsburgh Courier*, January 25, 1941, 1.

2. "Federal Discrimination," *Carolina Times*, April 6, 1940.

3. There is an ongoing and essential discussion on African American protest and its effectiveness during the Second World War. While historian Harvard Sitkoff pointed to the radicality of the movement early on, he later rescinded his argument and stated that once the United States entered the war, black protest almost vanished. Harvard Sitkoff, "Racial Militancy and Interracial Violence in the Second World War," *Journal of American History* 58, 3 (December 1971): 662; Harvard Sitkoff, "African American Militancy in the World War II South: Another Perspective," in *Remaking Dixie: The Impact of World War II on the American South*, ed. Neil McMillen (Jackson: University Press of Mississippi, 1997), 70–92. For a more recent look at the question of the persistence and effectiveness of the African American fight for civil rights see Kevin M. Kruse and Stephen Tuck, eds., *Fog of War: The Second World War and the Civil Rights Movement* (Oxford: Oxford University Press, 2012).

4. The most detailed studies of the MOWM are Lucy G. Barber, *Marching on Washington: The Forging of an American Political Tradition* (Berkeley: University of California Press, 2002); Herbert Garfinkel, *When Negroes March: The March on Washington Movement in the Organizational Politics for FEPC* (Glencoe, Ill.: Free Press, 1959); John H. Bracey, Jr., and August Meier, "Allies or Adversaries? The NAACP, A. Philip Randolph and the 1941 March on Washington," *Georgia Historical Quarterly* 75 (1991): 1–17. Glenda Gilmore provides research on the more radical and pro-Communist activists in the movement, in *Defying Dixie: The Radical Roots of Civil Rights, 1919–1950* (New York: Norton, 2009), 356–78.

5. On internationalism, African Americans, and Indian liberation: Gerald Horne, *The End of Empires: African Americans and India* (Philadelphia: Temple University Press, 2008).

6. Lauren Rebecca Sklaroff, "Constructing G.I. Joe Louis: Cultural Solutions to the 'Negro Problem' During World War II," *Journal of American History* 89, 3 (December 2002): 958–83.

7. Randolph, "'Defense Rotten'—Randolph." It was a call to nonviolent protest, but, according to Ruth Feldstein, "the march with a 'Call to Negro America' [that] carefully balanced gendered images of aggression and restraint. The march would be, he [Randolph] wrote, a 'mass action that is orderly and lawful, but aggressive and militant.'" Ruth Feldstein, *Motherhood in Black and White: Race and Sex in American Liberalism, 1930–1965* (Ithaca, N.Y.: Cornell University Press, 2000), 74.

8. A. Philip Randolph, "Why Not Issue an Executive Order?" *Norfolk Journal and Guide*, April 12, 1941, 8; A. P. Randolph. "Prejudice Bottlenecking U.S. Defense—Randolph: Leaders Need Mass Support, He Declares South Not Alone in Unfairness, Says Labor Leader," *Norfolk Journal and Guide*, February 1, 1941, 1.

9. See "A. Philip Randolph," *Chicago Defender*, February 8, 1941, 14; "Opinion," *Afro-American*, March 15, 1941, 4; "10,000 to March on Washington," *Philadelphia Tribune*, May 8, 1941, 1.

10. *Chicago Defender* quoted in Feldstein, *Motherhood in Black and White*, 74. Harboring a deep suspicion of Communism, Randolph feared as well that white communists would infiltrate the movement and co-opt the march, thereby discrediting its cause. "Communists Not Wanted in March to Washington, Declares Randolph," *New York Amsterdam Star-News*, June 21, 1941, 1.

11. A. Philip Randolph, "Let the Negro Masses Speak," *Norfolk Journal and Guide*, March 15, 1941, 8; Randolph, "Let the Negro Masses Speak," *New York Amsterdam Star-News*, April 12, 1941, 17.

12. Whether 100,000 people would have attended is rather questionable, but organizers were certain the march would produce a mass turnout of black protesters. Barber, *Marching on Washington*, 128.

13. See Gilmore, *Defying Dixie*, esp. 359–62; Kimberley S. Johnson, *Reforming Jim Crow: Southern Politics and State in the Age Before Brown* (New York: Oxford University Press, 2010), 225.

14. See E. Rhodes, "Under the Microscope," *Philadelphia Tribune*, June 26, 1941, 4; "Executive Act Halts March of 100,000 to Capital," *New York Amsterdam Star-News*, June 28, 1941, 1; "Why Shouldn't They March," *New York Amsterdam Star-News*, June 28, 1941, 14; "Postponed," *Pittsburgh Courier*, July 5, 1941, 6; "Randolph's Speech Explains Why He Called Off March," *New York Amsterdam Star-News*, July 19, 1941, 15.

15. "Negroes to Fight Employment Bias," *New York Times*, June 13, 1942, 21.

16. Dwight MacDonald and Nancy MacDonald, *The War's Greatest Scandal: The Story of Jim Crow in Uniform* (New York: March on Washington Movement, 1943), 1.

17. On African American anti-interventionism before the war, see Daniel W. Aldridge, III, "A War for the Colored Races: Anti-Interventionism and the African American Intelligentsia, 1939–41," *Diplomatic History* 18, 3 (June 2004): 321–52.

18. See Simon Topping, "Supporting Our Friends and Defeating Our Enemies: Militancy and Nonpartisanship in the NAACP, 1936–1948," *Journal of African American History* 89, 1 (Winter 2004): 22; Kruse and Tuck, eds., *Fog of War*.

19. Aldridge, "A War for the Colored Races," 323.

20. Penny von Eschen, *Race Against Empire: Black Americans and Anticolonialism, 1937–1954* (Ithaca, N.Y.: Cornell University Press, 1997), 8.

21. Brenda Gayle Plummer, *Rising Wind: Black Americans and U.S. Foreign Affairs, 1935–1960* (Chapel Hill: University of North Carolina Press, 1996), 103; see also Sitkoff, "Racial Militancy and Interracial Violence," 662. Gene Roberts and Hank Klibanoff confirm this assessment with their in-depth study of the relationship between and influence of the press on the civil rights movements and their eventual success, *The Race Beat: The Press, the Civil Rights Struggle, and the Awakening of a Nation* (New York: Vintage, 2007).

22. "The Courier's Double 'V' for a Double Victory Campaign Gains Country-Wide Support," *Pittsburgh Courier*, February 12, 1942, 1; first call for "Double V" a week earlier in the *Courier*. Penny von Eschen argues that the campaign could have also been called "Triple V" as African Americans' fight against Jim Crow was "seen as inseparably linked to the fight against both imperialism and fascism." Von Eschen, *Race Against Empire*, 34.

23. "Let's Defend Democracy Right Here and Now (An Editorial)," *Chicago Defender*, August 30, 1941, 1.

24. "The Negro Soldier," *Chicago Defender*, August 30, 1941, 14.

25. Johnpeter Horst Grill and Robert L. Jenkins, "The Nazis and the American South in the 1930s: A Mirror Image?" *Journal of Southern History* 58, 4 (November 1992): 668; Gilmore, *Defying Dixie*, 157–201.

26. Charles W. Harris, "For or Against Nazism," *Chicago Defender*, June 6, 1936, 7.

27. Wilkins quoted in Grill and Jenkins, "The Nazis and the American South," 689.

28. Aldridge, "A War for the Colored Races," 326.

29. George Schuyler quoted in Grill and Jenkins, "The Nazis and the American South," 690.

30. Soldier, Camp Rucker, Alabama, "Soldier Tells of Life Down South," *Chicago Defender*, July 8, 1944, 12.

31. Letter from Claude Barnett to President Roosevelt, January 31, 1942, The Claude A. Barnett Papers: Associated Negro Press News Releases, 1928–1964, Part III: Subject File on Black Americans, 1918–1967; Series F Reel 1 (hereafter Barnett Papers).

32. Marc Gallicchio, *The African American Encounter with Japan and China: Black Internationalism in Asia, 1895–1945* (Chapel Hill: University of North Carolina Press, 2000).

33. Soldier, Camp Rucker, Alabama, "Soldier Tells of Life Down South"; Hamilton Johnson, "Bemoans Lack of Race Pride," *Chicago Defender*, July 8, 1944, 12; Frank D. Griffin, "What the People Say," *Chicago Defender*, September 6, 1941, 14.

34. See Christina S. Jarvis, *The Male Body at War: American Masculinity During World War II* (DeKalb: Northern Illinois University Press, 2004), 147.

35. George Q. Flynn, "Selective Service and American Blacks During World War II," *Journal of Negro History* 69, 1 (Winter 1984): 15.

36. Col. Householder, Chief Miscellaneous Division, Tag Dept., in Morris J. MacGregor and Bernard C. Nalty, eds., *Blacks in the United States Army: Basic Documents*, vol. 5 (Wilmington, Del.: Scholarly Resources, 1977), 144–48, 146.

37. George Lipsitz, "'Frantic to Join . . . the Japanese Army': Black Soldiers and Civilians Confront the Asia-Pacific War," in *Perilous Memories: The Asia-Pacific War(s)*, ed. T. Fujitani, Geoffrey M. White, and Lisa Yoneyama (Durham, N.C.: Duke University Press, 2001), 348.

38. Richard M. Dalfiume, *Desegregation of the U.S. Armed Forces: Fighting on Two Fronts, 1939–1953* (Columbia: University of Missouri Press, 1969), 81.

39. Sherie Mershon and Steven Schlossman, *Foxholes and Color Lines: Desegregating the U.S. Armed Forces* (Baltimore: Johns Hopkins University Press, 1998), 77–81; see also Ulysses Lee, *The United States Army in World War II: The Employment of Negro Troops* (Washington, D.C.: Government Printing Office, 1966).

40. Lisa Lowe, *Immigrant Acts: On Asian American Cultural Politics* (Durham, N.C.: Duke University Press, 1996), 11–12; see also Richard Stillman, *Integration of the Negro in the U.S. Armed Forces* (New York: Praeger, 1968), 5; Jarvis, *The Male Body at War*, 151.

41. Steve Estes, *I Am a Man! Race, Manhood, and the Civil Rights Movement* (Chapel Hill: University of North Carolina Press, 2005), 13. During World War I, the General Staff advised different uniforms for service and combat units signifying their difference in importance. Jennifer D. Keene, *Doughboys, the Great War, and the Remaking of America* (Baltimore: Johns Hopkins University Press, 2003), 92. For information on uniforms for blacks in World War II, Alexander Bielakowski and Raffaele Ruggeri, *African American Troops in World War II* (Oxford: Osprey, 2007), 67.

42. Bill Stevens, member of the 25th Infantry Regiment of the 93rd Division, in Jarvis, *The Male Body at War*, 148.

43. George Roeder, Jr., *The Censored War: The American Visual Experience During the Second World War* (New Haven, Conn.: Yale University Press, 1993), 79.

44. Olivier Wieviorka, *Normandy: The Landings to the Liberation of Paris* (Cambridge, Mass.: Harvard University Press, 2008), 314–15.

45. Pastor William H. Jernagin quoted in Maggi M. Morehouse, *Fighting in the Jim Crow Army: Black Men and Women Remember World War II* (Lanham, Md.: Rowman & Littlefield, 2000), 131.

46. "Mr. President . . . It's Up to You!!" *Chicago Defender*, April 4, 1942, 1.

47. On white violence see Herbert Shapiro, *White Violence and Black Response: From Reconstruction to Montgomery* (Amherst: University of Massachusetts Press, 1988), esp. 301–48.

48. Estes, *I Am a Man!*, chap. 1.

49. "Are Negroes Fighting This War?" *Norfolk Journal and Guide*, October 21, 1944, 6.

50. "Is the War Department Responsible?" *Pittsburgh Courier*, January 29, 1944, 6; "Newsreels 'Cut' Negro Fighters: Public Is Kept in the Dark on Role," *New York Amsterdam News*, January 8, 1944, A1.

51. Roeder, *The Censored War*, esp. 44–47, 57

52. Gunnar Myrdal, *An American Dilemma: The Negro Problem and American Democracy* (New Brunswick, N.J.: Transaction, 1996), lxxxiii, 419–20. Its first edition was published in 1944. According to historian David W. Southern, some white officers took notice of the book and rethought their assessment of blacks in the armed forces. But ultimately, social scientists did not have profound influence on the integration of the American military. David W. Southern, *Gunnar Myrdal and Black-White Relations: The Use and Abuse of an American Dilemma 1944–1969* (Baton Rouge: Louisiana State University Press, 1987), 121–22.

53. Memo on The Negro Problem in the Armed Forces, quoted in Matthias Reiss, *"Die Schwarzen waren unsere Freunde": Deutsche Kriegsgefangene in der amerikanischen Gesellschaft 1942–1946* (Paderborn: Schöningh, 2002), 204n 42.

54. Claude Barnett's exchange of letters with editors of leading black press organs, Barnett Papers, Part III: Subject File on Black Americans, 1918–1967, Series F Reel 1. On the NAACP position, Roy Wilkins to Carl Murphy, publisher and editor of the *Afro-American*, April 26, 1943, NAACP Records, Part II, Box A 497, Folder Publicity Negro Troops 1942–1943.

55. The ANP became the longest-running African American news service.

56. Barnett to William Hastie, Civilian Aide to the Secretary of War, August 11, 1941, Barnett Papers, Part III: Subject File on Black Americans, 1918–1967; Series F Reel 1.

57. Barnett to Hastie, December 15, 1941.

58. The working agreement ended abruptly when Hastie quit his position as civilian aide in 1943 after a falling out with the War Department over its continuously racist treatment of black soldiers. Military officials, especially secretary of war Henry Stimson, considered him too radical and impatient. Hastie, on the other hand, could not accept the military's willful perpetuation of segregation. Their segregated status and treatment as scapegoats for negative military performances, and the military's and politicians' unwillingness to ameliorate black soldiers' position and image, among others, made it impossible for Hastie to continue his work. See Jerry N. Hess Interview with Judge William H. Hastie, January 5, 1972, *Harry S. Truman Library*; Dalfiume, *Desegregation of the U.S. Armed Forces*, esp. 81–83.

59. On the need to further study Barnett's possible influence on Wallace see: Adam Green, *Selling the Race: Culture, Community, and Black Chicago, 1940–1955* (Chicago: University of Chicago Press, 2007), 116–17.

60. "An Effective Progress: For Improving Negro Morale," Memorandum Henry A. Wallace, April 16, 1942; Barnett Papers, Part III: Subject File on Black Americans, 1918–1967; Series F Reel 1; see also Barnett, ANP, to Office of Facts and Figures, to the attention of Ulrie Bell, January 15, 1942, in ibid.

61. Roy Wilkins to William H. Hastie, January 11, 1943, Papers of the NAACP Microfilm Edition, Part 9, Series A: General Office Files on Armed Forces' Affairs, 1918–1955, Reel 14 (hereafter NAACP Papers MF).

62. Charley Cherokee, "National Grapevine," *Chicago Defender*, March 14, 1942, 15.

63. Lieutenant Christopher Sturkey quoted in Peter S. Kindsvatter, *American Soldiers: Ground Combat in the World Wars, Korea, and Vietnam* (Lawrence: University Press of Kansas, 2003), 267–68.

64. Speech by Marshall Field, Capital Press Club, Washington, D.C., June 21, 1944, Philleo Nash Papers, White House File, Box 55, Folder: Minorities—Negro—General: Negro Press and Issues of Democracy Speech by Marshall Field at the Capital Press Club, Washington, D.C., June 21, 1944, Harry S. Truman Papers, Harry S. Truman Library, Independence, Mo. (hereafter Nash Papers).

65. See "American Newspapers Can Rid the Country of Race Animosities," *Philadelphia Tribune*, July 1, 1944, 4; "PM-Chicago Sun Publisher Says: 'One-Sided View of War Given to White America,'" *Pittsburgh Courier*, July 1, 1944, 1.

66. Thomas Cripps and David Calbert, "The Negro Soldier (1944): Film Propaganda in Black and White," *American Quarterly* 31, 5 (Winter 1979): 616–40; Clayton Koppes and Gregory D. Black, "Blacks, Loyalty, and Motion-Picture Propaganda in World War II," *Journal of American History* 73, 2 (September 1986): 383–406. If blacks were portrayed at all in motion pictures, their portrayal was questionable at best. New York Public Library researcher C. D. Reddick looked at over one hundred Hollywood films with black characters and found 75 percent were "anti-Negro." Thomas Doherty, *Projections of War: Hollywood, American Culture and World War II* (New York: Columbia University Press, 1999), 207.

67. Alex L. Hinton, "Hinton: 'The Nero Soldier' Film Tells a Needed Story," *Norfolk Journal and Guide*, May 6, 1944, 6; Herman Hill, "Reviewer Praises Film on Colored Soldiers: Pic Traces Negro's Part in War," *Pittsburgh Courier*, February 26, 1944, 15; Tuck, "You Can Sing and Punch," 110–13.

68. See "The Negro as a Soldier," *New York Times*, August 6, 1944, E8; "Gen. Eisenhower Lauds Negro Troops," *New Journal and Guide*, August 5, 1944, C1.

69. Dalfiume, *Desegregation of the U.S. Armed Forces*, 98–102. For importance of these events and discussions, Robert F. Jefferson, *Fighting for Hope: African American Troops of the 93rd Infantry Division in World War II and Postwar America* (Baltimore: Johns Hopkins University Press, 2008), Epilogue; Gerald Astor, *A Blood-Dimmed Tide: The Battle of the Bulge by the Men Who Fought It* (New York: Bantam Doubleday Bell, 1999).

70. Mershon and Schlossman, *Foxholes and Color Lines*, 59–61.

71. See Ollie Barrington, "92nd Unit Leads 5th in Arno Crossing," *Pittsburgh Courier*, September 9, 1944, 1; "Negroes Now Killing Nazis," *New York Amsterdam News*, September 16, 1944, 10A; Art Carter, "92nd Division Units Cross the Arno River: Nine Wounded in Initial Battle Action by All-Colored Team with Fifth Army 92nd Division Fires Shot for Freedom at Nazis Negro Quizzes Nazi," *New York Amsterdam News*, September 9, 1944, 1.

72. "U.S. at War: Reports on the Negro Soldier," *Time*, March 26, 1945.

73. Milton Bracker, "Americans Lose Ground in Italy," *New York Times*, February 14, 1945, 5; Dalfiume, *Desegregation of the U.S. Armed Forces*, 86–87.

74. John H. Burma, "Analysis of Present Negro Press," *Social Forces* 26, 2 (December 1947): 177.

75. See Dalfiume, *Desegregating the U.S. Armed Forces*, 95–97.

76. Dale E. Wilson, "Recipe of Failure: Major General Edward M. Almond and Preparation of the U.S. 92nd Infantry Division for Combat in World War II," *Journal of Military History* 56, 3 (1992): 474.

77. "The Luckless 92nd," *Newsweek*, February 26, 1945, 34–35.

78. Letter George Fairchild to ANP, September 1943. Gibson answered Fairchild and sent his letter cc to Barnett: He argued that "Your reference to the report filed by General Davis and myself in the War Department is grossly untrue. . . . I have answered you in complete detail because the cause of the Negro soldier will be immeasurably harmed if you and others continue the spread of mischievous and baseless rumors. Certainly there are enough grievances that are founded in fact to keep all of us busy. If in the future you have occasion to write about the Army, I hope for the sake of hundreds of thousands of Negro soldiers on active duty that you confine your statements to material based on fact." Barnett Papers, Part III: Subject File on Black Americans, 1918–1967; Series F Reel 1.

79. Morris J. MacGregor, Jr., *Integration of the Armed Forces, 1940–1965* (Washington D.C.: Center of Military History of the United States Army, 1985); Mershon and Schlossman, *Foxholes and Color Lines*, 103–4.

80. Report on Visit to 92nd Division (Negro Troops) to Major General O. L. Nelson, March 12, 1945, Truman K. Gibson Papers, Box 3, Folder 3, Library of Congress, Manuscript Division, Washington, D.C. (hereafter Gibson Papers).

81. First quote: Milton Bracker, "Americans Lose Ground in Italy," *New York Times*, February 14, 1945, 5; second and last quote: "Negro Soldiers," *Washington Post*, March 18, 1945, B4; third quote: "U.S. at War: Report on the Negro Soldier," *Time*, March 26, 1945.

82. Milton Bracker, "Negroes' Courage Upheld in Inquiry," *New York Times*, March 15, 1945, 12; "Army Studying More Effective Negro Training," *New York Herald Tribune*, March 15, 1945.

83. Lem Graves, Jr., "Truman Gibson Finds Commanders in Italy Know of Race Feelings," *Norfolk Journal and Guide*, March 17, 1945; Collins George, "Facts Are Exposed by Aide," *Pittsburgh Courier*, March 24, 1945, 4.

84. Earl Brown, "Timely Topics," *New York Amsterdam News*, April 14, 1945, 14A.

85. Adam Clayton Powell, "Soapbox in Washington," *People's Voice*, March 31, 1945; "'Gibson Sold Out'—Powell," *Chicago Defender*, March 31, 1945, 1.

86. Ramona Lowe, "Demand Gibson Ouster; Nationwide Protest Slurs on 92nd Division," *Chicago Defender*, March 24, 1945, 1.

87. Grant Reynolds, "Questions Illiteracy Charges Against 92nd Division," *New York Amsterdam News*, March 24, 1945, 1A.

88. Roy Wilkins to Editor of the *New York Times*, March 20, 1945, NAACP Records, Part II , Box A 648, Folder 92nd Division 1945. The NUL joined the NAACP in the protest; Lowe, "Demand Gibson Ouster."

89. "The Negro Soldier Betrayed," *The Crisis*, April 1945, 97.

90. Roy Wilkins to Eustace Gay, March 27, 1945. In a letter to Thomas W. Young, editor of the *Norfolk Journal and Guide*, Roy Wilkins noted that the *Pittsburgh Courier*, though not fully "incompatible" with the philosophy of the NAACP, was also "'collaborationist' with the War department" and therefore should be "mindful of the immediate and long-range interests of Negro soldiers and civilians" and more "skeptical of the War department." Roy Wilkins to Thomas W. Young, May 5, 1945. Both letters in NAACP Records, Part II, Box A 648, Folder 92nd Division 1945.

91. "The conclusion is inescapable that Mr. Gibson betrayed the Negro soldier and rendered himself ineffective as representative of Negro citizens in the War department. Mr. Gibson ought to resign and forthwith." Roy Wilkins quoted in "'Gibson Sold Out'—Powell"; Lowe, "Demand Gibson Ouster."

92. Truman K. Gibson to Roy Wilkins, April 9, 1945. Truman K. Gibson, Sr., Gibson's father and president of Supreme Liberty Life Insurance Co., interfered and discontinued all support for the NAACP over the organization's criticism of his son. Truman K. Gibson, Sr., to Walter White, April 25, 1945. All in NAACP Records, Part II, Box A 648, Folder 92nd Division 1945

93. First quote: Complaint, Truman K. Gibson to Walter White, April 12, 1945; second quote of board decision: Minutes of the Meeting of the Board of Directors, April 9, 1945. Second and third quote: Minutes of the Meeting of the Board of Directors, May 14, 1945. All in NAACP Records, Part II, Box A 648, Folder 92nd Division 1945. See also Roy Wilkins, "The Old Army Game?" *The Crisis*, May 1945, 130–31, 140, 145; "Editorials," *The Crisis*, June 1945, 161. Fourth quote: "Truman Gibson Rebuffed by NAACP Board," *Chicago Defender*, June 2, 1945, 1.

94. SSG Donn V. Hart to the NAACP New York Office, August 31, 1945, NAACP Records, Part II, Box A 648, Folder 92nd Division 1945.

95. See "Is the 92nd a Failure?" *Chicago Defender*, April 14, 1945, 12; "Too Much Ado About the 92nd Division Episode," *New Journal and Guide*, April 14, 1945, B8; John Jordan, "The Truth About the 92nd," *New Journal and Guide*, April 21, 1945, A1; John H. Young, III., "Gibson Praises Troops," *Pittsburgh Courier*, April 14, 1945, 15; Eustace Gay, "Facts and Fancies: The Gibson Interview," *Philadelphia Tribune*, April 7, 1945, 4.

96. Marlon B. Ross has pointed out that emasculation for African American men was not only a "metaphorical threat," but a physical threat of castration. See Ross, *Manning the Race: Reforming Black Men in the Jim Crow Era* (New York: New York University Press, 2004), 7.

97. The gender-specific epithet "Uncle Tom" has a long tradition and "challenges opponents by feminizing them, and therefore linking them to 'weakness.'" Estes, *I am a Man!*, 8. According to Irene Visser, it is "a cultural byword for black spineless and soulless acquiescence. . . . his masculinity has been denied and his femininity emphasized instead." "(In) Famous Spirituality: Harriet Beecher Stowe's Uncle Tom," *Spiritus* 8 (2008): 1. The opposing stereotype of black men virulent in white circles was that of the hypersexual, primitive beast. See, e.g., Robert Staples, "Stereotypes of Black Male Sexuality: The Facts Behind the Myth," in *Men's Lives*, ed. Michael S. Kimmel and Michael A. Messner (Boston: Pearson, 2004), 428–32; Riché Richardson, *Black Masculinity and the U.S. South: From Uncle Tom to Gangsta* (Athens: University of Georgia Press, 2007), esp. 3–17.

98. "Somebody's Gotta Go!" *Chicago Defender*, March 24, 1945, 12; see also "Gibson Finds Some Friends," *Chicago Defender*, March 31, 1945, 1.

99. First quote: Hoffman Gardner, "Soldier Protests Gibson's Remarks," *Chicago Defender*, April 14, 1945, 12; second quote: Iola Stensen, "Save 92nd Has Great Record"; third quote: Janis Lee Brissey, "Gibson's 'Gotta Go'; Coast Youth Agrees," *Chicago Defender*, May 5, 1945, 12; James L. Stuart, "Gibson Report Aids Negro Haters," *Chicago Defender*, April 21, 1945, 12.

100. A Supreme Liberty Life Policyholder, "Negroes Have Lost Faith in Gibson," *Chicago Defender*, May 5, 1945, 12; see also T-Cpl. E. H. White, "Overseas Soldier Has His Say on Gibson," *Chicago Defender*, June 30, 1945, 12.

101. "Is the 92nd a Failure?" *Chicago Defender*, April 14, 1945, 12; "92nd Hits Back to Foe!" *Chicago Defender*, April 14, 1945, 1; "Rhine Infantry Comes Through,"

Atlanta Daily World, March 27, 1945, 1; Max Johnson, "Heroic Action Against Nazis Brings Awards," *New York Amsterdam News*, March 24, 1945, 6A.

102. Luther A. Townsley, "Gen'l, Clark Praises Brave 92nd Division," *Atlanta Daily World*, June 7, 1945, 1; see also "General Clark Hails 'Glorious' Record," *Chicago Defender*, June 9, 1945, 1.

103. "A Medal for a General," *Chicago Defender*, June 16, 1945, 15.

104. Gibson quoted in "Gibson and the 92nd," *Afro-American*, April 14, 1945, 4; see also Paul Sann, "Candid Troubleshooter," *Post Weekly Picture Magazine*, August 25, 1945.

105. Quote from Jordan, "The Truth About the 92nd"; see also John H. Young III, "Gibson Praises Troops," *Pittsburgh Courier*, April 14, 1945, 15; Venice T. Spraggs," Captures Two Towns in New Drive to Answer Slurs," *Chicago Defender*, April 14, 1945, 1; "92nd Has Not Failed in Combat, Gibson Answers," *Norfolk Journal and Guide*, April 14, 1945, A1.

106. Memorandum from Walter White to Thurgood Marshall, June 28, 1948, NAACP Records, Part II, Box A 648, Folder 92nd Division 1945.

107. Memorandum to Mr. Wilkins from Mr. White, August 27, 1945; see also "Is the 92nd a Failure?" *Chicago Defender*, April 14, 1945, 12.

108. Julius Adams, "Truman Gibson: 'Uncle Tom' or Useful Public Servant," *New York Amsterdam News*, April 14, 1945, 2A; Gay, "Facts and Fancies"; "Debunks Lie About Negro GI in Action," *New York Amsterdam News*, April 14, 1945, 1A; Charley Cherokee, "National Grapevine," *Chicago Defender*, April 28, 1945, 11.

109. "There's an Outside Chance," *Chicago Defender*, December 1, 1945, 12. Always a Gibson supporter, the *Norfolk Journal and Guide*, on the other hand, praised him for his exceptional service. "A Difficult Job Exceptionally Well Done," *Norfolk Journal and Guide*, November 24, 1945, B 12.

110. Fred Atwater, "Dixie Echoes 92nd Slurs," *Chicago Defender*, April 7, 1945, 1.

111. John Modell, Marc Goulden, and Sigurdur Magnusson, "World War II in the Lives of Black Americans: Some Findings and an Interpretation," *Journal of American History* 76, 3 (December 1989): 838. See also Walter White, *A Man Called White* (New York: Viking, 1948), 322–28; Jennifer E. Brooks, *Defining the Peace: World War Veterans, Race, and the Remaking of Southern Political Tradition* (Chapel Hill: University of North Carolina Press, 2004); Timothy B. Tyson, *Radio Free Dixie: Robert F. Williams and the Roots of Black Power* (Chapel Hill: University of North Carolina Press, 1999). Political scientist Christopher Parker supports this argument in his book on blacks and their fight against white supremacy after the Second World War. Political scientist Ronald Krebs, however, contests this radicalization argument. Christopher Parker, *Fighting for Democracy: Black Veterans and the Struggle Against White Supremacy in the Postwar South* (Princeton, N.J.: Princeton University Press, 2009), esp. 132, 195; Ronald R. Krebs, *Fighting for Rights: Military Service and the Politics of Citizenship* (Ithaca, N.Y.: Cornell University Press, 2006).

Chapter 2. Coming Home

1. Walter White, "People, Politics and Places: Nation in Fear," *Chicago Defender*, August 17, 1946.

2. For a detailed study on white segregationist fight against the civil rights movement since the New Deal see, e.g., Jason Morgan Ward, *Defending White Democracy: The Making of a Segregationist Movement and the Remaking of Racial Politics, 1936–1965* (Chapel Hill: University of North Carolina Press, 2011).

3. Harvard Sitkoff, "Harry Truman and the Election of 1948: The Coming of Age of Civil Rights in American Politics," *Journal of Southern History* 37, 4 (November 1971): 598.

4. Ward, *Defending White Democracy*, 84; on the fallout between African Americans and moderate whites over social equality, Jane Dailey, "The Sexual Politics of Race in World War America," in *Fog of War: The Second World War and the Civil Rights Movement*, ed. Kevin M. Kruse and Stephen Tuck (Oxford: Oxford University Press, 2012), esp. 168–70.

5. Theodore Bilbo before the Senate, Cong. Rec. 79th Cong., 1st sess., 6803–24 (1945); relocation to Africa in speech, 6818, 6886 (1945).

6. Robert L. Fleegler, "Theodore G. Bilbo and the Decline of Public Racism, 1938–1947," *Journal of Mississippi History* 66, 1 (Spring 2006): 15–16.

7. Sen. James Eastland before the Senate, Cong. Rec. 79th Cong., 1st sess., 6991–7005, 6992 (1945). On Eastland, the FEPC, and Germany, Chris Myers Asch, "Revisiting Reconstruction: James O. Eastland, the FEPC, and the Struggle to Rebuild Germany, 1945–1946," *Journal of Mississippi History* 67, 2 (2005): 1–28.

8. Eastland, Senate, 6994–95. Bilbo extended his racist slurs to Japanese in the discussion of the FEPC, claiming, "Personally, I think the Jap is a heathen. He is an animal. He is a mongrel. He is an off-breed. I think he is hopeless. If I had my way about it I would enforce sterilization of the whole damn race." 6999.

9. Eastland, Senate, 7002. On the changes and consistencies in white segregationists' fight against the African American freedom struggle see Ward, *Defending White Democracy*.

10. See Bilbo, Senate, 6816.

11. On the rape myth, Jacquelyn Dowd Hall, *Revolt Against Chivalry: Jessie Daniel Ames and the Women's Campaign Against Lynching* (New York: Columbia University Press, 1993), esp. 140; Lisa Lindquist Dorr, *White Women, Rape, and the Power of Race in Virginia, 1900–1960* (Chapel Hill: University of North Carolina Press, 2004); on rape, female civil rights activists, and African American women in general, see Danielle L. McGuire, *At the Dark End of the Street: Black Women, Rape, and Resistance—A New History of the Civil Rights Movement from Rosa Parks to the Rise of Black Power* (New York: Knopf, 2010), esp. 21–24. During World War I and World War II, a disproportionate number of African Americans were court-martialed and severely punished for rape. For World War I see Chad Williams, *Torchbearers of Democracy: African American Soldiers in the World War I Era* (Chapel Hill: University of North Carolina Press,

2010), 190pp. There is only a sociological study on rape and the American occupational troops in Europe: J. Robert Lilly, *Taken by Force: Rape and American GIs in Europe During WWII* (New York: Palgrave Macmillan, 2008). The book has serious flaws, but it is the first of its kind.

12. See "Eastland Hits Army for Denial of Stuttgart Rape Charges," *Washington Post*, July 18, 1945, 3; on Wheeler's trip, Marquis Childs, "Washington Calling," *Washington Post*, June 11, 1945, 6.

13. Eastland, Senate, 6996.

14. Eastland, Senate, 6997.

15. Eastland, Senate, 6996.

16. Quoted in Eric J. Sundquist, *To Wake the Nations: Race in the Making of American Literature* (Cambridge, Mass.: Harvard University Press, 1993), 425. The black "rape myth" had been a powerful argument after the First World War, when French troops, among them black soldiers from France's African colonies, occupied the Rhineland. Germans described these black men as "fürchterliche Marrokanerhorden" (dreadful Moroccan hordes), "wilde Tiere" (wild animals), and "betrunkene Neger" (drunken Negroes). They were often scapegoated for sexual violence and other offenses following the arrival of French troops. According to Heide Fehrenbach, there existed "sustained attention to racialized rape" that shifted from vilification of Jews to vilification of Soviets, Africans, and black Americans after the war. Heide Fehrenbach, *Race After Hitler: Black Occupation Children in Postwar Germany and America* (Princeton, N.J.: Princeton University Press, 2005), 53. According to historian Timothy Schroer, accusations against blacks, especially against African Americans, often resulted from expectations rather than experience. Timothy Schroer, *Recasting Race After World War II: Germans and African Americans in American-Occupied Germany* (Boulder: University Press of Colorado, 2007), 28–30; rape libel in German politics, e.g., David B. Posner, "Afro-America in Western German Perspective, 1945–1966" (Ph.D. dissertation, Yale University, 1997), 40; Sandra Mass, "Von der 'schwarzen Schmach' zur 'deutschen Heimat': Die Rheinische Frauenliga im Kampf gegen die Rheinlandbesetzung, 1920–1929," *WerkstattGeschichte* 32 (2002): 44–57; Robert Nowatzki, "Race, Rape, Lynching, and Manhood Suffrage: Constructions of White and Black Masculinity in Turn-of-the-Century White Supremacist Literature," *Journal of Men's Studies* 3, 2 (1994): 161–70.

17. See Asch, "Revisiting Reconstruction," esp. 18–19.

18. "1st Sgt. Washington Davis, What the People Say: Finds Americans, Not Germans His Enemy," *Chicago Defender*, September 1, 1945, 12. On the liberating effect of the open relations between German women and African Americans see Maria Höhn and Martin Klimke, *A Breath of Freedom: The Civil Rights Struggle, African American GIs, and Germany* (New York: Palgrave Macmillan, 2010), 39–54; Maria Höhn, *GIs and Fräuleins: The German-American Encounter in 1950s West Germany* (Chapel Hill: University of North Carolina Press, 2002).

19. Timothy B. Tyson, *Radio Free Dixie: Robert F. Williams and the Roots of Black Power* (Chapel Hill: University of North Carolina Press, 1999), 58–59.

20. Dailey, "The Sexual Politics of Race in World War II America," 145–70.

21. "Impeachment of Hate Senators Is Requested," *Atlanta Daily World*, July 4, 1945, 1.

22. Letters to NAACP and Senator Eastland, NAACP Records, Part II, Box A 649, Folder Eastland 1945, Box A 370, Folder United States Army Soldier Letters Senators Bilbo and Eastland 1945, and Box A 242, Folder Eastland, James, 1945–1955. *Stars and Stripes*, the daily newspaper of the U.S. armed forces, received numerous letters from soldiers attacking Eastland. Mail Call, *Stars and Stripes*, July 9, 1945, 2. The Eastland Papers at the University of Mississippi contain numerous letters of African American soldiers and American citizens, especially women, condemning the senator's thesis. James O. Eastland Collection, File Series 3, Subseries 1, Box 30, Folders 1944 Civil Rights, 1945 Civil Rights 1–3: Press Clippings, University of Mississippi, Department of Archives and Special Collections, Oxford, Mississippi.

23. S. B. Simmons, "Guide's Reply to Eastland Draws Favorable Comment," *Norfolk Journal and Guide*, July 21, 1945, C2; SGT M. H. Jones, Cpl. H. L. Clover, "Letter to the Editor: Soldiers Protest Eastland Attack," *Atlanta Daily World*, July 25, 1945, 6; "Letters from Amsterdam News Readers," *New York Amsterdam News*, July 28, 1945, 12; "Eastland's Insult Shocks Soldiers," *Norfolk Journal and Guide*, July 21, 1945, 11; "Embittered GIs Protests Eastland Racial Smear and Nazi Tactics: NAACP Receives Hundreds of Protest Letters Soldiers Pledge Themselves to Get Rights at Home." *Atlanta Daily World*, August 1, 1945, 1; "Colored Troops Denounce Senator Eastland's Smear," *Philadelphia Tribune*, August 4, 1945, 1.

24. John H. Young, III., "EASTLAND INSULTS 13,000,000 CITIZENS: Mississippi Senator in Vicious Attack, Says Negro Soldiers "Won't Fight, Won't Work," *Pittsburgh Courier*, July 7, 1945, 1. Another group wrote to the president on behalf of impeachment of Eastland and Bilbo. "Impeachment for Eastland, & Bilbo Urged: Asks President Truman to Take Action Against Race Baiting Mississippians," *New York Amsterdam News*, July 14, 1945, A1.

25. "Grandmother Takes on Eastland," *Philadelphia Tribune*, July 14, 1945, 1. On more grassroots activism, "Citizens Wax Anger over Eastland Slur," *Atlanta Daily World*, July 17, 1945, 4.

26. Marjorie McKenzie, "Pursuit of Democracy," *Pittsburgh Courier*, July 14, 1945, 7. On spread of segregation in occupied countries see, e.g., Höhn and Klimke, *A Breath of Freedom*, 54–62; Graham Smith, *When Jim Crow Met John Bull: Black American Soldiers in World War II Britain* (London: Tauris, 1987).

27. Evelyn Swann, "The Feminine Viewpoint: Dear Colored Servicemen," *Norfolk Journal and Guide*, July 7, 1945, 6; see also Warren Smadbeck, "Hitlerism and Eastland," *New York Amsterdam News*, July 14, 1945, A12.

28. "Dr. Goebbels Rides Again," *Pittsburgh Courier*, July 7, 1945, 6; see also "Eastland's Tale of 'Rape' a Lie, Say 7 Officers—They Were There," *Chicago Defender*, August 18, 1945, 2.

29. Both quotes in "Dr. Goebbels Rides Again."

30. "The South Is in The Saddle!" *Pittsburgh Courier*, July 7, 1945, 6.

31. Jarvis, *The Male Body at War*, 151; Susan Bordo, *Unbearable Weight: Feminism, Western Culture, and the Body*, 2nd ed. (Berkeley: University of California Press, 2004).

32. "The South Is in the Saddle!"

33. "Sen. Eastland's Attack Greeted by Silence," *Philadelphia Tribune*, July 14, 1945, 4.

34. Sen. James Mead, Cong. Rec. 79th Cong., 1st sess., 7424–28 (1945); Sen. Wagner, 7420–22.

35. Harry McAlpin, "Wagner and Mead Defend Negro Soldier on Floor of Congress," *Atlanta Daily World*, July 19, 1945, 1; Earl Brown, "Timely Topics," *New York Amsterdam News*, July 21, 1945, A12; Harry McAlpin, "New York's Senators Vindicate Honor of Negro GIs in Debate," *Pittsburgh Courier*, July 21, 1945, 12; "Defends Negro GI's: Wagner Says Eastland's Views Are Not Those of General Staff," *New York Times*, July 13, 1945, 9.

36. Helen Gahagan Douglas, "The Negro Soldier Extensions of Remarks," Cong. Rec. 79th Cong., 2nd sess., A428–43 (1946); Helen Gahagan Douglas, *The Negro Soldier: A Partial Record of Negro Devotion and Heroism in the Cause of Freedom, Gathered from the Files of the War and Navy Departments* (Washington, D.C.: Government Printing Office, 1946). Douglas on the concept of the book, Helen Gahagan Douglas Project: Oral History Transcript, interview by Amelia Fry, 1973/1974/1976, *Women in Politics Oral History Project*.

37. Isaac Woodard, Sworn Testimony for Civil Law Suit, November 1947, NAACP Papers MF, Series B, Reel 30.

38. Harvard Sitkoff, "Racial Militancy and Interracial Violence in the Second World War," *Journal of American History* 58, 3 (December 1971): 667.

39. Quotes from "Nation Aroused over Blinding of Negro Veteran," *Chicago Defender*, July 27, 1946, 1; "Veteran's Eyes Gouged Out by Hate-Crazed Dixie Police," *Chicago Defender*, July 20, 1946, "Veteran, Beat by Aiken Officers, Totally Blind," *Atlanta Daily World*, May 3, 1946, 4.

40. Kari Frederickson, *The Dixiecrat Revolt and the End of the Solid South, 1932–1968* (Chapel Hill: University of North Carolina Press, 2001), 54–55.

41. Quotes from "Nation Aroused over Blinding of Negro Veteran"; "Veteran's Eyes Gouged Out by Hate-Crazed Dixie Police"; "Veteran, Beat by Aiken Officers, Totally Blind."

42. "Blinding of Vet Shocks the Nation," *Atlanta Daily World*, July 21, 1946, 1.

43. "Federal Help Sought for Blinded Veteran," *New York Times*, July 25, 1946, 23; P. V. Hammond, "Isaac Woodard," *Washington Post*, July 23, 1946, 12; J. G. Frain, "Isaac Woodard," *Washington Post*, August 5, 1946, 6; "Chief Shull Is Acquitted in Columbia," *Augusta Chronicle*, November 6, 1946, 1.

44. Telegram Alliance of Postal Employees to President Truman, September 28, 1946, Papers of Harry S. Truman General File, Box 2701, Folder D, Harry S. Truman, Harry S. Truman Library, Independence, Missouri (hereafter Truman Papers). The majority of letters and telegrams were referred to the Justice Department or the Veterans Administration, as the White House felt unable to cater to or answer the requests.

45. "It's a Laugh Son," *Chicago Defender*, July 20, 1946, 14.

46. J. G. Frain, "Isaac Woodard," *Washington Post*, August 5, 1946, 6; Hammond, "Isaac Woodard."

47. See, e.g., Adriane Lentz-Smith, *Freedom Struggles: African Americans and World War I* (Cambridge, Mass.: Harvard University Press, 2009), 206–37; Williams, *Torchbearers of Democracy*, 223–60.

48. *The Crisis*, October 1946, 298–301. For a general overview of racial violence, Herbert Shapiro, *White Violence and Black Response: From Reconstruction to Montgomery* (Amherst: University of Massachusetts Press, 1988), 301–77; Allen D. Grimshaw, *Racial Violence in the United States* (Chicago: Aldine, 1969), 136–84.

49. "The Defender Pledge," *Chicago Defender*, August 3, 1946, 1, 6; see also "Courier Verse: Atrocity," *Pittsburgh Courier*, November 16, 1946, 6; "Freedom to Lynch" and "The Patton Revolution," *Pittsburgh Courier*, September 27, 1947, 6.

50. "Southern Bestiality," *Chicago Defender*, July 20, 1946, 14.

51. See "Georgia Weighs Monroe Murders," *New York Times*, August 4, 1946, 77. Although racial violence and lynching grew in numbers after the Second World War as after the First World War, they never increased as significantly. For a current look at lynching and an explanation for the decrease in numbers see e.g. Manfred Berg, "Das Ende der Lynchmorde im amerikanischen Süden," *Historische Zeitschrift* 283, 3 (2006): 583–616; Tyson, *Radio Free Dixie*, 58.

52. "Carol Brice and Husband Planning Benefit Concert for Isaac Woodard," *Atlanta Daily* World, July 30, 1946, 4.

53. "Woodard Tells Bitter Story," *Chicago Defender*, July 27, 1946, 3.

54. "Star Studded Show Ready," *New York Amsterdam News*, August 10, 1946, 1.

55. "Isaac Woodard Is Dreaming of Justice," *New York Amsterdam News*, August 10, 1946, 4.

56. Myers, "Black, White, and Olive Drab," 191.

57. Gerald Edwin Shenk, "Work or Fight: Selective Service and Manhood in the Progressive Era" (Ph.D. dissertation, University of California, San Diego, 1992), 27. Shenk distinguishes between "masculine men" and "more effeminate men" (dichotomized chart): Men—Non-men; Agency—Latency; Powerful—Powerless; Volition—Instinct, Impulse; Structure—Chaos; Organization—Disorganization; Self-discipline—Controlled by others; Physical Perfection—Illness, Crippled. Balance—Distortion; Fairness—Unfairness; see also Kathleen Kennedy, "Manhood and Subversion During World War I: The Cases of Eugene Debs and Alexander Berkman," *North Carolina Law Review* 82, 5 (June 2004): esp. 1661–68.

58. On the trope of the dysfunctional African American family, Ruth Feldstein, *Motherhood in Black and White: Race and Sex in American Liberalism, 1930–1965* (Ithaca, N.Y.: Cornell University Press, 2000), 40–85.

59. Nora Holt, "Blinding of Isaac Woodard American Hero," *New York Amsterdam News,* August 17, 1946, 9.

60. "Looking to the Future," *New York Amsterdam News,* July 27, 1946, 8.

61. "Southern Bestiality."

62. "Benefit Tickets A-Goin," *New York Amsterdam News,* August 6, 1946, 2.

63. See Ollie Stewart, "Acquit Eye-Gouging Cop," *Afro-American,* November 16, 1946, 1; A. H. Calloway, "Isaac Woodard Loses Suit for $50,000 Damages: Greyhound Not Liable for Beating," *Pittsburgh Courier,* November 22, 1947, 21.

64. Over time, the press lost interest and his death in 1992 went almost unnoticed. Most history books on postwar United States mention the Isaac Woodard case as representative of the position of black soldiers in the South.

65. Paul C. Davis, "The Negro in the Armed Services," *Virginia Quarterly Review* 24 (1948): 506. When he lists positive character traits of black soldiers, he argues within traditional black stereotypes of docility, servitude, and dedication to white men. "Gratitude, loyalty, and religious feeling are very pronounced."

66. "Headed Negro Troops: Believes Them Inferior," *AVC Bulletin,* August 1, 1946, 5; rebuttals: "Sachs' Opinions Scored by Colored Ex-Officer," *AVC Bulletin,* September 1, 1946, 5.

67. Quote from Grant Hauskins, transcript of interview by Nathan Stanley, transcript of interview with Grant Hauskins, http://mcel.pacificu.edu, accessed July 21, 2011. See also Bill Smith, "Few GIs Eager to Return to States," *Pittsburgh Courier,* February 22, 1947, 1. In more detail, Höhn and Klimke, *A Breath of Freedom,* 21–38.

68. NAACP quoted in "Mass Lay-Offs Follow V-J Day," *Atlanta Daily World,* August 19, 1945, 1; "V-J Day Shows Up Unfair Discharges for Negroes," *Philadelphia Tribune,* August 25, 1945, 1; "V-J Day Shows Unfair Army Discharge System," *Chicago Defender,* August 25, 1945, 4. On the high number of discharges, Ulysses Lee, *The United States Army in World War II: The Employment of Negro Troops* (Washington, D.C.: Government Printing Office, 1966), esp. 298–300.

69. On blue discharges, *Investigations of the National War Effort: Report of the Committee on Military Affairs House of Representatives,* 79th Cong. (June 1946), H.R. Rep. No. 2740.

70. Margot Canaday, *The Straight State: Sexuality and Citizenship in Twentieth-Century America* (Princeton, N.J.: Princeton University Press, 2009), esp. 154; Margot Canaday, "Building a Straight State: Sexuality and Social Citizenship Under the 1944 G.I. Bill," *Journal of American History* 90, 3 (2003): 940.

71. John H. Young, "Limit on Army Blue Discharges," *Pittsburgh Courier,* October 27, 1945, 1. See also "The Army Blue Discharge Certificate," *Atlanta Daily World,* November 27, 1947; "Marines Charge Discharge Bias," *New York Amsterdam News,* April 20, 1946, 20. Passed in 1944 as the Servicemen's Readjustment Act of 1944, the

GI Bill provided numberous benefits and assistance to returning World War II veterans in order to smooth their transition to civilian life. See Suzanne Mettler, *Soldiers to Citizens: The G.I. Bill and the Making of the Greatest Generation* (New York: Oxford University, 2005).

72. Jennifer E. Brooks, *Defining the Peace: World War Veterans, Race, and the Remaking of Southern Political Tradition* (Chapel Hill: University of North Carolina Press, 2004), 20.

73. Both quotes from Young, "Limit on Army Blue Discharges," *Pittsburgh Courier*, October 27, 1945, 1.

74. Edward F. Witsell, Adjutant General, to Jesse D. Dedmon, Jr., Secretary Veterans Affairs National Association for the Advancement of Colored People, December 3, 1945; Phillip McGuire, ed., *Taps for a Jim Crow Army: Letters from Black Soldiers in World War II* (Lexington: University Press of Kentucky, 1983), 146.

75. White quoted in "Says Peoples Determined to End Exploitation Walter White Makes Report at Annual Meeting," *Atlanta Daily World*, January 10, 1946, 1.

76. Edwin C. Johnson, "Blue Discharge," November 8, 1945, 78th Cong., 2nd Sess., A4778.

77. *Investigations of the National War Effort*, 13–14.

78. "House Committee Acts on 'Blue Discharges'," *Pittsburgh Courier*, February 9, 1946, 1.

79. Benjamin E. Mays, "Veterans: It Need Not Happen Again," *Phylon* 6 (Third Quarter 1945): 209; Joseph D. Bibb, "Life Magazine Gives Scant Credit to Our Soldiers in War History," *Pittsburgh Courier*, November 4, 1950, 7.

80. "Dustin' Off the News," *Chicago Defender*, January 26, 1946, 6.

81. *Los Angeles Sentinel*, March 21, 1946, 6.

82. "Facts on the Negro in World War Two [Comic Strip]," *Black Dispatch*, March 19, 1948, 7.

83. "NAACP Historian," *Chicago Defender*, February 23, 1946, 6. A reader of the *Chicago Defender* expressed his discontent over the fact that Jean Byers was white. Scolding the choice as "almost absurd," he demanded to hire an African American college graduate for this task. L. F. Cole, "Letter to the Editor: Asks for Negro Historian of World War II," *Chicago Defender*, March 16, 1946, 14.

84. A telling title of an article in *Our World*: Ex.-Sgt. George N. Constable, "A Different Story: We All Helped to Win the War . . . Remember?" *Our World* 2, 1, February 1947.

85. William Jordan, *Black Newspapers and America's War for Democracy, 1914–1920* (Chapel Hill: University of North Carolina Press, 2001), 5.

86. "Were Negro Soldiers Cowards?" *Our World* 2, 2, March 1947, 9ff.

87. Ibid.

88. Charley Cherokee, "National Grapevine: Tra La and Hey Nonny, You All," *Chicago Defender*, March 29, 1947, 13.

89. The event had been introduced by black historian Carter G. Woodson in 1926 to remember and celebrate the achievements of black America.

90. L. D. Reddick to President Truman, January 21, 1947, Truman Papers, President's Personal File, Box 130, Folder PPF 30.

91. Letter from Truman to Reddick, February 4, 1947, ibid.

92. David K. Niles, Memorandum for the Honorable William D. Hassett, March 4, 1947, ibid.

93. L. D. Reddick, "What Should the American Negro Reasonably Expect as the Outcome of a Real Peace," *Journal of Negro Education* 12, 3 (Summer 1943): 568–78.

94. Letter from L. D. Reddick to Eisenhower referenced in Colonel J. W. Bowen, Secretary General Staff, December 17, 1948; Letter from Eisenhower to L. D. Reddick, February 13, 1947, RG 407, Records of the Adjunct General's Office, Box 718, National Archives and Record Administration (NARA), College Park, Maryland.

95. L. D. Reddick, "Letters to the Editor: Race Relations in the Army," *Journal of American Sociology* 53, 1 (July 1947): 41–42.

96. E. T. Hall, Jr. "Race Prejudice and Negro-White Relations in the Army," *American Journal of Sociology* 52, 5 (March 1947): 401–9.

97. L. D. Reddick, "Race Relations in the Army," *American Journal of Sociology* 53, 6 (July 1947): 41.

98. A. B. Tourtellot, *Life's Picture History of World War II* (New York: Time, 1950).

99. Joseph D. Bibb, "Life Magazine Gives Scant Credit to Our Soldiers in War History," *Pittsburgh Courier*, November 4, 1950, 7.

100. Quotes from Letter from Roy Wilkins to Andrew Heiskell, Publisher *Life*, October 4, 1950, Papers of Roy Wilkins, Library of Congress Manuscript Division, Washington D.C., Box 3, Folder Correspondence 1950 (hereafter Wilkins Papers); Roy Wilkins also quoted in "Life Publisher Says: 'Role of Negro GI Was Not Ignored,'" *Pittsburgh Courier*, November 11, 1950, 2.

101. Letter from Roy Wilkins to *Life*, December 12, 1950, apologizing for his late payment for *Life's Picture History of World War II*. The letter was made public by Homer Roberts, a Chicago businessman, who claimed the book "outraged Negroes in this country." E. R. Noderer, "Not Mentioned in War History, Negroes Object," *Chicago Daily Tribune*, October 21, 1950, 6.

102. Roy Wilkins to Andrew Heiskell, Publisher *Life*, October 4, 1950; see also Wilkins quoted in "Life Publisher Says," 2.

103. Roy Wilkins to *Life*, December 12, 1950, Wilkins Papers, Box 3, Folder Correspondence 1950.

104. Joseph D. Bibb, "Our GIs Slighted: Life Magazine Gives Scant Credit to Our Soldiers in War History," *Pittsburgh Courier*, November 4, 1950, 7.

105. Susan Faludi, *Stiffed: The Betrayal of the American Man* (New York: William Morrow, 1999), 16; see Andrew Huebner, *The American Warrior Image: Soldiers in American Culture from the Second World War to the Vietnam Era* (Chapel Hill: University of North Carolina Press, 2008).

106. Roy Wilkins quoted in "Gillem Report Called Failure by Roy Wilkins," *Chicago Defender*, April 20, 1946; see also *Los Angeles Sentinel*, March 21, 1946, Editorial Page.

107. "The Gillem Report," *Chicago Defender*, March 23, 1946, 15; see also "New Army Order Tricks Whites Also," *Chicago Defender*, July 27, 1946, Editorial Page.

108. E.g., *Pittsburgh Courier*, May 11, 1946; *Norfolk Journal and Guide*, March 9, 1946, 1; Roy Wilkins, "Still a Jim Crow Army," *The Crisis*, April 1946, 106–89, 125.

109. For more information, Richard M. Dalfiume, *Desegregation of the U.S. Armed Forces: Fighting on Two Fronts, 1939–1953* (Columbia: University of Missouri Press, 1969) and Morris J. MacGregor, Jr., *Integration of the Armed Forces, 1940–1965* (Washington D.C.: Center of Military History of the United States Army, 1985).

110. Truman quoted in David McCullough, *Truman* (New York: Simon and Schuster, 1992), 588. On Truman and civil rights, William C. Berman, *The Politics of Civil Rights in the Truman Administration* (Columbus: Ohio State University Press, 1970); Sitkoff, "Harry Truman and the Election of 1948," 597–616; Michael R. Gardner, *Harry Truman and Civil Rights: Moral Courage and Political Risks* (Carbondale: Southern Illinois University Press, 2002); Donald R. McCoy and Richard T. Ruetten, *Quest and Response: Minority Rights in the Truman Administration* (Lawrence: University Press of Kansas, 1973).

111. President Harry S. Truman to Thomas C. Clark, Attorney General, September 20, 1946, Harry S. Truman Civil Rights Vertical File, Truman Papers.

112. See, e.g., Gardner, *Harry Truman and Civil Rights*, 28.

113. President's Committee on Civil Rights, *To Secure These Rights: The Report of the Civil Rights Committee on Civil Rights* (New York: Simon and Schuster, 1947).

114. Both quotes in ibid., 46- 47.

115. Confidential memorandum Clark M. Clifford to Harry S. Truman, November 19, 1947, *Harry S. Truman Library*, May 17, 2012. African Americans formed one of many voting blocs Clifford covered in the memorandum, but they took on an essential place in the electoral considerations.

116. The speech did not mention the end of segregation, only discrimination.

117. Channing H. Tobias, President Truman's Message on Civil Rights, February 11, 1948, Nash Papers, White House File, Box 38, Folder: Correspondence Philleo Nash, Personal and Miscellaneous, 1947–1952.

118. Niles, Memo Public Interest in the President's Civil Rights Program; see also Berman, *The Politics of Civil Rights in the Truman Administration*, 90.

119. Thomas Jefferson Murray, House of Representatives, February 25, 1948, Cong. Rec., 80th Cong., 2nd sess., 1702.

120. John Hope Franklin, *From Slavery to Freedom: A History of African Americans* (New York: Knopf, 1994), 461–62; on the unprecedented nature of Truman's civil rights rhetoric, Garth E. Pauley, "Harry Truman and the NAACP: A Case Study in Presidential Persuasion on Civil Rights," *Rhetoric and Public Affairs* 2, 2 (1999): 211–41.

Chapter 3. Stepping up the Fight

1. Grant Reynolds before NAACP War Emergency Conference in 1944, "NAACP's Wartime Conference Centers on Post-War Demands," *Pittsburgh Courier*, July 22, 1944, 1; see also Timothy B. Tyson, *Radio Free Dixie: Robert F. Williams and the Roots of Black Power* (Chapel Hill: University of North Carolina Press, 1999), 48.

2. Douglass L. Conner, World War II veteran, quoted in Neil McMillen, "How Mississippi's Black Veterans Remember World War II," in *Remaking Dixie: The Impact of World War II on the American South*, ed. Neil McMillen (Jackson: University Press of Mississippi, 1997), 108; see also Jennifer E. Brooks, *Defining the Peace: World War Veterans, Race, and the Remaking of Southern Political Tradition* (Chapel Hill: University of North Carolina Press, 2004), 14; Tyson, *Radio Free Dixie*, 51–52.

3. See "'Red Scare' Raised by Chaplain in N.Y. Race Against Powell," *Chicago Defender*, May 18, 1946, 4; "All's Still Quiet on the Congressional War-Fronts," *New York Amsterdam News*, October 5, 1946, 1; "We Want Teamwork," *New York Amsterdam News*, October 26, 1946, 10; "Meet Speakers Hits Adams for Doing Nothing," *New York Amsterdam News*, November 2, 1946, 25. On Dewey and blacks, "Do Your Duty: Vote!" *New York Amsterdam News*, November 2, 1946, 10.

4. The leading veterans' organization in the United States, the American Legion, refused to integrate as a whole, but left it up to the individual chapters and state organizations. The Veterans of Foreign Wars, American Veterans Committee, and United Negro and Allied Veterans of America were founded as interracial organizations that demanded the integration of the military. "Vet Organizations Bid for Negro Membership," *Chicago Defender*, November 2, 1946.

5. Alex Lubin, *Romance and Rights: The Politics of Interracial Intimacy 1945–1954* (Jackson: University Press of Mississippi, 2005), x.

6. The general outline of UMT is mainly based on Michael J. Hogan, *A Cross of Iron: Harry S. Truman and the Origins of the National Security State* (Cambridge: Cambridge University Press, 2000), chap. 4; William A. Taylor, "Every Citizen a Soldier: The U.S. Army's Campaign for Universal Military Training Following World War II" (Ph.D. dissertation, George Washington University, 2010).

7. "Postwar Training," *Washington Post*, January 8, 1945, 6.

8. President Harry S. Truman, "Address Before a Joint Session of the Congress on Universal Military Training," October 23, 1945, *New York Times*, October 24, 1945, 3. Gerhard Peters and John T. Woolley, The American Presidency Project, http://www.presidency.ucsb.edu.

9. Mark R. Grandstaff, "Making the Military American: Advertising, Reform, and the Demise of an Antistanding Military Tradition, 1945–1955," *Journal of Military History* 60, 2 (April 1996): 304.

10. Documents on and of the committee, White House Office Files 109-B, Box 641, Folder President's Advisory Committee on Universal Military Training, Truman Papers.

11. Sidney Shalett, "UMT Bill Action Sought in House," *New York Times*, May 9, 1947, 11.

12. National Security Act of 1947: Hearings before House Committee on Expenditures in the Executive Departments, 80th Cong., 1st sess. (June 20, July 16, 1947); Hearings before Committee on Expenditures in the Executive Departments, 80th Cong., 2nd sess. (January 14, 1948).

13. See, e.g., Universal Military Training, Digest of H.R. 4278 (a Bill to Enact the National Security Training Act of 1947) H.R. Rep. No. 1107; Letters from Secretary of Defense, dated February 9 and February 10, 1948; Letter to Chairman, Senate Armed Services Committee, Discussing Universal Military Training Costs; Letter from Secretary of Defense, Dated February 26, 1948, to Chairman, Senate Armed Services Committee, Discussing Costs of Reserves, Senate Committee Print, 80th Cong., 2nd sess. (1948).

14. James Forrestal before Senate Armed Services Committee, March 18, 1948, *Vital Speeches of the Day* 14, 12 (April 1, 1948): 364–66.

15. "Harry McClain, Legion, V.F.W. Urge Full Year Training Plan," *Chicago Daily Tribune*, February 7, 1945, 6.

16. The Gallup poll on UMT, as well as on other topics, was conducted over a long span of time. Although published independently, it was widely used in newspapers and magazines across the country. The percentile of support went up 12 points after a short slump in January 1948: "Public Support for Both Draft and UMT Shown," *Los Angeles Times*, April 9, 1948, 1.

17. William Gould, "Letter to the Editor—Not the Road to Peace: Universal Military Training Neither Prevents nor Wins Wars," *Hartford Courant*, January 2, 1945, 6. A large number of people joined the debate on the continuation of the draft and UMT right from the start. Not only did they write letters to the editor, they also flooded President Truman and their representatives with mail on their personal take on the draft and the pending introduction of UMT. Papers of Harry S. Truman Official File 245, Box 845, 846, 847, 848.

18. On the discussion in the general public see, e.g., "Universal Military Training," *New Republic*, December 12, 1947, 12; William L. Bratt, Jr., "Why Advocate U.M.T.," *Nation*, April 24, 1948; *Congressional Digest*, 26, 10 (October 1947); Hanson W. Baldwin, "19 Million in World Armies, Forty-Nation Survey Shows," *New York Times*, May 4, 1947, 1; Josephus Daniels, "Should U.S.A. Adopt a Program of Universal Military Training? Con," *Congressional Digest*, 26, 10 (October 1947): 241–43.

19. Timothy Stewart-Winter, "'Not a Soldier, Not a Slacker': Conscientious Objectors and Male Citizenship in the United States During the Second World War," *Gender & History* 19, 3 (November 2007): 519–42.

20. For his general take on UMT and the draft, Langer's Radio Broadcast on UMT, June 13, 1948; Langer, "Extension of Remarks: Universal Military Training," 80th Cong., 2nd sess., Cong. Rec., August 7, 1948, A45030–31.

21. On the importance of military service in the transition to manhood see historians Patricia Thomas and Marie Thomas, who assert that the armed forces "represented a passage from boyhood to manhood for generations of American men" and that they "define what it means to be a man. . . . A major function of the military, therefore, is to create men—men defined by a traditional masculine ideology." Patricia J. Thomas and Marie D. Thomas, "Integrating Women in the Military: Parallels to the Progress of Homosexuals?" in *Out in Force: Sexual Orientation and the Military*, ed. Gregory M. Herek, Jared B. Jobe, and Ralph M. Carney (Chicago: University of Chicago Press, 1996), 65–85, 70.

22. See "Senatorial Nonsense," *New York Times*, December 25, 1946, 28; Sidney I. Simon, "For Military Training: Advocated as Teaching Tolerance and Building Character," *New York Times*, January 5, 1947, E10.

23. See Robert P. Patterson, Statement submitted to Congress, May 23, 1947, *Congressional Digest* 26, 10 (October 1947): 242. This response by the War Department came to an article by Hanson Baldwin in the *New York Times*.

24. Senator Gurney and Representative Oberton Brooks submitted almost identical proposals to the 80th Congress in the name of the two veterans' organizations. Charles Gotthart, "U.S. Must Stay Too Strong for Attack: Truman," *Chicago Daily Tribune*, August 29, 1947, 3.

25. "Educators Hit War Training in Peacetime," *Christian Science Monitor*, January 10, 1945, 3; Benjamin Fine, "Educators Oppose Peace-Draft Bill," *New York Times*, January 11, 1945, 21.

26. Harold Taylor, "Why I Oppose U.M.T.," *Nation*, April 17, 1948, 410–12; Henry Wallace, "Universal Military Training," *New Republic*, December 1, 1947, 12; Henry Wallace, "The Militarization of the United States," *New Republic*, January 26, 1948. For more on the radical site, "The Army Says—The Army Builds Men—But Let's See HOW It Builds Them"; "Is It Your Boy They're Planning to Train for This?"; National Council Against Conscription Papers (NCAC Papers), Series C, Box 6, Folder Outreach Published Literature 1945–1949, Swarthmore Peace Collection, Swarthmore College, Swarthmore, Pennsylvania.

27. One of the exceptions was Taylor, "Why I Oppose U.M.T."

28. "No Negroes at Knox Experimental Unit," *Pittsburgh Courier*, January 11, 1947, 1.

29. See "300,000 Negroes May Be Called: Immediate Action Is Urged by President," *Pittsburgh Courier*, March 27, 1948, 1&4; "Army Snipes at Bias as UMT Fight Grows," *Pittsburgh Courier*, January 31, 1948, 1; "Brass Hats and Jim Crow," *Pittsburgh Courier*, January 10, 1948, 6.

30. See Charles H. Houston to Lester B. Granger, April 21, 1948, NAACP Papers MF, Part 9, Series A, Reel 9; "Sees Conflict in New Army Training Program," *Chicago Defender*, June 21, 1947, 9.

31. Rep. Arthur Capper (R-Kan.), "The Negro and the Postwar Military Policy Extension of Remarks," 79th Cong., 1st sess., NAACP Papers MF, Part 9, Series A, Reel 7.

32. "Universal Military Training," *Pittsburgh Courier*, January 3, 1948, 6. If not stated otherwise, the following quotes are from this article.

33. "Truman Asks Action 'Now' on Racism," *Chicago Defender*, July 5, 1947.

34. "In Nation's Capital," *New York Amsterdam News*, July 12, 1947, 10.

35. Quoted Julius Thomas, Director of Industrial Relations National Urban League, Statement in front of the Fahy Committee, Washington, D.C., April 25, 1949, in NAACP Papers MF, Part 9, Series A, Reel 7.

36. Capper, "The Negro and the Postwar Military Policy Extension of Remarks."

37. Roy Wilkins to *Negro Digest*, Against Peacetime Conscription, January 1946, NAACP Records, Part II, Box A 655, Folder Universal Military Training General 1944–49.

38. The newspaper went so far as to demand that the training of black troops take place in the North, a proposal African Americans particularly contested. Opponents of this idea felt that—despite it being understandable in light of violent, if not fatal, attacks on black soldiers in the South—white Southerners could interpret the move as a retreat of black civil rights activists and a victory for segregation and white supremacy. "No Jim Crow Universal Training," *New York Amsterdam News*, January 25, 1947, 8. See also interview with Judge William H. Hastie, January 5, 1972, interview by Jerry N. Hess, *Harry S. Truman Library*, January 14, 2008, http://www.trumanlibrary.org/oralhist/hastie.htm.

39. "What About Racial Integration," *Pittsburgh Courier*, June 14, 1947; see also "Bias Still Stands in Military Training," *Pittsburgh Courier*, July 26, 1947, 22.

40. Letter Roy Wilkins to Ed Sanders, Committee to Prevent Compulsory Military Training, April 29, 1947, NAACP Records, Part II, A 112, Folder Bills Armed Forces Compulsory Military Conscription, 1946–1948.

41. "No Jim Crow Universal Training."

42. Report of the President's Advisory Commission on Universal Military Training: *A Program for National Security* (Washington, D.C.: Government Printing Office, 1947); partly quoted in *Pittsburgh Courier*, June 7, 1947, and in President's Committee on Civil Rights, *To Secure These Rights: The Report of the Civil Rights Committee on Civil Rights* (New York: Simon and Schuster, 1947), 43; see also Richard M. Dalfiume, *Desegregation of the U.S. Armed Forces: Fighting on Two Fronts, 1939–1953* (Columbia: University of Missouri Press, 1969), 154.

43. Quoted in Lem Graves, "Segregated Army Must Go, Says Truman's Committee," *Pittsburgh Courier*, June 7, 1947, 1.

44. Gibson quoted in Graves, "Segregated Army Must Go, Says Truman's Committee," *Pittsburgh Courier*, June 7, 1947, 1.

45. The two latest comprehensive books on the NAACP, Sullivan's *Lift Every Voice* and Berg's *Ticket to Freedom*, mention the fight for integration in military service and training only in passing. Patricia Sullivan, *Lift Every Voice: The NAACP and the Making of the Civil Rights Movement* (New York: New Press, 2009), 358–59, 365; Manfred

Berg, *The Ticket to Freedom: The NAACP and the Struggle for Black Political Integration* (Gainesville: University Press of Florida, 2007), 125–30.

46. Chad Williams, *Torchbearers of Democracy: African American Soldiers in the World War I Era* (Chapel Hill: University of North Carolina Press, 2010), 42–43.

47. B. F. McLaurin, international field organizer of the Brotherhood of Sleeping Car Porters quoted in "Brotherhood Official Vigorously Opposes Peacetime Conscription," *Black Worker* 11, 6 (June 1945): 1, 3. In his invitation to the meeting that would later form the Committee Against Jim Crow in Military Service and Training, Randolph expressed his "democratic objections" to conscription in general, but the main issue for him was segregation. See, e.g., Randolph to Layle Lane, September 3, 1947, Papers of A. Philip Randolph Microfilm Edition, ed. John H. Bracey and August Meier (Bethesda, Md.: University Publications of America, 1990) (hereafter Randolph Papers MF), Reel 12. The BSCP was an important networking tool for the later, very intense fight for military desegregation.

48. He founded the committee with Willard Townsend of the United Transport Service Employment of America, Morrish Millard, national secretary of the Workers Defense League, and Wilfried Lynn, chairman of the Lynn Committee to Abolish Segregation in the Armed forces. "Ask Truman End Jim Crow," *Chicago Defender*, May 12, 1945. Quote from Press Release, Planning Committee of the National Committee to Abolish Segregation in the Armed Forces, April 30, 1945, NAACP Papers MF, Part 9, Series A, Reel 7.

49. See Worthy to Randolph, August 14, 1947, Randolph Papers MF, Reel 12.

50. Paula F. Pfeffer, *A. Philip Randolph, Pioneer of the Civil Rights Movement* (Baton Rouge: Louisiana State University Press, 1990), 134. Pfeffer provides an invaluable study of the campaign in his biography on Randolph.

51. Committee Against Jim Crow in Military Service and Training, Press Release, February 16, 1948, The Papers of the Congress of Racial Equality, 1941–1967, Series III:19, Reel 9 (Bethesda, Md.: Microfilming Corporation of America, 1980) (hereafter CORE Papers).

52. Committee Against JimCrow in Military Service and Training, "Negroes Threatened by U.M.T. Segregation," n.d., NAACP Records, Part II, Box A 370, Folder Committee Against Jim Crow in Military Service Training.

53. "Equality Advocated in Training Measure," *New York Times*, November 26, 1947, 25. The effectiveness of the FEPC remained mainly on paper. Discrimination still dominated the defense industries and the Administration.

54. Committee Against JimCrow in Military Service, "Negroes Threatened by U.M.T. Segregation."

55. Lem Graves, "Washington Notebook," *Pittsburgh Courier*, November 29, 1947, 21.

56. Letters from A. Philip Randolph and Grant Reynolds to President Harry S. Truman, Letter from A. Philip Randolph to Harry S. Truman, January 12, 1948, in a letter dated January 1948, from A. Philip Randolph, National Treasurer, Committee

Against Jim Crow in Military Service and Training, to President Harry S. Truman (Alexandria, Va.: Alexander Street Press, 1948), n.p.; letters to various congressmen, one of the first ones Robert Taft, Randolph Papers MF, Reel 12. Documents of committee requests for a meeting with the president can also be found, among others, in *Documentary History of the Truman Presidency*, vol. 31, *The Truman Administration's Civil Rights Program: The Desegregation of the Armed Forces*, ed. Dennis Merrill (Bethesda, Md.: University Publications of America, 2001); Dalfiume, *Desegregation of the U.S. Armed Forces*, 162–63.

57. Randolph to Attorney General Tom C. Clark, February 27, 1948, Randolph Papers MF, Reel 12.

58. Randolph, Senate Committee Hearings 1948, 686.

59. Transcript, A. Philip Randolph Oral History Interview I, October 29, 1969, interview by Thomas H. Baker, Internet Copy, Lyndon B, Johnson Library, http://www.lbjlib.utexas.edu (hereafter Randolph LBJ Interview).

60. David K. Niles to Matt Connelly, January 20, 1948, Merrill, *Documentary History of the Truman Presidency*, vol. 31, 153.

61. Harry S. Truman, "Special Message to the Congress on Civil Rights," February 2, 1948. Gerhard Peters and John T. Woolley, *The American Presidency Project*, http://www.presidency.ucsb.edu.

62. Pfeffer, *Randolph*, 124. On Truman, civil rights, and the South, Harvard Sitkoff, "Harry Truman and the Election of 1948: The Coming of Age of Civil Rights in American Politics," *Journal of Southern History* 37, 4 (November 1971), esp. 599–604, 612–16. Sitkoff argues that the 1948 election "legitimized the issue of civil rights" that now became "part of the agenda of respectable urban liberalism in 1948 and was identified with both national parties and the President of the United States" (615).

63. Randolph LBJ Interview.

64. Randolph quoted in "Negro Defense View Told; Truman Advised of Hesitancy to Serve without Anti-Bias Pledge," *New York Times*, March 23, 1948, 28.

65. Donald B. Cloward, representing the Northern Baptist Convention, Dr. W. H. Jernagin, director of the Washington Bureau of the National Fraternal Council of Negro Churches of America, Truman K. Gibson, a lawyer and member of the President's Advisory Committee on Universal Training, Elwood S. McKenney from the Massachusetts Fair Employment Practice Commission, Jesse O. Dedmon, Jr., of the Veterans Affairs NAACP, Albert Black and Pauline E. Myers of the Provisional Committee to Abolish Segregation from the Universal Military Training Program; Adam Clayton Powell, 22nd Congressional District of New York.

66. All speeches from Senate Committee Hearings 1948.

67. Pauline E. Myers, March 31, 1948, Senate Committee Hearings, 701.

68. Statement of Truman K. Gibson, Chicago, March 30, 1948, Senate Committee Hearings, 642–47, 645.

69. Reynolds, March 31, 1948, Senate Committee Hearings, 669–85. Reynolds appeared before the House Committee on Armed Services two weeks later and

repeated the demands in impatient and daring language. Grant Reynolds, Hearings before the House Committee on Armed Services, 80th Cong., 2nd sess., H.R. 6274 and H.R. 6401: An Act to Provide for the Common Defense by Increasing the Strength of the Armed Forces of the United States, and for Other Purposes, 12–23 April and 3 May 1948, 6422–32 (hereafter HR Hearings 1948).

70. A. Philip Randolph before Senate Armed Services Committee, March 31, 1948, 687–88.

71. Ibid.

72. Quote from his article on American conscientious objectors in World War II, Stewart-Winter, " 'Not a Soldier, Not a Slacker'," 520.

73. Randolph, Senate Committee Hearings 1948, 687–88. Reynolds used the same phrase, "take a Jim Crow draft lying down" in a letter written to Republican senator Arthur H. Vandenberg, March 24, 1948 (letter reprinted following Reynolds's statement before the Senate Armed Services Committee, 682).

74. Reynolds, HR Hearings 1948, 6423. Reynolds's statement was widely publicized, e.g., "Services Blamed for Delay on Fund," *New York Times*, April 20, 1948, 17.

75. On the cooperation and problems between pacifists and original organizers in the two movements see A. J. Muste, Memorandum in Executive and Administrative Arrangements Involving the Committee Against JIM CROW and the League for Non-Violent Civil Disobedience, A. J. Muste, 1948, NAACP Papers, DG 052, Series D Program Work, Box 7, Folder Race Relations and Universal Military Training; Pfeffer, *Randolph*.

76. Minutes of a Meeting to Explore the Possibility of Establishing a Committee to Give Support to Those Who Refuse to Register and Serve in JimCrow Armed Services: Letter Bayard Rustin to Gregory Votaw, June 14, 1948, both in League for Non-Violent Civil Disobedience Against Military Segregation December 1941–June 1948, CDGA Collective Box, Swarthmore College Peace Collection, Swarthmore College, Swarthmore, Pa. (hereafter League Papers), Folder 2; Letter A. J. Muste, Fellowship of Reconciliation to A. Philip Randolph, June 9, 1948, Randolph Papers MF, Reel 12.

77. Muste, Memorandum in Executive and Administrative Arrangements in NCAC Papers, DG 052, Series D Program Work, Box 7, Folder Race Relations and Universal Military Training.

78. Letters A. Philip Randolph to George M. Houser, June 19, 1946, and October 6, 1947; CORE Papers, Series III:3, Reel 8.

79. "Conscription is TOO HIGH a PRICE to Pay for Prejudice: A Report on Racial Segregation in the Armed Forces" NCAC Papers, DG52, Series C, Box 6, Folder Outreach Published Literature 1945–1949.

80. John M. Swomley to Morris Hilgram, December 12, 1944, National Council Against Conscription Papers (NCAC Papers), DG52, 052 Series D, Box 7, Folder Work re: race relations and UMT: involvement with Committee Against Jim Crow in Military Service and Training, 1947–1949. See also NCAC Papers on further interaction and communication between groups.

81. "Negro Youth Leader Pledges Support to Randolph Civil Disobedience Program," Press Release, Race Relations Department, Fellowship of Reconciliation, League Papers, Folder 1.

82. Randolph took a pacifist stance in World War I and was charged with violating the Sedition Act, but over time he came to consider war as the last resort and as being unpreventable. Andrew Kersten, *A. Philip Randolph: A Life in the Vanguard* (Lanham, Md.: Rowman & Littlefield, 2007), 20; Pfeffer, *Randolph*, 9–10.

83. Recent News Stories on Jim Crow Draft, Memorandum Charles Lawrence to Bayard Rustin, William Worthy, and George Houser, n.d., CORE Papers, Series III:19, Reel 3.

84. See also John H. Stanfield, "The Dilemma of Conscientious Objection for African Americans," in *The New Conscientious Objection: From Sacred to Secular Resistance*, ed. Charles C. Moskos and John Whiteclay Chambers, II (New York: Oxford University Press, 1993), 47–56.

85. On Bayard Rustin, Steven J. Niven, "Bayard Rustin," in *African American National Biography*, vol. 7, ed. Henry Louis Gates, Jr., and Evelyn Brooks Higginbotham (Oxford: Oxford University Press, 2007), 51–53, 52; John D'Emilio, *The Lost Prophet: The Life and Times of Bayard Rustin* (Chicago: University of Chicago Press, 2003), 37–38.

86. Muste, Memorandum in Executive and Administrative Arrangements.

87. Various messages between Grant Reynolds and A. Philip Randolph and A. J. Muste and Randolph in July and early August 1948, Randolph Papers MF, Reel 12.

88. Community Organization, League for Non-Violent Civil Disobedience Against Military Segregation, *Bulletin* 5, July 7, 1948, League Papers, Folder 2.

89. For term elites see Taeku Lee, *Mobilizing Public Opinion: Black Insurgency and Racial Attitudes in the Civil Rights Era* (Chicago: University of Chicago Press, 2002), 9.

90. Community Organization, League for Non-Violent Civil Disobedience Against Military Segregation, *Bulletin* 5; *Bulletin* 8, July 2, 1948, League Papers, Folder 2.

91. Morris J. MacGregor, Jr., *Integration of the Armed Forces, 1940–1965* (Washington D.C.: Center of Military History of the United States Army, 1985), http://www.history.army.mil.

92. "Organization Backs APR," *Black Worker*, April 1948, 6; Pfeffer, *Randolph*, 146.

93. Victor G. Reuther, Director Education Department UAW-CIO, to Walter White, June 16, 1948, NAACP Records, Part II, Box A 370, Folder Committee Against Jim Crow in Military Service and Training, 1947–1948.

94. NAACP, Region I, Records 1942–1986 1945–1977, Bancroft Library, University of California, Berkeley, Box 1, Folder 1:68: Committee Against Jim Crow; Memorandum Walter White to all Branches, April 1, 1948; Letter N. W. Griffin, Regional Secretary, West Coast Regional Office NAACP, San Francisco, to A. Philip Randolph, May 17, 1948, Box 1, Folder 1:79: Segregation in Armed Services.

95. See George M. Houser to Bayard Rustin, July 23, 1948, NCAC Papers, DG 052 Series D, Box 7, Folder Work re Race relations and UMT: Involvement with Committee Against Jim Crow in Military Service and Training, 1947–1949; see also Bayard Rustin to Marvin Young, Warren, Ohio, August 9, 1948, League Papers, Folder 2.

96. On the WAC, M. Michaela Hampf, *Release a Man for Combat: The Women's Army Corps During World War II* (Köln: Böhlau Verlag, 2010).

97. Charissa Threat, "Re-Imagining Civil Rights: The Campaign to Integrate the Army Nurses Corps, 1940–1966" (Ph.D. dissertation, University of Iowa, 2008). Threat focuses on the integration of black females and white males into the Army Nurse Corps, painting a riveting picture of gender, race, and service in postwar America; see her forthcoming book with the University of Illinois Press.

98. Second Report, League for Non-Violent Civil Disobedience Against Military Segregation, Bulletin 8; Argument of the Boston Tea Party also in a letter from Randolph to Senator William Langer, July 22, 1948.

99. Second Report.

100. See Letter communication League Papers, Folder 1 and 2.

101. Letter Lela M. Lee to Randolph, July 23, 1948, Randolph Papers MF, Reel 12; see also Draft of a Letter to go out to Brotherhood locals and women's auxiliaries on Brotherhood stationary, Randolph Papers MF, Reel 3; Letter to Ladies Auxiliary New York, April 17, 1948, Reel 12.

102. See Steve Estes, *I Am a Man! Race, Manhood, and the Civil Rights Movement* (Chapel Hill: University of North Carolina Press, 2005), 3.

103. On subversion of gender roles in the black freedom struggle see, e.g., bell hooks, et al., "The Crisis of African American Gender Relations," *Transition* 5, 66 (1995): 91–175.

104. See "Blast at Army Bias Jolts Entire Nation," *Pittsburgh Courier*, April 10, 1948, 1, 5.

105. Morse's allegations of "treason" and Randolph's reaction, Senate Committee Hearings 1948, 691.

106. Senator Wayne Morse, April 12, 1948, 80th Cong., 2nd. sess., 4314, 4316.

107. Randolph's reaction to Morse, Senate Committee Hearings 1948, 691.

108. Randolph, Senate Committee Hearings 1948, 689.

109. Ruth Feldstein, *Motherhood in Black and White: Race and Sex in American Liberalism, 1930–1965* (Ithaca, N.Y.: Cornell University Press, 2000), 74.

110. Reynolds, HR Hearings 1948, 6425; quoted in "Revolt Threat Voiced Against 'Jim Crowism'," *Los Angeles Times*, April 20, 1948, 12.

111. Quoted in "Protest Made on Jim Crow Draft Law," *Hartford Courant*, April 20, 1948, 9.

112. Michael Geyer, "War and the Context of General History in an Age of Total War: Comment on Peter Paret, 'Justifying the Obligation of Military Service; Michael Howard, "World War One: The Crisis in European History," *Journal of Military History* 57, 5 (October 1993): 154.

113. Reynolds, HR Hearings 1948, 6423.

114. Assistant Attorney General T. Vincent Quinn, Criminal Division, Director, FBI, A. Philip Randolph, Treason, July 7, 1948, A. Philip Randolph FBI File (hereafter Randolph FBI File), Reel 1. The *New York Times* also reported on the League recommendation on "subterfuge." "Segregation Foes Fight Draft Law," *New York Times*, June 27, 1948, 35.

115. Press Release, League for Non-Violent Civil Disobedience Against Military Segregation, League Papers, Folder 1.

116. League for Non-Violent Civil Disobedience Against Military Segregation, "Memorandum on Penalties Contained in Draft Law as Applied to Persons Who Are Conscientiously Unwilling to Serve in a Jimcrow Military Program," *Bulletin* 3, July 7, 1948, League Papers, Folder 1.

117. "Negroes Must Stand Firm," *Black Worker*, August 1946, 3.

118. "Means by Which an Individual Can Indicate His Refusal to Participate in the Jimcrow Draft," League for Non-Violent Civil Disobedience Against Military Segregation, *Bulletin* 4, July 7, 1948, League Papers, Folder 2.

119. Wayne M. Blake and Carola A. Darling, "The Dilemmas of the African American Male," *Journal of Black Studies* 24, 4 (June 1994): 402.

120. Randolph's reference to Gandhi also "kept the nonviolent alternative in focus" and "important lessons in the practice of nonviolent direct action were learned," as historian Sudarshan Kapur has pointed out in *Raising up a Prophet: The African American Encounter with Gandhi* (Boston: Beacon Press, 1992), 162. Kapur does not go into detail about Randolph's postwar civil disobedience campaign, but mentions it in passing as evidence for the persisting influence of Gandhi's ideas in African American circles.

121. Randolph, Senate Committee Hearings 1948, 687–88.

122. A. Philip Randolph, "An Open Letter: Randolph Replies on Civil Disobedience," *New York Amsterdam News*, July 31, 1948, 3, reprinted, e.g., in "In Defense of Civil Disobedience Campaign," *New York Tribune*, August 8, 1948. Michael G. Long points out that Bayard Rustin wrote the letter. Michael G. Long, ed., *I Must Resist: Bayard Rustin's Life in Letters* (San Francisco: City Lights Books, 2012), 116.

123. Andrew K. Sandoval-Strausz, "Travelers, Strangers, and Jim Crow: Law, Public Accommodations, and Civil Rights in America," *Law and History Review* 23, 1 (Spring 2005): 93.

124. League for Non-Violent Civil Disobedience Against Military Segregation, Questions on Civil Disobedience, *Bulletin* 2, June 17, 1948, League Papers, CDGA Box, Folder 1.

125. Bayard Rustin on his first meeting with A. Philip Randolph, *The Reminiscences of Bayard Rustin*, no. 2: Interview of Bayard Rustin by Ed Edwin, January 24, 1985 (Alexandria, Va.: Alexander Street Press, 2003), 63.

126. Reynolds and Randolph's statements were read by Alfred Black, a young black World War II veteran.

127. Felix Hébert, HR Hearings 1948, 6428, discussion, 6429–32.

128. Randolph FBI, Reel 1.

129. William A. Venerable, Randolph FBI, Reel 1. On Communists and civil rights, see Glenda Gilmore, *Defying Dixie: The Radical Roots of Civil Rights, 1919–1950* (New York: Norton, 2009).

130. Reynolds, HR Hearings 1948, 6423; Albert Black, Washington Chairman Committee Against Jim Crow in Military Service and Training, Press Release: House Committee Hears Civil Disobedience Appeals from Reynolds and Randolph, April 19, 1948, NCAC Papers, DG 052, Series D Program Work, Box 7, Folder Race Relations and Universal Military Training: Involvement with Committee Against Jim Crow in Military Service and Training. The question who committed treason was a recurring one. See, e.g.: Charles H. Lewis, Jr., "Letter to the Editor, *Boston Herald*, n.d. in NAACP Records, Part II, Box A 370, Folder Committee Against Jim Crow in Military Service Training; "Who is Treasonable Now!" *Los Angeles Sentinel*, May 27, 1948, Editorial Page.

131. On the importance of the Cold War as a tool for the African American civil rights struggle, see, e.g., Mary L. Dudziak, *Cold War Civil Rights: Race and the Image of American Democracy* (Princeton, N.J.: Princeton University Press, 2000).

132. Letter from A. Philip Randolph, National Treasurer, Committee Against Jim-Crow in Military Service and Training, to President Harry S. Truman, January 12, 1948 (Alexandria, Va.: Alexander Street Press, 1948), n.p.

133. Earl Brown's article for *New York Amsterdam News*, April 10, reprinted in *Congressional Record*, July 12, 1948, 4418–22. However, neither the microfilm nor the Proquest reprint of the newspaper contains an article with these quotes for all 1948. See also, e.g., *New York Amsterdam News*, April 10, 1948, Editorial page.

134. George S. Schuyler, "Views and Reviews," *Pittsburgh Courier*, April 10, 1948, 7. Schuyler was listed as one of the founding members of the committee. Press Release Committee, November 23, 1947, CORE Papers, Series III:19, Reel 9. Schuyler wrote two articles comparing the discriminatory and segregationist situation in the American military with the Venezuelan and Colombian military allegedly free of racial segregation and discrimination. "Segregation Does Not Exist in Venezuelan Armed Forces; Latins Frown on Bias in U.S.," *Pittsburgh Courier*, July 24, 1948, 1; "Colombia's Army Gives . . . to U.S. Brass Hats," *Pittsburgh Courier*, August 14, 1948, 1.

135. Howard W. Coles to Randolph, July 20, 1948 Randolph Papers MF, Reel 12.

Chapter 4. Mass Civil Disobedience

1. C. P. Trussell, "Congress Told UMT Racial Bars Would Unleash Civil Disobedience: Congress Warned on UMT Race Bars," *New York Times*, April 1, 1948, 1–2; John G. Norris, "Negroes May Ignore Draft, Leaders Say: Congress Warned of 'Sit-Down' If Military Service Keeps Race Bars Negroes May Ignore Draft," *Washington Post*, April 1, 1948, 1. For status of civil rights reports in the white press, Gene Roberts and Hank Klibanoff, *The Race Beat: The Press, the Civil Rights Struggle, and the Awakening of a*

Nation (New York: Knopf, 2006), 12; "Randolph Warns of Draft," *Philadelphia Tribune*, April 3, 1948, 1.

2. See "Negro Threat Against Draft Causes Alarm," *Anniston Star*, April 1, 1948, 20; "Negroes Warned They Will Face Treason Charge," *Landmark*, April 1, 1948, 3; "Pullman Porter Chief at White House," *Delta Democrat-Times*, April 5, 1948, 6; "Negro Leaders Defy Possible Military Draft," *Statesville Daily Record*, April 19, 1948, Front Page; "Threatens Army Boycott," *Florence Morning News*, April 20, 1948, 1.

3. "Crisis in the Making: U.S. Negroes Tussle with Issue . . . ," *Newsweek*, June 7, 1948, 28. The article was reprinted in condensed form in *Negro Digest*, August 1948.

4. Walter White to Malcolm Muir, Editor *Newsweek*, June 29, 1948, NAACP Records, Part II, Box A 370, Folder Committee Against Jim Crow in Military Service and Training, 1947–1948. On the problematic cooperation between Randolph and the NAACP, John H. Bracey, Jr., and August Meier, "Allies or Adversaries? The NAACP, A. Philip Randolph and the 1941 March on Washington,'" *Georgia Historical Quarterly* 125, 1 (1991): 1–17.

5. White to Muir, NAACP Records, Part II, Box A 370, Folder: Committee Against Jim Crow in Military Service and Training, 1947–1948.

6. Reynolds to *Newsweek*, June 5, 1948, Randolph Papers MF, Reel 12.

7. "The Draft on Its Merits," *New York Times*, May 28, 1948, 22.

8. "Nonsegregated Draft," *Washington Post*, May 13, 1948, Editorial Page; "Negroes in the Draft," *Washington Post*, April 2, 1948, 24.

9. Bruce Mcm. Wright, a World War II veteran who had experienced segregation firsthand, angrily replied to the *New York Times* editorial: "What is a man to fight for when he is denied human rights as an individual and as a race by the army which drafts him to fight for freedom and democracy? . . . Perhaps the time has come to abandon unreasoning chauvinism; perhaps one should not blindly say, 'My country, right or wrong'; and civil disobedience may be the answer after all, since official reason gives no response and Congress filibusters." To the Editors of the *New York Times*: "For a Democratic Draft Act: Civil Rights Legislation Advocated to Ban Discriminatory Practices," *New York Times*, June 2, 1948, 28. For articles agreeing with the *Post* and *Times*, "Not by Threat to Rebel," *St. Louis Star-Times*, April 9, 1948, 1; "Misrepresenting Negroes," *New York World-Telegram*, April 1, 1948, reprinted in April edition of the *Black Worker*, 6; "Army Segregation," *Anniston Star*, 4.

10. Letter Ellen Hunt to A. Philip Randolph, May 12, 1948, Randolph Papers MF, Reel 12.

11. Jane Dailey, "The Sexual Politics of Race in World War II America," in *Fog of War: The Second World War and the Civil Rights Movement*, ed. Kevin M. Kruse and Stephen Tuck (Oxford: Oxford University Press, 2012), 146. On interracial marriage after the Second World War and before *Loving v. Virginia* see Alex Lubin, *Romance and Rights: The Politics of Interracial Intimacy, 1945–1954* (Jackson: University Press of Mississippi, 2005).

12. Marjorie McKenzie, "Pursuit of Democracy: Randolph-Reynolds Testimony May Have Given Big-Wigs Something to Think About," *Pittsburgh Courier*, April 10, 1948, 6. McKenzie (1912–1980) held law degrees from Terrell Law School and Columbia University. She worked as a columnist for the *Pittsburgh Courier*, supported John F. Kennedy, and later served on his Commission on Equal Employment Opportunities and as a judge in the juvenile court of the District of Columbia. Clayborne Carson et al., eds., *The Papers of Martin Luther King, Jr.*, vol. 5, *Threshold of a New Decade* (Berkeley: University of California Press, 2005), 276.

13. Marjorie McKenzie, "Pursuit of Democracy: Reaction to Randolph's Stand Exposes Division of Opinion Within Race," *Pittsburgh Courier*, April 17, 1948, 6; Marjorie McKenzie, "Pursuit of Democracy: Negro Leaders Refuse to Arbitrate Army Bias . . . What Comes now?" *Pittsburgh Courier*, May 8, 1948, 6.

14. E.g., NAACP Records, Part II, Box A 370, Folder: Committee Against Jim Crow in Military Service and Training.

15. McKenzie, "Pursuit of Democracy: Randolph-Reynolds Testimony May Have Given Big-Wigs Something to Think About."

16. John H. Stanfield, "The Dilemma of Conscientious Objection for African Americans," in *The New Conscientious Objection: From Sacred to Secular Resistance*, ed. Charles C. Moskos and John Whiteclay Chambers, II (New York: Oxford University Press, 1993), 52.

17. Adam Clayton Powell, Jr., Statement before Senate Armed Services Committee, April 2, 1948, Senate Committee Hearings 1948, 964–67, Powell's comments were reprinted in various newspapers, e.g., "Powell Blasts Army Policy," *Pittsburgh Courier*, April 10, 1948, 1; 60,000 Ministers Urged to Fight Jim-Crow Army," *Afro-American*, April 10, 1948, 5. Bayard Rustin collected articles on the events: Fellowship of Reconciliation Records (hereafter FOR Records) (DG013), Bayard Rustin Files Series D, Campaign to Resist Military Segregation: Press Clippings, Swarthmore Peace Collection, Swarthmore, Pennsylvania.

18. See also interviews in Christopher Parker, *Fighting for Democracy: Black Veterans and the Struggle Against White Supremacy in the Postwar South* (Princeton, N.J.: Princeton University Press, 2009).

19. Robert Ingram Reed, World War II Veteran, New York, "What the People Think: Randolph Program Depends on Support," *Pittsburgh Courier*, July 24, 1948, 2; William A. Richardson, Ex-Navy Veteran, "Will Hang Together or Hang Separately," *Pittsburgh Courier*, June 5, 1948, 7.

20. "Men or Mice," The *Sun*, April 10, 1948, in FOR Records, Bayard Rustin Files, Campaign to Resist Military Segregation: Press Clippings, 1948.

21. Joe Nettles, Oklahoma City, "Agrees with Randolph," *Chicago Defender*, August 7, 1948, 14.

22. George McGray, "Labor View: Labor Leaders Are Strong Men," *Los Angeles Sentinel*, April 8, 1948, Editorial Page.

23. Joe Louis Statement to Senate Committee on Armed Services provided in written form by A. Philip Randolph, Senate Committee Hearings 1948, 1085.

24. On the importance of Joe Louis and his military service during World War II in the African American community and armed forces see Lauren Rebecca Sklaroff, "Constructing G.I. Joe Louis: Cultural Solutions to the 'Negro Problem' During World War II," *Journal of American History* 89, 3 (December 2002): 958–83.

25. Quote in J. A. Rogers, "Rogers Says: Opposition to Constituted Power Is Always Treason," *Pittsburgh Courier*, May 1, 1948, 6; copy in CORE Papers, Reel 3.

26. Horace R. Cayton, "You Can Like Him or Dislike Him, But He Has Unadulterated Courage," *Pittsburgh Courier*, April 17, 1948.

27. *Norfolk Journal and Guide*, April 10, 1948, Editorial Page. "Randolph Statement Scored," *Norfolk Journal and Guide*, April 10, 1948, A1; cf. Letter to the editors: all in *New York Amsterdam News*, April 10, 1948, Editorial Page; Jack Branch, "This Is still America," *Philadelphia Tribune*, April 6, 1948, 4.

28. Quote in P. L. Prattis, "The Horizon: Randolph's Threat Can Serve a Great Purpose as a 'Bluff Tactic'," *Pittsburgh Courier*, April 17, 1948, Editorial Page; Ralph A. Reynolds, Council for Civic Unity, "Letter to the Editor," *San Francisco Chronicle*, n.d.; Charles H. Lewis, "Letter to the Editor," *Boston Herald*, n.d. Both critics personally informed Walter White on their letters to the editors. NAACP Records, Part II, Box A 370, Folder: Committee Against Jim Crow in Military Service and Training.

29. William A. Fowlkes, "Seeing and Saying: Dynamite," *Atlanta Daily World*, April 4, 1948, 4.

30. Lem Graves, Jr., "Washington Notebook," *Pittsburgh Courier*, April 10, 1948, 3. In mid-May, Graves wrote a letter to Randolph in which he vehemently rejected the latter's recommendation to already enlisted soldiers to lay down their guns and refuse to fight. Lem Graves Letter to A. Philip Randolph, May 15, 1948, Randolph Papers MF, Reel 12.

31. "Fighting the Jim Crow Army," *The Crisis*, May 1948, 136.

32. Ibid.

33. NAACP Press Release, April 15, 1948, NAACP Papers MF, Part 9, Series A, Reel 11.

34. See Paula F. Pfeffer, *A. Philip Randolph, Pioneer of the Civil Rights Movement* (Baton Rouge: Louisiana State University Press, 1990), 159–60; Berg notes that "the NAACP leaders did not eagerly welcome new players on the civil rights field. They had given many years of service to the association and were deeply convinced that their own goals and methods represented the best interest of the black community at large." Manfred Berg, *The Ticket to Freedom: The NAACP and the Struggle for Black Political Integration* (Gainesville: University Press of Florida, 2007), 168.

35. Questionnaire and news release on outcome in NAACP Papers MF, Part 9, Series A, Reel 7.

36. On the NAACP's suspicions of newer strategies and the generational shift see, e.g., Derek Catsam, *Freedom's Main Line: The Journey of Reconciliation and the Freedom Rides* (Lexington: University Press of Kentucky, 2009), esp. 23–24.

37. "Loyalty Pledged for ROTC Negroes," *New York Times*, April 3, 1948, 3. On the development and position of ROTC programs in black colleges see Charles Johnson, *African Americans and ROTC: Military, Naval, and Aeroscience Program at Historically Black Colleges* (Jefferson, N.C.: McFarland, 2002).

38. Walter White to Victor G. Reuter, Director of Education UAW-CIO, June 22, 1948; Walter White to Mr. Muir, *Newsweek*, June 29, 1948; NAACP Records, Part II, Box A 370, Folder: Committee Against Jim Crow in Military Service and Training.

39. Telegram Walter White to Wayne Morse, April 1, 1948, Ibid.

40. On Walter White: Kenneth Roberts Janken, *White: The Biography of Walter White, Mr. NAACP* (New York: New Press, 2003), esp. 219. The same held for Thurgood Marshall and Roy Wilkins. Both remained suspicious of new approaches to civil rights; see Catsam, *Freedom's Main Line*, 23–24; Berg, *Ticket to Freedom*, 170–72.

41. Marie G. Baker, Secretary of Decatur Branch NAACP, to Walter White, April 1, 1948, NAACP Records, Part II, Box A 370, Folder: Committee Against Jim Crow in Military Service and Training.

42. Walter White Telegram to Senator Morse, NAACP Records, Part II, Box A 370, Folder: Committee Against Jim Crow in Military Service and Training, included in the *Congressional Record*, April 12, 1948. See also Lamar Perkins, "Segregation and Civil Disobedience," n.d., Randolph Papers MF, Reel 12. White replied and issued a press release on April 22 claiming that politicians who had long fought integration and civil rights used Randolph's campaign "shamelessly . . . as an excuse for nonaction." "Press Release: Civil Rights Retreat Denounced by White," April 22, 1948, NAACP Records, Part II, Box A370, Folder: Committee Against Jim Crow in Military Service and Training 1947–1948.

43. Morse hoped to be able to convene with White and talk about the current situation of civil rights in the United States. Letter Senator Wayne Morse to Walter White, May 5, 1948. There was a number of letters exchanged between White and Morse on the possible disservice of the civil disobedience campaign on the cause of civil rights and the effectiveness of pro-civil rights politicians in Congress. In NAACP Records, Part II, Box A 370 Folder: Committee Against Jim Crow in Military Service and Training 1947–1948 or NAACP Papers MF, Part 9, Series A, Reel 7.

44. W. W. Law to Walter White, April 21, 1948, NAACP Records, Part II, Box A 370, Folder: Committee Against Jim Crow in Military Service and Training.

45. Draft of Letter to Senator Morse, April 7, 1948, ibid.

46. See, e.g., "'Cheap Politics' Charged in Dealing with Civil Rights Law," *Norfolk Journal and Guide*, May 1, 1948, D1.

47. Both quotes from Letter Walter White to Wayne Morse, April 14, 1948, NAACP Records, Part II, Box A 370, Folder: Committee Against Jim Crow in Military Service and Training.

48. Roy Wilkins, "The Watchtower," *Michigan Chronicle*, April 10, 1948, Wilkins Papers, Box 50, Folder: The Watchtower; Wilkins, "The Watchtower," *Los Angeles Sentinel*, April 8, 1948, Editorial Page.

49. Memorandum to Mr. White from Mr. Wilkins, April 9, 1948, NAACP Records, Part II, Box A 644, Folder: Conference on Negroes in the Armed Services, 1948–1949.

50. "Segregation in the Armed Forces," *Pittsburgh Courier*, April 10, 1948, 6.

51. "Invitation to Disaster," *Evening Star*, April 1, 1948, Editorial Page.

52. "Protest, Yes; Treason, No!" *Norfolk Journal and Guide*, April 10, 1948, Editorial Page; "Letter to the Editors," *New York Amsterdam News*, April 10, 1948, Editorial Page; Jack Branch, "This Is Still America," *Philadelphia Tribune*, April 6, 1948, 4; "Senator Gets Letter Opposing Randolph's View," *Norfolk Journal and Guide*, April 17, 1948, C18.

53. See "The Negro U.S. Citizen," *New York Amsterdam News*, April 10, 1948, Editorial Page; "Leaders Close Rank," *New York Amsterdam News*, May 1, 1948, Editorial Page; "Randolph Statement Scored: Threat of Treason Resented," *Norfolk Journal and Guide*, April 10, 1948, A1.

54. Arthur Davis, "With a Grain of Salt: Civil Disobedience Threat Considered Untimely and Harmful to Civil Rights," *Norfolk Journal and Guide*, April 17, 1948, E10.

55. Letter Gibson to President Truman, March 24, 1948, Truman Papers, White House Official Files 109, Box 611, Folder: Miscellaneous (1948–1949).

56. Statement of Truman K. Gibson, Chicago, Senate Committee Hearings 1948, Universal Military Training. Hearings, 642–47, 645. William L. Dawson, a black Democrat from Illinois and avid supporter of Truman, pledged his full-fledged support to the long-established obligations of male citizenship. He pointed out: "I positively believe it is my duty at all times to defend my native land. I was among the first volunteers in the First World War and feel it is a patriotic must." Cong. Rec. 94:4, April 12, 1948, 4314.

57. The first black general, Benjamin O. Davis, Sr., was attacked in a similar manner for his alleged lack of activism against discrimination and segregation of blacks in the armed forces during the war. See, e.g., "Goodbye, General Davis," *Sun*, July 6, 1948.

58. Steven J. Niven, "Gordon B. Hancock," in *African American National Biography*, vol. 4, 48–50.

59. Gordon B. Hancock, "Between the Lines: A. Philip Randolph and the Anti-Gradualists," *Los Angeles Sentinel*, April 22, 1948, Editorial Page. The article was reprinted under a different title a week later: "Between the Lines: Anti-Gradualism," *Atlanta Daily World* and *Birmingham World*, April 27, 1948.

60. Senator Morse, April 12, 1948, Cong. Rec. 94:4, 4317.

61. Memorandum Niles to Matthew J. Connelly, April 5, 1948, Truman Papers, White House Official Files 109, Box 611, Folder: Miscellaneous (1948–1949).

62. Adam Clayton Powell, Jr., quoted in "60,000 Ministers Urged to Fight Jim-Crow Army," *Afro-American*, April 10, 1948, 5; see also "Somebody's Gotta Go," *Chicago Defender*, March 24, 1945, 12; "Truman Gibson Rebuffed by NAACP Board," *Chicago Defender*, June 2, 1945, 2.

63. Grant Reynolds, HR Hearings 1948, 6425. The term "Quisling" refers to Vid-kun Quisling, the Norwegian prime minister who cooperated with the Nazis. Reynolds equated Gibson with Quisling to identify further his behavior as a betrayal of the race and cooperation with white oppressors. The British press appropriated the term to refer to all factions collaborating with Nazis. See Hans Fredrik Dahl, *Quisling: A Study in Treachery* (New York: Cambridge University Press, 1999).

64. Lem Graves, "Gibson, Reynolds Nearly Swap Blows," *Pittsburgh Courier*, April 10, 1948, 1; on the fallout between Reynolds and Gibson see also Phillip McGuire, *He, Too, Spoke for Democracy: Judge Hastie, World War II, and the Black Soldier* (New York: Greenwood Press, 1988), 104.

65. When their cooperation fizzled out in the early 1950s, Reynolds worked as a lawyer and civil rights organizer in White Plains, New York. The Schomburg Center for Research in Black Culture holds an interview with Reynolds. More info on Reyn-olds: Christine Knauer, "Grant Reynolds," in *African American National Biography*, vol. 6.

66. In his 2005 memoir, Gibson called Reynolds "an erratic black chaplain during the war whom I tried to help out when he frequently landed in trouble but who would constantly denounce me as not being extreme enough in prodding the army toward more enlightened racial policies." Truman K. Gibson with Steve Huntley, *Knocking Down Barriers: My Fight for Black America—A Memoir* (Evanston, Ill.: Northwestern University Press, 2005), 230.

67. Since the Republican Party controlled the Senate in 1948, Russell was the highest ranking Democratic member of the committee, not chairman. When the Dem-ocrats took control of Congress, he became chairman.

68. Louis Lautier, "Treasonable Disloyalty Suggested by Randolph," *Norfolk Jour-nal and Guide*, April 10, 1948, D2.

69. Russell, Senate Committee Hearings 1948, 647.

70. General Dwight D. Eisenhower, April 3, 1948, Senate Committee Hearings 1948, 995–96.

71. To explain the high number of courts-martial, Wilkins argued that black sol-diers were persecuted for resisting Jim Crow or chose Absence Without Official Leave (AWOL) "when they go sick of being pushed around." Wilkins, "The Watchtower," *Los Angeles Sentinel*, April 15, 1948, Editorial Page.

72. Eisenhower, April 3, 1948, Senate Committee Hearings 1948.

73. Despite Eisenhower's attempts to justify the negative data on black soldiers to a certain degree, parts of the African American community grew more incensed by his adherence to segregation. See, e.g., "Gen. 'Ike' Blasted for Jimcrow Army Stand," *Los Angeles Sentinel*, May 6, 1948, 12.

74. Henry Lee Moon to Jack Kroll, Director Congress of Industrial Organiza-tions—Political Action Committee (CIO-PAC), May 8, 1948, Records of the National Urban League (hereafter NUL Records), Lester Granger Papers, Box 153, Series 1,

Folder Personal Correspondence April–July 1948, Manuscript Division, Library of Congress, Washington, D.C.

75. See Harvard Sitkoff, "Harry Truman and the Election of 1948: The Coming of Age of Civil Rights in American Politics," *Journal of Southern History* 37, 4 (November 1971): 597–616. Sitkoff does not explicitly consider Executive Order 9981 an influence on African Americans in their decision in the 1948 presidential election. Based on an interview with George M. Elsey, a member of the Truman White House staff, historian Ken Hechler claims Randolph's campaign had no influence on Truman's civil rights decisions, Executive Order 9981 in particular. Ken Hechler, "Truman Laid the Foundation for the Civil Rights Movement," in *The Civil Rights Legacy of Harry S. Truman*, ed. Raymond H. Geselbracht (Kirksville, Mo.: Truman State University Press, 2007), 51–66, 59, Dudziak, *Cold War Civil Rights*.

76. "Democrats Act to Curb Party Strife," *Chicago Daily Tribune*, March 22, 1948, 1.

77. "Lester Granger Won't Be Aide," *Atlanta Daily World*, July 7, 1945, 1; "Lester Granger Named Civilian to the Secretary of the Navy," *Norfolk Journal and Guide*, June 23, 1945, B1.

78. Lester Granger to Jack Kroll, CIO-PAC, May 7, 1948, NUL Papers, Series I, Box 153, Folder Personal Correspondence Apr–July 1948. Granger and the NUL later even established a special navy recruiting program for African Americans in segregated schools. Granger cooperated closely with Lieutenant Dennis Nelson, the civilian aide to the secretary of the navy, to get more black men to join the navy ROTC. See NUL Papers, Southern Regional Office, esp. Box A 100, 111, 123.

79. Granger quoted in Louis Lautier, "In Nation's Capital," *New York Amsterdam News*, May 8, 1948, 10.

80. Telegram Walter White to James Forrestal, April 21, 1948, NAACP Records, Box A 644, Folder Conference on Negroes in the Armed Services, 1948–1949.

81. Letter Lester Granger to Walter White, April 23, 1948, NUL Papers, Series I, Box 152, Folder Correspondence January–June 1948.

82. Lester Granger to Marx Leva, Special Assistant to the Secretary of Defense, May 16, 1948, NUL Papers, Series I, Box 161, Folder Secretary of Defense 1948.

83. Stephen J. Wright, dean of Hampton Institute, paraphrased in "Just Forget the Status Quo Argument," *Norfolk Journal and Guide*, May 8, 1948, 4.

84. "Forrestal Asks 15 Negro Leaders to Meet on Bias," n.n., April 21, 1948, 1, NAACP Papers MF, Part 9, Series A, Reel 9.

85. Lester Granger, Chairman, Introductory Statement National Defense Conference, April 26, 1948; and Minutes of Press Conference on Negro Affairs, NUL Papers, Series I, Box 153, Folder: National Defense Conference on Negro Affairs.

86. Report of Conference on Racial Policy of the Armed Services held in Washington, D.C., April 26, 1948 (Tentative Draft), NAACP Papers MF, Part 9, Series A, Reel 9. Pfeffer notes that "Randolph's militant stand gave punch to the protest of the more moderate black betterment groups." Pfeffer, *Randolph*, 160.

87. Wilkins, "The Watchtower"; see also "The Army Won't Learn," *Los Angeles Times,* May 6, 1948.

88. "Negroes Ban Advisory Unit for Military," *Washington Post,* May 5, 1948, 1.

89. "Negro Leaders Quit Army Advisory Role," *New York Times,* April 27, 1948, 17.

90. Charley Cherokee, "National Grapevine: The Uninvited," *Chicago Defender,* May 8, 1948, 13; see also, "Mr. Forrestal and Company," *Chicago Defender,* May 8, 1948, 14. The participants of the conference included Lester B. Granger, Sadie Alexander, John Davis, Truman Gibson, Bishop Greeg, Charles Houston, Reverend John Johnson, Loren Miller, Hopson Reynolds, Channing Tobias, Roy Wilkins, and Geo Weaver.

91. "Leaders Close Ranks," *New York Amsterdam News,* May 1, 1948, 10.

92. Hubert Humphrey, the liberal senator from Minnesota, joined the picketers and included his findings successfully in his speech before the DNC. William C. Berman, *The Politics of Civil Rights in the Truman Administration* (Columbus: Ohio State University Press, 1970), 111–12; John D'Emilio, *The Lost Prophet: The Life and Times of Bayard Rustin* (Chicago: University of Chicago Press, 2003), 154.

93. Reynolds and Randolph to Harry S. Truman, June 21, 1948, Truman Papers, Official Files, Box 848, Folder R.

94. This section is in language and wording partially based on my article on Langer and civil rights: Christine Knauer, "'A Man Who Fancies Abraham Lincoln': Senator William Langer's Civil Rights Record," *North Dakota History* 76, 3–4 (2011): 22–40.

95. Quote from Letter Randolph to Langer, May 16, 1948, Randolph Papers, Reel 12; "Randolph to Urge Negroes in Army to Drop Guns if Russell Segregation Amendment Passes," Press Release, Committee Against Jim Crow in Military Service and Training, May 14, 1948, Randolph Papers, Reel 12.

96. "Another Back-to-Africa," *Afro-American,* July 23, 1949, 4.

97. Robert L. Fleegler, "Theodore G. Bilbo and the Decline of Public Racism, 1938–1947," *Journal of Mississippi History* 66, 1 (Spring 2006): 1; on Southern fears, Jason Sokol, *There Goes My Everything: White Southerners in the Age of Civil Rights, 1945–1975* (New York: Vintage, 2006).

98. Gilbert C. Fite, *Richard B. Russell, Jr., Senator from Georgia* (Chapel Hill: University of North Carolina Press, 1991), 501.

99. See Jason Morgan Ward, *Defending White Democracy: The Making of a Segregationist Movement and the Remaking of Racial Politics, 1936–1965* (Chapel Hill: University of North Carolina Press, 2011), 118–21.

100. "Draft Bill Fate More Doubtful," newspaper article n.n., n.d. (presumably *New York Post,* mid- to late May), William Langer Papers, Orin G. Libby Manuscript Collection, University of North Dakota, Grand Forks (hereafter Langer Papers).

101. The amendments would ban all segregation from any form of the draft and would include anti-lynching legislation applicable to all draftees, anti-Jim Crow legislation in interstate travel, a bar to all companies or individuals with Jim Crow employment from having contracts with the armed forces or the government, and a bar to discrimination against people in uniform in public places and facilities. Langer amendments, see, e.g., "Draft Bill Facing Civil Rights Rider," *Washington Post*, May 27, 1948, 5; C. P. Trussell, "Senate Votes to Bar Draft of 18-Year-Olds for Training," *New York Times*, June 5, 1948, 1.

102. Charles M. Barber, "A Diamond in the Rough: William Langer Reexamined," *North Dakota History* 64 (Fall 1998): 3; Lawrence H. Larsen, "William Langer: A Maverick in the Senate," *Wisconsin Magazine of History* 44 (Spring 1961): 189–98; Agnes Geelan, *The Dakota Maverick: The Political Life of William Langer, also Known as "Wild Bill"* (Fargo, N.D.: Geelan, 1975); Robert Wilkins, "Senator William Langer and National Priorities: An Agrarian Radical's View of American Foreign Policy, 1945–1952," *North Dakota Quarterly* 42 (Autumn 1974): 42–59.

103. Langer, June 4, 1948, 80th Cong., 2nd sess., Cong. Rec., 7150; see also 7149.

104. Ibid., 7148; Langer quoted in John G. Norris, "Senate Chiefs Predict Defeat for Civil Rights Draft Riders," *Washington Post*, June 5, 1948, 1.

105. Langer, "Extensions of Remarks: Universal Military Training," Address on ABC, June 13, 1948, 80th Cong., 2nd sess., Cong. Rec., August 7, 1948, A5031.

106. Langer quoted in "Bitter Fight Shapes over Service J'Crow," *Atlanta Daily World*, May 30, 1948, 1; see also "Draft Program Faces New Hurdle as Civil Rights Riders Loom," *New York Times*, May 27, 1948.

107. Langer also submitted a statement on "Americans Don't Want Peacetime Conscription" that laid out the reasons for his opposition to the draft, calling it an "un-American system." Langer, "Extensions of Remarks," A5021–22.

108. "Draft Bill Faces New Hurdle as Civil Rights Rider Looms," *New York Times*, May 28, 1948, 1.

109. Trussell, "Senate Votes to Bar Draft of 18-Year-Olds for Training"; Norris, "Senate Chiefs Defeat for Civil Rights Draft Riders."

110. "Draft Bill Faces New Hurdle as Civil Rights Rider Looms."

111. John G. Norris, "Draft Riders Due to Raise Senate Storm," *Washington Post*, June 4, 1948, 1.

112. "Anti-Poll Tax Amendment in Draft Passed," *Washington Post*, June 8, 1948, 1.

113. John G. Norris, "GOP to Block Rights Rider if Delay in Draft Threatens," *Washington Post*, May 29, 1948, 1; see also "Senate Heads into Racial Rights Battle over Draft," *Los Angeles Times*, June 5, 1948, 4.

114. Harry M. Ward, "Crispus Attucks," *African American National Biography*, vol. 1, 196.

115. Senator Russell before Senate, June 4, 1948, 80th Cong., 2nd sess., Cong. Rec., 7148.

116. Quoted in Claudette Bennett, "Racial Categories Used in the Decennial Censuses, 1790 to Present," *Government Information Quarterly* 17, 2 (2000): 169–70; see also C. Matthew Snipp, "Racial Measurement in the American Census: Past Practices and Implications for the Future," *Annual Review of Sociology* 29 (2003): 568; Sarah E. Chinn, *Technology and the Logic of American Racism: A Cultural History of the Body as Evidence* (London/New York: Continuum, 2000), 1–22, 93–140.

117. Historian Kevin M. Kruse argues that "segregationists were instead fighting *for* rights of their own—such as the 'right' to select their neighbors, their employees, and their children's classmates, the 'right' to do as they pleased with their private property and personal businesses, and, perhaps most important, the 'right' to remain free from what they saw as dangerous encroachments by the federal government. To be sure, all of these positive 'rights' were grounded in a negative system of discrimination and racism." Kevin M. Kruse, *White Flight: Atlanta and the Making of Modern Conservatism* (Princeton, N.J.: Princeton University Press, 2005), 9.

118. Senator Russell before the Senate, June 8, 1948, 80th Cong., 2nd sess., Cong. Rec., 7358.

119. Statement of Senator Richard B. Russell, May 11, 1948, Richard B. Russell, Jr., Collection (hereafter Russell Papers), Series 2 Civil Rights IA, Box 30, Folder 8, Richard B. Russell Library for Political Research and Studies University of Georgia, Athens.

120. Russell before the Senate, June 8, 1948, 7361–64.

121. Ibid., 7364.

122. Ibid., 7360.

123. Senator Maybank before the Senate, 7366.

124. The discussion on the Russell-Maybank Amendment continued the following day with pledges of support from senators John McClellan (Ark.), Allen Ellender (La.), and James Eastland (Miss.). Ellender before the Senate, June 9, 1948, 7489, 7491; McClelland, 7494–95.

125. "The Draft on Its Merits," *New York Times*, May 28, 1948, 22; see also "Nonsegregated Draft," *Washington Post*, May 13, 1948, 10.

126. Bertha Walsh Letter to Russell, May 20, 1948, Russell Papers, Ser. 10 Civil Rights, Box 185, Folder 4. Another correspondent called Russell and his followers "Southern Crackers" and celebrated the role of African Americans in building and perceiving the American nation. Letter n.d., not signed, Folder 5.

127. A Real Southerner Letter to Russell, May 25, 1948, Russell Papers, Ser. 10 Civil Rights, Box 185, Folder 5. Senator James O. Eastland received numerous letters on the possible desegregation of the American military that often referenced his speech on the failure of black soldiers in 1945. James O. Eastland Collection, File Series 3, Subseries 1: Issue Correspondence, Box 33, Folder: 1948 (1–3), University of Mississippi, Oxford.

128. A. Philip Randolph and Grant Reynolds to President Truman, June 29, 1948, Harry S. Truman Official Files, 93-B, *Harry S. Truman Library*, February 15, 2009. Incessant letter writing campaign reflected in Truman's White House Official Files 93, Box 544, Folder 1948 [2 of 3]; "Truman Urged to Issue Order Ending Army Segregation," *Afro-American*, July 24, 1948, 1; "Truman Urged to End Racial Segregation in Army," *Norfolk Journal and Guide*, July 24, 1948, 1; "End Army Bias, Randolph Tells Pres. Truman," *Pittsburgh Courier*, July 24, 1948, 1.

Chapter 5. Truman's Order

1. Unsigned memorandum, dated June 29, 1948, titled "Should the President Call Congress back?" Truman Library Personal Papers Collection, Papers of Samuel I. Rosenman, 1944–1966, Box 9, Subject File; 1948; Campaign 1948; HST Acceptance Speech.

2. The order was accompanied by Executive Order 9980, "Regulations Governing Fair Employment Practices within the Federal Establishment" that called for the desegregation of the federal workforce. For more information on the second order see, e.g., William C. Berman, *The Politics of Civil Rights in the Truman Administration* (Columbus: Ohio State University Press, 1970), 79–137.

3. Executive orders "are, loosely speaking, presidential directives that require or authorize some action with the executive branch (though they often extend far beyond the government). They are presidential edicts, legal instruments that create or modify laws, procedures, and policy by fiat." Kenneth Mayer, *With the Stroke of a Pen: Executive Orders and Presidential Power* (Princeton, N.J.: Princeton University Press, 2002), 4. Executive orders have traditionally been used to pass controversial laws without the Congress debating or authorizing them.

4. On the work and efforts of the Fahy Committee see, e.g., Morris J. MacGregor, Jr., *Integration of the Armed Forces, 1940–1965* (Washington, D.C.: Center of Military History of the United States Army, 1985), http://www.history.army.mil; Sherie Mershon and Steven Schlossman, *Foxholes and Color Lines: Desegregating the U.S. Armed Forces* (Baltimore: Johns Hopkins University Press, 1998); Donald R. McCoy and Richard T. Ruetten, *Quest and Response: Minority Rights in the Truman Administration* (Lawrence: University Press of Kansas, 1973), 221–36.

5. First quote: Oral History Interview with Clark Clifford, July 27, 1971, interview by Jerry N. Hess, *Harry S. Truman Library*, http://www.trumanlibrary.org, 261, 269. Clark Clifford quoted in Richard M. Yon and Tom Lansford, "Political Pragmatism and Civil Rights Policy: Truman and Integration of the Military," in *The Civil Rights Legacy of Harry S. Truman*, ed. Raymond H. Geselbracht (Kirksville, Mo.: Truman State University Press, 2007), 103–16, 107.

6. Michael R. Gardner, *Harry Truman and Civil Rights: Moral Courage and Political Risks* (Carbondale: Southern Illinois University Press, 2002), 112. Berman argues that Truman had his party's and his own success in mind when pushing civil rights. Gardner, on the other hand, underlines his moral convictions as the main force behind

the moves. Berman, *The Politics of Civil Rights in the Truman Administration*. Berg goes so far as to call Gardner's take on Truman "an almost hagiographic account that sees only moral forces behind Truman's actions and denies that politics played any role." Manfred Berg, *The Ticket to Freedom: The NAACP and the Struggle for Black Political Integration* (Gainesville: University Press of Florida, 2007), 288 n28. Whereas Gardner celebrates Truman for his civil rights stance, Carol Anderson argues that "Truman's efforts did not even come close to what needed to be done." He gave "the aura of action . . . with no enforcement mechanism and no serious repercussions for noncompliance." Carol Anderson, *Eyes off the Prize: The United Nations and the African American Struggle for Human Rights, 1944–1955* (Cambridge: Cambridge University Press, 2003), 3.

7. Oral History Interview with Philleo Nash, October 18, 1966, interview by Jerry N. Hess, *Harry S. Truman Library*, http://www.trumanlibrary.org, 351–52. See also Richard M. Dalfiume, *Desegregation of the U.S. Armed Forces: Fighting on Two Fronts, 1939–1953* (Columbia: University of Missouri Press, 1969), 172–74; Berman, *The Politics of Civil Rights in the Truman Administration*, 116–19.

8. Brenda Gayle Plummer, *Rising Wind: Black Americans and U.S. Foreign Affairs, 1935–1960* (Chapel Hill: University of North Carolina Press, 1996), 187; see also Mary L. Dudziak, *Cold War Civil Rights: Race and the Image of American Democracy* (Princeton, N.J.: Princeton University Press, 2000), 82; Berman, *The Politics of Civil Rights*, 117–20.

9. A new biography of Wallace and the 1948 presidential election is Thomas W. Devine, *Henry Wallace's 1948 Presidential Campaign and the Future of Postwar Liberalism* (Chapel Hill: University of North Carolina Press, 2013). The book extensively covers Wallace's tour through the South and his attempts at garnering the black vote. However, it does not consider military integration or Executive Order 9981.

10. Dudziak, *Cold War Civil Rights*, 82; Michael S. Sherry, *In the Shadow of War: The United States Since the 1930s* (New Haven, Conn.: Yale University Press, 1997), 147.

11. MacGregor, *Integration of the Armed Forces, 1940–1965*.

12. Quote from Louis Lautier, "Order Intended to Wipe out Army Jim Crow," *Atlanta Daily World*, August 1, 1948, 1. See also Mary Spargo, "End of Troop Segregation Eventual Aim, Truman Says," *Washington Post*, July 30, 1948, 1; John G. Harris, "Dixie Talkathon Ties Up Senate, Stalls Off Price Curb: But Truman Only Smiles at Filibuster," *Boston Daily Globe*, July 30, 1948, 1.

13. Dalfiume, *Desegregation of the U.S. Armed Forces*, 117–18.

14. "21 Southern Senators Map a Filibuster on Civil Rights," *New York Times*, July 28, 1948, 1.

15. See Chapter 6.

16. Bradley quoted in "Army Segregation to Go," *New York Times*, July 30, 1948, 2.

17. In his autobiography, Bradley stated he had to discourage "instant integration" in the U.S. army, for "it would have utterly destroyed what little Army we had." Furthermore, the "many senior Southerners in Congress" and predominant white Southerners in the army would have withdrawn their support for the military. According to Bradley, Truman's executive order was, therefore, "much watered down." Omar N. Bradley with Clay Blair, *A General's Life: An Autobiography* (New York: Simon and Schuster, 1983), 485.

18. "NAACP Requests General Bradley Repudiate Statement on Segregation in the Armed Forces," August 8, 1948, NAACP Records, Part II, A 646, Folder: US Army General 1948.

19. Hanson W. Baldwin, "Segregation in the Army: Gen. Bradley's View Is Held to Put Morale Above Compulsory Change," *New York Times*, August 8, 1948, 51.

20. Richard B. Russell, Jr., Collection, Series 10 Civil Rights Box 185, Folder 2, Richard B. Russell Library for Political Research and Studies University of Georgia, Athens.

21. Walter White to Editor of the *New York Times*, August 11, 1948, NAACP Records, Part II, A 646, Folder: U.S. Army General 1948.

22. Roy Wilkins, Papers of Roy Wilkins, , Box 22, Folder Desegregation Armed Forces (1948), Manuscript Reading Room, Library of Congress, Washington D.C.

23. Randolph Dear Friend Letter, July 27, 1948, League for Non-Violent Civil Disobedience Against Military Segregation December 1941–June 1948, CDGA Collective Box, Swarthmore College Peace Collection, Swarthmore College, Swarthmore, Pennsylvania, Folder 2.

24. Press Release: On First Reading Randolph Denounces Truman's Army Executive Order as Political and Misleading, League for Non-Violent Civil Disobedience Against Military Segregation, July 27, 1948. On the problematic origin and wording of the press release, see John D'Emilio, *The Lost Prophet: The Life and Times of Bayard Rustin* (Chicago: University of Chicago Press, 2003), 158.

25. Reynolds even set October 15 as a deadline for hearing back from the White House. Memorandum, Reynolds to Senator James Howard McGrath, August 1, 1948, Randolph Papers MF, Reel 12.

26. Randolph Dear Friend Letter, August 24, 1948, Randolph Papers, Reel 12; also quoted in D'Emilio, *Lost Prophet*, 158.

27. Telegram Walter White to the *Los Angeles Sentinel*, August 27, 1949, NAACP Papers, Part 9 Series A, Reel 12; "Truman Proclamation Splits Negro Leaders," *Los Angeles Sentinel*, July 29, 1948, 1.

28. Arthur M. Fine to Walter White, July 28, 1948. NAACP Records, Part II, Box A 646 or NAACP Papers MF, Part 9, Series A, Reel 11; see also "Probe of Organization Requested: NAACP Political Activity Charged," *Norfolk Journal and Guide*, October 9, 1948, 1.

29. "Defender Editor Hails Truman's Historic Order," *Chicago Defender*, July 31, 1948, 1; see also "Mr. Truman Makes History," *Chicago Defender*, August 7, 1948,

Editorial Page; "Truman Is Triumphant," *Chicago Defender*, July 24, 1948, Editorial Page; Let's Put Up or Shut Up," *Chicago Defender*, July 31, 1948, 1.

30. "Mr. Randolph Takes a Walk," *Afro-American*, August 28, 1948, Editorial Page; "Truman's Wretched Performance," *California Eagle*, August 5, 1948, Editorial Page; see also "Little Civil Rights Order Issued by President Truman," *California Eagle*, July 29, 1948, 18.

31. See, e.g., "The Order Mr. Truman Did Not Issue," *Pittsburgh Courier*, August 7, 1948; "A Challenge to Mr. Truman," *Pittsburgh Courier*, August 21, 1948; "Tips for the Veteran," *Norfolk Journal and Guide*, August 7, 1948; "No Whoops, Just Waiting," *New York Post*, July 29, 1948. The *Chicago Defender* was exuberant and headlined right from the start "President Truman Wipes Out Segregation in Armed Forces," *Chicago Defender*, July 31, 1948.

32. James L. Hicks, "Veteran's Whirl," *Atlanta Daily World*, July 31, 1948, 3; see also "Veterans Whirl: Truman's Weak Army Order Indicates He's 'Off Target," *Afro-American*, August 7, 1948, B10.

33. "Randolph Halts Civil Disobedience," *Black Dispatch*, August 21, 1948, Editorial Page; Arthur P. Davis, "With a Grain of Salt: Truman Credited with Playing Smart Game of Politics with the White House," *Norfolk Journal and Guide*, August 7, 1948, D10.

34. "Editorial: Vote for Gov. Dewey," *Pittsburgh Courier*, October 30, 1948; Lem Graves, Jr., "Lem Graves Sees Dewey' Electoral Vote Doubling Truman's Victory Certain," *Pittsburgh Courier*, October 30, 1948, 2; see also "John L. Clark Says May Win Vote in 23 States, But Still Won't Have Enough"; "Our Choice for President!" *New York Amsterdam News*, October 2, 1948, 10; "Do We Want to Take a Chance on Mr. Barkley as President?" *Afro-American*, October 16, 1948, 4; "The Sentinel's Choices: An Editorial Vote for Dewey," *Los Angeles Sentinel*, October 28, 1948, 1; "The Negro Vote and the Presidency," *Norfolk Journal and Guide*, October 16, 1948, 1; "Vote Wisely—No Candidate Holds a Mortgage on Our Vital Votes," *Norfolk Journal and Guide*, October 30, 1948, B24A. The *Chicago Defender* and the *Atlanta Daily World*, otherwise Republican papers, and the *Black Dispatch* favored Truman.

35. See, e.g., quote in "Dissolution Splits Foes of Draft Bias," *New York Times*, August 19, 1948; "Civil Disobedience Drive Abandoned," *Norfolk Journal and Guide*, August 28, 1948, 1; "Blot Draft Despite Randolph," *Chicago Defender*, August 28, 1948, 1.

36. Grant Reynolds, "A Triumph for Civil Disobedience," *Nation*, August 18, 1948, 228–29; quote from Press Release Statement of Grant Reynolds and A. Philip Randolph, Wednesday, August 18, 1948, William Langer Papers, Civil Rights Folder, Orin G. Libby Manuscript Collection, University of North Dakota, Grand Forks. All major black newspapers printed the press release or parts of it. Even white publications picked it up and expressed their satisfaction with the end of the campaign.

37. Randolph to Henry Lee Moon, November 18, 1948, NAACP Papers MF, Part 9, Series A, Reel 11.

38. Reynolds, "Triumph for Civil Disobedience," 229.

39. "The Education of A. Philip Randolph," Editorials, *Pittsburgh Courier*, August 28, 1948; see also "End Disobedience Campaign," *New York Age*, August 28, 1948, Editorial Page. On the fallout see Paula F. Pfeffer, *A. Philip Randolph, Pioneer of the Civil Rights Movement* (Baton Rouge: Louisiana State University Press, 1990), 148–61.

40. George M. Houser to A. Philip Randolph, March 30, 1949, National Council against Conscription Papers (NCAC Papers), Swarthmore Peace Collection, Swarthmore College, DG52, Series D, Program Work, Box 7, Folder Race Relations and Universal Military Training: Involvement with Committee Against Jim Crow in Military Service and Training. Copies of the letter were sent to Muste, Rustin, Swomley, and Worthy.

41. Letter A. Philip Randolph to Reverend J. Raymond Henderson, August 24, 1948, Randolph Papers MF, Reel 12.

42. Statement by Grant Reynolds, National Chairman, and A. Philip Randolph, National Treasurer of the Committee Against Jim Crow in Military Service and Training, NAACP Records, Region I, Box 1, Folder 1:79: Segregation in Armed Services; see also *Black Worker*, November 1948, 1; "Randolph, Reynolds Say Pacifists Sabotaged Campaign," *Afro-American*, October 16, 1948, C4; "Truman's Anti-Bias Drive Okeyed; Randolph and Reynolds Say Mission Done Civil Disobedience Accomplished Mission, Move Leaders Opine," *Atlanta Daily World*, October 15, 1948, 1.

43. The rift between Rustin and Randolph began to close again in the late 1950s, after they had successfully cooperated on various civil rights campaigns. Their cooperation climaxed in the March on Washington in 1963. Rustin's homosexuality was never an issue between the two. According to Rustin, Randolph only focused on his work and intellect and always showed him the highest respect. Interview of Bayard Rustin by Ed Edwin, April 3, 1985, in *The Reminiscences of Bayard Rustin, No. 4: Interview of Bayard Rustin*, ed. Ed Edwin (Alexandria, Va.: Alexander Street Press, 2003), 135–36.

44. "Randolph and Reynolds," *Chicago Defender*, August 28, 1948, 14. See also "No Civil Disobedience," *Los Angeles Sentinel*, August 26, 1948, Editorial Page. George S. Schuyler, "Views and Reviews: 'What Caused 'Buddy' and 'Slick' to Drop Army Fight?'" *Pittsburgh Courier*, August 28, 1948, 19.

45. "The Education of A. Philip Randolph," 18.

46. Schuyler, "Views and Reviews: 'What Caused 'Buddy' and 'Slick' to Drop Army Fight?'" *Pittsburgh Courier*.

47. Willard Townsend, "The Other Side," *Chicago Defender*, September 11, 1948, 15. Townsend did not consider civil disobedience an adequate approach to ending segregation and discrimination in the military service, but he embraced the freshness and fervor of the younger generation of whites and blacks in turning America into a real democracy.

48. Lester Granger, Final Report on the National Defense Conference on Negro Affairs, to James Forrestal, August 26, 1948, NUL Papers, Series I, Box 152, Folder

National Defense Conference on Negro Affairs 1948, Manuscript Division, Library of Congress, Washington, D.C.

49. Correspondence between Loren Miller and Lester B. Granger, September 24, 29, 1948, NUL Papers, Series Granger Papers, Series 1, Box 153, Folder Personal Correspondence August–December.

50. Letter Lester B. Granger to A. Philip Randolph, October 5, 1948, Randolph Papers MF, Reel 12.

51. Roy Wilkins, "The Watchtower," *Los Angeles Sentinel*, August 26, 1948, Editorial Page.

52. Wilkins, "No Civil Disobedience."

53. John H. Young, III, "Truman Stock Rises as President Takes People's Side vs. Congress," *Chicago Defender*, June 19, 1948, 1.

54. See Lester Granger to Marx Leva, Special Assistant to the Secretary of Defense, May 16, 1948, NUL Papers, Series 1, Box 161, Folder Secretary of Defense 1948; Lem Graves, Jr., "Negro Issue Splits Dems," *Pittsburgh Courier*, July 10, 1948, 1; e.g., "Editorial: Vote for Gov. Dewey," *Pittsburgh Courier*, October 30, 1948, 1.

55. On Dewey, civil rights, and the election of 1948, Simon Topping, "'Never Argue with the Gallup Poll': Thomas Dewey, Civil Rights and the Election of 1948," *Journal of American Studies* 38, 2 (2004): 179–98. See also, e.g., *New York Amsterdam News* quoted in "Others' Opinions," *Pittsburgh Courier*, January 27, 1948, 6; Roy Wilkins, "The Watchtower," *Los Angeles Sentinel*, July 8, 1948, 7; "In the Nation's Capital: The Decision," *Atlanta Daily World*, July 25, 1948, 4; "Power of Negro Vote Proved by Reaction at 3 Conventions," *Pittsburgh Courier*, August 14, 1948; Drive Against Jim Crow," *New York Amsterdam News*, July 31, 1948, 10; "Our Choice for President!" *New York Amsterdam News*, October 2, 1948, 10.

56. See reports and election advice of the *California Eagle* in the months immediately preceding the 1948 election.

57. "Truman Challenges," *Black Dispatch*, November 13, 1948, Editorial Page; see also "Negroes Vote for Truman," ibid.

58. See "Democratic Victory Puts Southern Reactionaries Back In Power," *Norfolk Journal and Guide*, November 6, 1948, A24; "New Political Line-up," *Los Angeles Sentinel*, November 11, 1948, 23; "Our Opinions: The Winner and Still Champion," *Chicago Defender*, November 14, 1948, 6.

59. "A Victory for the People," *Atlanta Daily World*, November 4, 1948, 6.

60. "Our Opinions: The Winner and Still Champion," *Chicago Defender*, November 14, 1948, 6.

61. Marcus H. Ray to Walter White, April 4, 1949, NAACP Papers MF, Part 9, Series A, Reel 11.

62. See "The Army Stumbles on," *The Crisis*, February 1950, 101.

63. Drew Pearson, "Royall for Segregation to Limit," *Washington Post*, May 18, 1948, in Papers of Stephen J. Spingarn, Civil Rights File, Box 40, Folder Civil Rights File Civil Rights, Newspaper Clippings, Harry S. Truman Library.

64. Dalfiume, *Desegregation of the U.S. Armed Forces*, 179; see also "Truman to Meet Committee on Bias in Armed Forces," *Chicago Defender*, January 8, 1949, 1.

65. Lem Graves, "Army Bias Probe Starts; It Can End Segregation—Will It?" *Pittsburgh Courier*, January 15, 1949, 1. The *Chicago Defender* trusted that President Truman and the Fahy Committee were actually intent on ending segregation once and for all. "End of Military Jim Crow," *Chicago Defender*, February 12, 1949, Editorial Page.

66. On the limitations of the Fahy Committee: MacGregor, *Integration of the Armed Forces*, 350, 312–14; Desmond King, *Separate and Unequal: Black Americans and the U.S. Federal Government* (New York: Oxford University Press, 1995), 139.

67. Randolph to Henry Moon, November 18, 1948, NAACP Papers MF, Part 9, Series A, Reel 11.

68. Letter A. Philip Randolph to Simon Cross, Manager Marshall Civil Liberties Trust, August 19, 1948, Randolph Papers MF, Reel 12; see also Pfeffer, *Randolph*, 164.

69. See, e.g., Transcripts in Fahy Committee Hearings, U.S. Army Heritage and Education Center, U.S. Army War College, Carlisle Barracks, Carlisle, Pennsylvania.

70. President's Committee on Equality of Treatment and Opportunity in the Armed Services, April 25, 1949, Morning Session. Ibid. See also "Play to Show How Jim Crow Affects GI's," *New York Amsterdam News*, January 8, 1949, 21.

71. Grant Reynolds, *Hearings of the President's Committee on Equality of Treatment and Opportunity in the Armed Services*, Pentagon, April 25, 1949, Washington, D.C., Morning Session, 68.

72. Ibid., 71.

73. See A. L. Wirin to Roger Baldwin, ACLU, June 29, 1949, American Civil Liberties Union Records (hereafter ACLU Records), MC#001 Box 1100 Folder 4: Segregation in the Armed Forces. Information on ACLU and Fahy Committee; Public Policy Papers, Department of Rare Books and Special Collections, Princeton University Library; Letter Lester B. Granger, NUL, to Roger Baldwin, ACLU, March 21, 1949; and Reply Baldwin to Granger, March 23, 1949, ibid.

74. "Paul Robeson's Story," *Pittsburgh Courier*, September 17, 1949, 1. On Robeson's role and symbolism before 1939, see, e.g., Hazel V. Carby, *Race Men* (Cambridge, Mass.: Harvard University Press, 2000), chap. 4. Since the remarks were unscripted, the news was based on an AP reporter who quoted Robeson. The singer later claimed that his statements were taken out of context and distorted. He maintained that he had stated that working people across the world should only fight for peace, since war merely exploited them for the benefits of a ruling minority. "Robeson Misquoted? He Says So," *Chicago Defender*, May 21, 1949, 12.

75. "Robeson Speaks for Robeson," *The Crisis*, May 1949, 137.

76. Mary E. Cygan, "A Man of His Times: Paul Robeson and the Press, 1924–1976," in *Paul Robeson: Essays on His Life and Legacy*, ed. Joseph Dorinson et al. (Jefferson, N.C.: McFarland, 2004), 81–97, 87.

77. George S. Schuyler, "Views and Reviews: So, Along Comes Paul Robeson with the Clincher," *Pittsburgh Courier*, May 7, 1949, Editorial Page; see also "Mr. Robeson Goes to Town," *Pittsburgh Courier*, April 30, 1949, 14.

78. The *Los Angeles Sentinel* published statements by local influential African Americans who repudiated Robeson's statement in "Negro Will Never Be Traitor— Says Leaders," *Los Angeles Sentinel*, May 5, 1949, C9.

79. See, e.g., "Robeson as Speaker for Negroes Denied," *New York Times*, April 25, 1949, 16; "Peace Is Wonderful—But Not Moscow's Brand," *Los Angeles Times*, April 26, 1949, A4; "The Case of Paul Robeson," *New York Times*, April 25, 1949, 22; Cygan, "A Man of His Times," 87.

80. An exception was the *Pittsburgh Courier*. A front page editorial pointed out that Robeson had never served his country in any war and, therefore, never proved willing and able to be man enough for the most virile and honorable tasks a man could possibly perform. He was described as not brave enough and willing to fight for "the rights and privileges of American life" others were willing to fight for, "cognizant they did not enjoy the rights which were vouchsafe to other Americans," but "nevertheless fought to make the dream of full equality a wonderful reality." The editorial vilified Robeson and removed his right to call himself American and moreover a "Negro American" for whom he claimed to speak. "Mr. Robeson Goes to Town"; see also Schuyler, "Views and Reviews: So, Along Comes Paul Robeson with the Clincher."

81. Powell quoted in "Robeson as Speaker for Negroes Denied."

82. "Robeson Blasted for Paris Speech," *Chicago Defender*, April 30, 1949, 1; "Committing National Suicide," *Black Dispatch*, April 8, 1950, editorial; "Will Not Fight Russia—Robeson NAACP Challenges Statement," *Los Angeles Sentinel*, April 28, 1949, A1; Dean Gordon Hancock, "Between the Line: The Robeson Riot," *Los Angeles Sentinel*, September 29, 1949, Editorial Page.

83. Randolph quoted in "Randolph, on Tour, Hits Robeson, Reds," *Chicago Defender*, February 4, 1950, 4; see also "Would Negroes Fight in a War Between the USA and USSR," *Black Worker*, September 1949, 1.

84. Walter White quoted in Daniel W. Aldridge, "A Militant Liberalism: Anti-Communism, the African American Intelligentsia, 1939–1955," paper for 2004 American Historical Association, December, *World History Archives*, http://www.hartford-hwp.com, accessed December 24, 2011.

85. "Robeson Blasted for Paris Speech"; "Committing National Suicide"; Hancock, "Between the Lines."

86. "The Careless Paris Remark," *Black Dispatch*, April 30, 1949, Editorial Page.

87. "Group Opposes Hearing," *New York Times*, July 13, 1949, 21.

88. Hancock, "Between the Lines."

89. Paul Robeson, speech at rally sponsored by Civil Rights Congress, "Robeson Denounces Korean Intervention," in *Paul Robeson Speaks: Writings, Speeches, and Interviews, a Centennial Celebration*, ed. Philip Sheldon Foner (New York: Citadel

Press, 2002), 252–53. Robeson had been long under FBI surveillance. *FBI File on Paul Robeson* (microform) (Wilmington, Del.: Scholarly Resources, 1987), http://foia.fbi .gov. Robeson never swerved from his interpretation of American interference in Korea and repeatedly scolded African Americans for participating in an intervention he considered an attempt to oppress colonial peoples under American imperialist rule. "Speech to Youth" Address, First National Convention of Labor Youth League, November 24, 1950, in *Paul Robeson Speaks*, 254–59, 259.

90. See Lucius C. Harper, "Is Communism Better Than Democracy? If Not, Why Be Afraid of It?" *Chicago Defender*, August 12, 1950, 7; "Muzzling Paul Childish," *Afro-American*, August 26, 1950, 4.

91. "In Spite of Handicaps," *Atlanta Daily World*, August 25, 1950, 6.

92. In her book on war and African Americans since the Second World War, historian Kimberley Phillips often focuses on left-wing protest. *War! What Is It Good for? Black Freedom Struggles and the U.S. Military from World War II to Iraq* (Chapel Hill: University of North Carolina Press, 2012).

93. See Senator Russell, June 21, 1950, 81st Cong., 2nd sess., Cong. Rec., 8974.

Chapter 6. A Country They Never Knew

1. Bruce Cumings, *The Korean War: A History* (New York: Modern Library, 2010), 4.

2. Quotes in Melinda Pash, *Standing in the Shadow of the Greatest Generation: The Americans Who Fought the Korean War* (New York: New York University Press, 2012), 91–92.

3. Japan declared Korea a protectorate in 1905 after the Russo-Japanese War, and five years later annexed it.

4. A 1950 Gallup poll in August 1950 reported that 57 percent of respondents believed the United States was now involved in World War III; 28 percent believed the Koreans would stop short of war; 15 percent expressed no opinion. *The Gallup Poll: Public Opinion 1935–1971*, vol. 2, *1949–1958* (New York: Random House, 1969), 933. See, e.g., John Fousek, *To Lead the Free World: American Nationalism and the Cultural Roots of the Cold War* (Chapel Hill: University of North Carolina Press, 2000), 165; Michael S. Sherry, *In the Shadow of War: The United States Since the 1930s* (New Haven, Conn.: Yale University Press, 1997), 177.

5. Omar N. Bradley with Clay Blair, *A General's Life* (New York: Simon and Schuster, 1983), 476–77, 476.

6. Since prime minister of North Korea Kim Il Sung continuously pressured Stalin for military equipment to which the Soviet Union agreed. See, e.g., Telegram from Shtykov to Vyshinski regarding Meeting with Kim Il Sung, March 21, 1950, Wilson Center, Digital Archive, http://digitalarchive.wilsoncenter.org/document/112044.

7. On the interconnectedness of Korea and cooperation with South Africa's apartheid regime, Thomas Borstelmann, *Apartheid's Reluctant Uncle: The United States and Southern Africa in the Early Cold War* (New York: Oxford University Press, 1993),

chap. 7, esp. 143, 161, 167. Fifteen other UN members ultimately participated in the mission in Korea, but the United States and South Korea supplied "more than 90% of manpower." William Stueck, *The Korean War: An International History* (Princeton, N.J.: Princeton University Press, 1997), 3. To abstain from all too tedious repetitions, the terms "American" and "UN" are often used interchangeably despite the problematic nature of this equation.

8. George Elsey, Summary of a telegram dated June 29, 1950, from the U.S. ambassador to the Soviet Union to secretary of state Dean Acheson, *Harry S. Truman Library*; "Washington Holds Russia to Account," *New York Times*, June 25, 1950, 1. Historians have lengthily debated to what extent the Soviet Union was involved in or even spurned the North Korean attack. While internal factors that brought about the war are no longer ignored, the opening of the Soviet archives has also shown that Russia had an important role and interest in the invasion. In his 2001 essay, Alan R. Millett points out that the dichotomy between calling it an "international" or "civil" war is not only "false" but also "irrelevant." "The Korean War should be treated as one of several Asian wars of decolonization that began during World War II, not a war encouraged by design or inadvertently started by the Soviet Union and the United States," Millett, "The Korean War," 193–94. For a detailed look at and reassessment of the internal conflicts and reasons for the Korean War, see Bruce Cumings, *The Origins of the Korean War I: Liberation and the Emergence of Separate Regimes 1945–1947* (Princeton, N.J.: Princeton University Press, 1981).

9. "Radio and Television Address to the American People on the Situation in Korea," July 19, 1950, *Public Papers of the President of the United States, Harry S. Truman, Containing the Public Messages, Speeches, and Statements of the President, January 1 to December 31, 1950* (Washington, D.C.: Government Printing Office, 1965), 537. Numerous books and articles exist on the military course of the Korean War; for a first overview see Clay Blair, *The Forgotten War: America in Korea* (New York: Times Books, 1987); Cumings, *The Origins of the Korean War I*; Cumings, *The Origins of the Korean War II: The Roaring of the Cataract 1947–1950* (Princeton, N.J.: Princeton University Press, 1990); Bruce Cumings and Kathryn Weathersby, "An Exchange on Korean War Origins," *Cold War International History Project Bulletin 6/7* (Winter 1995/96): 120–22; Alan R. Millett, "The Korean War: A 50-Year Critical Historiography," *Journal of Strategic Studies* 24, 1 (March 2001): 188–224.

10. "'Aggression Will Be Met with Force'," *Los Angeles Times*, July 20, 1950, A4; Bruce E. Bechtol, Jr., "Paradigmenwechsel des Kalten Krieges: Der Koreakrieg 1950–1953," in *Heiße Kriege im Kalten Krieg*, ed. Bernd Greiner, Christian Th. Müller, and Dierk Walter (Hamburg: Hamburger Edition, 2006), 151–54.

11. Gallup poll, 942. Relying on public opinion polls at that time is problematic. See Lee, *Mobilizing Public Opinion*, 43–90. But the polls are still indicative of a trend in public opinion. The Gallup polls usually did not break down their findings by race or gender. There is, for instance, no polling information specifically on African Americans.

12. See, e.g., Sherry, *In the Shadow of War*, 178.

13. "War Is Declared by North Koreans, Fighting on Border," *New York Times*, June 25, 1950, 1.

14. "Korea: Danger Spot," *Washington Post*, June 26, 1950, 8; see also "Saving Korea," *Washington Post*, June 27, 1950, 10; "U.S. Troops Rushing to Stem Red Koreans' Push," *Los Angeles Times*, July 3, 1950, 1.

15. *New Republic*, July 3, 1950, 5, emphasis original.

16. Willard Shelton, "Notes from Capitol Hill," *Nation*, July 1, 1950, 6. "The Shape of Things," *Nation*, July 1, 1950, 1–2. The analogy between the German invasion of Poland and the North Korean attack on South Korea was a common one; see, e.g., "Red Blitzkrieg Dooms Free Korea," *Los Angeles Times*, June 26, 1950, 6. The (mis)use of historical analogies has been a frequent device in politics and the press; see, e.g., Ernest R. May, *"Lessons" of the Past: The Use and Misuse of History in American Foreign Policy* (New York: Oxford University Press, 1973).

17. On June 27, the *New York Times* referred to it as a "Soviet-Sponsored 'Civil War'": Hanson W. Baldwin, "Korea Weakness Internal," June 27, 1950, 10.

18. Gallup poll, 955.

19. "'Aggression Will Be Met with Force'."

20. General Douglas MacArthur quoted in "MacArthur Pledges Victory in 'Shortest Possible Time'," *New York Times*, July 17, 1950, 1.

21. "The News of the Week in Review," *New York Times*, July 9, 1950, E1.

22. Max Hastings, *The Korean War: A History* (New York: Simon and Schuster 1987), 83.

23. Both quotes in "The United Nations at War," *New York Times*, July 10, 1950, 20; see also "The Meaning of Korea," *Washington Post*, July 18, 1950, 12. Lieutenant Colonel Robert L. Wadlington quoted in Ralph Reatsorth, "Yank Tells of Struggle for Taejon," *Hartford Courant*, July 23, 1950, 16. For climate and territory see, e.g., Hanson Baldwin, "Korea's Battle Picture: Our Defense Is Stiffer," *New York Times*, July 23, 1950, E5.

24. Sherry, *In the Shadow of War*, 130.

25. Ibid., 177.

26. See, e.g., ibid., 179–80; in more detail see John W. Dower, *War Without Mercy: Race & Power in the Pacific War* (New York: Pantheon, 1986).

27. Fletcher Pratt, "Korea Will Be a Months-Long Job," *Washington Post*, July 9, 1950, B1.

28. Sherie Mershon and Steven Schlossman, *Foxholes and Color Lines: Desegregating the U.S. Armed Forces* (Baltimore: Johns Hopkins University Press, 1998), 218.

29. Mark Hyman, "People Are Talking About," *Philadelphia Tribune*, July 4, 1950, 9.

30. Lester B. Granger, "The National Emergency and Community Welfare," Speech, May 3, 1951, Minnesota Welfare Conference, NUL Papers, Series 1, Box 169, Folder Miscellaneous Speeches 1948–1951.

31. Randolph to President Truman, August 4, 1950, Truman Papers, PPF, Box 553, Folder PPF 2540. The White House remained suspicious of Randolph due to his previous civil rights activism. In April 1950, David K. Niles, administrative assistant to the president, characterized Randolph as having "misbehaved occasionally, but fortunately he is not in the Paul Robeson class . . ." Memo David K. Niles to John Steelman, April 25, 1950, ibid.

32. A. Philip Randolph quoted in "Randolph Says Negroes, Other Minorities, Have Stake in Korean Struggle," *Black Worker*, July 1950, 1, reprinted in "'Hands off Korea'—Robeson 'Smash the Reds'—Randolph," *Pittsburgh Courier*, July 8, 1950, 2.

33. "Black United States and the United Nations on Korea," *Black Worker*, August 1, 1950, 2.

34. From 1936 to 1940, Randolph acted as president of the National Negro Congress (NNC) in which communists and noncommunists cooperated. After the Hitler-Stalin Pact in August 1939 the coalition began to fall apart. Randolph decried NNC support for communist Russia. A clear rift developed when he left the congress in 1940, protesting the organization's communist affiliation and proclaiming his fervent anticommunist stance. Glenda Gilmore, *Defying Dixie: The Radical Roots of Civil Rights, 1919–1950* (New York: Norton, 2009), 307–11.

35. "Vital Stake in Korea—Randolph," *Atlanta Daily World,* July 2, 1950, 1.

36. A. Philip Randolph, "Letter to the Editor: Soviet Liberation Propaganda to Involve Minorities Denounced," *New York Times*, July 1, 1950, 9.

37. Von Eschen maintains that the black press showed "an absence of attention to the Korean War" and produced only sparse coverage. Penny von Eschen, *Race Against Empire: Black Americans and Anticolonialism, 1937–1954* (Ithaca, N.Y.: Cornell University Press, 1997), 146.

38. George Schuyler, "Views and Reviews: Our Independence Is in Greater Peril Than Ever," *Pittsburgh Courier*, July 8, 1950, 15. However, once the war was in full swing, Schuyler was quick to make clear that African Americans were willing and able to fight like every other American.

39. Charlotta Bass, "Uncle Tom Is Not Dead," *California Eagle*, July 14, 1950, 1–2; Raphael Konigsberg, "In Honor of the American Revolution," *California Eagle*, July 14, 1950, Editorial Page; "The Obligation of the Government," *California Eagle*, July 14, 1950, Editorial Page; Paul Robeson, *Paul Robeson Speaks*, ed. Philip Sheldon Foner (New York: Citadel Press, 2002), 252–53, 254–59, 259; Kimberley Phillips, *War! What Is It Good for? Black Freedom Struggles and the U.S. Military from World War II to Iraq* (Chapel Hill: University of North Carolina Press, 2012), 157; David Widener, "Seoul City Sue and the Bugout Blues: Black American Narratives of the Forgotten War," in *Afro Asia: Revolutionary Political and Cultural Connections Between African Americans and Asians*, ed. Fred Ho and Bill V. Mullen (Durham, N.C.: Duke University Press, 2008), esp. 72–76.

40. On anti-interventionism between 1939 and 1941 see Daniel W. Aldridge, III, "A War for the Colored Races: Anti-Interventionism and the African American Intelligentsia, 1939–41," *Diplomatic History* 18, 3 (June 2004): 321–52.

41. See Fousek, *To Lead the Free World*, 182.

42. "United Front on Korea," *Los Angeles Sentinel*, July 13, 1950, Editorial Page. In a follow-up editorial, the *Los Angeles Sentinel* vehemently refuted the idea that it was a mere "family dispute" in which the United States had no stake in. "The Korean Crisis," *Los Angeles Sentinel*, July 27, 1950, Editorial Page.

43. "Was It Worth It?" *Los Angeles Sentinel*, August 17, 1950, Editorial Page; ". . . And Still Korea," *Los Angeles Sentinel*, June 19, 1952, Editorial Page.

44. "Korea: World Trouble Spot," *Norfolk Journal and Guide*, July 15, 1950, editorial page.

45. "Calling the Red Bluff," *Chicago Defender*, July 8, 1950, 6. In its next editorial, it called Stalin "the biggest dictator of our times." "The Big Lie," *Chicago Defender*, July 15, 1950, 6. The *Birmingham World* and *New York Amsterdam News* embraced Truman's argumentation and course of action. Compared with other major African American newspapers, they focused less on a critical assessment of the state of foreign policy, or the faults of the United States in its domestic and anticommunist strife, but rather on the involvement of black troops in Korea.

46. This contradicts Plummer's statement that the *Pittsburgh Courier* opposed the intervention. Brenda Gayle Plummer, *Rising Wind: Black Americans and U.S. Foreign Affairs, 1935–1960* (Chapel Hill: University of North Carolina Press, 1996), 206. "Korea, United Nations, Peace," *Pittsburgh Courier*, July 8, 1950, Editorial Page.

47. No one seemed to recognize the other UN member states as full partners in the endeavor. "What We Face in Korea," *Afro-American*, July 15, 1950, Editorial Page.

48. "Cold War Grows Hotter," *Afro-American*, July 1, 1950, Editorial Page.

49. "What We Face in Korea."

50. "Our Opinions: The Call of Our Country," *Chicago Defender*, December 23, 1950, 6.

51. A multitude of articles, editorials, and columns were published on the question of national unity. See Alice Dunnigan, "FEPC Defeat Echoes Around World During Freedom Talk," *Atlanta Daily World*, July 23, 1950, 1; "Shriners End Conclave on Civil Rights Pledge," *New Journal and Guide*, August 26, 1950, 1; "Our Stand on Korea," *Philadelphia Tribune*, August 15, 1950, 4; Lucius C. Harper, "Dustin' Off the News: Some Sidelights on the Korean War That Might Be Interesting," *Chicago Defender*, August 5, 1950, 7.

52. See Rudolph Spencer, "The Tragedy of Korea," *Black Dispatch*, September 23, 1950, 1.

53. John Q. Observer, "Political Digest," *Los Angeles Sentinel*, August 17, 1950, A2.

54. J. A. Rogers, "Rogers Says: Harry Truman's Veto of the Barden Bill Was True Statesmanship," *Courier*, November 24, 1951, 15.

55. "Koreans Non-White," *Pittsburgh Courier*, July 8, 1950, 4.

56. Reference to and first, more profound studies of African American discourse on the racial character of the war see: Widener, "Seoul City Sue and the Bugout

Blues," 55–87, esp. 61; Michael C. Green, *Black Yanks in the Pacific: Race in the Making of American Military Empire After World War II* (Ithaca, N.Y.: Cornell University Press, 2010), 121.

57. Mary L. Dudziak, *Cold War Civil Rights: Race and the Image of American Democracy* (Princeton, N.J.: Princeton University Press, 2000), esp. 18–46; Stueck, *The Korean War*, 187; Steven Casey, *Selling the Korean War: Propaganda, Politics, and Public Opinion 1950–1953* (Oxford: Oxford University Press, 2008), 320–22.

58. Roy Wilkins to Thurgood Marshall, February 20, 1951, Wilkins Papers, Box 3, Folder Correspondence 1951.

59. "Sensible War Strategy," *Black Dispatch*, July 8, 1950, Editorial Page.

60. Roy Wilkins to Frank Pace, Jr., July 21, 1950, NAACP Papers MF, Part 9, Series A, Reel 14.

61. "Is It a War of Color?" *Ebony*, October 1950, 94; see also Alfred Baker Lewis, "Not a Racial War," *Afro-American*, September 13, 1950, Editorial Page; Plummer, *Rising Wind*, 206.

62. "This Is No Race War," *Los Angeles Sentinel*, August 31, 1950, Editorial Page; see also P. L. Prattis, "The Horizon: American Attitudes Making Enemies of Many South Koreans," *Courier*, September 1, 1951, 18; "Have We Lost the Koreans?" *Philadelphia Tribune*, August 21, 1951, 4.

63. "National Grapevine: It's Now Perhaps or Never," *Chicago Defender*, August 5, 1950, 6. Lucius C. Harper attacked the United States more aggressively and asked what Asians could hope "'under democracy' if what they know about the Negro's plight here to be true? . . . We even had the audacity to fight on foreign soil with a Jim Crow army in the name of democracy. What could be more contradictory?" Harper, "Dustin' off the News."

64. "Colored Troops Win First Victory for U.S. in Korea: The 24 Takes Yechon in 16 Hours," *Afro-American*, July 29, 1950, 1–2.

65. "This Is No Race War"; Prattis, "The Horizon"; "Have We Lost the Koreans?" *Philadelphia Tribune*, August 21, 1951, 4.

66. "Death in Korea," *Our World*, December 1950, 30; see also "Is It a War of Color?", *Ebony*, October 1950, 94; Alfred Baker Lewis, "Not a Racial War," *Afro-American*, September 13, 1950, Editorial Page.

67. A. J. Siggins, "Korean Flare-Up May Be Trap for U.S. Diplomacy," *Black Dispatch*, July 8, 1950, 8; see also "Sensible War Strategy," *Black Dispatch*, July 8, 1950, Editorial Page; "Korean Clash Seen as Fight Between White and Colored," *Black Dispatch*, July 22, 1950, 8.

68. Gordon B. Hancock, "Between the Lines: Getting Our Country Told," *Atlanta Daily World*, August 5, 1950, 6.

69. "National Grapevine: There's Still Time," *Chicago Defender*, July 15, 1950, 6.

70. Gordon B. Hancock, "Between the Lines: Getting Our Country Told," *Atlanta Daily World*, August 5, 1950, 6; see also Gordon B. Hancock, "Between the Lines," *Black Dispatch*, July 29, 1950, August 5, 1950, Editorial Page; "Between the Lines:

Bully-Ism Backfires," *Philadelphia Tribune,* July 29, 1950, 4; Gordon B. Hancock, "Between the Lines: Over Confidence," *Atlanta Daily World,* August 3, 1950, 4; "Koreans Won't Like This," *Afro-American,* August 26, 1950, 4.

71. All quotes from Trezzvant W. Anderson, "World News: Putting the Finger on Korea," *Pittsburgh Courier,* July 22, 1950, 31.

72. Sherry, *In the Shadow of War,* 179.

73. Cartoon, "Sabotaging Our Right to World Leadership," *New York Amsterdam News,* June 24, 1950.

74. Dower, *War Without Mercy,* 173–74. Historian Bruce Cumings has also argued that there existed an "ubiquitous racism of whites coming from a segregated American society, where Koreans were 'people of color' subjugated to apartheid-like restrictions." Cumings, *The Korean War: A History,* 15.

75. "Is This White Chauvinism?" *The Crisis,* February 1951, 103. The *Los Angeles Times,* for instance, noted that soldiers used the term "gooks" for North Koreans, but explained that it was merely a "soldier's word for anyone racially different from himself," thereby completely ignoring the racist and offensive quality of the term. "Soldiers Revive 'Gook' as Name for Korean Reds," *Los Angeles Times,* August 6, 1950, 6. Yet again, the *Pittsburgh Courier* published the widest range of opinions in its editorial and opinion pages. Its columnists extensively elaborated on the significance of race and domestic race relations in the war and increased its pressure on the U.S. government.

76. "Koreans Won't Like This." "The word gook is a contemptuous derisive term corresponding in meaning to a degrading name sometimes applied to Negroes in certain areas of the United States." See also Rudolph Spencer, "The Tragedy of Korea," *Black Dispatch,* September 23, 1950, 1; Ralph Matthews, "How Sex Demoralized Our Army in Korea," *Afro-American,* August 5, 1950, 7.

77. Quote from "Human Rights Day," *Courier,* December 16, 1950, 21.

78. Robert P. Martin, "Chinese Reds Prove They're Tough Men," *New York Amsterdam News,* January 6, 1951, 6.

79. Marjorie McKenzie, "Pursuit of Democracy: America Must Realize That Beyond the Atlantic Circle the World Is Yellow, Black," *Courier,* July 15, 1950, Editorial Page.

80. Horace Cayton, "Split-Thinking Hurls Our Foreign Policy and Affects Our Attitude to Both Asia and Africa," *Courier,* July 15, 1950, Editorial Page.

81. "National Grapevine: There's Still Time," *Chicago Defender,* July 15, 1950, 6.

82. Martin, "Chinese Reds Prove They're Tough Men."

83. Dower argues that "much rhetoric of World War Two was readily adaptable to the cold war." Dower, *War Without Mercy,* 29, 180–200.

84. "Cartoonist Reaction to Current Events in Korea," *Los Angeles Times,* May 3, 1953, B5.

85. "The Wounded," *Saturday Evening Post,* September 23, 1950, 32–33, 144–46; "Negro Troops Win 16-Hr. Fight for Road Center; Infiltering Cut," *Washington Post,* July 22, 1950, 1.

86. See "American Attitudes Towards Other Races Worries Army," *Philadelphia Tribune*, July 29, 1950, 1; GI's Warned Not to Use Word 'Gook', *Afro-American*, September 2, 1950, 5.

87. "'Our Little War with the Heathen'," *Chicago Daily Tribune*, August 27, 1950, 20; see also Walter Sullivan, "G.I. View of Koreans as 'Gooks' Believed Doing Political Damage," *New York Times*, July 26, 1950, 1; Fradley H. Garner, "Letters to the Time: G.I. View of Koreans: Program of Psychological Orientation Advocated for Troops," *New York Times*, August 2, 1950, 23; "Friends over Force," *Christian Science Monitor*, August 7, 1950, 18; "Mirror of World Opinion: When 'Gooks' Become 'Roks'," *Christian Science Monitor*, September 21, 1950, 22.

88. Hanson W. Baldwin, "Korea Shows Need of U.S. Policy Unity," *New York Times*, October 31, 1950, 4. Despite these critical insights, however, many of his colleagues often remained unable or unwilling to refrain from racist stereotyping when he designated Koreans as having a "volatile quality," a lack of morale, and untrustworthiness.

89. As an ANP dispatch, the article was widely distributed in the African American newspapers. "Japanese Hero-Worship Many Korean Vets," *New York Amsterdam News*, October 28, 1950, 19; "Display Hero Worship to Korean War Vet," *Atlanta Daily World*, October 31, 1950, 4.

90. Ralph Matthews, "A Strange Item from the Front," *New York Amsterdam News*, November 17, 1951, 1.

91. "Bunche Thinks U.N. Can Solve Korean War," *Atlanta Daily World*, November 16, 1950, 1; "Dr. Bunche Suggested as Mediator for Korean War," *Norfolk Journal and Guide*, December 23, 1950, 1; "Stassen Likes Bunche for Korean Mediation," *Courier*, December 16, 1950, 1.

92. "Dr. Bunche Needed Now," *Chicago Defender*, December 16, 1950, 6; reference in "The Other Way Out," *Afro-American*, November 4, 1950, 4; "The Guide Post: It's Time for the UN to Play Its Ace; Dr. Ralph Bunche Is Usually a Winner," *New Journal and Guide*, January 13, 1951, 12.

93. "Negro General for M'Arthur," *Chicago Defender*, July 15, 1950, 1.

94. Information on Milton A. Smith, "Correspondent on Korean War Front," *New Journal and Guide*, November 18, 1950, D28A. Quotes in "Negro Soldiers Good Will Ambassadors, Writer Says," *Atlanta Daily World*, February 27, 1951, 2; "Tan GI's in Korea Envoys of Good Will," *Afro-American*, March 3, 1951, 1; "Colored Soldiers Called America's Best Ambassadors," *Norfolk Journal and Guide*, March 3, 1951, 7.

95. "Such Intelligence," *Chicago Defender*, December 9, 1950, 6.

96. In his book on blacks and World War I, Chad Williams shows African American soldiers' complicated relationship with Africans. He argues that "African Americans remained historically tied to and often politically invested in the United States. And as Americans, they had internalized many of the stereotypes and misconceptions of African peoples popularized by the West . . . African American servicemen often continued to fall back upon stereotype, caricature, and exoticization. Pervasive notions

of African inferiority, held by white and black Americans alike, proved difficult to overcome. Americanness regularly trumped Africanness." Chad Williams, *Torchbearers of Democracy: African American Soldiers in the World War I Era* (Chapel Hill: University of North Carolina Press, 2010), 190–91, 195.

97. Gordon Hancock, "Between the Lines," *Atlanta Daily World*, October 22, 1950, 4.

98. "National Grapevine," *Chicago Defender*, December 9, 1950, 6.

99. Alvin E. White, "All Soldiers Caught in Whirlpool of Korean War," *Atlanta Daily World*, December 13, 1950, 8.

100. Langston Hughes, "Colored Asia Makes Highly Colored News These Days," *Chicago Defender*, August 15, 1953, 11.

101. On the connections see Phillips, *War!*, 156–60.

102. On acting as a negotiator see Ralph Matthews, "Rambling Thoughts of a War Reporter," *Afro-American*, November 24, 1951, 14.

103. L. Alex Wilson, "Wilson Paints Picture of 'Beautiful' Korea thru the Eyes of Battered GI Joes," *Chicago Defender*, September 30, 1950, 4; "Story of Korea Is Shocking Saga of a Nation Living in the Past," *Chicago Defender*, December 23, 1950; see also "Korean Assignment No Bed of Roses; Too Much Lacking," *Afro-American*, July 29, 1950, 7.

104. James Hicks, "This Is Korea: Natives, Cows, Dogs, Chickens Live in the Same Huts, Conditions Shocking," *Afro-American*, September 30, 1950, 12; see also "24th Quickly Learns New-Style Fighting," *Afro-American*, August 5, 1950, 3; Milton A. Smith, "What Happened to Kilroy? He Is Not About in Korea," *Norfolk Journal and Guide*, January 5, 1951, 5.

105. Ralph Matthews, "A Correspondent Leads a Dog's Life Too in Korea," *Norfolk Journal and Guide*," September 1, 1951, 1.

106. "Story of Korea Is Shocking Saga of a Nation Living in the Past."

107. Milton Smith, "No Welcome Mat Out for U.S. in Korea," *Afro-American*, December 16, 1950, 13.

108. Vincent Tubbs, "Korea Is Not the Place for a Modern War," *Afro Magazine Section*, August 19, 1950, 3.

109. Nora Waln, "Our Softhearted Warriors," *Saturday Evening Post*, December 23, 1950, 28; "Lonely GIs Aid Korean War Orphans," *Philadelphia Tribune*, March 13, 1951, 13; "Korean Kids Learn Yanks Mean Sweets," *Afro-American*, August 26, 1950, 12.

110. "Story of Korea is Shocking Saga of a Nation Living in the Past."

111. "Korea Pictured as a Sick Friend Struggling for Life," *Norfolk Journal and Guide*, September 1, 1951, 24.

112. Ralph Matthews, "Korean War National Tragedy: 212,554 Dead, Wounded, 600,000 Homes Wrecked," *Afro-American*, September 1, 1951, 14.

113. Ralph Matthews, "Soldiers Forget Their Hating Many Times to Aid the Young," *New York Amsterdam News*, September 8, 1951, 7.

114. Ralph Matthews, "A Lesson, Korean Style," *New York Amsterdam News*, September 15, 1951, 17.

115. Sgt. Bob Philips, "Army Decorates Savannah's Joe Jinks for Heroism in Korea War," *Chicago Defender*, December 23, 1950, 2.

116. See "Steering Wheel Is GI's Souvenir of Korean Reds Attack," *Philadelphia Tribune*, September 19, 1950, 3; "GI Has Prized Souvenir of Korean War," *Atlanta Daily World*, September 20, 1950, 3; Mark Hyman, "City Men Returned to Naval Hospital Tell of Battle," *Philadelphia Tribune*, September 23, 1950, 1.

117. Green, *Black Yanks in the Pacific*, 124–25. In her book and article, Phillips often only touches on the derogatory language and orientalist attitude shown in African American publications. She focuses on highlighting soldiers and activists, like Du Bois and Robeson, who protested openly or at least questioned the war. See Kimberley Phillips, " 'Did the Battlefield Kill Jim Crow?' The Cold War Military, Civil Rights, and Black Freedom Struggles," in *Fog of War: The Second World War and the Civil Rights Movement*, ed. Kevin M. Kruse and Stephen Tuck (Oxford: Oxford University Press, 2012), 213–15; *War!* reference to African American racism toward Japanese during occupation, 127–28; otherwise see, e.g., 134

118. "Operation Negro," *Courier*, January 13, 1951, 6.

119. "GI Wipes Out Enemy Column," *Courier*, August 5, 1950, 1; James Hicks, "Heroic Five Kill 125," *Afro-American*, September 23, 1950, 1.

120. Wilson, "Wilson Paints Picture of 'Beautiful' Korea"; Bradford Laws, "How Can You Tell Friend from Foe Plagues Tanks," *Afro-American*, August 26, 1950, 13. White soldiers felt the same way. See Hastings, *The Korean War*, 82, 241.

121. See Wilson, "Wilson Paints Picture of 'Beautiful' Korea"; Laws, "How Can You Tell Friend from Foe Plagues Tanks; Green, *Black Yanks in the Pacific*, 130.

122. L. Alex Wilson, "Fresh Troops, Planes Help 24th Overcome Red Gains," *Chicago Defender*, September 9, 1950; 1; Frank Conniff, "Red Army Using Korean Children to Spy on UN Forces," *Norfolk Journal and Guide*, February 1, 1951, 7.

123. "Joe Koats" also "Jo Kos" was used for North Koreans. L. Alex Wilson, "Front Line Grapevine: Late, But News Just the Same," *Chicago Defender*, September 8, 1950, 6; "Lt. Gilbert Thinks He Was Right," *Afro American*, October 21, 1950, 13. Green has rightly pointed out that African Americans, like whites, "fell back upon imagery of the American West and Native Americans," Green, *Black Yanks in the Pacific*, 128.

124. L. Alex Wilson, "Forces Afloat Give Excellent Support to Ground Troops," *Norfolk Journal and Guide*, September 16, 1950, 1; "Ramblin' in Korea," *Norfolk Journal and Guide*, October 7, 1950, 11.

125. "Fight or Die Is Army's Decision," *Afro-American*, August 12, 1950, 12.

126. Dower, *War Without Mercy*. Dower analyzes the mainstream discourse and racist constructions of the enemy soldier, but does not extensively cover American minorities. A number of researchers claim, however, that there existed a special African American assessment of Asians during World War II due to their racial otherness.

See Marc Gallicchio, *The African American Encounter with Japan and China: Black Internationalism in Asia, 1895–1945* (Chapel Hill: University of North Carolina Press, 2000); Nathaniel Deutsch, "'The Asiatic Black Man': An African American Orientalism?" *Journal of Asian American Studies* 4, 3 (October 2001): 193–208; George Lipsitz, "Frantic to Join . . . the Japanese Army": Black Soldiers and Civilians Confront the Asia Pacific War," in *Perilous Memories: The Asia-Pacific War(s)*, ed. T. Fujitani, Geoffrey M. White, and Lisa Yoneyam (Durham, N.C.: Duke University Press, 2001), 347–77.

127. "North Koreans Go 'Blackface' to Confuse Troops," *Atlanta Daily World*, August 8, 1950, 4. Quote from Wilson, "Wilson Paints Picture of 'Beautiful' Korea"; "Can't Trust those Gooks," *Chicago Defender*, September 30, 1950, both 4; "N. Korean Use 'Blackface to Confuse 24th Infantry," *Afro-American*, August 12, 1950, 3.

128. See "24th Quickly Learns New-Style Fighting," *Afro-American*, August 5, 1950, 3.

129. Helen H. Jun, *Race for Citizenship: Black Orientalism and Asian Uplift from Pre-Emancipation to Neoliberal America* (New York: New York University Press, 2011), 23. Jun points to Gaines's book in developing her argument: Kevin Gaines, *Uplifting the Race: Black Leadership, Politics, and Culture in the Twentieth Century* (Chapel Hill: University of North Carolina Press, 1996).

130. bell hooks, *Black Looks: Race and Representation* (Boston: South End Press, 1992), 7.

131. Historian Green presents similar findings, however, he fails to analyze the African American claim to racial sensitivity in more detail. Green, *Black Yanks in the Pacific*, 110, 124.

132. Milton Smith, "We've Been Licked: Defeat in Korea Stunning to Yanks," *Afro-American*, December 16, 1950, 1.

133. The concept of "Orientalism" was first developed by Edward Said, *Orientalism: Western Conceptions of the Orient* (New York: Penguin, 2003). Historian Christina Klein purports a more positive and empowering idea of Orientalism, *Cold War Orientalism: Asia in the Middlebrow Imagination, 1945–1961* (Berkeley: University of California Press, 2003). On associating with the Koreans, P. L. Prattis, "Fort Devens GI Inquires About Freedom, Jim Crow in the United States," *Courier*, July 14, 1951, 20. Kimberley Phillips underlines the repulsion of black soldiers in segregated units toward killing enemy soldiers and civilians. First, linking segregation to a general unwillingness to kill proves problematic. Some white soldiers might have had reservations to kill, too. Second, the quote she presents to support her claim refers to a different problem entirely: "What the hell had we black people ever done to them that merited such inhumane treatment?" In Curtis Morrow's memoir, *What's a Commie Ever Done to Black People?*, "them" refers back to white people and their racist attitudes and treatment of blacks, not Koreans and Chinese as Phillips claims. However, Morrow certainly questioned—at least in retrospect—why he should fight other racial minorities and give his life for a racist country. But one also has to keep in mind that

Morrow intentionally constructed himself in his autobiography. Curtis James Morrow, *What's a Commie Ever Done to Black People? A Korean War Memoir of Fighting in the U.S. Army's Last All Negro Unit* (Jefferson, N.C.: McFarland, 1997), 12; discrepancy see Phillips, "Did the Battlefield Kill Jim Crow," 213.

134. On "black orientalism" in the nineteenth century, Jun, *Race for Citizenship*. Jun argues that black Orientalism is "a heterogeneous and historically variable discourse in which the contradictions of black citizenship engage with the logic of American Orientalism" (18). On Afro-Orientalism, Billy V. Mullen, *Afro-Orientalism* (Minneapolis: University of Minnesota Press, 2006).

135. Katherine Moon's general study on the relation of American soldiers and Korean women does not specifically consider African Americans. Moon, however, supports the argument that that the American racial ideology was responsible for Korean racism, *Sex Among Allies: Military Prostitution in U.S.-Korean Relations* (New York: Columbia University Press, 1997), esp. 1–56; Maria Höhn and Seungsook Moon, eds., *Over There: Living with the U.S. Military Empire from World War Two to the Present* (Durham, N.C.: Duke University Press, 2010), 39–77, 51–53.

136. Alex Lubin, *Romance and Rights: The Politics of Interracial Intimacy 1945–1954* (Jackson: University Press of Mississippi, 2005), 116.

137. War correspondent Ralph Matthews described American women in Japan as spoiled and condescending toward locals. "GI's Ponder Peace Moves," *Afro-American*, September 22, 1951, 5.

138. The average age of soldiers was 23 compared to 26 during the Second World War. Pash, *In the Shadow of the Greatest Generation*, 46.

139. Ralph Matthews, "Wacs and Pom Pom Wage War in Yokohama," *Afro-American*, September 22, 1950, 8; cf. "Tan WACs Blue, Korea GIs Don't Bother to Date Them," *New York Amsterdam News*, September 22, 1951, 1; James L. Hicks, "Officer Says Our Girls in Japan Not Attractive," *Afro-American*, November 25, 1950, 13.

140. Alan Berube, *Coming out under Fire: The History of Gay Men and Women in World War II* (New York: Free Press, 1990), cf. 30.

141. Ralph Matthews, "Wacs and Pom Pom Wage War in Yokohama," *Afro-American*, September 22, 1950, 8; cf. "Tan WACs Blue, Korea GIs Don't Bother to Date Them," *New York Amsterdam News*, September 22, 1951, 1.

142. The black war correspondent contended that it was a combination of "Ancient customs" and hatred for the racism of white Americans, which withheld Korean women from associating with soldiers. Ralph Matthews, "Why Did Army Flop? AFRO Editor Blames Its Collapse on Sex NO FRATERNIZATION," *Afro-American*, August 5, 1950, 7.

143. Moon, *Sex Among Allies*, 16.

144. On sexual availability and occupation, on prostitution and militarization: Cynthia Enloe, *Maneuvers: The International Politics of Militarizing Women's Lives* (Berkeley: University of California Press, 2000), esp. chap. 3; Enloe, *Bananas, Beaches*

and Bases: Making Feminist Sense of International Politics (Berkeley: University of California Press, 2000 updated ed.).

145. Ralph Matthews, "How Sex Demoralized Our Army in Korea," *Afro-American*, August 5, 1950, 7.

146. L Alex Wilson, "Why Tan Yanks Go for Japanese Girls," *Chicago Defender*, November 11, 1950, 1; James L. Hicks, "Officer Says Our Girls in Japan Not Attractive," *Afro-American*, November 25, 1950, 13.

147. First quote: James Hicks, "Japanese or American Girls: Which? Why?; Soldiers Say They Prefer Type Which Acknowledges Man as Head of the House," *Afro-American*, October 7, 1950, 1; second quote: "Tan GIs Seeking Permits to Marry Japanese Women," *Black Dispatch*, November 11, 1950, 1; Frank Whisonant, "'Moosey Mae' Wins Hearts of Negro GIs," *Courier*," December 9, 1950, 3; L. Alex Wilson, "Chatter About GIs in Korea," *Chicago Defender*, February 3, 1951, 2.

148. Ethel Payne, "Says Japanese Girls Playing GI's for Suckers," *Chicago Defender*, November 18 and 25, 1950, 12.

149. "Let GIs Wed Japanese Girls," *Courier*, November 18, 1950, 1 and 5. An article in *Jet* in 1952 painted black soldiers as victims of conniving prostitutes. "Is Vice Menacing Our GIs?," *Jet*, May 8, 1952, 14–17.

150. On reports on the problematic position of black women with respect to interracial relationships see Lubin, *Romance and Rights*, 118.

151. Ole Nosey, "Everybody Goes When the Wagon Comes," *Chicago Defender*, November 25, 1950, 20; see also L. Alex Wilson, "Why Tan Yanks Go for Japanese Girls," *Chicago Defender*, November 11, 1950, 1; Ralph Matthews, "GI's Sing Inflation Blues: Spiraling Cost of Love Is Joe's Biggest Gripe," *Afro-American*, September 8, 1951, 14.

152. Ralph Matthews, "Wacs and Pom Pom Wage War in Yokohama," *Afro-American*, September 22, 1951, 8; see also "Tan WACs Blue, Korea GIs Don't Bother to Date Them," *New York Amsterdam News*, September 22, 1951, 1.

153. Editorial Cartoon, "Battle Between Wac's and Native Girls Rages in Japan," *Afro-American*, September 22, 1951, 8.

154. L. Alex Wilson, "G.I.'s Disappointed and Disgusted: Land below 38th Parallel 'Black Hole of Calcutta'," *Norfolk Journal and Guide*, September 30, 1950, D15.

155. L. Alex Wilson, "Front Line Grapevine; Note to Wives and Sweethearts," *Chicago Defender*, September 9, 1950, 6. UN comfort stations grew in number during the course of the Korean War. "What is clear about the institution of UN comfort stations is the persistence of the instrumental use of women's sexual labor by military and civilian authorities to entertain (and essentially control) soldiers, the agents of imperial and local political powers. . . . In the face of dire wartime poverty, the Korean government viewed prostitution as an inevitable means to feed its population. In the midst of war, the government also viewed it as a necessary means to entertain foreign soldiers who were fighting the war against North Korea." Seoungsook Moon, "Regulating Desire, Managing the Empire: US Military Prostitution in South Korea, 1945–1970," in Höhn and Moon, *Over There*, 39–77, 51–53.

156. On relationships, prostitution, and venereal diseases in Korea see, e.g., Pash, *Standing in the Shadow of the Greatest Generation*, 130pp.

157. Milton A. Smith, "GIs Spurn Korean Gals, Wait for Jap Lassies," *Chicago Defender*, December 16, 1950, 19.

158. Ralph Matthews, "A Strange Item from the Front," *New York Amsterdam News*, November 17, 1950, M1.

159. "Would You Object If Your Son Married a Korean Girl," *Afro Magazine*, October 30, 1954, 9.

160. "Buddy System Integrates South Koreans, 'Bobo,' 'Casey' et al into US Army," *Washington Post*, October 10, 1950, 4.

161. "South Koreans Put in U.S. Army Units: Republican Troops Trained at Special Camps and Then Fight Alongside G.I.'s: Their Bravery Acclaimed Language Problem Overcome by Signs," *New York Times*, August 25, 1950, 3.

162. See Jun, *Race for Citizenship*, 16–17.

163. "An Insult in Korea," *Courier*, September 2, 1950, 3; "Abolish 'Negro' Units," *Courier*, September 9, 1950, Editorial Page.

164. Ralph Matthews, "This Week," *Afro-American*, September 23, 1950, 7.

165. Horace Cayton, "Cayton: North Koreans Are Not So Undemocratic That We Should Forget Their Racial Problem," *Courier*, September 16, 1950, 20.

Chapter 7. Black Men at War

1. Marjorie McKenzie, "Pursuit of Democracy: America Must Realize That Beyond the Atlantic Circle the World Is Yellow, Black," *Courier*, July 15, 1950, Editorial page.

2. For his selfless actions and acclaimed heroism, Hudner received the Congressional Medal of Honor in April 1951. "Congressional Medal for Pilot," *Los Angeles Sentinel*, April 5, 1951, A1.

3. "Grim Rescue Drama Revealed in Enemy Territory," *Norfolk Journal and Guide*, March 10, 1951, 24. "First Negro Naval Pilot Dies as Plane Is Downed," "Rescue Efforts Fail: 1st Tan Navy Flier Dies in Korea," *Afro-American*, December 16, 1950, 1.

4. White press, see, e.g., Roscoe Simmons, "The Untold Story," *Chicago Daily Tribune*, December 17, 1950, SW20; "Flier Wins Honor Medal: Truman Will Present Award to Navy Pilot for Korea Rescue," *New York Times*, March 31, 1951, 4.

5. See Lauren Rebecca Sklaroff, "Constructing G.I. Joe Louis: Cultural Solutions to the 'Negro Problem' During World War II," *Journal of American History* 89, 3 (December 2002): 958–83.

6. The navy did everything to disseminate this positive image. See Lester Granger Papers, NUL Papers. The papers contain an array of sources on Granger's activism on behalf of the navy that speak of his influence on the positive image of the navy in the African American community. A more thorough study of these papers is warranted.

7. Roy Wilkins, "The Watchtower," *Los Angeles Sentinel*, March 3, 1949, C7; "Ambitious Mississippi Youth Makes Grade as Navy Pilot," *Philadelphia Tribune*, April 30, 1949, 2; "Hard Work Paid off for Navy Flier Jesse L. Brown," *Norfolk Journal and Guide*, May 7, 1949, 20. C1.

8. "Rescue Efforts Fail: 1st Tan Navy Flier Dies in Korea."

9. James Hicks, "Lest We Forget: Whom Do They Mean? Whom Are They Talking About?" *Afro-Magazine*, November 10, 1951, 22H.

10. "Ace Naval Pilot Killed," *Norfolk Journal and Guide*, December 16, 1950, C1.

11. See "Medal of Honor Winner Meets Widow of Pilot He Tried to Save," *Norfolk Journal and Guide*, April 28, 1951, 1; "Mrs. Brown Thanks Lieutenant for Heroic Effort," *Afro-American*, April 21, 1951; "Dead Pilot's Widow Sobs at Ceremony, Mates Aid Daughter," *Philadelphia Tribune*, April 17, 1951, 1.

12. "Medal of Honor Winner Meets Widow."

13. "Risked Life for Ensign Jesse Brown, First Colored Naval Pilot," *Norfolk Journal and Guide*, April 7, 1951, C2.

14. "Democracy Alive in Navy: Leyte Pilots Raise $2,700 for Late Buddy's Daughter," *Afro-American*, April 28, 1951, 19.

15. Albert Barnett, "Names in the News: 'Jo' Baker, Lt. Hudner, Dr. Rufus Clement," *Chicago Defender*, April 14, 1951, 7.

16. Mary Whittaker, "A Life for a Cause," *Chicago Defender*, April 28, 1951, 6.

17. Quote in L. Alex Wilson, "Along the Korean War Front: Southern Whites, Negroes Give Jim Crow Hard Time in Mixed Tank Group," *Chicago Defender*, September 2, 1950, 1; L. Alex Wilson, "Battlefront Commander Says Integration Works," *Norfolk Journal and Guide*, September 30, 1950, C1; L. Alex Wilson, "Does Integration Work In Korea? Along the Korean War Front Wilson Finds Sailors Fighting, Living Together Aboard Vessels," *Chicago Defender*, September 16, 1950, 1.

18. L. Alex Wilson, "Freed by Tan Yanks, Dixie Raps Bias," *Chicago Defender*, October 7, 1950, 1; L. Alex Wilson, "GIs Learn Democracy Lesson on Front Line," *Norfolk Journal and Guide*, October 14, 1950, 10. A similar story, "Heroic Five Kill 125," *Afro-American*, September 23, 1950, 1.

19. See, e.g., "Radical Change of Policy to Affect Nation's Fliers; Air Force to Open Up Personnel Would Be Integrated Complete Use of Personnel Planned, Washington Reports," *Norfolk Journal and Guide*, January 22, 1949, D23; "Air Force, Plans to End Segregation," *Philadelphia Tribune*, January 22, 1949, 3; "The Army's Out of Step," *Afro-American*, June 3, 1950, Editorial Page; James L. Hicks, "Integration a Fact as We Fight Koreans," *Afro-American*, August 19, 1950, 1.

20. President's Committee, *Freedom to Serve: Equality of Treatment and Opportunity in the Armed Services—A Report by the President's Committee* (Washington, D.C.: Government Printing Office, 1950). Monroe Billington, "Freedom to Serve: The President's Committee on Equality of Treatment and Opportunity in the Armed Forces, 1949–1950," *Journal of Negro History* 51, 4 (October 1966), 262–74.

21. Lester Granger to President Truman, quoted in Donald R. McCoy and Richard T. Ruetten, *Quest and Response: Minority Rights and the Truman Administration* (Lawrence: University Press of Kansas, 1973), 232.

22. "Armed Services Integration," *The Crisis*, July 1950, 443; see also "Join the Navy, Dodge Jim Crow," *Black Dispatch*, November 4, 1950, Editorial page; James L. Hicks, "Air Forces Best Deal," *Afro-American*, June 26, 1951, 1.

23. "Fear and Army Integration," *Afro-American*, December 23, 1953, Editorial Page; see also "Mixed Units, GI Victories: Jolt Dixie Brass Hats," *Chicago Defender*, August 26, 1950, 1; "Combat Soldiers High in Praise of Infantry Integration," *New Journal and Guide*, October 28, 1950, 11; "Jim Crowism in the Army," *Chicago Defender*, March 24, 1951, 6; Charles Armstrong in Yvonne Latty, Ron Tarver, *We Were There: The Voices of African American Veterans, from World War II to the War in Iraq* (New York: HarperCollins, 2004), 58.

24. See Sherie Mershon and Steven Schlossman, *Foxholes and Color Lines: Desegregating the U.S. Armed Forces* (Baltimore: Johns Hopkins University Press, 1998), 218.

25. Charles Rangel, *And I Haven't Had a Bad Day Since: From the Streets of Harlem to the Halls of Congress* (New York: Thomas Dunne, 2007), 59.

26. Lucius C. Harper, "Dustin' Off the News: Some Sidelights on the Korean War That Might Be Interesting," *Chicago Defender*, August 5, 1950, Editorial Page; "24th Escapes Korean Trap: MacArthur Lauds Negro Unit's Action Unit's Escape Called One of Heroic Tales of Far Eastern War," *New York Amsterdam*, July 15, 1950, 1; "Publishers Laud MacArthur Policy," *Afro-American*, October 21, 1950, 1; Frank Whisonant, Jim Crow Operates Among GIs in Nippon," *Courier*, December 9, 1950, 3.

27. "Jim Crow Blood Again! UN Raps Race Tag on Blood," *Courier*, September 16, 1950, 1. On blood donations and segregation esp. during World War II, see Sarah E. Chinn, *Technology and Logic of American Racism: A Cultural History of the Body as Evidence* (London: Continuum, 2000), chap. 4.

28. See A. M. Rivera, Jr.,". . . Flags in Korea!: Confederate Banners Fly Anywhere!!!," *Courier*, September 22, 1951, A1; "Defender Rips Rebel Flags in Korea," *Chicago Defender*, January 19, 1952, 3; Ralph Matthews, "Rebel Flags Flooding Korea," *Afro-American*, December 1, 1951, 1.

29. "24th Infantry Called into Action in Korea," *Atlanta Daily World*, July 1, 1950, 1; "Thousands of Negro Troops Among U.S. Forces Alerted in Japan," *Philadelphia Tribune*, July 1, 1950, 1.

30. "Negro GI's Hit Korean Beaches," *New York Amsterdam News*, July 8, 1950, 1.

31. See "24th Infantry Called into Action in Korea," *Atlanta Daily World*, July 1, 1950, 1 The article was dispatched by the NNPA and printed in numerous black papers. See "24th Infantry Called into Action in Korea: Negro Troops First to Face Battle Fire," *Birmingham World*, July 4, 1950, 1.

32. The deferment system certainly favored college students. The number of black deferments is difficult to assess, as the armed forces did not keep deferment statistics by race after 1950. On deferments during the Korean War, see Melinda Pash, *Standing*

in the Shadow of the Greatest Generation: The Americans Who Fought the Korean War (New York: New York University Press, 2012), 39–45; African Americans and the draft during Korea, Paul T. Murray, "Blacks and the Draft: A History of Institutional Racism," *Journal of Black Studies* 2, 1 (September 1971): 67–74.

33. The army did not fully abolish the quota system until April 1950, but tried to resist any changes to the method procedure that excluded blacks based on test scores. President Truman had to interfere to get the army to acquiesce. Numbers in Kimberley Phillips, *War! What Is It Good for? Black Freedom Struggles and the U.S. Military from World War II to Iraq* (Chapel Hill: University of North Carolina Press, 2012), 147; Murray, "Blacks and the Draft: A History of Institutional Racism," 57–76, 67–69; Christian G. Appy, *Working-Class War: American Combat Soldiers and Vietnam* (Chapel Hill: University of North Carolina Press, 1993), 18, 30. William T. Bowers, William M. Hammond, and George L. MacGarrigle, *Black Soldier, White Army: The 24th Infantry Regiment in Korea* (Washington, D.C.: Center of Military History, 1996), 37–38.

34. "More Negroes Expected to Enlist in the Army," *Chicago Defender*, June 15, 1946, 12. Historian Green elaborates lengthily on the needs and necessities of blacks and their enlistment in the armed forces. Michael C. Green, *Black Yanks in the Pacific: Race in the Making of American Military Empire After World War II* (Ithaca, N.Y.: Cornell University Press, 2010), chap. 1; Phillips, *War!* 146–49.

35. After his return from Korea, Wilson continued to work as a successful journalist covering and participating in the civil rights movement. During the coverage of the integration of black students in Little Rock, Arkansas, in 1957, he was severely beaten by a white mob. In a later interview on the events, he stated that his training as a marine and experiences as a war correspondent in Korea had prepared him to stay calm in dangerous situations and not flee from the mob. He died in 1960 from what his wife believed to be the long-term effects of the head injuries sustained during the attack. "Defender Ace to Korea," *Chicago Defender*, July 15, 1950, 1; "Alex Wilson, Defender Editor-in-Chief, Dies," *Chicago Defender*, October 12, 1960, A1, 3; on the cause of death, *Jackson Sun*, n.d., *Jackson Sun Homepage*, April 27, 2009, http://orig.-jacksonsun.com; Gene Roberts and Hank Klibanoff, *The Race Beat: The Press, the Civil Rights Struggle, and the Awakening of a Nation* (New York: Vintage, 2007); the beating, 176–79; his death, 243. On reporters in Korea see, e.g., Susan D. Moeller, *Shooting War: Photography and the American Experience of Combat* (New York: Basic, 1989); Phillips, *War!* 131ff.

36. "Albert L. Hinton's First and Tragically, Last War Story," *Norfolk Journal and Guide*, August 1, 1950, 1.

37. Ralph Matthews, "A Correspondent Leads a Dog's Life Too in Korea," *Norfolk Journal and Guide*, September 1, 1951, B1; "Editorial Cartoon: Headaches of Korean Correspondents," *Afro-American*, September 22, 1951, Editorial Page. Phillips provides details on James Hicks and his work during the Korean War. Phillips, *War!* 131ff.

38. Vivian Carter Mason, "The Guide Post," *Norfolk Journal and Guide*, August 5, 1950, D14.

39. The *Afro-American* continued to follow African American soldiers rather thoroughly throughout the war.

40. "24th Infantry Called into Action in Korea"; "Thousands of Negro Troops Among U.S. Forces Alerted in Japan."

41. "Tan GI's Go into Action! " *Chicago Defender*, July 8, 1950, 1.

42. "25,000 Negroes Face Draft; Thousands of Others Volunteering," *Courier*, July 22, 1950, 1.

43. Roy Wilkins, "The Watchtower," *Los Angeles Sentinel*, March 3, 1949, C7; see also "Ambitious Mississippi Youth Makes Grade as Navy Pilot," *Philadelphia Tribune*, April 30, 1949, 2; "Hard Work Paid Off for Navy Flier Jesse L. Brown," *Norfolk Journal and Guide*, May 7, 1949, 20 C1.

44. "Defender Ace to Korea," *Chicago Defender*, July 15 1950, 1; "With Troops in Korea," *Afro-American*, July 29, 1950, 1; "Courier Reporter to Korea," *Pittsburgh Courier*, July 29, 1950, 1; Vincent Tubbs, "Covering a War Is No Bed of Roses," *Afro-Magazine*, September 30, 1950.

45. "To Break Up the 24th Infantry," *Afro-American*, September 23, 1950, Editorial Page.

46. See Marion B. Campfield, "Mostly About Women," *Chicago Defender*, October 2, 1950, 10.

47. Richard Bartell, somewhere in Korea, "Soldier Says Letters Would Boost Morale," *Courier*, January 13, 1951, 22.

48. "What to Put in Letters Mailed to Soldiers Overseas," *Afro-American*, September 30, 1950, 13.

49. Robert Westbrook, "'I Want a Girl, Just like the Girl That Married Harry James': American Women and the Problem of Political Obligation in World War II," *American Quarterly* 42, 4 (December 1990): 587–614, 589; more on pin-ups and female sexuality during World War II: Maria Elena Buszek, *Pin-Up Grrrls: Feminism, Sexuality, Popular Culture* (Durham, N.C.: Duke University Press, 2006); Marilyn E. Hegarty, *Victory Girls, Khaki-Wackies, and Patriotutes: The Regulation of Female Sexuality During World War II* (New York: New York University Press, 2008).

50. Master Sergeant Theodore Senior and Sergeant Edgar Anderson to Walter White, December 20 1943, NAACP Papers MF, Part 9, Series A, Reel 14, quoted in Charissa Threat, "Searching for Colored Pin-Up Girls: Race, Gender and Sexuality During World War II," paper, Berkshire Conference, University of Massachusetts Amherst, June 2011.

51. "These GI's Want Letters and Pin-Up Pictures," *Afro-American*, September 30, 1950, 13; "Soldiers Want Letters and Pictures from Town," *Atlanta Daily World*, December 29, 1950, 5. The article was reprinted under different headings in all major newspapers: "Our Girls Let Us Down," *Afro-American*, January 13, 1951, 4.

52. See Cynthia Enloe, *Maneuvers: The International Politics of Militarizing Women's Lives* (Berkeley: University of California Press, 2000), 56; on venereal disease, morality, and war, Allen Brandt, *No Magic Bullet: A Social History of Venereal Disease in the United States Since 1880* (Oxford: Oxford University Press, 1987).

53. James Hicks, "Lonesome Lads in the 159th Field Artillery Beg Girls Back Home to Write Them," *Afro-American*, September 2, 1950, 1; "Our Readers Say: You Won't Be Old Maids," *Afro-American*, January 13, 1951, 4.

54. Robert A. Nye, "Western Masculinities in War and Peace," *American Historical Review* 112, 2 (2007), 420, 417.

55. "Combat Engineers Do Backbreaking Work to Conceal Troops and Guns, Get Bombed Out and Start Over Again," *Afro-American*, September 16, 1950, 1; "Service Troops Backing Up Korean Combat Units," *Afro-American,* July 22, 1950, 1; "Medics Rendering Excellent Services to Wounded on Battlefields in Korea," *Afro-American*, September 16, 1950, 1; "Medics the Angels with Dirty Faces," *Afro-American*, October 7, 1950, 20.

56. Small selection of hundreds of articles: "Tan GI's See Action on Korean Front," *Chicago Defender*, July 8, 1950, 1; cf. "Tan Fliers over Korea: Negro Ground Troops Await Call," *Pittsburgh Courier*, July 8, 1950, 1; "'Info' About Local GIs," *Courier*, September 16, 1950, 17; The 665th Trucking Co. Takes Leading Part in Korean War," *Birmingham World*, June 1, 1951, 1.

57. L. Alex Wilson, "Private in 24th Regiment Hailed: Greatest Hero of War," *Norfolk Journal and Guide*, September 30, 1950, 1; see also "Heroes in Korea Are Made Not Born," *Afro-American*, December 22, 1951, 14.

58. "What Is the Answer?" *California Eagle*, September 29, 1950, Editorial Page. However, with anti-Communist frenzy and political pressure on the rise, Charlotta Bass, the long-time owner and publisher, sold the paper in 1951 and it moved toward the mainstream.

59. In *Project Clear*, Leo Bogart asserted that white as well as black observers saw "a sharp distinction . . . between Negroes in all-Negro units and those who are integrated in white units." Morale and performance were seen to increase substantially when placing black soldiers in white outfits. Leo Bogart, ed., *Project Clear: Social Research and the Desegregation of the United States Army* (New Brunswick, N.J.: Transaction, 1992), 11. This was often not the case with respect to black observers. Although it was essential to underline the positive effects of integration on morale, lauding all-black units remained a cornerstone in war reporting and the black community. This widely differing style of reporting is what Dalfiume called "confused." This assessment is dispelled, I maintain, when considering manhood and race pride as essential elements into the analysis. Richard M. Dalfiume, *Desegregation of the U.S. Armed Forces: Fighting on Two Fronts, 1939–1953* (Columbia: University of Missouri Press, 1969), 206–7.

60. "Black Segregationists," *Black Dispatch*, September 23, 1950, Editorial Page.

61. With the war progressing and China entering it, censorship increased. See, e.g., "Information for Correspondents Eighth Army Censorship Regulations," January 14, 1951, ACLU Records, MC#001, Box1172, Folder 39 Korea Cases—News Censorship; Mason Edward Horrell, "Reporting the Forgotten War: Military-Press Relations in Korea, 1950–1954" (Ph.D. dissertation, University of Kentucky, 2002); Steven Casey, *Selling the Korean War: Propaganda, Politics, and Public Opinion 1950–1953* (Oxford: Oxford University Press, 2008), esp. 41–66; Moeller argues that correspondents wanted more censorship than less " 'to keep them clean of error.' " Moeller, *Shooting War*, 278–79.

62. Andrew Huebner, *The American Warrior Image: Soldiers in American Culture from the Second World War to the Vietnam Era* (Chapel Hill: University of North Carolina Press, 2008), 100.

63. "The Wounded," *Saturday Evening Post*, September 23, 1950, 32–33, 144–46.

64. "The Ugly War," *Time*, August 21, 1950.

65. See, e.g., "Korean Balance Sheet," *New York Times*, July 25, 1950, 26; see also Huebner, *The Warrior Image*, esp. 100–107; see also his article: "Kilroy Is Back," 103–29.

66. See Huebner, *The Warrior Image*, 104–7.

67. On the changing iconography and portrayal of soldiers during the Korean War, see Huebner, *The Warrior Image*, Part II, esp. 130; Moeller, *Shooting War*, chapter on Korea.

68. "Death in Korea," *Our World*, December 1950, 27–31; "All UN Korea War Casualties Not Due to Enemy; Some Are Killed by Own Comrades," *Afro-American*, November 10, 1951, 9.

69. See, e.g., James LaFourche, "Mississippi GI Tells Graphic Story of Bloody Struggle with Reds in Korean Heights Escape Death Following Shot in Shoulder and Hand Almost Blown Off During Battle Was Under Enemy Fire for 26 Days," *Black Dispatch*, October 21, 1950, 2.

70. L. Alex Wilson, "Front Line Grapevine: Late, But News Just the Same," *Chicago Defender*, September 9, 1950, 6.

71. L. Alex Wilson, "Front Line Grapevine: Where Are the Replacements?" *Chicago Defender*, September 23, 1950, 4.

72. See Frank Whisonant, "Was 24th Used as a Scapegoat," *Courier*, September 23, 1950, 1.

73. L. Alex Wilson, "Front Line Grapevine: Say Mister, This Is War," *Chicago Defender*, September 16, 1950, 3; L. Alex Wilson, "Forces Afloat Give Excellent Support to Ground Troops," *Norfolk Journal and Guide*, September 16, 1950, 10; Frank Whisonant, "Heavy Blows Hit Tan GIs: Count Rows of Wounded," *Courier*, August 19, 1950, 1.

74. James Hicks, "Boys Go into Battle, Come out as Men," *Afro-American*, September 23, 1950, 9; Bradford P. Laws, "Liberated GI's 'Cried like Babies'," *Courier*, October 20, 1951, 12A

75. "M-Sgt. Push Just 'Having Fun' Killing Reds in Korea," *Atlanta Daly World*, September 21, 1950, 1; "159th Sharpshooters Slay 650," *Afro-American*, September 16, 1950, 1.

76. See Dalfiume, *Desegregation of the U.S. Armed Forces*, e.g., 17–18.

77. Roy E. Appleman, *South to the Naktong, North to the Yalu: United States Army in the Korean War (June to November 1950)* (Washington, D.C.: Government Printing Office, 1961), 190.

78. Bowers, Hammond, and MacGarrigle note that "the press and politicians sought to play up Yech'on for reasons of their own." William T. Bowers, William M. Hammond, and George L. MacGarrigle, *Black Soldier, White Army: The 24th Infantry Regiment in Korea* (Washington, D.C.: Center of Military History, 1996), 93.

79. "U.S. Hails Tan Warriors," *Chicago Defender*, July 29, 1950, 1–2. On the victory in Yechon see Lt. Col. Bradley Biggs, "The 24th Infantry Regiment: The Deuce-Four in Korea," *Military Review* 83, 5 (September/October 2003): 58–62.

80. "Mixed Units, GI Victories: Jolt Dixie Brass Hats," *Chicago Defender*, August 26, 1950, 1.

81. "Negro GIs First Heroes: 24th Takes City in Bloody Battle," *Pittsburgh Courier*, July 29, 1950, 1–2.

82. "Our Opinions: Our Boys Lead the Way," *Chicago Defender*, July 29, 1950, Editorial Page; "Holding that Line," *Chicago Defender*, August 5, 1950, 6.

83. Lucius C. Harper, "Dustin' Off the News: Negro Soldiers Capture Korean Town; Georgia Soldiers Resign in Droves," *Chicago Defender*, July 29, 1950, 7.

84. See Dalfiume, *Desegregation of the U.S. Armed Forces*, 206–7.

85. "U.S. Hails Tan Warriors," *Chicago Defender*, July 29, 1950, 1–2.

86. "Our Opinions: Our Boys Lead the Way," *Chicago Defender*, July 29, 1950, Editorial Page. The front and editorial pages of African American newspapers were filled with demands for first-class citizenship and integration based on the black outfit's victory. "That Jim Crow Army," *Black Dispatch*, July 29, 1950, Editorial Page; "Colored Troops Win First Victory for U.S. in Korea," *Afro-American*, July 29, 1950, 1; William Gordon, "Reviewing the News: Loyalty of the Negro," *Birmingham World*, August 18, 1950, 6.

87. "'Give Us Everything to Fight for,' Says GI in Letter to Folks Back Home," *Afro-American*, September 9, 1950, 12.

88. Powell quoted in "Powell Fights JC Military Clause," *Afro-American*, April 14, 1951, 12.

89. "That Jim Crow Army," *Black Dispatch*, July 29, 1950, Editorial Page.

90. Not all agreed with this argumentation and pledged wholehearted allegiance to the nation even if segregation continued for a while. William L. Dawson, April 14, 1951, 82nd Cong., 1st sess., Cong. Rec., 3765.

91. "White Demands Probe of Army Bias in Japan," *Black Dispatch*, August 5, 1950, 1; see also R. E. Eley, "The Pulse of the Public: 'Segregation in Draft Called Insult'," *New York Amsterdam News*, April 7, 1951, Editorial Page; Clarence Mitchell,

Hearings on H.R. 1752 before House Committee on Armed Services, 82nd Cong. 844–56 (1951), January 23–26, 29–31, February 5, 6, 26, 28, March 1, 2, 5–8, 1951.

92. "Army Studies Negro Troops' Combat Record," *Los Angeles Times*, September 12, 1950, 4.

93. "Negro Troops Win 16-Hr. Fight for Road Center; Infiltering Cut," *Washington Post*, July 22, 1950, 1; see also "GIs Capture City on Korean Coast," *Chicago Daily Tribune*, July 22, 1950, 1; "U.S. Troops Seize Iowa Red Centers," *Los Angeles Times*, July 22, 1950, 1; "Yongdok Regained," *New York Times*, July 22, 1950, 1; *Newsweek*, July 31, 1950; "Two Armies for One?" *New Republic*, November 6, 1950, 11–12. See also Huebner, *The Warrior Image*, 112. Huebner quotes *Time* as a source to back up his argument that the white press praised black troops. Quoting from an article, he claims that the 24th Infantry Regiment was called "brave, battered." Although the article focuses on the fight surrounding Yech'on and mentions the warfare of "Negro troops," *Time* did not call the all-black unit "brave, battered," but referred to the 24th Division, a still all-white unit. "Battle of Korea: A Question of Tomatoes," *Time*, August 21, 1950, 19.

94. "Afro, Wrapped in Cellophane, Making Rounds of Korean Front," *Afro-American*, September 9, 1950, 1.

95. See *Fort Worth Star-Telegram*, "U.S. Negro Troops Mirror of World Opinion," *Christian Science Monitor*, August 17, 1950, 18.

96. Ibid.; "On Congratulations," *Gastonia Gazette*, July 24, 1950, 4; "Negro Soldiers Beat off Reds," *Aniston Star*, July 27, 1950, 16; "Reds Mass for New Attack on U.S. Lines," *Daily Times-News*, July 27, 1950, 1; "MacArthur Visits the Warfront; Has Optimistic Outlook," *Landmark*, July 27, 1950, 1–2.

97. John M. Hightower, "Valiant U.S. Negro Troops Refute Red Color Claims," *Hartford Courier*, August 20, 1950, 13.

98. Rep. Frances Payne Bolton (R-Oh.), "The Negro Question Without Propaganda," August 31, 1950, Cong. Rec., 81st Cong., 2nd Sess., A6282–84.

99. "24th Infantry Praised for Capture of Yechon," *Atlanta Daily World*, July 26, 1950, 1.

100. Rep. Hon. Thomas J. Lane (D-Mass.), July 24, 1950, 81st Cong., 2nd sess., 10867, reprinted in "24th Infantry Praised for Capture of Yechon"; Sen. Herbert R. O'Conor (D-Md.), August 21, 1950, 12852.

101. See Sen. Herbert H. Lehman (D-N.Y.), August 23, 1950, 13183; Rep. Walter H. Judd (R-Minn.), "Negro Troops Fighting Valiantly in Korea Give Lie to Soviet Propaganda," July 31, 1950, 81st Cong., 2nd sess., Cong. Rec., A5531. Judd submitted an article from the *Minneapolis Tribune* that emphasized the propaganda value of the African American presence in Korea in the struggle for the support of minority people and called on black soldiers to inform the world about their willingness to fight, which supposedly belied any race war allegations.

102. "Truman Praises Negro Soldiers," *Los Angeles Times*, September 12, 1950, 4.

103. See in general Mary L. Dudziak, *Cold War Civil Rights: Race and the Image of American Democracy* (Princeton, N.J.: Princeton University Press, 2000), 12–13.

104. "Let's Tell the World," *Afro-American*, September 9, 1950, 4.

105. Gordon B. Hancock, "Between the Lines," *Los Angeles Sentinel*, August 31, 1950, A8; see also Benjamin E. Mays, "Mays: We Should Continue to Fight for Civil Liberties During Any and All Crises," *Pittsburgh Courier*, September 9, 1950, 21; "'Give Us Everything to Fight For,' Says GI in Letter to Folks Back Home."

106. J. H. Jenkins, "Rather Inconsistent," *Afro-American*, September 9, 1950, 4.

107. Lynn Landrum, "Thinking out Loud," *Dallas News*, July 27, 1950, 3.

108. Extended quote from *The Crisis*: "Here is high praise of the 24th Regiment from its own commander mixed in the same dispatch with slurs on their bravery and skill as soldiers. This looks to us like a build up to justify continual segregation of Negro troops in Korea. Is it because some of the former officers of the old 92nd Division are now on General MacArthur's staff? Are these slurs to be forerunners of a campaign of slander against Negro fighters as came out of the last war?" "Army Brass and the 24th Regiment," *The Crisis*, October 1950, 578–79.

109. C. R. M. Sheppard to President Truman, attached to a letter to Senator Russell pledging support for the halt to integration, July 5, 1950, Russell Papers, Box 185, Folder 2.

110. C. E. Griffith to Richard B. Russell, January 22, 1951, Russell Papers, Box 175, Folder 1.

111. George T. Laney to Richard B. Russell, May 30, 1951, in ibid.

112. William A. Fowlkes, "Seeing and Saying: Our Two-Front Warfare," *Atlanta Daily World*, July 30, 1950, 4; see also "Keep the Home Fires Burning," *Philadelphia Tribune*, July 25, 1950, 4; P. L. Prattis, "Today is the Time to Fight for Full Citizenship, a Vital Issue," *Courier*, June 7, 1953, Editorial Page.

113. Gordon B. Hancock, "Between the Lines," *Black Dispatch*, August 5, 1950, Editorial Page. On the African American hope for change through war see Joseph D. Bibb, "Children of Destiny," *Courier*, May 24, 1952, Editorial Page.

114. See "Putting Something over Race Bias Hinted in Snub to Nurse," *Pittsburgh Courier*, July 15, 1950, Editorial Page; "Our Boys Lead the Way," *Chicago Defender*, July 29, 1950, 6.

115. George A. Sewell, "Dots and Dashes: FEPC: Voluntary or Compulsory?" *Atlanta Daily World*, December 16, 1951, 4.

116. See Randolph to Catharine D. Leated, January 22, 1952, Randolph Papers MF, Reel 1.

117. Quoted in "FEPC Vote Shows Need to Alter Senate Rule Rule—White: To Formulate Course of Action in Elections," *Atlanta Daily World*, July 16, 1950, 1.

118. Alice Dunnigan, "FEPC Defeat Echoes Around World During Freedom Talk," *Atlanta Daily World*, July 23, 1950, 1; see also Horace Cayton, "Cayton: Total Mobilization of America's Manpower Will Be Impossible if Jim Crow is Upheld," *Courier*, December 23, 1950, 16.

119. Randolph to David K. Niles, August 7, 1950; see also Randolph to Harry S. Truman, August 4, 1950, Harry S. Truman President's Personal File, Box 553, Folder PPFO 2540, Truman Papers. His request was backed by Senator Lehman, whom Randolph had asked for support. Senator Lehman to Matthew Connelly, secretary of the president, August 11, 1950, ibid.

120. "FEPC Foes, Friends Set for Battle," *Chicago Defender*, May 13, 1950, 1; Dudziak, *Cold War Civil Rights*, 89.

121. Historian Berman maintains that Korea kept the FEPC "issue alive as far as Negro leaders were concerned," but Truman was too involved in foreign affairs to give it much attention. According to Berman, he "was no longer subject to pressure from civil rights organizations" and therefore could ignore civil rights. William C. Berman, *The Politics of Civil Rights in the Truman Administration* (Columbus: Ohio State University Press, 1970), 178–79.

122. White's wire to Russell reprinted in "Forego Talkiest in Crisis, NAACP Bids Sen. Russell," *Atlanta Daily World*, July 9, 1950, 1.

123. Walter White, "South Can't Escape Race Showdown," *Chicago Defender*, August 5, 1950, 7; "Set FEPC Vigil to Hit Congressmen," *New York Amsterdam News*, July 8, 1950, 3.

124. "Surrendering the Filibuster," *Pittsburgh Courier,* July 15, 1950, Editorial Page.

125. "Lucas Moves to Take up FEPC Bill July 10," *Atlanta Daily World*, June 16, 1950, 1.

126. Senator Lucas paraphrased in "Senate Coalition Knifes F.E.P.C. Bill Again," *Chicago Defender*, July 22, 1950, 1.

127. An editorial accompanied the cartoon "Setting a Poor Example," *Afro-American*, July 22, 1950, 4; similar argument with respect to a different issue, the desegregation of higher education: "Knifing Democracy," *Los Angeles Sentinel*, Los Angeles, August 24, 1950, Editorial Page.

128. There was some opposition in African Americans' own ranks. George S. Schuyler once again represented the conservative, almost reactionary, voice. Amid his general rejection for Truman and the Korean War in particular, he called the FEPC "a tool which New Deal politicians could use to destroy the American system." "News and Reviews: One-Sided NAACP Must Become Construction," *Courier*, December 30, 1950, 19.

129. Louis Lautier, "Capital Spotlight," *Atlanta Daily World*, April 11, 1951, 6.

130. Alice Dunnigan, "Defeat of FEPC Does Grave Injury to U.S. Prestige," *Philadelphia Tribune*, July 25, 1950, 2.

131. Louis Lautier, "The Capital Spotlight," *Afro-American*, August 26, 1950, 4; Louis Lautier, "Capital Spotlight: Jealousy Among National Leaders Hinted in D.C.," *Norfolk Journal and Guide*, September 9, 1950, 13.

132. William Gordon, "Reviewing the News, *Atlanta Daily World*, July 26, 1950, 1.

133. White, "South Can't Escape Race Showdown."

134. Ibid.

135. Joseph D. Bibb, "Mr. Taft Fails," *Courier*, December 29, 1951, 7.

136. Arnold de Mille, "R. R. Porters Ask Truman for Emergency FEPC," *Chicago Defender*, September 23, 1950, 5; "FEPC Up to the President," *Courier*, July 7, 1951, 20.

137. M. Moran Weston, "Talk on Price Controls," *New York Amsterdam News*, August 12, 1950, 6.

138. Letter Roy Wilkins to C. W. Mackay, Managing Editor Afro-American Newspapers, December 14, 1950, in Wilkins Papers, Box 3, Folder Correspondence 1950.

139. Joseph D. Bibb, "Harry's Failure," *Courier*, August 19, 1950, 17.

140. See Robert L. Harris, Jr., "Lobbying Congress for Civil Rights: The American Council on Human Rights, 1948–1963," in *African American Fraternities and Sororities: The Legacy and the Vision*, ed. Tamara L. Brown, Gregory Parks, and Clarenda M. Phillips (Lexington: University Press of Kentucky, 2005), 211–30.

141. "Booklet Questions Party's Intentions Back of FEPC," *Atlanta Daily World*, May 30, 1951, 1; see also Arthur Moore, "Negro's War Record Offers a Challenge," *New York Amsterdam News*, July 29, 1950, 6; "Korea and the FEPC," *Philadelphia Tribune*, January 23, 1951, 4.

142. "500 in Wisconsin Ask Truman to Issue War-Time FEPC," *Afro-American*, September 9, 1950, 15.

143. "National Grapevine: Gap Widens," *Chicago Defender*, April 21, 1951, 6.

144. Louis Lautier, "FEPC Need Greater Than During FDR's ERA," *Afro-American*, January 13, 1951, 3.

145. Communication with the White House requesting an emergency meeting with the president discussing the situations of blacks. Quotes from Arnold de Mille, "Set White House Race Meet," *Chicago Defender*, January 20, 1951, 1; Letter Randolph, February 6, 1951, in Randolph Papers, Reel 25.

146. "Equality in National Defense," *The Crisis*, February 1951, 102.

147. Harry S. Truman: "Executive Order 10210—Authorizing the Department of Defense and the Department of Commerce to Exercise the Functions and Powers Set Forth in Title II of the First War Powers Act, 1941, as Amended by the Act of January 12, 1951, and Prescribing Regulations for the Exercise of Such Functions and Powers," February 2, 1951. Gerhard Peters and John T. Woolley, *The American Presidency Project*, http://www.presidency.ucsb.edu/ws/?pid=60785.

148. Berman, *Truman and Civil Rights*, 186.

149. Bethune, Mays, White, Tobias, and Randolph Meeting President Truman, Statement to President Truman at White House Conference on February 28, 1951, in Randolph Papers, Reel 25.

150. See "Boost for Defense," *Philadelphia Tribune*, June 30, 1951, 4; "A Timely Solution," *Philadelphia Tribune*, July 10, 1951, 4.

151. One special case was that of John Derrick, whom white policemen killed in New York shortly after he left the Korean front. He was not the only African American

killed by New York police, but his status as a Korean War veteran made the case a particularly sensitive one. "The Pulse of the Public: 'Is This What They Fight for in Korea?'" *New York Amsterdam News*, December 30, 1950, Editorial Page; "Discharged GI Killed by Harlem Cops," *New York Amsterdam News*, December 16, 1950; "Justice for John Derrick," *New York Amsterdam News*, December 30, 1950, 1. Briefly covered in Martha Biondi, *To Stand and Fight: The Struggle for Civil Rights in Postwar New York City* (Cambridge, Mass.: Harvard University Press, 2003), 192.

152. Ralph Matthews, "Inside Riot in Cicero Felt in Korea: Morale of Troops on War Front Affected," *Afro-American*, September 8, 1951, 14; see also Ralph Matthews, "U.S. Bigotry Deadlier Than Communist Bullets," *Norfolk Journal and Guide*, September 8, 1951, A6C; "Cicero Riot Felt Even in Korean Scene," *New York Amsterdam News*, September 8, 1951, 1; "Yanks Bitter over Reports from U.S.A," *Courier*, August 19, 1950, 1

Chapter 8. A Mixed Army

1. War correspondent James Hicks reported that American planes mistakenly bombed their own troops and caused some to leave their positions. "Air Officer at Rear as 24th Is Bombed," *Afro-American*, September 16, 1950, 1. On the failure of the 24th Infantry Regiment, Richard M. Dalfiume, *Desegregation of the U.S. Armed Forces: Fighting on Two Fronts, 1939–1953* (Columbia: University of Missouri Press, 1969), 204; Morris J. MacGregor, Jr., *Integration of the Armed Forces, 1940–1965* (Washington D.C.: Center of Military History, 1985).

2. For details on the events on Battle Mountain see William T. Bowers, William M. Hammond, and George L. MacGarrigle, *Black Soldier, White Army: The 24th Infantry Regiment in Korea* (Washington, D.C.: Center of Military History, 1996), 145–56.

3. MacGregor, *Integration of the Armed Forces*.

4. Frank Whisonant, "Was 24th 'Framed'?," *Courier*, September 23, 1950, 1, 2; see also Frank Whisonant, "Charge Discontent Riddling 'Fighting 24th,'" *Courier*, September 2, 1950; 8; James Booker, "Army Victimizes Tan GI's: Widespread Frameup Charged by Heroes of Korean Campaign," *New York Amsterdam News*, November 25, 1950, 1; James Hicks, "Army Passes Buck," *Afro-American*, August 26, 1950, 1.

5. Frank Whisonant, "Will 24th Be Broken Up?," *Courier*, September 16, 1950, 1; "Final Argument Against Segregation," *Courier*, September 30, 1950, 6.

6. Major General William B. Kean letter to commanding General of the 8th Army, Subject: Combat Effectiveness of the 24th Infantry Regiment, September 9, 1950, MacArthur Memorial Archives, Norfolk, Va., RG 15 Box 89, Folder 1; see also MacGregor, *Integration of the Armed Forces*, 436; Roy E. Appleman, *South to the Naktong, North to the Yalu: United States Army in the Korean War (June to November 1950)* (Washington, D.C.: Government Printing Office, 1961), 485–86. Without considering the circumstances and African American protest, military historian Appleman accepts Kean's interpretation as fully reliable. His book caused black veterans to vehemently protest.

7. Black units certainly struggled in Korea, but white officers often overemphasized their failures. See Sherie Mershon and Steven Schlossman, *Foxholes and Color Lines: Desegregating the U.S. Armed Forces* (Baltimore: Johns Hopkins University Press, 1998), 220–23.

8. Lieutenant colonel Bradley Biggs, a member of the 24th Infantry Regiment during the Korean War, also admits to the problems the outfit had, but argues that failures occurred in black and white units alike. Furthermore, the lack of equipment and leadership wore hard on all soldiers on the front lines fighting against an enemy with "superior firepower, tanks, and sheer aggressiveness." Bradley Biggs, "The 24th Infantry Regiment: The Deuce-Four in Korea," *Military Review* 83, 5 (September/October 2003): 57.

9. Whisonant, "Was 24th 'Framed'?"; "The 24th Is Good," *Afro-American*, August 26, 1950, 4; James Hicks, "Army Passes Buck," *Afro-American*, August 26, 1950, 1.

10. Whisonant, "Was 24th 'Framed'?"

11. Quoted in "What Gives in Korea," *Afro-American*, September 16, 1950, 1; later in the war see Bradford Lewis, "Negro Serviceman Valiant in Korea," *Philadelphia Tribune*, September 22, 1951, 9; David Widener, "Seoul City Sue and the Bugout Blues: Black American Narratives of the Forgotten War," in *Afro Asia: Revolutionary Political and Cultural Connections Between African Americans and Asians*, ed. Fred Ho and Bill V. Mullen (Durham, N.C.: Duke University Press, 2008), 58.

12. "The Latest GI Smear," *Courier*, November 18, 1950, B18.

13. In his study on Ivory Perry, a civil rights activist and Korean War veteran, Lipsitz covers the Gilbert case rather extensively. It gives great insight into the emotions involved, but is somewhat limited in its critical assessment of the black and white reports on the case. George Lipsitz, *A Life in the Struggle: Ivory Perry and the Culture of Opposition*, 2nd ed. (Philadelphia: Temple University Press, 1995), 41.

14. "Big-Hearted U.S.A. Pleads for Life of Lt. Gilbert," *Norfolk Journal and Guide*, October 14, 1950, 1.

15. E. Washington Rhodes, "Under the Microscope: Justice for Negro Soldiers," *Philadelphia Tribune*, December 9, 1950, 4.

16. Thurgood Marshall, "Summary Justice—The Negro GI in Korea," *The Crisis*, May 1951. According to numbers of the General Headquarters, Far East Command, Report of Investigations Regarding Irregularities in the Administration of Military Justice in the 25th Division, March 27, 1951, fifty-five blacks were charged and thirty-two convicted in the time from July to October 1950. Bowers, Hammond, and MacGarrigle, *Black Soldier, White Army*, 173.

17. Widener, "Seoul City Sue and the Bugout Blues," 58. During World War II, 141 men had been executed after courts-martial. The overwhelming majority received the death penalty for rape and murder cases, whereas only one soldier, a multiple offender, was executed for desertion. *Investigations of the National War Effort: Report of the Committee on Military Affairs House of Representatives*, 79th Cong. (June 1946), H.R. Rep. No. 2740. 3.

On the overlooked field of military justice and courts-martial see Elizabeth Lutes Hillman, *Defending America: Military Culture and the Cold War Court-Martial* (Princeton, N.J.: Princeton University Press, 2005), on Gilbert 95–96.

18. "The Gilbert Case," *Courier*, December 9, 1950, 18; "What the People Think: Gilbert Case Brings Army Attitude in Sharp Focus," *Courier*, November 18, 1950, 6; sympathetic, but no reference to race, "Courage and Cowardice on the Korean War Front," *New Journal and Guide*, October 14, 1950, 12.

19. Charles M. Bussey, *Firefight at Yechon: Courage and Racism in the Korean War* (Lincoln: University of Nebraska Press, 1991, 2002), 117; "Courage and Cowardice on the Korean War Front," D16: see also Michael C. Green, *Black Yanks in the Pacific: Race in the Making of American Military Empire After World War II* (Ithaca, N.Y.: Cornell University Press, 2010), 130–31.

20. As Bussey put it, the soldier would "be used as object to further denigrate all Negroes." Bussey, *Firefight at Yechon*, 117–18.

21. See "Truman Asked to Bar Death for Officer," *New York Times*, September 23, 1950, 32; "Officer Sentenced to Death in Korea, Wife Appeals to President for Mercy," *Hartford Courant*, September 23, 1950, 1.

22. "Lieut. Gilbert's Offense," *Washington Post*, October 23, 1950.

23. Ibid.; "Justice and Discipline," *Christian Science Monitor*, October 19, 1950, 22; "The Case of Lt. Gilbert," *New York Post*, October 3, 1950, n.p.; "Truman Asked to Bar Death for Officer," 32; "Officer Sentenced to Death in Korea, Wife Appeals to President for Mercy."

24. Booker T. Washington Public High School to President Truman, October 31, 1950, Truman Papers, White House Central Files, Official File Box 1710, OF 2715. Countless letters with regard to Gilbert were sent to Truman. All in Truman Papers White House Central Files, Official File, Boxes 1710–13, OF 2715.

25. Calman Buk [?] to President Truman, November 9, 1950, Truman Papers, OF 1710, 2715. Buk wrote to Truman multiple times, always referring to the discrepancies between the treatment of blacks and the official claim to be fighting for democracy. Calman Buk to Truman, November 19, 1950.

26. Booker, "Army Victimizes Tan GI's: Widespread Frameup charged by Heroes of Korean Campaign", 1; see also "Fair Play Urged," *New York Amsterdam News*, November 25, 1950, 8; Gordon Hancock, "Between the Lines: The High Cost of Face-Saving," *Black Dispatch*, January 27, 1951, 7.

27. Frank Whisonant, "Courier Had Story; Couldn't Break It," *Courier*, September 30, 1950, 1, 5;; see also "Convicted Soldiers in Korea Beg NAACP for Aid," *Norfolk Journal and Guide*, November 25, 1950, 1; "Pretty Pictures and Ugly Truth," *Chicago Defender*, December 30, 1950, Editorial Page; "What Is the Answer?" *California Eagle*, September 29, 1950, Editorial Page; "Commentator Slurs Negroes and Koreans," *California Eagle*, July 21, 1950, 2.

28. Milton A. Smith, "Lt. Gilbert's Story: Condemned Officer Not Afraid to Die," *Afro-American*, November 25, 1950, 1; Milton A. Smith, "Exclusive Interview with Lt.

L. A. Gilbert in Stockade," *Norfolk Journal and Guide*, December 2, 1950, 11;"Truman Orders Stay of Death for Lieutenant Gilbert," *Atlanta Daily World*, November 28, 1950, 1; Langston Hughes, "World in Need of Peace, Not of the Troubled Sort," *Chicago Defender*, December 30, 1950, Editorial Page.

29. "Still Hope for Lt. Gilbert", *Afro-American*, 9 December 1950, 4.; see also "Convicted Soldiers in Korea Beg NAACP for Aid," *Norfolk Journal and Guide*, November 25, 1950, 1; "Pretty Pictures and Ugly Truth," *Chicago Defender*, December 30, 1950, Editorial Page.

30. "Letter to Father Tells of Situation with Tragic End," *Philadelphia Tribune*, September 26, 1950, 1.

31. Cf. "Lt. Gilbert Thinks He Was in Right," *Afro-American*, October 21, 1950, 13; "I Am Not A Coward: Lieut. Gilbert Cries," *Courier*, October 21, 1950, 1, 4. Also printed in white newspapers, "Doomed Officer Tells Why He Defied Orders: Asserts Advance Meant Death for His Men," *Chicago Daily Tribune*, October 15, 1950, 3.

32. Smith, "Lt. Gilbert's Story: Condemned Officer Not Afraid to Die"; "Exclusive Interview with Lt. L. A. Gilbert in Stockade," 1. Gilbert's wife was pregnant with a third child at the time of the court-martial. Born premature, the baby died. See also "Town Prays for Doomed Soldier," *Afro-American*, September 30, 1950, 1; "Courageous Wife Fights for Husband's Life," *Norfolk Journal and Guide*, November 4, 1950, D1; "Don't Let My Son Die: Mother of Condemned Combat Officer Appeals to Truman," *Pittsburgh Courier*, September 30, 1950, 1, 5; "Doomed GI's Family Fight to Save Life: Record of Soldiers in Family Lounge," *New York Amsterdam News*, October 7, 1950, 2.

33. Smith, "Lt. Gilbert's Story: Condemned Officer Not Afraid to Die."

34. Hughes, "World in Need of Peace, Not of the Troubled Sort"; "The Pulse of the Public: 'Start Democracy at Home Says a Reader," *New York Amsterdam News*, January 27, 1951, Editorial Page.

35. John G. Norris, "Truman Commutes Gilbert Sentence," *Washington Post*, November 28, 1950, 4.

36. "Defense of Convicted GI's in Korea NAACP's No. 1 Task," *Afro-American*, December 2, 1950, 1

37. Stanley Roberts, "NAACP Sends Aid to Korean GIs," *Courier*, December 9, 1950, 1.

38. Marshall to Wilkins, n.d., Wilkins Papers, Box 3, Folder General Correspondence 1951.

39. "Gen. MacArthur Bans Defense of Negro GIs," *New York Amsterdam News*, December 23, 1950, 1.

40. Quoted in "Marshall to Leave for Japan on Jan. 11," *Courier*, January 6, 1951, 1; see also "'Mac' Calls Off Ban on Marshall," *Chicago Defender*, December 30, 1950, 1.

41. "MacArthur Relents," *Black Dispatch*, January 12, 1951, Editorial Page; see also John Howard, "Justice in the Army," *Chicago Defender*, December 16, 1950, 6; Hughes, "World in Need of Peace, Not of the Troubled Sort."

42. See Letter exchange between Wilkins and Marshall during Marshall's investigations in Asia, Papers of Roy Wilkins, Box 4, Folder Correspondence 1951.

43. See Roy Wilkins to Thurgood Marshall, February 20, 1951, Wilkins Papers, Box 3, Folder Correspondence 1951.

44. Marshall, "Summary Justice—The Negro GI in Korea," 297–304, 350–55; "Mr. Marshall Reports," *The Crisis*, March 1951, 181.

45. Marshall, "Summary Justice," 355. On Gilbert and Marshall see also Phillips, *War!* 136ff.

46. "Profiles: Mr. President II-Ten O'Clock Meeting," *New Yorker*, April 14, 1951, 50–51. This piece was part of a series of articles on Truman and his presidency.

47. Letter Walter White to President Truman, May 17, 1951, Truman Papers OF Box 1711, OF 2751 N.

48. A grueling report on the situation of UN troops in Korea after China's entrance: Hank Walker, "Once More 'We Got a Hell of a Beating," *Life*, December 11, 1950; *The Gallup Poll: Public Opinion 1935–1971*, vol. 2, *1949–1958* (New York: Random House, 1969), 961.

49. "MacArthur Is Greeted by Rebel Flags," *New York Amsterdam News*, May 5, 1951, 2.

50. James L. Hicks, "Segregation Allowed Under His Command: Tan Yanks Won't Shed Any Tears over His Removal," *Afro-American*, April 21, 1951, 1.

51. See "Mixed Guard Greets Gen. MacArthur," *Chicago Defender*, May 5, 1951, 1; Cliff Mackay, "The Week's," *Afro-American*, May 19, 1951, 4; Cliff Mackay, "The Week's," *Afro-American*, June 23, 1951, 4; "Insubordination," *Black Dispatch*, April 21, 1951, Editorial Page; "MacArthur Is Greeted by Rebel Flags."

52. "Stay-Down Pilots," *Washington Post*, April 20, 1952, B4.

53. See Letter Thurgood Marshall to Major General Harry H. Vaughn, Military Aid to the President, May 28, 1952, Truman Papers, OF Box 1711, OF 2751 N; "Renew Appeal to Truman for Release of Lt. Gilbert," *Chicago Defender*, June 7, 1952, 1; "Cite Koje, Air Force Sitdown in Gilbert Plea," *Philadelphia Tribune*, 3 June 1952, 2; "Immediate Release of Lt. Gilbert Asked," *Afro-American*, June 21, 1952, 3.

54. Since the 1980s, Attorney Herman (Hy) Lieberman worked to clear Gilbert's name. He collected great stacks of documents and interviews with Gilbert on tape that speak of the quality of the accusations, the sentence, and its repercussions on Gilbert and his later life. Lieberman's collection is located with his heirs in Brookline, Massachusetts. At the time of my research neither the boxes nor the folders had been processed. It was impossible to establish a retraceable citation. Despite these reservations, the documents, especially the taped interviews, will be invaluable when working on the Gilbert case in more detail, which this study cannot provide.

55. Harold H. Martin, "How Do Our Negro Troops Measure Up?" *Saturday Evening Post*, June 16, 1951, 139–41. On the persistence of the stereotypes see also: Phillips, *War!* 139–42.

56. The *Saturday Evening Post* was not the only mainstream newspaper or magazine that made such an appraisal. Two months after Martin's piece, *Time* magazine published an article on the soon-to-be-dissolved all-black 24th Infantry Regiment, claiming that, although the unit had produced "individual heroes . . ., and it routed the North Koreans at Yechon in the first days of the war," its "Korea battle record was spotty." But blacks, the article claimed, improved their record when serving in integrated units under white guidance. "National Affairs: Side by Side," *Time*, August 6, 1951. The military historians Bowers et al. have noted that "the already battered reputation of the 24th fell to the lowest point it would ever reach in the Korean War." Bowers, Hammond, and MacGarrigle, *Black Soldier, White Army*, 218.

57. Martin, "How Do Our Negro Troops Measure Up?" 141.

58. Frank M. Gossett, "Letters to the Editor: Our Negro Troops," *Saturday Evening Post*, July 28, 1951, 4; see also Sid S. Champion Edwards, Mississippi, "Letters to the Editor," *Saturday Evening Post*, July 28, 1951, 4.

59. On the decline of public racism Robert L. Fleegler, "Theodore G. Bilbo and the Decline of Public Racism, 1938–1947," *Journal of Mississippi History* 66, 1 (Spring 2006): 1–26.

60. Criticism in "The Libel May Pay Off," *Philadelphia Tribune*, June 23, 1951, 4.

61. The image of black soldiers failing in combat, which had been a fixture in the mainstream press, even made it to Great Britain as well. Alistair Cooke of the *Manchester Guardian* wrote an extensive piece on integration in the armed forces. Although apprehensive of the racial situation and position of blacks in the United States, the author nonetheless relied on questionable assessments made by black soldiers' superiors. He stressed that the high degree of black illiteracy was problematic in combat and reproduced the concept that black soldiers were afraid in the dark and maintained: "The tacit rule of thumb in Korea has developed into an understanding that coloured troops had better stay out of night-fighting, unless they are tough enough to sprinkle in with the scared, but better disciplined, whites." Countering Thurgood Marshall's findings, Cooke asserted that the civil rights drive in the United States made punishment of black soldiers more problematic and less severe than that of whites. Alistair Cooke, "Black and White in the Forces: 'Integration' in the United States," *Manchester Guardian*, July 31, 1951, 6.

62. White explicitly referred to Truman's Executive Order 9981, he incorrectly claimed to have been issued in 1946 instead of 1948. Quotes in Walter White, "The Post Piece of Negro GIs Will Make You Angry, Sad, Thoughtful," *Chicago Defender*, July 7, 1951, 7; see also "A Step But Only a Step," *Atlanta Daily World*, August 8, 1951, 6.

63. P. L. Prattis, "The Horizon," *Courier*, June 30, 1951, 22.

64. "Full Speed Ahead for Integration," *New York Amsterdam News*, August 4, 1951.

65. Frank Whisonant, "The Truth About the 24th Inf.: Whisonant's Reply," Col. John T. Corley, "The Truth About the 24th Inf.: Col. Corley's Story," both in *Courier*,

June 30, 1950, 1, 5; L. Alex Wilson, "Wilson Answers Post's Slap at 24th," *Chicago Defender*, June 30, 1951, 14; "Our GI's Meet the Test," *Chicago Defender*, June 30, 1951, 6.

66. Both quotes from "Are Negroes Inferior Soldiers?," *Ebony*, September 1951, 96. George S. Schuyler also criticized the move to question African Americans' reasons for fighting and to explain blacks' alleged lack of morale and fighting spirit that presumably was reflected in their poor combat record. In an oral history interview in 1962, he retrospectively commented on this, in his eyes, questionable and doubtful move on the part of civil rights activists that rubbed off on their supporters. "The first victory won on the Korean Front was won by an all-Negro unit there, which all of the writers on the subject, or most of them, have been disposed to pass over entirely; in their zeal to favor racial integration they denigrated the conduct of Negro troops." *The Reminiscences of George S. Schuyler, 1962*, int. William T. Ingersoll (Alexandria, Va.: Alexander Street Press, 2003), 465.

67. Dalfiume, *Desegregation of the U.S. Armed Forces*, 203–4.

68. Biggs, "The 24th Infantry Regiment," 64.

69. Mary McLeod Bethune to James C. Evans, August 10, 1951, Mary McLeod Bethune Papers [microform]: the Bethune-Cookman College collection, 1922–1955 (Bethesda, Md.: University Publications of America, 1995), Reel 4.

70. Walter Simmons, "Negro Soldiers Sad at Breakup of Their Outfit," *Chicago Daily Tribune*, July 29, 1951, 2. See also "Ridgeway Ends Segregation in all Army Units," *Chicago Defender*, August 4, 1951, 1, which used many of the same quotes, but relayed a much more pleased impression of black soldiers' reaction.

71. "LAST ALL-NEGRO ARMY REGIMENT TO BE DISBANDED: 24th to Be Absorbed by Mixed Unit," *Chicago Daily Tribune*, July 27, 1951, A15;

72. Quotes: "The Glorious 24th," *Los Angeles Sentinel*, July 26, 1951, Editorial Page; see also "Army Finally Learns," *Afro-American*, August 4, 1951, Editorial Page; "The Big Brass Learns Vital Lesson During Korean Fight," *Norfolk Journal and Guide*, August 11, 1951, 14; "Kill 24th To End Army Segregation," *Chicago Defender*, July 28, 1951, 1

73. "Farewell to the 24th," *Courier*, August 4, 1951, Editorial Page.

74. Quotes from "They Also Ran," *Courier*, February 7, 1953, Editorial Page; see also George S. Schuyler, "Views and Reviews: A Rap at the Revival of 'Lies' About Negro GIs," *Courier*, March 6, 1954, 9.

75. Ralph Matthews, "This Week," *Afro-American*, September 23, 1950, 7; Biggs, "The 24th Infantry Regiment," 65. Two months into the war, and amidst mounting casualties, the *Philadelphia Tribune* had commented on white discourse surrounding integration. "If white soldiers are sent to the 24th . . ., it will be to strengthen the unit's combat effectiveness by giving it 'better' soldiers. When Negro troops are sent to white units, such transfers are gratifyingly hailed as an example of Army democracy"; "Double-Talk in Korea," *Philadelphia Tribune*, September 19, 1950, 4.

76. In May 1952, James Michener, World War II veteran and famed author, reflected extensively in the *Saturday Evening Post* on what he called the "forgotten heroes" of the "unpopular war," "The Forgotten Heroes of Korea," *Saturday Evening Post*, May 10, 1952, 19; E. Mueller, "Trends in Popular Support for the Wars in Korea and Vietnam," *American Political Science Review* 65, 2 (June 1971): 361. See Gallup polls from 1949 to 1958.

77. Martin Medhurst, "Text and Context in the 1952 Presidential Campaign: Eisenhower's 'I Shall Go to Korea' Speech," *Presidential Studies Quarterly* 30, 3 (September 2000): 464–84. Eisenhower's pledge to go to Korea and eventually end the war certainly struck a chord with African Americans. But military integration and Eisenhower's position on civil rights played a greater role in his assessment among most African Americans. When Eisenhower ran for president in 1952, the black press reminded its readers of his problematic appearance before the Senate Armed Services Committee in spring 1948. See "National Grapevine: By Their Deeds," *Chicago Defender*, February 9, 1952, 10; see also "Our Opinions: Eisenhower, Taft and Truman," *Chicago Defender*, January 19, 1952, 10; "General Eisenhower and Domestic Issues," *Norfolk Journal and Guide*, January 19, 1952, A22; Louis Lautier, "Looking at the Record of General Eisenhower," *Norfolk Journal and Guide*, June 14, 1952, 14; "We Like Stevenson," *Afro-American*, November 1, 1952, 1, A22; "National Grapevine: By Their Deeds," *Chicago Defender*, February 9, 1952, 10; "Our Opinions: Eisenhower, Taft and Truman," *Chicago Defender*, January 19, 1952, 10; "Speak out, Gen. Ike!," *Afro-American*, January 26, 1952, 4; "Gen. Ike's Own Words Prove He's a Segregationist," *Afro-American*, February 16, 1952, 5; "Eisenhower Disappointing," *Afro-American*, June 14, 1952, 4.

78. On the truce talks see Walter G. Hermes, *Truce Tent and Fighting Front* (Washington, D.C.: Office of the Chief of Military History, U.S. Army, 1966); Barton J. Bernstein, "The Struggle over the Korean Armistice: Prisoners of Repatriation," in *Child of Conflict: The Korean-American Relationship, 1943–1953*, ed. Bruce Cumings (Seattle: University of Washington Press, 1983); Steven Casey, *Selling the Korean War: Propaganda, Politics, and Public Opinion 1950–1953* (Oxford: Oxford University Press, 2008), Part III.

79. Harry S. Truman, "Executive Order 10308—Improving the Means for Obtaining Compliance with the Nondiscrimination Provisions of Federal Contracts," December 3, 1951. Online by Gerhard Peters and John T. Woolley, *The American Presidency Project*. http://www.presidency.ucsb.edu.

80. Joseph D. Bibb, "Mr. Taft Fails," *Courier*, December 29, 1951, 7.

81. Joseph D. Bibb, "Political Showdown: Candidates Will Have to Show Where They Stand on Racial Issues," *Courier*, December 22, 1951, 5; "FEPC up to the President," *Courier*, July 7, 1951, 20.

82. See Jason Morgan Ward, *Defending White Democracy: The Making of a Segregationist Movement and the Remaking of Racial Politics, 1936–1965* (Chapel Hill: University of North Carolina Press, 2011).

83. See Leo Bogart, ed., *Project Clear: Social Research and the Desegregation of the United States Army* (New Brunswick, N.J.: Transaction, 1992).

84. In 1951, the House Armed Services Committee passed the then-called Winstead Amendment 21 to 12 after voting against the Javits Amendment, which would have added integration to the draft bill. "Committee Tacks Racial Amendment to Draft Bill," *Norfolk Journal and Guide*, March 24, 1951, E3.

85. Marjorie McKenzie, "Pursuit of Democracy," *Courier*, December 2, 1950, 20.

86. On the limits of World War II as leverage for the civil rights movement see Kevin M. Kruse and Stephen Tuck, eds., *Fog of War: The Second World War and the Civil Rights Movement* (Oxford: Oxford University Press, 2012).

87. Gallup poll, 1140.

88. Peter S. Kindsvatter, *American Soldiers: Ground Combat in the World Wars, Korea, and Vietnam* (Lawrence: University Press of Kansas, 2003), 134.

89. See Robert Schakne, "Gen. Clark Summons Aides to Top Secret Meeting," *Atlanta Daily World*, July 2, 1953, 1; Robert E. Clark, "Korean Truce Crisis End Seen by Pres. Eisenhower," *Atlanta Daily World*, July 2, 1953, 1.

90. Adam J. Zweiback, "The 21 'Turncoat GIs': Nonrepatriations and the Political Culture of the Korean War," *The Historian* 60, 2 (Winter 1998): 345–62; H. H. Wubben, "American Prisoners of War in Korea: A Second Look at the 'Something New in History' Theme," *American Quarterly* 22, 1 (Spring 1970): 3–19; Charles S. Young, "Name, Rank, and Serial Number: Korean War POWS and the Politics of Limited War" (Ph.D. dissertation, Rutgers University, 2003); Gary Harold Rice, "The Lost Sheep of the Korean War" (Ph.D. dissertation, University of Texas at Austin, 1998); Susan L. Carruthers, *Cold War Captives: Imprisonment, Escape, and Brainwashing* (Berkeley: University of California Press, 2009), 174–216.

91. Chalmers M. Roberts, "The GIs Who Went Red: A Portrait of Poverty, Ignorance and Strife," *Washington Post*, December 29, 1953, 11.

92. "Korea: The Sorriest Bunch," *Newsweek*, February 8, 1954, 40; see also Chalmers M. Roberts, "The GIs Who Went Red: A Portrait of Poverty, Ignorance and Strife," *Washington Post*, December 29, 1953, 11; Mary Lou Downer, "'21 Stayed' Tells Story of GI Turncoats," *Los Angeles Times*, November 13, 1955, C15; "One Who Won't Return," *Time*, October 26, 1953; Zweiback, "The 21 Turncoat GIs," 3; Kyle A. Cuordileone, *Manhood and American Political Culture in the Cold War* (New York: Routledge, 2005), 81–82.

93. On McCarthyism, Ellen Schrecker, *Many Are the Crimes: McCarthyism in America* (New York: Little, Brown, 1998).

94. Lewis H. Carlson, *Remembered Prisoners of a Forgotten War* (New York: St. Martin's, 2002). See also Young, "Name, Rank, and Serial Number," and Zweiback, "The 21 Turncoat GIs"; Richard Joseph Fallace, "Prisoners of Cold War: Soviet and US Exploitation of American Korean War Prisoners" (Ph.D. dissertation, Oklahoma State University, 2000), 9–10.

95. On the centrality of race in the debates on POWs, Zweiback, "The 21 'Turn-coat GIs.'"

96. Roberts, "The GIs Who Went Red."

97. Edward Hunter covered African Americans in a separate chapter. *Brainwashing: The Story of Men Who Defied It* (New York: Farrar, Straus & Cudahy, 1956), 89–116, 90. See also Widener, "Seoul City Sue and the Bugout Blues," 67.

98. Frederic Sondern, Jr., "U.S. Negroes Make Reds See Red," *Reader's Digest* (January 1954): 37–42.

99. "Freed POWs Tell of Dope Addiction," *Los Angeles Times*, August 9, 1953, 1.

100. Green, *Black Yanks in the Pacific*, 184 n88.

101. Virginia Pasley, *21 Stayed* (New York: Farrar, Straus & Cudahy, 1955), 133. In his 2007 memoir, Clarence Adams, one of the black defectors, called this comment "an insult to any thinking African American." *An American Dream: The Life of an African American Soldier and POW Who Spent Twelve Years in Communist China*, ed. Della Adams and Lewis H. Carlson (Amherst: University of Massachusetts Press, 2007), 2.

102. "Who Are GIs Who Fell for Red Line? Why Did They Turn down 'Come Home' Plea?," *Chicago Defender*, January 9, 1954, 4; Roi Ottley, "One of Twenty-One," *Chicago Defender*, October 1, 1955, 8; "GI's on Semi-Official List of War Prisoners," *Atlanta Daily World*, January 1, 1954, 1.

103. NAACP Press Release, December 17, 1953: "Come Home to Fight Jim Crow Walter White Urges 3 P.O.W.'s," NAACP Records, Box A 649, Folder Prisoners of War, 1952–1955; see also "The Misguided Three," *Afro-American*, February 6, 1954, Editorial Page.

104. C. A. Irvin, "Reds Segregated Negro GIs in North Korea Prison Camps," *Courier*, June 6, 1953, 18; John J. Casserly, "Reds Played Race vs. Race," *Chicago Defender*, August 15, 1953, 1; "Repatriated POW Describes 4 Days of Brain 'Washing'," *Norfolk Journal and Guide*, May 23, 1953, 1; "Returning Prisoners Allege Communism and Marijuana Were Daily Diets in Prisons," *Black Dispatch*, August 29, 1953, 7.

105. Chuck Davis, "PW's Back Home, Tell Horrors of Red Slavery," *Chicago Defender*, September 5, 1953, 3.

106. "Colored Soldiers Rated High in Resistance to Red Bait," *Norfolk Journal and Guide*, August 22, 1953, 24.

107. See W. Fitzhugh Brundage, "The Roar on the Other Side of Silence: Black Resistance and White Violence in the American South, 1880–1940," in *Under Sentence of Death: Lynching in the South*, ed. W. Fitzhugh Brundage (Chapel Hill: University of North Carolina Press, 1997), 271–91.

108. William Worthy, "Red Bid to Negro PW's Muffed," *Christian Science Monitor*, July 8, 1955, 12; also published in a slightly altered version: "POW's Two Years Later: The Other Side of the Coin," *Afro-American*, March 12, 1955, A10. Second

quote: C. D. Halliburton, "South of the Mason-Dixon Line," *Philadelphia Tribune*, February 16, 1954, 4.

109. "Negro PWs Segregated: "Pounded" By Propaganda," *Norfolk Journal and Guide*, August 15, 1953, 1; James Hicks, "Two Ex-Pow's Give Answer: What Caused 3 Korean War Prisoners to Stay with the Reds?" *Afro-American*, May 1, 1954, 22.

110. William Worthy, "POWs Two Years Later," *Afro-American*, February 12, 1955, A6; quote Worthy, "POWs Two Years Later: The Other Side of the Coin," *Afro-American*, March 12, 1955, A10.

111. "Our Opinions: Imagine You're a Negro PW," *Chicago Defender*, August 22, 1953, 11; see also "The Case of Cpl. Holder," *New York Amsterdam News*, October 10, 1953, 16.

112. William Worthy, "No Campus in Red China Universities," *Afro-American*, March 23, 1957, A4; see also William Worthy, "Seven Out, Fourteen to GO!" *Afro-American*, March 16, 1957, A4; William Worthy, "Some Day, They'll Come Home," *Afro-American*, April 13, 1957, A4.

113. "The Misguided Three," *Afro-American*, February 6, 1954, Editorial Page.

114. Roi Ottley, "Roi Ottley Says," *Chicago Defender*, October 1, 1955, 8.

115. Gordon B. Hancock, "Between the Lines: Somewhere America Failed GIs Who Prefer Communism," *Philadelphia Tribune*, January 16, 1954, 4; J. A. Rogers, "Rogers Says: What the Reds Taught Will Remain in the Brains of Americans," *Courier*, May 23, 1953, 9; see also *Black Dispatch*, January 16, 1954, Editorial Page; William Worthy, "Returnees Test U.S. Negro Ex-PWs Pose Challenge," *Christian Science Monitor*, July 5, 1955, 12. On protest and radicalization see, Phillips, *War!*, 162–65; Christopher Parker, *Fighting for Democracy: Black Veterans and the Struggle Against White Supremacy in the Postwar South* (Princeton, N.J.: Princeton University Press, 2009), 151.

116. The Pentagon had to revise the number from 54,246 to 36,940 due to a clerical error. The Korean War Veterans Memorial still displays the earlier number. *Time*, June 12, 2000.

117. See Marilyn Young, "An Incident at No Gun Ri," in *Crimes of War: Guilt and Denial in the Twentieth Century*, ed. Omer Bartov, Atina Grossmann, and Mary Nolan (New York: New Press, 2002), 242–58; see also Bruce Cumings, *The Korean War: A History* (New York: Modern Library, 2010), 149–203.

118. "No Shouting in the Streets," *Philadelphia Tribune*, 28 July 1953, 4.

119. "End of Korean War Hailed by Race," *Courier*, August 1, 1953, 3; The Truce in Korea," *Afro-American*, August 9, 1953, 4; John B. Henderson, "The Korean Conflict: Cost and Accomplishment," *Norfolk Journal and Guide*, August 15, 1953, 14.

120. Quotes from "Ike's Word Means Something," *Courier*, February 14, 1953, 8; see also "So Long, Harry," *Los Angeles Sentinel*, January 15, 1953, A8; "Wanted: A Sensible Solution," *Los Angeles Sentinel*, March 5, 1953, A8; "Korea: Still a Misadventure," *Los Angeles Sentinel*, June 11, 1953, A8; "Freedom to Eat," *Courier*, June 20, 1953, 8.

121. "The Truce in Korea," *Afro-American*, August 9, 1953, 4.

122. "'Korea Has Taught Us You Can't Win War with JC Units'—Ridgway," *Afro-American*, August 4, 1951, 1; see also Bernard C. Nalty, *Strength for the Fight: A History of Black Americans in the Military* (New York: The Free Press, 1986), 259. Junior officers had started to integrate before Ridgway's official order. Phillips, *War!*, 139–43.

123. First quote: "The Lesson of Korea," *Afro-American*, August 8, 1953, 4: second quote: Roi Ottley, "Army Mixes Races, Morale Rises," *Chicago Daily Tribune*, March 21, 1954, SW12.

124. "The Lesson of Korea," *Afro-American*, August 8, 1953, 4; L. Alex Wilson, "Wilson Says Mixed Army Big Gain of Korean War," *Chicago Defender*, August 8, 1953, 1.

125. Number of black soldiers is an estimate by the Department of Defense, *Department of Defense*, http://koreanwar.defense.gov, accessed October 20, 2012.

126. "Cartoon: He's Got a Good Left, But No Right," *Afro-American*, April 18, 1953, Editorial Page.

127. "Louisiana Furnishes a Korean Hero," *Atlanta Daily World*, March 25, 1953, 4.

128. Sid White, "Heroic GI Gets Silver Star For Saving Colonel's Life," *Norfolk Journal and Guide*, March 21, 1953, 1; "Fast-Shooting GI. Called 'Bravest' by Man He Saved," *Philadelphia Tribune*, March 21, 1953, 1; see also Sid White, "American GI Kills Eight, Rescues CO," *Atlanta Daily World*, March 19, 1953, 1; "Soldier, 19, Saves Officers From Red Fury," *Los Angeles Sentinel*, March 19, 1953, 1; "Tan GI Saves Wounded Colonel From Korea Reds: 8 Chinese Killed in Capture Attempt," *Courier*, March 21, 1953, 1.

129. "National Grapevine: With Malice Toward Some," *Chicago Defender*, April 4, 1953, 2.

130. "Heels and Heroes," *Chicago Defender*, April 4, 1953, 11.

131. John Bodnar, "Private Ryan and Postwar Memory in America," *American Historical Review* 106, 3 (June 2001): 809.

132. Robert K. Chester, "'Negroes' Number One Hero': Doris Miller, Pearl Harbor, and Retroactive Multiculturalism in World War II Remembrance," *American Quarterly* 65, 1 (March 2013): 37.

133. Roi Ottley, "Army's Mixing of Races Refutes Prophets," *Chicago Daily Tribune*, March 21, 1954, S4.

134. See Lipsitz, *A Life in the Struggle*; Timothy B. Tyson, *Radio Free Dixie: Robert F. Williams and the Roots of Black Power* (Chapel Hill: University of North Carolina Press, 1999); Charles Rangel, *And I Haven't Had a Bad Day Since: From the Streets of Harlem to the Halls of Congress* (New York: Thomas Dunne, 2007). The involvement of Korean War veterans in the postwar civil rights movement warrants more research, which this study cannot provide. Many have touched on it, but no historian has specifically focused on it.

135. Charles Sumner Stone, Jr., "Unsegregated Army," *Saturday Evening Post*, January 31, 1953, 4.

136. "Services Abolish All-Negro Units: Defense Department Report Says Integration Program Is Ahead of Schedule," *New York Times*, October 31, 1954, 23.

Epilogue

1. An earlier, longer version of the epilogue appeared as "Don't Ever Distort My History: Conflicting Interpretations of the African American Performance in the Korean War," in *The American Experience of War*, ed. Georg Schild (Paderborn: Franz Schöningh, 2010), 235–61.

2. Author's transcript of Colin Powell's speech at the Harry S. Truman Library and Museum, July 26, 1998, National Public Radio.

3. E. J. Dionne, Jr., "Korea: The Bitter War Americans Forgot; Impact Proved Profound in U.S.," *Washington Post*, June 24, 1990, A27. Early on, the Korean War garnered the name often still used, "the forgotten war." Joanne Bourke discards the term in general, stating: "The Korean War, for example, was not the 'Forgotten War,' a lapse of a freefloating 'national memory': political and cultural factors rendered it the 'Ignored War.'" Bourke, "Introduction, 'Remembering' War," *Journal of Contemporary History* 39, 4 (2004): 473. Critical assessment of the term also in Marilyn Young, "An Incident at No Gun Ri," in *Crimes of War: Guilt and Denial in the Twentieth Century*, ed. Omer Bartov, Atina Grossmann, and Mary Nolan (New York: New Press, 2002), 242–58.

4. On remembering the Korean War: Christine Knauer, "A Victory After All: Remembering the Korean War in the United States," in *We Are What We Remember: The American Past Through Commemoration*, ed. Jeffrey L. Meriwether and Laura Mattoon D'Amore(Cambridge: Cambridge Scholars Publishing, 2012), 154–75.

5. Kirk Savage, *Monument Wars: Washington D.C., the National Mall, and the Transformation of the Memorial Landscape* (Berkeley: University of California Press, 2009), 282.

6. William J. Clinton: "Remarks at the Dedication Ceremony for the Korean War Veterans Memorial," July 27, 1995, in Gerhard Peters and John T. Woolley, *The American Presidency Project*, http://www.presidency.ucsb.edu.

7. Richard Slotkin, "Unit Pride: Ethnic Platoons and the Myths of American Nationality," *American Literary History* 13, 3 (2001): 469.

8. William J. Clinton, "Remarks on the Observance of the 50th Anniversary of the Korean War," June 25, 2000, in Peters and Woolley, *The American Presidency Project*.

9. Historian Robert K. Chester calls this distorted remembrance "retroactive multiculturalism" that "offer[s] counterweight recuperating nonwhite service into a teleology of egalitarian reform," Chester, "'Negroes' Number One Hero': Doris Miller, Pearl Harbor, and Retroactive Multiculturalism in World War II Remembrance," *American Quarterly* 65, 1 (March 2013): 35.

10. See Rudolph W. Stephens, *Old Ugly Hill: A G.I.'s Fourteen Months in the Korean Trenches, 1952–1953* (Jefferson, N.C.: McFarland, 1995); William D. Dannenmaier, *We Were Innocents: An Infantryman in Korea* (Urbana: University of Illinois Press, 1999). It is not uncommon for soldiers or veterans to feel insufficiently honored and commemorated by the people for whom they put their life on the line. Veterans of World War II who have been recognized locally and nationally have felt national ingratitude toward their sacrifices. See Erika Doss, "War, Memory, and the Public Mediation of Affect: The National World War II Memorial and American Imperialism," *Memory Studies* 227, 1 (2008): 227–50.

11. The term "sandwiched" is often used in public discourse when describing the position of the Korean War in the public consciousness. See, e.g., Cynthia Koury, "Sacrifices Are Not Forgotten, After All," *Telegram & Gazette*, May 1, 2000, A1; Charles Rangel, "On Korean War Memorial Day, Congressman Rangel Urges America to Remember the Forgotten War," News Release, Charles Rangel, June 25, 2008, *United States House of Representative Press.* TV journalist Tom Brokaw shaped the term "Greatest Generation." *The Greatest Generation* (New York: Random House, 1998).

12. Roy E. Appleman, *South to the Naktong, North to the Yalu: United States Army in the Korean War (June to November 1950)* (Washington, D.C.: Government Printing Office, 1961); William T. Bowers, William M. Hammond, and George L. MacGarrigle, *Black Soldier, White Army: The 24th Infantry Regiment in Korea* (Washington, D.C.: Center of Military History, 1996). Bernard C. Nalty, *Strength for the Fight: A History of Black Americans in the Military* (New York: The Free Press, 1986).

13. Both men had already attained a respectable status in the black press during the war. See L. Alex Wilson, "Tan Yank Engineer Outfit Lauded by General for Record Breaking Feat," *Chicago Defender*, October 14, 1950, 19; "Angeleno's Son Hero in Combat," *Los Angeles Sentinel*, November 16, 1950, A3.

14. David K. Carlisle, "Letter to the Editor 16," *Los Angeles Times*, October 28, 1984, S14; see also Charles M. Bussey, *Firefight at Yechon: Courage and Racism in the Korean War* (Lincoln: University of Nebraska Press, 2002).

15. Bussey, *Firefight at Yechon*, Acknowledgments.

16. Ibid., xv–xviii, xvii, xviii.

17. Carlisle quoted in Bryan Brumley, "Army Reconsidering Historical Accounts Disparaging Black Soldiers," *Associated Press*, July 24, 1988, AMC Cycle.

18. Carlisle quoted in Philip Shenon, "Veterans of Black Unit Threaten Suit over Army's Account of Their Service," *New York Times*, May 7, 1996, A16.

19. Gerald Horne, "Nalty, Bernard C., 'Strength for the Fight: A History of Black Americans in the Military' (Book Review)," *Historian* 50, 2 (February 1988): 294–95; Clay Blair quoted in "Column One: War and Black GIs' Memories: Veterans of the Action in Korea Set Out on a Painful Journey to Erase a Record of ShameThe Quest Proves Elusive," *Los Angeles Times*, November 15, 1989, 1. Blair's assessments of black soldiers in *The Forgotten War* was to a large part based on Bussey's and Carlisle's oral

histories. Clay Blair, *The Forgotten War: American in Korea, 1950–1953* (New York: Times Books, 1987), esp. 150–53.

20. Carlisle quoted in Philip Shenon, "Veterans of Black Unit Threaten Suit over Army's Account of Their Service," *New York Times*, May 7, 1996, A16.

21. Curtis James Morrow, *What's a Commie Ever Done to Black People: A Korean War Memoir of Fighting in the U.S. Army's Last All-Negro Unit* (Jefferson, N.C.: McFarland, 1997), esp. 34–36, quote 35.

22. Donald E. Franklin, "Soldiers of Misfortune," *St. Louis Post-Dispatch*, July 22, 2002, B1. Retired major general Oliver Dillard quoted in ibid. In 2002, the *Post-Dispatch* published a number of articles on African American soldiers' experiences in the Korean War and seemed to be eager to assist in the struggle for altering the prevalent image of black Korean War soldiers. Bill Smith, "Black Soldiers Fully Shared Korean War's Bloody Cost," *St. Louis Post-Dispatch*, February 20, 2002, A1.

23. Jack A. Green, "Korean War Conference Highlights Contributions and Sacrifices of Black Americans," *Navy Newsstand: The Source for Navy News*, hrrp://www.news.navy.mil, accessed April 28, 2003. The conference, held April 16–19, 2003, was taped and later broadcast by CSPAN. CSPAN released a DVD set that is in the author's possession. All subsequent quotes transcribed by the author from the DVD broadcasts. *African Americans in the Korean War* (Washington, D.C.: C-SPAN, 2005).

24. Bob Fletcher, ibid.

25. All panelists and speakers from the audience repeated these arguments incessantly throughout the conference.

26. Michael Taylor, "Obituaries: Charles M. Bussey—Member of the Tuskegee Airmen," *San Francisco Chronicle*, April 20, 2004, B7; "His Actions Speak Louder Than Words," *38th Parallel* 1, 4: 12.

Index

Acknowledgments

Writing a book is a marathon, not a sprint; and although it is a lonely struggle, one needs a lot of help from start to finish.

It has been a great privilege to work with the University of Pennsylvania Press, especially Bob Lockhart, Rachel Taube, and Alison Anderson, who helped tremendously on the last steps of the way.

I owe thanks to Professor Udo Sautter and Professor Georg Schild, who showed the patience and support that I needed. I also want to thank Professor Dieter Langewiesche and Professor Bernd Engler. The SFB 437 at the Eberhard Karls University Tübingen provided me with a great environment for my research and the writing process.

I give heartfelt thanks to Professor Glenda Gilmore at Yale University, who took me under her wings when I was a mere visiting assistant of research at Yale. She has helped me in every possible way ever since. Her brilliance and selfless dedication are awe-inspiring.

This book would not have been possible without generous funding from the Deutsche Forschungsgemeinschaft, the German Historical Institute Washington, D.C., and the Truman Library.

The staff at all the libraries and archives I researched in over the years was invaluable for this project. I am greatly indebted to them. Robert Caulkins and Leslie R. Miller did tremendous jobs as my proxy researchers at the G. Libby Manuscript Collection, University of North Dakota, Grand Forks, and the Richard B. Russell Library for Political Research and Studies, University of Georgia, Athens, for which I owe them greatly.

I would also like to thank the panelists and audiences at the various meetings of the AHA, ASALH, OAH, ASA, Aim Gender, HOTCUS, UCD Clinton Institute of American Studies, and Heidelberg Spring Academy. There I was fortunate enough to meet and befriend Daniel Siemens, to whose knowledge of and dedication to history and writing I can only aspire.

So many people helped me on the long and rocky path. Without them this book would not have been possible: Andra Vosteen, Thorsten Schimming, Elena Schwan, Maria Schubert, Professors David Godshalk, Mary Stewart, Maria Höhn, and Bryant Simon, Charissa Threat, Melinda Pash, Gisela Kampermann, Katrin Kampermann, Evi Draxl, Anne Overbeck, Liam van Beek, Andrew Johnston, Christian Sauer, Linda Oechsle, Rainer Brang, Florian Herbert, Nursen Cinar, Murat Cinar, Figen Ongun, Matthias Speidel, Helga von der Kettenburg, Marina Dold, Sonia Lee, Andreas Kraft, Susanne Wiedemann, Daniela Hoegg, Roswitha Ade, Nina Höhnle, Margarete Dengler, Dr. Kai Schörner, Dr. Kirsten Klein, Barbara Bickel, and especially Professor Arthur Melms.

Niki Rodusakis and Margaret Hass acted as great proofreaders of earlier versions. Angela Allmendinger was kind enough to read through various versions of the manuscript in its late stages more than once and made it so much better with her insights and feeling for language. Special thanks go out to Miriam Leypoldt for helping me with the index. I also owe a lot to KC Anderson who is one of the kindest people I know. She was willing to provide me with her sharp wit and proofreading skills, even if time was short.

Ilyana Karthas has been a wonderful friend and inspiration over the years, and showed me how to finish.

Five amazing women deserve special thanks. They have been with and there for me since high school: Bettina Veit, Corinna Schmid, Esther Hori, Julika Jäger, and Sandra Brang. Bettina was kind enough to accompany me on one of my many research trips and helped me find my way.

Jan David Ott has been cheering me on since we met in a seminar in Tübingen. One could not ask for a better friend.

It takes a village to raise a child and for me it took a loving family to finally finish my work. They grounded me and never left my side, even in the hardest times. My uncles and cousins deserve special mentioning: Hermann Knauer helped me whenever I needed help. Werner and Philipp Sommer always managed to save my computer files when I, yet again, thought they were gone for good; and my cousins Friederike and Greta dropped everything to go on research trips with me.

Ultimately, I owe everything to my father, Armin Knauer, and my sister, Sabine, whom I love with all my heart. Without them, I would have never finished. They encouraged and distracted me when I needed it, and they have never given up on me. Sabine is my travel companion, my confidante, my shoulder to cry on, and simply the best sister and friend one can imagine.

I offer my greatest gratitude to my mother, Hannelore Knauer, who died before I could finish. But this book would have never existed if it had not been for her unconditional love, support, sacrifice, and belief in me. She is my inspiration. To her memory this book is dedicated.